Sports Racing
CARS

Sports Racing CARS

EXPERT ASSESSMENT OF FIFTY MOTOR RACING GREATS

Anthony Pritchard

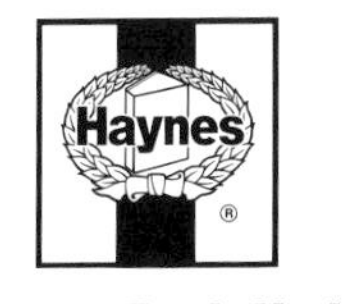

Haynes Publishing

First published in March 2005

A catalogue record for this book is available from the British Library

ISBN 1 84425 138 1

Library of Congress catalog card no 2004 117 157

Haynes North America Inc., 861 Lawrence Drive, Newbury Park, California 91320, USA.

Published by Haynes Publishing, Sparkford, Nr Yeovil, Somerset BA22 7JJ, UK.
Tel: 01963 442030 Fax: 01963 440001
Int.tel: +44 1963 442030 Int.fax: +44 1963 440001
E-mail: sales@haynes.co.uk
Website: www.haynes.co.uk

Designed and typeset by Christopher Fayers

Printed and bound in Great Britain by J. H. Haynes & Co. Ltd., Sparkford

CONTENTS

INTRODUCTION

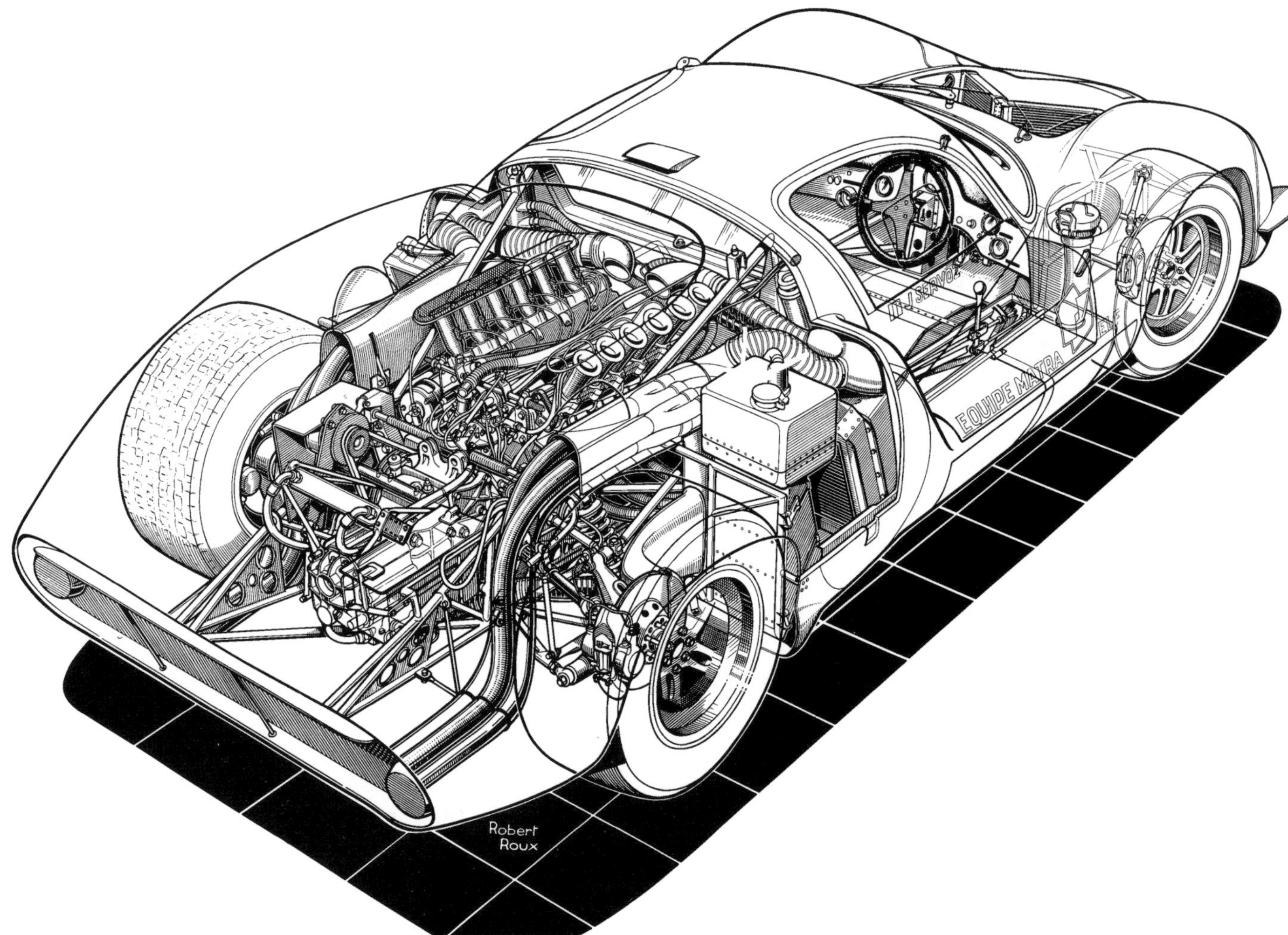

The space-frame M630 was the first Sports Prototype Matra to use the team's V12 engine and from this car Matra developed the open models that won at Le Mans in three successive years.

By a sports-racing car I mean cars that were built, developed or adapted for sports car racing. I do not mean cars which were modified to give a little more oomph with better roadholding than their basic production contemporaries, but were 'reworked' to produce a significantly different car. An example is the Jaguar C-type that retained the existing XK120 engine and gearbox, the former substantially modified, within a new chassis that had different suspension and body.

I have relied on manufacturers' power output figures, except where I have better information, and those of Italian manufacturers should be treated with especial caution. Perspex and Plexiglas are the British and American terms for the same product. I have opted to use Plexiglas in this book. FIA is the abbreviation for *Fédération Internationale de l'Automobile*, the governing body of motor sport.

Le Mans has been pivotal to sports car racing for many years, although it was not so to begin with, but just another obscure Continental race for touring cars, held over a longer distance than most. It has been included as a round in the World Sports Car Championship ever since the inauguration of the first in 1953, except for three years: 1956 when the race was run to the *Automobile Club de l'Ouest*'s own rules following the previous year's disaster and for 1989 and 1990 when the organisers refused to comply with the requirements of *FISA*, the abbreviation for *Fédération Internationale du Sport Automobile*, then the division of the FIA responsible for the administration of motor sporting events. Previously such power had been handled by a body known as the CSI, the abbreviation for *Commission*

Sportive Internationale. Currently, and in recent years, the FIA itself holds this responsibility.

Other important races over the years have been the Mille Miglia (the Italian road race held between 1927 and 1957) and the Targa Florio (the Sicilian road race that survived until 1973, but it should be remembered that although it was first held in 1906, it was not consistently held as a sports car race until post-World War Two days). Other important races were the Belgian 24 Hours, originally known as the Belgian Touring Car Grand Prix, which survived from 1924 to 1949 and there was a final event in 1953.

It was that year that the World Sports Car Championship was first held and the rounds then were the Sebring 12 Hours, the Mille Miglia, Le Mans, the Nürburgring 1,000Km race (first held in 1953 and then revived in 1956), the Tourist Trophy at Dundrod in Northern Ireland (1953–55) and the Carrera Panamericana Mexico road race (1953–54). Other races joined the series, as others dropped out, and some were rounds of the Championship for only a very brief while.

Although Le Mans had worldwide recognition and the Mille Miglia was of especial importance to Italian constructors and a lure to those outside Italy, the inauguration of the Championship became an important focal point for teams competing in sports car racing, and in its early days attracted many important competitors. All things are relative though and it has to be said that sports car racing has never, unlike Grand Prix racing, been a major focus of interest, even when 'works' teams such as Alfa Romeo, Jaguar and Mercedes-Benz were competing.

Over the years the *Fédération Internationale de l'Automobile* and its successors have, generally, made a success of Grand Prix racing, but in sports car racing have persistently introduced new regulations, sometimes sweeping changes, that have destroyed much of the character, interest and support of manufacturers and enthusiasts. The first change of this nature was the imposition of the 3,000cc capacity limit in Championship sports car racing from 1958 onwards. It resulted in the almost total loss of interest in the category and it ground to a halt in 1961.

The powers-that-be proposed replacing it with GT racing, but the organisers of some of the most important races collaborated in introducing a 'Championship' for Prototype or Experimental cars and for a while there was confusion about exactly what they meant! From this grew the battles between Ferrari and Ford that, together with the appearance of Chaparral, raised racing to a new and exceptionally exciting level.

When the decision was made to limit Prototypes to 3,000cc from 1968 onwards (a move intended to 'assist' French constructors Alpine and Matra), a wonderful loophole was built into the regulations. This permitted cars of up to 5,000cc of which at least 25 examples (originally 50) had been built. So, we then had another couple or so seasons (1969–71) of fast and competitive racing, but it was only really exciting in 1970 when Porsche and Ferrari were locked in close combat.

This exciting scenario of racing was destroyed at the end of 1971 when the 5,000cc Competition sports cars were banned. There followed two years of good racing, when Ferrari totally dominated in 1972 and a year-long battle between Ferrari and Matra in 1973. Ferrari withdrew at the end of 1973 and Matra carried on for another almost all-conquering year.

Thereafter it was virtually oblivion, as sports car racing largely died, despite the efforts of Porsche (in particular), Alfa Romeo and Mirage. The plan was to have a new standardised formula for Europe and North America for 1982 onwards. Sadly, the relevant authorities could not agree, so there was Group C in Europe and IMSA racing in the United States. Both categories attracted strong interest – despite constantly changing regulations – and these categories survived until 1992 by which time sports car racing in Europe was to all intents and purposes buried.

The final blow was the introduction of the unblown 3,500cc category, where sports cars became virtually grand prix cars, but with much greater ground-force. Exceptionally, Le Mans has retained its prestige and support and the *Automobile Club de l'Ouest* has led the way with its own specific categories and attracted major manufacturers to compete. I think that sports car racing is at another crossroads and desperately needs long-term stability and greater excitement for the spectator.

Anthony Pritchard
Wooburn Green, Bucks
2005

ACKNOWLEDGEMENTS

I would like to take this opportunity of expressing my greatest appreciation for all the kindness and help that I received from photographer Guy Griffiths over a period of forty years. He is deeply missed. There are many others to whom I would like to express my appreciation for their help, in particular: Cliff Allison; Richard Attwood; Bob Berry; Paul Fearnley (Editor of *Motor Sport*, for consent to use the extract from the interview with Jim Hall); Phillippe Leroux; Pete Lyons; David Piper; and Roy Salvadori.

Lorraine-Dietrich

1923–26

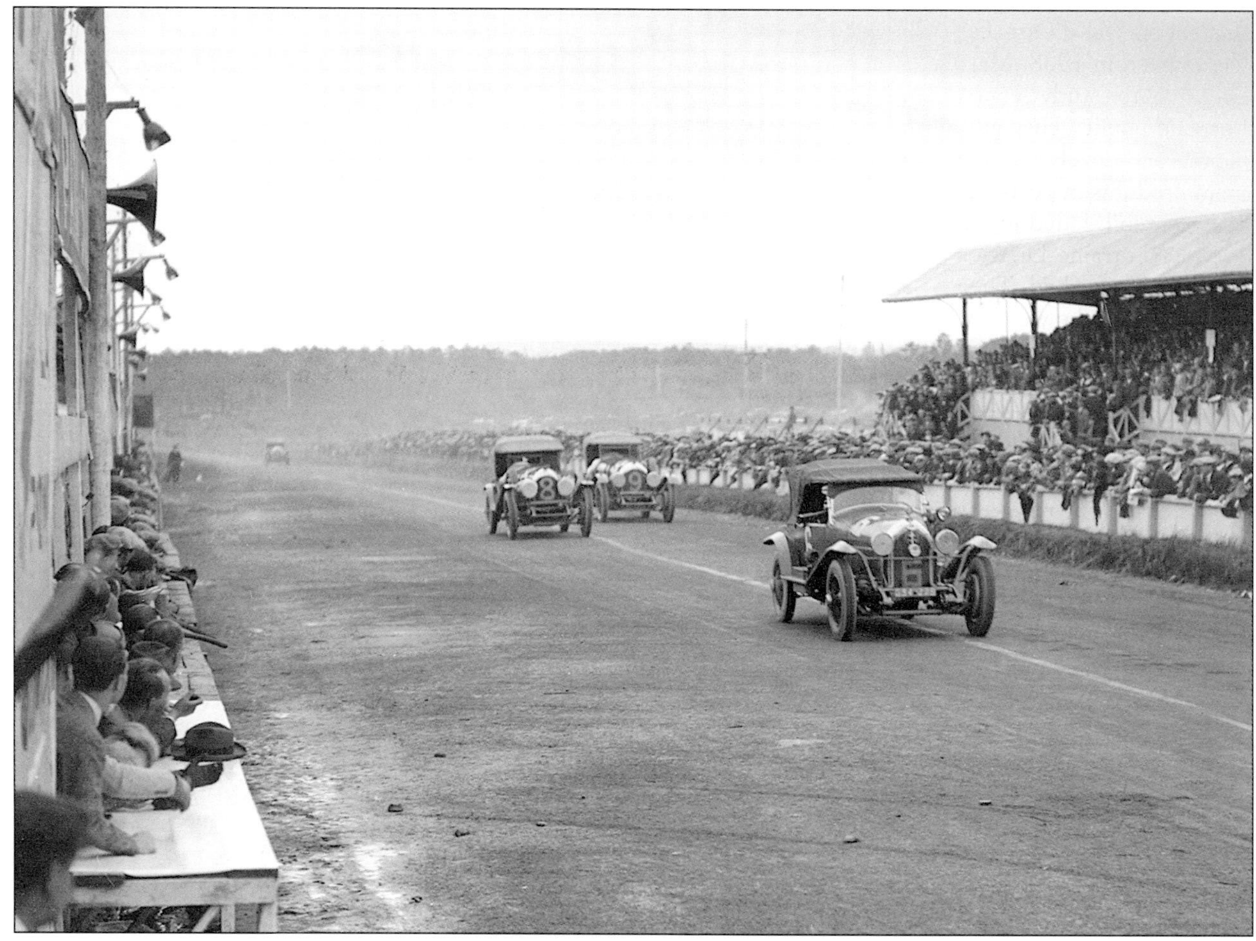

Early in the 1926 Le Mans race the winning Lorraine-Dietrich of Bloch/Rossignol leads the three works Bentleys past the pits. (LAT)

The marque manufactured cars over a 37-year period, and was a regular competitor in the early days of motor racing, but it built only one sports model and it was this car which achieved its greatest competition successes. Lorraine-Dietrich had its origins in de Dietrich et Cie, a successful engineering company that was founded in the 18th century. It became a maker of railway stock and track with factories in Lunéville in Lorraine and Niederbronn in Alsace.

Following the Franco-Prussian war of 1870–71 and the defeat of France, the new German state signed the Treaty of Frankfort in the Hall of Mirrors at Versailles on 10 May 1871. As a term of this France conceded Alsace and that part of Lorraine near the border with Germany. De Dietrich found itself with one factory in France and one in Germany. The two arms of de Dietrich split in 1905. The Lunéville factory changed its name to Societé Lorraine des Établissements de Dietrich et Cie and the cars were now marketed under the name Lorraine-Dietrich.

The best racing performance of these early years was in the 1906 Circuit of the Ardennes in which Lorraine-Dietrich drivers took first, third, fifth and seventh places with monster four-cylinder 18,146cc 130hp cars. As late as 1912 Lorraine-Dietrich contested the French Grand Prix with cars of primitive chassis design, chain-drive and powered by four-cylinder 15,095cc engines. One of these cars came to England for record-breaking at Brooklands and in post-World

War One days Malcolm Campbell, Douglas Hawkes and others raced it at the banked Surrey track where it became known as *Vieux Trois Charles*. It is now displayed in the Brooklands Museum.

Following the German invasion of France early in the First World War, Lorraine-Dietrich lost its Lunéville factory and all work then centred on the Argenteuil factory in the Val d'Oise *Département* that the company had opened in 1908. Marius Barbarou joined Lorraine-Dietrich to study captured German aero engines. Lorraine built Hispano-Suiza aero engines under licence and developed its own designs. These were the main products in post-war days and the cars, built only at Argenteuil, faded in importance.

Most Lorraine-Dietrich production cars were dull and undistinguished. The one exception was the B-3-6 15CV model, the work of Barbarou, which entered full production in 1921. The original, sluggish, ugly ducking turned into a very beautiful and very potent swan. The engine was a six-cylinder 3,446cc (75×130mm) unit with fixed cylinder head, exposed and very long needle pushrods and coil ignition. In some ways it was a precursor of the engines designed later by Georges Ruesch at Talbot. In original form, the 15CV engine developed 40bhp or so. Transmission was by a single-plate clutch, a three-speed gearbox and a spiral bevel final drive.

The front axle was suspended on semi-elliptic leaf springs and there were cantilever springs at the rear. The steering was left-hand and there were artillery wheels. For this model Lorraine-Dietrich adopted a rounded radiator shell that, coincidentally, resembled that of the Bentley, but carried the cross of Lorraine. Wheelbase length ranged from 9ft 6in (2,895mm) to 10ft 8in (3,250mm). Unlike the 3-litre Bentley that was to become its closest rival, the 15CV had no sporting pedigree, but that was all to change.

Barbarou introduced a semi-sporting version of the 15CV with few mechanical changes in 1923. When details of the Le Mans 24 Hours race, intended to demonstrate the reliability of ordinary touring cars was announced, many French manufacturers showed serious interest, including Lorraine-Dietrich. For any production car to survive 24 hours of racing, day and night, on the very badly surfaced, ill-maintained, dusty roads of the time was something well worth advertising. That there was no outright annual winner mattered little, for a win in the Triennial Cup would provide even greater publicity.

So three 15CV tourers lined up for the start of the first 24 hours held on 26–27 May 1923, all entered by private owners, but with the works providing enthusiastic support. However, the Lorraines lacked the speed to challenge for the lead, and two 3-litre Chenard-Walckers led throughout hotly pursued by the Bentley of Duff/Clement. Conditions worsened as the roads broke up more and more and there were gusting winds accompanied by rain-squalls during the night hours.

The Lorraine of Gérard de Courcelles/André Rossignol covered eighth highest distance, 1,158.417 miles (1,863.893km) at 48.267mph (77.662kph), about 40 miles less than the Bentley, which was joint fourth on distance. Robert Bloch/Stalter had a troubled race, covering 19th highest distance, 943.896 miles (1,518.729km), jointly with a 2-litre Rolland-Pilain. The third Lorraine-Dietrich driven by Gonzague/Lecuereuil/Flaud retired.

In 1924 Lorraine fitted the 15CV with front-wheel brakes as standard and Barbarou had developed a Sports version on the short chassis. The Sports had a multi-plate clutch, the Perrot-type brakes were much larger than those fitted to the standard model and there was a Dewandre servo. A tachometer and Rudge-Whitworth centre-lock, wire-spoked wheels were usually fitted.

The body was either a four-seater tourer by Labourdette or a sports saloon. With a 3.5:1 axle ratio, the makers guaranteed 80mph (129kph). The engines of the Le Mans cars had dry-sump lubrication. Because of the similar radiator designs, you might think that a Lorraine coming at you head-on was a Bentley, but the wings, body-style and general proportions were all different from those of the British car.

Three Sports models ran in the 1924 Le Mans race, which was postponed until 14–15 June in the hope of better weather conditions. All the entries in the race were French apart from the 3-litre Bentley of Duff/Clement. There was a new regulation that required drivers of open cars to stop after five laps to erect the hood and this had to stay in place for 20 laps. The 3-litre Chenard-Walckers led initially, but after six hours both had caught fire and were out of the race. Bloch/Stalter (Lorraine) led from Duff/Clement, with the other Lorraines third and fourth but during the Sunday morning Duff in the Bentley took the lead.

Just before 1pm the second-place Lorraine retired because of valve trouble, the result of over-driving by Bloch/Stalter in their efforts to catch the Bentley. About 2½ hours before the finish, the Bentley came into the pits for a precautionary change of rear wheels, which took far too long and dropped the British car to second place. Duff spent the rest of the race making up lost ground and at the finish had covered 1,290.44 miles (2,076.32km) to win, only marginally greater than that of the surviving Lorraines of Stoffel/Brisson which had completed 1,280.49 miles (2,060.31km) and de Coucelles/Rossignol 1,276.77 miles (2,054.32km).

Lorraine-Dietrich had learned that Le Mans required

After 24 hours of pounding on rough, badly surfaced roads and hard racing, the 1925 Le Mans-winning 3.4-litre Lorraine-Dietrich of de Courcelles/Rossignol is seen after the finish.

a combination of speed, mechanical toughness, good preparation and testing. Three Sports models were entered in the 1925 Le Mans race held on 20–21 June and the car driven by Stalter/Brisson had twin Zenith carburettors. The opposition included two 3-litre Bentleys and two new 3-litre twin overhead camshaft Sunbeams. Bentley and Lorraine fought a fierce duel, which led to mechanical problems and the Lorraine of Bloch/St Paul was in third place when it spun three times and overturned.

By 4am on the Sunday morning de Courcelles/Rossignol and Stalter/Brisson with their Lorraines led from Chassagne/'Sammy' Davis with the surviving Sunbeam. The Sunbeam drivers were still pushing hard and by 6am had moved into second place. These were the positions at the finish and the leading Lorraine had covered 1,388.129 miles (2,233.500km) at 57.838mph (93.061kph). Stalter/Brisson with their Lorraine covered third greatest distance. It was a superb performance in the face of very strong opposition.

Three Lorraines again ran in the 1926 Le Mans race held on 18–19 June where there was a hard-fought battle between Ariès, Bentley and Lorraine-Dietrich. The Lorraines were catalogued as the 'Le Mans' model, but only four were built, the three race-cars and a spare. The 'Le Mans' had twin-plug ignition, twin Zenith carburettors and torpedo bodies by Kelsch. A feature of these bodies was a flexible joint between the bonnet and the fabric tourer body and this reduced vibration and shake. Lorraine still used a three-speed gearbox, more than adequate for Le Mans, as its high gearing gave a maximum speed in bottom gear of 50mph (80kph) and top speed was about 96mph (154kph).

In 1926 the Lorraines displayed exceptional reliability and speed. Two Bentleys retired and in the closing stages the order was Lorraine-Lorraine-Bentley-Lorraine. 'Sammy' Davis with the surviving Bentley was instructed to try to catch and pass the second-place Lorraine, but 20 minutes before the finish he slid into a sandbank at *Mulsanne*. Bloch/Rossignol, who covered 1,585.993

miles (2,551.863km) at 66.082mph (106.326kph), de Courcelles/Mongin and Stalter/Brisson with their Lorraines took first three places on distance ahead of two 2-litre OMs. De Courcelles/Mongin won the second Biennial Cup and there was, of course, no overall winner of each annual race until 1928.

Lorraine-Dietrich increasingly concentrated on aero engines and after 1926 ceased to support entries at Le Mans. A Sports Lorraine returned to the Sarthe circuit in 1931 and finished fourth in the hands of Trebor/Balart. They covered 1,763.074 miles (2,836.786km) compared with the 1,875.079 (3,017.002km) of the winning 8C Alfa Romeo of Tim Birkin/Lord Howe. Increased distances were due to improved road conditions as much as rising performance. The last appearance of a 15CV at Le Mans was in 1934 when Vernet entered a car for himself and Daniel Porthault. They retired early in the race.

In 1929 Lorraine joined a government-sponsored consortium of airframe and engine builders known as Société Génerale Aeronautique, intended to be the Aerospatiale of its day. Wisely, many other companies declined to join, the consortium was unsuccessful and in 1932 Lorraine's bankers appointed a receiver who sold off most of the company in parts. The 15CV was finally fitted with a four-speed gearbox in 1930 and ceased production in 1932. The last Lorraine car was the side-valve 4-litre 20CV. Only a few hundred were built, there were no buyers for the car division and this closed in 1934.

The 1926 Le Mans Winner

The 1926 Le Mans-winning Lorraine-Dietrich as it is today, beautifully and accurately restored and with a delightful performance on the road. (FotoVantage)

This is the only genuine survivor of the Le Mans Lorraines. After the race, driver Robert Bloch acquired it as a touring car and cut off the tail, which he replaced with a platform to carry luggage and two spare wheels. The car passed through many hands before Serge Broussard discovered it in 1972, bought it and fully restored it. Madame Jeanne Leroux, whose father had worked for Lorraine, acquired it in 1995 and her son Phillippe and his wife Christine appear with it at historic events.

It is a long-legged car, still with a very robust performance, and the six-cylinder engine is remarkably smooth. Although the 'crash' gearbox needs the usual careful timing and the occasional 'crunch' is almost unavoidable, it is quiet and positive. By Vintage standards the steering is light and the very large servo-assisted brakes are firm and powerful. This Lorraine-Dietrich is an exceptionally handsome and potent car, a true greyhound with all the characteristics of the breed – plus proven endurance – and is a great survivor from a classic era.

Ariès 3-litre

1925–27

The 3-litre Ariès driven by Chassagne/Laly which came so close to winning the 1927 Le Mans race. (LAT)

The 3-litre Ariès built at Coubevoie has one claim to fame, and rightly so, and that is the challenge that it presented to Bentley at Le Mans in 1927. The make originated in 1903 and the name is the French version of the Greek *Ares* (equivalent of the Latin *Mars*, God of War). Much of Ariès production before the First World War was devoted to Aster-engined commercial vehicles, but it produced a very compact V4 1,130cc (60×100mm) engine in 1908 and two years later catalogued what was then the smallest six-cylinder production engine in the world. The 1913 car range included a model with the very fashionable Knight double sleeve-valve engine, although the company sold only a few of these.

During the war years Ariès built Hispano-Suiza aero engines under licence and the profits from this sustained post-First World War production, as it did with Ballot and others. The early post-war models had side-valve engines, but in 1922 the company introduced an overhead camshaft four-cylinder 1,085cc model, 5CV Type CC2, with front-wheel brakes. From 1924 they ran regularly at Le Mans. These cars finished on a couple of occasions.

The best performance was in 1924 when Gabriel/Lapierre took 11th place (and were the first 1,100cc finishers) at 40.82mph (65.68kph) and covered 979.708 miles (1,576.35km), while Rigal/Delano finished in 13th place with another of these cars. The marque was less successful in 1926 and the Gabriel/Paris car was 13th and last finisher at a speed of 45.540mph (73.274kph).

The 2,957cc (82×140mm) model originally appeared in side-valve form, but was re-engineered for 1922 with a single overhead camshaft cylinder head, incorporating drive to the camshaft by a vertical shaft as on Hispano-Suizas of the period. There was a four-speed gearbox and the chassis was the usual channel-section with rigid axles front and rear suspended on semi-elliptic leaf springs. The majority of sporting Ariès had four-seater tourer bodies of conventional type and in this form they competed at Boulogne, Le Mans, San Sebastian and Spa-Francorchamps without conspicuous success.

At Le Mans in 1925 a 3-litre Ariès driven by veteran Louis Wagner and Charles Flohot finished sixth, covering 1,227.296 miles (1,974.719km) at 53.22mph (85.63kph). Two cars ran the following year with an attempt at aerodynamics; flat curving tails and enclosed rear wheels, which led to this version becoming known as the *Pumaise* ('creeping bug'). Modifications to the engines included higher compression ratio, together with larger carburettors and power output was said to be 96bhp.

A change in the rules for the 1926 Le Mans race meant that now the first driver had to erect the hood at the start and then stop after 20 laps to lower it. *The Autocar* reported, ". . .the drivers of the two big light blue Ariès, Flohot and Laly, seemed absolutely lazy. They erected their hoods, fastened the straps and buttoned the side curtains as if they were about to start for a pleasure run in showery weather, while their team-mates, Chassagne and Duray, stood by impatiently."

Nor did these drivers show much speed, at least in the first few hours of the race. Suddenly it seemed as though Laly had cottoned on to the fact that he was at the wheel of a potent piece of machinery, and he increased his speed considerably, set a new lap record at just over 70mph (113kph) – beaten later in the race by de Courcelles (Lorraine-Dietrich) at 71.112mph

Another view of the Ariès at Le Mans in 1927. This photograph shows off well the smooth, full-width rear bodywork that contrasted so much with the traditional upright radiator and skimpy front wings. (LAT)

(114.42kph) – and worked his way up to eighth place. By midnight Laly/Chassagne were in sixth place and Flohot/Duray ninth.

Both Ariès retired during the Sunday morning; under acceleration from Arnage a carburettor blew back on the Flohot/Duray car. Duray switched off the petrol, stopped the car and put out the fire using the on-board extinguisher; damage was limited to burnt-out wiring. Later on the Sunday morning Chassagne was unable to restart on the starter motor after a routine pit stop; investigation revealed that the batteries were not holding their charge and Ariès retired the car.

In 1927 among other changes in the regulations, the organisers supplied the pump fuel, with a view to preventing the competitors from using their own special brews. The works Bentley team was competing in its third Le Mans race after two years of failure, but apart from Ariès, there were no other large-capacity cars in the race. Ariès entered only a single 3-litre car for Chassagne and Laly. Jean Chassagne was vastly experienced, having been a works Sunbeam driver and co-drove with 'Sammy' Davis the second-placed 3-litre Sunbeam in the 1925 race.

Initially the Bentleys held first three places, the 4½-litre of Clement/Callingham heading the 3-litre cars of d'Erlanger/Duller and 'Sammy' Davis/Benjafield, trailed by the 3-litre Ariès of Chassagne/Laly. At about 9.30pm a 2-litre Th. Schneider slid wildly at *White House*, and stopped, straddling the road; Callingham swerved into the ditch to avoid the French car, then the second Th. Schneider, Duller's Bentley and a 1,100cc Ariès piled into the debris.

Next on the scene was Davis, who had a premonition that all was not well, eased off but not enough to prevent his Bentley from sliding sideways into the wreckage under braking. He was the only driver able to motor from the scene and back in the pits he surveyed the Bentley. The chassis frame and front axle were bent, the offside front wing and running board were smashed and only the driver with tools carried on the car could carry out repairs. With Benjafield at the wheel, the Bentley rejoined the race after half-an-hour, but by then the 3-litre Ariès led by six laps.

During the rain-swept night the Bentley steadily closed the gap and by 11am on the Sunday morning it was four laps behind. W.O. Bentley then heard a peculiar noise from the engine of the French car as it passed the pits and urged Davis and Benjafield to speed up to bring pressure on the Ariès team. Laly then had difficulty in starting the car after a pit stop and now the gap was down to one lap and Chassagne increased his lap speed to keep the Bentley at bay. With less than two hours to the finish the Ariès came to rest out on the circuit, its race run because of a sheared camshaft drive.

The Bentley went on to cover the greatest distance at Le Mans for the second time. It was a defeat that shattered all Ariès aspirations and although the company withdrew from competition work, almost certainly the company's poor trading record had much to do with this decision. Before the end of the year Laly with a three-litre Ariès won the handicap Georges Boillot Cup at Boulogne, cut short that year to 70 miles (112km).

Despite the vast number of cars offered on the French market in the 1920s, Ariès flourished, selling mainly the small-capacity models, the sporting performance of which gave them considerable appeal. It is also a fact that, generally, manufacturers based in the Paris area, flourished to a greater extent than those based away from the capital. In 1929 the company introduced a very swift version of the 1,085cc car, the CC 4S sports model, that featured twin plugs per cylinder. As the economy worsened, so sales flagged and the company was just managing to keep afloat.

Ariès continued to manufacture commercial vehicles until 1934 and cars of largely undistinguished type and in small numbers until 1938. One of the company's final products was the four-cylinder 10CV Super that boasted a two-speed rear axle and this was built between 1934 and 1938. The majority of the later commercial vehicles were based on passenger chassis. Ariès's claim to fame is not just that it battled with Bentley and lost, but, like Chenard-Walcker, Voisin and others, it made pioneer attempts to introduce aerodynamics to motor racing.

The writer has made enquiries through contacts in France, but there seems to be no surviving three-litre Ariès, standard or competition. This is a very great pity, as they were cars of exceptionally good performance and, by the standards of the time, good handling and braking.

Alvis front-wheel drive
1925–30

Major C. M. Harvey heads the Alvis straight-eight entries at the start of the 1930 Tourist Trophy. Behind are Cyril Paul and Harold Purdy. Following his experiences in the First World War, during which he was gassed, Harvey suffered from severe depression and sadly in 1936 he shot himself.

When the Chief Engineer of Alvis, Captain G.T. Smith-Clarke, originally proposed a front-wheel-drive car, it was intended for use in hill climbs and sprints. With the greater proportion of weight on the front wheels, Smith-Clarke argued, if the car skidded, the driver could save time by being able to accelerate out of the skid, instead of having to ease off to avoid spinning. The car would also have greater stability because the absence of a prop-shaft would permit much lower construction.

The first FWD Alvis had a chassis made of duralumin and the usual production four-cylinder 1,496cc (68×103mm) push-rod engine reversed in the chassis. At the back of the engine, but at the front of the car, there was a single-plate clutch enclosed in a bell-housing, the four-speed gearbox and the straight-tooth bevel final drive. Alvis built two cars, the first of which was called *Tadpole* because of the way in which the front end was glued to the track, but the rear end danced about the road. Early in their racing career these cars were fitted with Roots-type superchargers at the front of the engine, driven from the nose of the crankshaft and protruding well into the cockpit.

During the 1925 British season the fwd Alvis cars, which were little more than low-cost specials, performed encouragingly, and the Alvis directors took it into their heads to build two Grand Prix cars for the 1,500cc formula that came into force for the 1926 season. Cars complying with the new formula had to weigh not less than 700kg (1,544lb) and have a minimum width of 80cm (31.52 inches). Two seats were compulsory, even though riding mechanics were no longer carried. One of these cars ran in a Shelsley Walsh hill climb, one was entered in the RAC Grand Prix at Brooklands and they both ran and retired in the JCC 200 Miles race at Brooklands in September.

Although these were Grand Prix cars, many of the features were adopted on the later sports-racing cars. The GP Alvis had an in-line eight-cylinder engine of 1,497cc (55×78.75mm) with fixed cylinder head, two high-mounted camshafts, one on each side of the engine, operating the horizontal valves through short vertical rockers. The crankcase was cast in aluminium-alloy split along the centre-line of the crankshaft, no flywheel was needed and the circular-web crankshaft ran in five plain bearings. There were duralumin connecting rods and plain big ends with duralumin bearing surfaces.

Ignition was by twin magnetos driven from the front of the camshafts and each fired four cylinders. A Roots-type supercharger was driven from the crankshaft and projected into the cockpit and there was a single Solex carburettor. Alvis used dry-sump lubrication. The company published no power output figures, but a conservative estimate would put the figure at about 115bhp. Transmission was by a small multi-plate clutch and a four-speed gearbox with drive to the front wheels through a straight-tooth bevel final drive and exposed drive-shafts with universal joints at each end.

The pressed-steel chassis had deep channel-section side members tapering to the rear, with a very substantial bulkhead behind the radiator that stiffened the chassis and served as a front engine mount and with tubular arms running from the chassis frame to the engine crankcase. Front suspension was, as on the 1925 cars, by pairs of quarter-elliptic springs parallel to the chassis each side and with a front axle consisting of two tubes, a form of reverse de Dion suspension that was also adopted on the 1925 fwd Miller. Single trailing quarter-elliptic springs each side, again as on the 1925 cars, were used at the rear.

It was clear that the Grand Prix cars were less than satisfactory and it was decided to rebuild them for 1927, fitting single-seater bodywork as now permitted under the regulations. Technically, the most important change was the adoption of twin overhead camshafts driven from the crankshaft by an enormous idler pinion over a foot in diameter. Other features were hemispherical combustion chambers, with the valves inclined at 90° and the springs enclosed in dashpots. The crankcase was a one-piece alloy casting. Power output was said to be 125bhp.

At the front, the four-speed gearbox now projected well into the air stream, so as to concentrate even more weight on the front wheels, and again there was a multi-plate clutch. The differential was mounted below the clutch and the gearbox and because of the car's very low construction, the input shaft passed under the differential and back into it at a slightly higher level. The inboard brakes were bolted on either side of the differential. The 1927 Alvis was one of the first racing cars with independent front suspension and it consisted of quarter-elliptic springs each side, paired above and below the drive-shafts and with twin Hartford dampers. The rear suspension was unchanged.

Once again Alvis had the cars ready only late in the year, but they were not raceworthy. The car entered for works driver Major C.M. Harvey in the RAC Grand Prix at Brooklands broke a piston in practice and non-started. The two cars ran in the JCC 200 Miles race at the same venue two weeks later, but both retired because of engine failure. The 1,500cc Grand Prix formula came to an end after its second year and Alvis withdrew from this form of racing, in reality, a venture that it could ill-afford. Alvis was a true pioneer of fwd, alongside Miller in the United States and Grégoire in France, and the lessons learned over three years were now put to more practical purposes.

In February 1928 Alvis announced production fwd cars typed the FA and FB 12/50, the sportier of which was the FA with 8ft 6in (2,590mm) wheelbase. The chassis was a channel-section structure, deep and narrow at the front and widening out at the rear. The front suspension followed that of the 1927 Grand Prix cars and at the rear there was a new independent system by leading arms with quarter-elliptic springs bolted underneath.

The 1,482cc (68×102mm) four-cylinder engine was derived from that used in the very successful, very conventional push-rod 12/50 sports model, but there was now a single overhead camshaft driven by a very noisy gear-train which also drove the supercharger (when fitted) and the engine ancillaries. As was becoming usual practice, the engine was reversed in the chassis and ahead of it were the clutch housing, the four-speed gearbox and rear of the differential housing all in a one-piece aluminium-alloy housing. With their very long bonnets, these cars had a very sleek, racy appearance.

Originally, Alvis entered five cars in the 1928 Le Mans race, but reduced the entry to two, both modified FA fwd cars, without superchargers as they doubted that they would last the 24 hours in 'blown form', and with Cross & Ellis fabric bodies. There were problems in practice, but both cars enjoyed a trouble free race. Harvey/Purdy finished sixth at 59.195mph (95.245kph), covering 1,420.689 miles (2,285.889km). Every car in front had an engine of over 4,000cc. 'Sammy' Davis/Urquhart-Dykes took ninth place. Interestingly, three of J.A. Grégoire's fwd Tractas, one of 1,500cc and two of 1,100cc took 12th, 16th and 17th places – the 1,100s were the last two finishers.

At the end of August Alvis entered five modified,

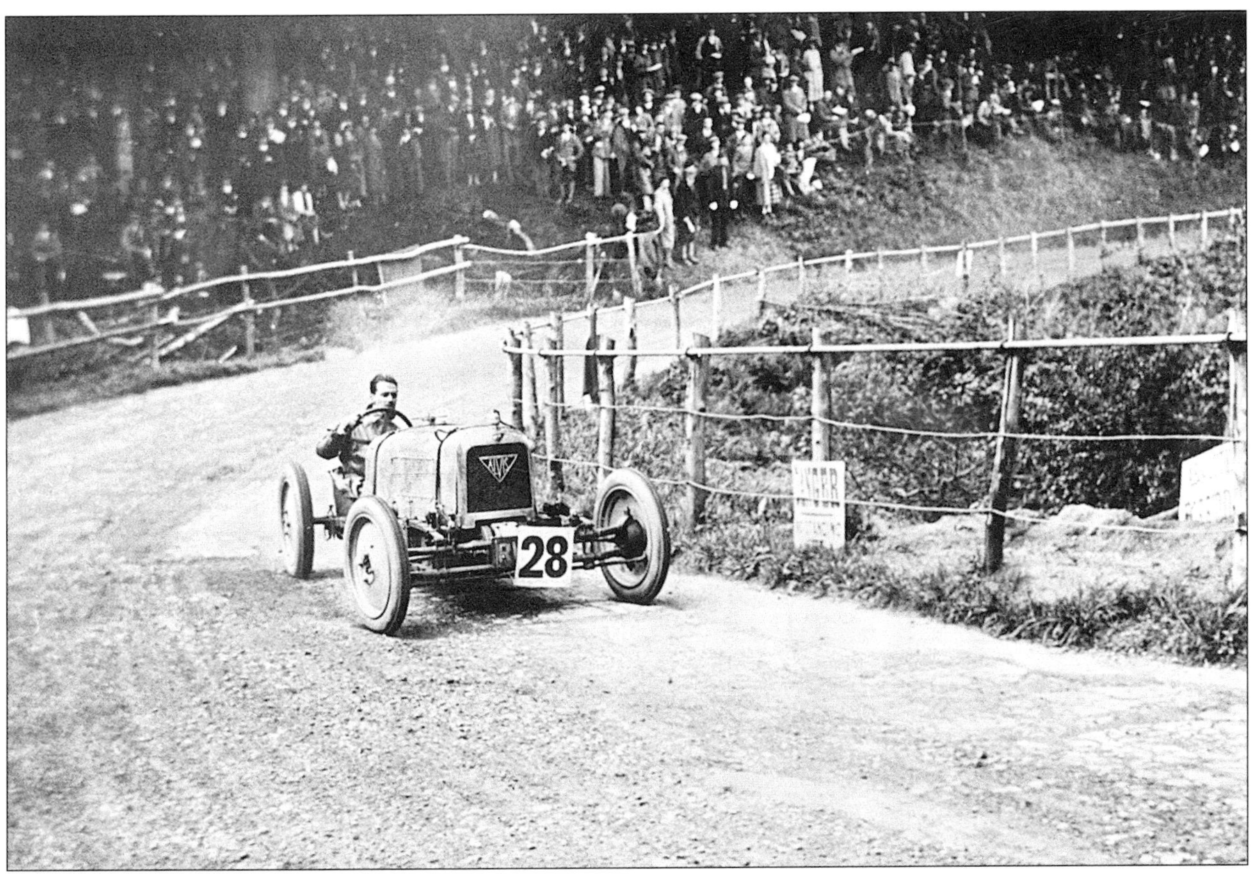

This is the first of the 1925 1,500cc front-wheel-drive cars, Tadpole, with C.M. Harvey at the wheel at Shelsley Walsh hill climb in May that year. Alvis later fitted a streamlined tail and made a number of modifications, including the installation of a supercharger.

supercharged cars known as the FC in the 410-mile (660km) handicap Tourist Trophy run on the Ards circuit in Northern Ireland. The FCs had a revised engine of 1,496cc (68×103mm) with fixed cylinder head, roller-bearing big ends and a special crankshaft. Power output was 72bhp at 4,470rpm. The gearbox had special constant-mesh ratios that narrowed the gap between third and top and there was a Carbodies aluminium-alloy two-seater body.

The FCs showed great promise, but only the car driven by Leon Cushman qualified as a finisher, in second place behind Kaye Don's supercharged Lea-Francis. Shortly afterwards Harvey drove this car in the 279-mile (449km) Georges Boillot Cup and he was in third place when a piston failed. The TT cars were sold off with standard engines and Alvis also sold a limited number of replicas of both the Le Mans and TT entries. Whatever the merits of these early fwd cars, they were too complicated and too 'new-fangled' for the buying public, even though they were good for 80mph in standard form. Production ceased in April 1929, but Alvis was not deterred.

The company now built four supercharged straight-eight sports-racing cars that they typed the FA 8/15. The engine was developed from that of the 1927 Grand Prix car, but had a shorter stroke of 78.5mm, giving a capacity of 1,491cc. Steel connecting rods with needle-roller big ends replaced the duralumin con-rods of the 1927 cars, the crankshaft ran in ball-and-roller main bearings and there was a wet sump, although it was almost separate from the engine and known as 'semi-dry.' Alvis reckoned the power output was still about 125bhp.

As on the 1927 Grand Prix cars, the gearbox was mounted ahead of the final drive, but the sports cars were of higher construction and the input shaft entered the final drive at a higher level. The 10ft (3,048mm) wheelbase-chassis was similar to that of the production cars, but at the rear there were twin transverse semi-elliptic springs. Again Carbodies were responsible for the short-tail two-seater bodies.

In 1929 the first JCC Double 12 Hours race was held at Brooklands. Because of the ban on the use of the track at night, it was not possible to hold a 24 hours' race and this was next best. Smith-Clarke acted as nominee for

Alvis and three cars ran in his name. It was another dismal race for Alvis and none of the cars survived. Willday/Griffiths retired early on the first day because of a broken oil pump drive, the Urquhart-Dykes's, husband and spouse, were eliminated on the second day because of a broken spring anchorage, while Cushman/Paul had gearbox problems that left them with top gear only until the clutch gave up just over an hour before the finish.

Two Alvis straight-eights with regulation four-seater bodies appeared at Le Mans. Cyril Paul/'Sammy' Davis non-started after it was discovered that the camshaft of their car was out of line following big-end failure. Paul replaced Cushman in the car to be shared with Urquhart-Dykes and they ran well early in the race until a water leak developed. The regulations did not allow water to be added until 210 miles (337km) had been completed and when this was done, the cylinder block cracked.

The third appearance of the straight-eights in 1929 was in the handicap Tourist Trophy held in August on the Ards circuit. These were two-seaters and were driven by Harvey, Paul and Cushman. The main opposition in the 1,500cc class came from five 6C 1500 Alfa Romeos. The FA 8/15s could match the lithe Italian cars for speed, but they were some 400lb (180kg) heavier.

These two slightly modified production front-wheel-drive cars with Cross & Ellis bodies ran at Le Mans in 1928. Harvey is pulling out of the pits with the car that he and Purdy drove into sixth place. The Alvis has lost a headlamp, not unusual in long-distance races of the period because of vibration and road shocks. These cars had seats in the dickey to comply with the requirements for four-seater bodywork and the compulsory hood enclosed both cockpit and dickey.

The Coventry cars ran well until rain began to fall when they were slowed by misfiring caused by the protruding carburettor intakes sucking in water. They finished well down the field in the order Cushman eighth, Harvey ninth and Paul 17th. Campari's Alfa Romeo took second place behind Caracciola's mighty 7-litre Mercedes-Benz and another Mercedes-Benz and other Alfas were fifth, sixth and seventh.

Alvis was not planning to race the straight-eights in 1930, but Charles Follett, now the London distributor, persuaded them to enter a team in the 1930 Tourist Trophy and probably helped finance it. The cars were similar to those raced in 1929, apart from new front suspension by two upper transverse semi-elliptic springs, lower radius arms and Hartford shock absorbers.

Weight had been substantially reduced since 1929 and there are good grounds for believing that three of the cars had Elektron alloy crankcases. The bodies, built by Cross & Ellis, were wider, with less sloping, beetle-back tails and there was a bulge in the bonnet side covering the carburettors to prevent a recurrence of the 1929 problem.

Three of the cars at Ards were works-entered for Harvey, Cushman and Paul, but the fourth car driven by Purdy was nominally a private entry by D.K. Mansell. *Scuderia Ferrari*-entered supercharged Alfa Romeo 6C 1750s driven by Campari, Nuvolari and Varzi took the first three places, but Paul took a fairly satisfactory fourth place at an average of 69.61mph (112.00kph) compared with Nuvolari's 70.88mph (114.95kph). Purdy and Cushman were sixth and seventh and Alvis took the first three places in the 1,500cc class.

Harvey, the Alvis front-runner, dropped out of contention in bizarre circumstances. At his first pit stop he left his car in neutral with the brakes on (the correct procedure was to leave the car in gear with the brakes off) and his mechanic had difficulty in turning the brake adjusters. In his haste to rejoin the race Harvey jumped into the car, fired the engine and started to move off. The mechanic narrowly avoided being run over and hastily joined his driver. The brakes had not, of course, been properly adjusted, a brake locked, Harvey hit a bank and the Alvis spun round, damaging its tail. He was able to carry on, but at the finish he was too far behind to be classified.

Alvis did not race the fwd cars again. It had been a bold and inspired effort to fly in the face of conventional design thinking, something that J.A. Grégoire did more successfully in racing with his smaller-capacity Tractas of less advanced design. The eight-cylinder models were pure sports-racing cars of impeccable breeding, having been directly developed from the Grand Prix cars.

Bentley 4½-litre Supercharged

1929–30

Tim Birkin, with W.O. Bentley as riding mechanic, drove this blown 4½-litre Bentley in the 1929 Tourist Trophy on the Ards circuit in Northern Ireland. They finished second on scratch behind the 7-litre Mercedes-Benz of Caracciola, but they were a poor 11th on handicap.

The competition cars from Cricklewood were developed during the 1920s from near-enough standard sports tourers to out-and-out sports racers – even though they were never purpose-built racers like the Alvis straight-eight cars. More comparable with Lorraine-Dietrich, they gradually evolved, but of course remained – always – characteristically Albion in concept. When a 3-litre Bentley ran in the first Le Mans race in 1923, it was a private entry by J.E. Duff, the London agent, but prepared at the works (which meant precisely what it said, for there was no attempt at development).

The Bentley, co-driven by Frank Clement, who was in charge of Bentley's Experimental Department and an official works driver, was the fastest car in the race, but plagued by minor problems, including running out of fuel, it covered fourth highest distance, jointly with a Bignan and an Excelsior. Duff and Clement returned to the Sarthe circuit in 1924 with the same car, now fitted with front-wheel brakes and headlamp stone-guards, and they covered the highest distance, ahead of two Lorraine-Dietrich entries.

In 1925 the works team took over the *oriflamme*, but the 3-litre cars entered in both that year and 1926 retired. In 1927 Bentley entered a 4½-litre car, together with two 3-litres and after the notorious *White House* crash that involved all three, the battered 3-litre of Benjafield/Davis covered the highest distance. In 1928 there was an outright winner at Le Mans for the first time and Barnato/Rubin with a 4½-litre Bentley won from a Stutz and two Chryslers, with another 4½-litre Bentley driven by Birkin/Chassagne in fifth place.

Tim Birkin challenged W.O. Bentley's conviction that the way forward in sports car racing was with the new 6½-litre Speed Six. Birkin believed that the answer was a supercharged version of the 4½-litre. Part of his thinking was that a supercharged car would have a better chance of beating the very successful supercharged 6C 1750 Alfa Romeos in handicap races. It would carry

In the 1930 Le Mans race Dr Benjafield, seen here at Pontlieue, cruises back to the pits with a stripped tread and much buckled rear wing. He drove solo after co-driver Giulio Ramponi was taken ill, but retired because of piston failure when in third place. (LAT)

a lower handicap than the Speed Six and would be faster than the standard 4½-litre car, although running in the same handicap class. Bentley argued that it was not good enough to simply tack a blower on to the existing engine, but a supercharged engine should be built from scratch.

In standard form the 4,398cc (100×140mm) Bentley engine featured a single overhead camshaft, four valves per cylinder, twin magnetos and two plugs per cylinder. The works team cars had special high-compression 'hour glass' aluminium-alloy pistons and developed 130bhp compared with the 105/110bhp of the production cars. Depending on the body fitted, tyres and gearing, these 3,800lb (1.723kg) behemoths had a maximum speed of up to 120mph.

C. Amherst Villiers carried out very extensive and expensive modifications to the 4½-litre engine that included a new and stronger cylinder block, crankshaft, connecting rods, pistons and oil pump. The Villiers-designed, Roots-type supercharger was fed by two SU carburettors and driven off the front of the crankshaft. The existing 10ft 10½in (3,315mm) chassis was retained, but a modified front cross-member carried the nose of the engine and the back of the blower was mounted between the front dumb-irons. A front tie-bar carried the front of the blower.

A further modification made in mid-1930 was the adoption of a larger-capacity ribbed sump to improve oil cooling. The power output of the 4½-litre blown cars as raced by Birkin was about 175bhp at the rear wheels. This made them around 12mph faster than the unblown Le Mans cars and the acceleration was much better. After the first blown car had been completed, Birkin demonstrated it to Bentley Chairman Woolf Barnato and he was sufficiently impressed to sanction the production of 50 examples, now necessary to comply with Le Mans regulations. It should be stressed that while W.O. Bentley did not approve of the supercharged cars, he was not actively opposed to them.

Birkin's three cars were prepared at Welwyn and Lofty England, later of Jaguar, was among those who worked on them. It had been hoped to run the cars at Le Mans in 1929, but they were not ready. Birkin, however, drove the prototype blown car in the BARC Six Hours race at Brooklands on 29 June. There were now two Bentley teams, the works cars and Birkin's blown entries. The Brooklands race was run on a short, 2.616-mile (4.21km) circuit with chicanes and on a handicap basis. Birkin had problems with the blower relief valve, but it is believed that oil starvation caused his retirement. Barnato/Dunfee won the race with the original works Speed Six.

Next was the Irish Grand Prix in Phoenix Park, Dublin on 12–13 July. On the first day there was the Saorstat Cup for cars up to 1,500cc and the following day the Eireann Cup for cars over 1,500cc took place. Both were 300-mile (482km) races and the Irish Grand Prix was decided on the results of both events. Birkin battled with Thistlewayte's 7-litre supercharged Mercedes-Benz until this blew a head gasket. Birkin's car started to overheat and Glen Kidston with a works Speed Six narrowly beat him on scratch. Rubin had plug problems with his blown car and finished eighth on scratch. Ivanowski with a 6C 1750 Alfa Romeo won on handicap and was also the winner of the Grand Prix.

In the Tourist Trophy at Ards on 17 August a single works Speed Six and blown cars driven by Birkin, Rubin and Harcourt-Wood, faced four 7-litre blown Mercedes and three works Alfa Romeo 6C 1750s. W.O. Bentley went as riding mechanic with Birkin because, "I thought our mechanics were beginning to consider themselves heroes. After the race I realised that they were." Kidston crashed the works car and Caracciola (works Mercedes-Benz) won on scratch and handicap at 72.82mph (117.17kph). Birkin was second on

Tim Birkin drove this stripped, blown Bentley, in his own words, "a Sealyham amongst greyhounds", in the 1930 French Grand Prix at Pau. He took second place to Etancelin driving a 2-litre Bugatti Type 35.

scratch at 69.01mph (111.04kph) after a trouble free run, but was relegated to 11th place on handicap. Rubin hit a bank and overturned his car, while Harcourt-Wood retired.

The 500 Miles race held on Brooklands Outer circuit on 12 October was the final race of the year. All the Bentleys ran in stripped form. Birkin/Harcourt-Wood shared the only blown car entered and after leading, it fell back because of an oil leak that spread everywhere including Birkin's goggles and retired after a broken exhaust ignited the fabric body. The works unsupercharged cars of Clement/Barclay (4½-litre) and Davis/Dunfee (6½-litre) took the first two places.

Birkin was in financial trouble and before the 1930 season he sold the blown cars to horse racing enthusiast, the Hon Dorothy Paget. She had the first car rebuilt as a single-seater and acquired a new road-racing car. Birkin/Chassagne, Kidston/Dunfee and Benjafield/Baron d'Erlanger drove the Paget entries in the Double Twelve race at Brooklands on 9–10 May. They ran well initially, but on the first day Birkin/Chassagne retired because of a broken chassis and Kidston/Dunfee were eliminated by a broken valve. On the second day Davis pushed his 'Blower' a mile back to the pits where a new rear axle was fitted, but this car later retired. Works 6½-litre cars took first two places.

At Le Mans, held on 21–22 June, the blown Bentleys were in immediate trouble because they overheated on the official fuel supplied. On two cars the compression plate was removed and they ran on pure benzole (apparently permitted under the regulations), but there was insufficient time to convert the third car and it was withdrawn. The driver pairings were Birkin/Chassagne and Benjafield/Ramponi. The blown cars showed a tremendous turn of speed, but were plagued by tyre problems.

Benjafield had continued single-handed after Ramponi was taken ill at about midnight on the Saturday. The Birkin/Chassagne car, in fourth place, retired because of a broken crankshaft at midday on the Sunday and less than an hour later Benjafield was out of the race because of a broken piston. Works 6½-litre cars took the first two places and shortly after Le Mans the Bentley company announced its withdrawal from racing.

All three Paget team cars ran in the Irish Grand Prix in July and they faced three 7-litre Mercedes-Benz entries. Early in the race Harcourt-Wood and Chassagne brought their 'Blowers' into the pits because of loss of oil pressure and although they continued, they were no longer serious contenders. Birkin and Caracciola battled furiously, and the German Mercedes driver had to cover two laps more than Birkin. On the day Caracciola was the superior driver, especially in the wet, and Birkin had to stop twice because of serious oil leaks. Caracciola went on to win from Campari (6C 1750 Alfa Romeo) with Earl Howe (7-litre Mercedes-Benz) third and Birkin fourth.

Next came the Tourist Trophy at Ards on 23 August. The Paget team was out in force with entries for Birkin, Kensington Moir and Benjafield/Chassagne. After Caracciola was disqualified for running an oversize supercharger, the Bentleys seemed to be in with a good chance. The Alfa Romeos were, however, faster than expected and exploited their handicap advantage to the full. Birkin moved steadily up the field, but at three-quarters' race distance made a bad mistake, hit a telegraph pole glancingly and spun into a wall. The Alfa Romeos took the first three places, while Kensington Moir was a poor 11th on handicap and Benjafield unclassified (Chassagne did not drive).

In September Birkin ran a stripped, blown Bentley in the very poorly supported 247-mile (397km) Formule Libre French Grand Prix at Pau. The two-ton Bentley had much the same performance as the 2-litre Bugattis, but vastly inferior roadholding. Etancelin (unblown Type 35) won by 3min 26sec from Birkin, who was a mere ten seconds ahead of Zanelli (blown Type 35C). The winning car was low on fuel. Just after the finish the last of the clutch-retaining bolts sheered and the Bugatti could not have completed another lap. Birkin's drive was spectacular, but had little to do with sports-car racing.

The final outing for the Paget sports car team was the 500 Mile race on the outer circuit at Brooklands on 4 October. The race was a Formule Libre event, Birkin/Duller sharing the single-seater, while Eyston/Wood and Benjafield/Eddie Hall drove stripped road-racing cars. Benjafield/Hall drove superbly to take second place on handicap behind the Austin Seven of 'Sammy' Davis/The Earl of March. Eyston/Wood retired because of magneto-drive failure and the blue single-seater had its problems and finished a poor ninth.

Brooklands marked the end of the blower Bentleys' serious racing days, for Dorothey Paget sold the road-racers at the end of the year. She retained the single-seater and Birkin vied for the record for the banked Brooklands track until his death in 1933. With it he set a record of 137.96mph in 1932. Although the blower Bentley has come to be regarded as the archetypal British Vintage car (and replicas have proliferated), it lacked the reliability for endurance racing and, as the new breed of cars such as Jano's Alfa Romeos reflected substantial technical progress, dinosaurs such as the Bentley and the 7-litre Mercedes-Benz soon disappeared from the circuits.

Alfa Romeo 8C 2300

1931–34

Nuvolari partnered by Guidotti with the new 8C 2300 Spyder Corsa seen before the start of the 1931 Mille Miglia. Two of these cars ran in this race, but they were untried and plagued by tyre problems. Victory went to Caracciola with a 7-litre Mercedes-Benz SSKL. (Centro Documentazione Alfa Romeo)

Vittorio Jano's eight-cylinder cars created an Alfa Romeo sporting tradition that persisted throughout the 1930s and they enjoyed a superb competition record. They were remarkably multi-faceted cars for they were suitable for fast touring, long-distance endurance racing and, in their most powerful form, won Grands Prix. They were the natural successors to the same designer's six-cylinder 1,500cc, 1,750cc and 1,900cc cars that dated back in single overhead camshaft form to 1925. When Jano designed the 8C 2300, he incorporated many design features from the earlier cars.

The 8C 2300 had a straight-eight engine of 2,336cc (65×88mm) cast in aluminium-alloy in two blocks of four cylinders with steel liners and there was an alloy crankcase. Between the blocks was a pair of helical gears, one of which drove the camshafts through intermediate gears and the other drove the supercharger, the oil and water pumps and the dynamo. There were separate detachable alloy cylinder heads and two valves per cylinder with triple valve springs at an included angle of 90°. The pistons were aluminium-alloy and the connecting rods were I-section steel. The two-piece crankshaft ran in ten main bearings.

A twin-choke Memini carburettor fed the mixture to the Roots-type supercharger mounted low down on the right of the engine and compressing at 5–6psi. Lubrication was dry-sump with a 4½-gallon (20-litre) oil tank. Ignition was by a Bosch coil and distributor and there was a manual retard and advance in the centre of the steering wheel. Despite the absence of a fan, the engine invariably ran cool. Compression ratio varied, but even in the mildest tune was 5.75:1. Power output of the competition versions was as high as 155bhp at 5,200rpm.

As on the earlier six-cylinder cars, transmission was by a four-speed, constant-mesh gearbox integral with the engine and a large multi-plate clutch. The channel-section chassis had rigid axles front and rear suspended on semi-elliptic springs, located by two radius rods and friction-type shock absorbers. Originally, the rear of the front springs slid in semi-cylindrical trunnions, but later they were shackled at both ends. Rod-operated brakes, as on the six-cylinder cars were used, but with enormous 15½in (400mm) finned light alloy brakes and cast iron liners that filled the wire-spoked wheels. The wheelbase of the *Corto* was 9ft 3in (2,820mm) and the *Lungo* 10ft 2in (3,099mm).

The model with shorter wheelbase, known in competition form as the *Spyder Corsa*, first appeared in the Mille Miglia road race in April 1931 and is also known as the *Mille Miglia* model. Because of the threat from Mercedes-Benz (Caracciola won the race with an SSKL), the new cars, driven by Nuvolari and Arcangeli, were raced before they were ready. They were in effect prototype cars and had the oil tank mounted at the front between the dumb-irons. They both led the race at times, but suffered problems with their Pirelli tyres, Arcangeli had clutch trouble and crashed, while Nuvolari also crashed, but carried on with cuts on his face bleeding to finish ninth.

As the *Monza* pure racing version of the 8C 2300 would not be ready to race until later in the month, two stripped *Spyder Corsas* ran in the 363-mile Targa Florio on 10 May. All the Alfa Romeo drivers except Arcangeli retained front mudguards to protect themselves from flying stones. Nuvolari (8C 2300) won from Borzacchini (6C 1750) and Varzi (Bugatti Type 51). Flying stones broke Arcangeli's goggles and lacerated his face, so he handed his 8C 2300 over to Zehender who finished sixth and last.

The exhaust side of the 8C 2300 straight-eight engine. The ribbed, cast exhaust manifold was a work of beauty in itself. (FotoVantage)

At the beginning of June Sir Henry Birkin raced a new *Lungo* in the Eireann Cup race, the second leg of the Irish Grand Prix held in Phoenix Park, Dublin. Although he won his race from Campari (8C 2500 Maserati in sports form), he was second on the handicap aggregate of the two races. Three 8C 2300 *Lungo* four-seaters ran at Le Mans in June. Earl Howe/Sir Henry Birkin with the former's private car, but running as part of the works team, won at a record 78.128mph (125.708kph) from Ivanowski/Stoffel with a 7-litre Mercedes. Both the works 2.3s retired. Because of this success the *Lungo* is usually known in Britain as the *Le Mans* model.

In July Birkin partnered by George Eyston ran his 8C 2300 *Lungo* in the Belgian 24 Hours race at Spa-Francorchamps. They built up a 40-minute lead, but the car developed a misfire and retired out on the circuit and a 7-litre Mercedes-Benz won the race. In the 410-mile (660km) handicap Tourist Trophy on the Ards circuit in Northern Ireland in August, Alfa Romeo entered three *Lungos* and Lord Howe and Sir Henry Birkin joined them with their private cars. Borzacchini drove magnificently with his 8C 2300, averaging 79.05mph (127.19kph) and was second on handicap to Black (MG). Campari finished sixth with his 8C 2300 and the other three Alfa Romeos retired.

In the Mille Miglia in April 1932 the works fielded three *Spyder Corsas* with Touring bodies for Borzacchini, Campari and Nuvolari, with Caracciola works-assisted. There was also a *Scuderia Ferrari* entry of five 8C 2300s with Zagato bodies. Portello faced no serious opposition and Alfa's only problem was a surfeit of rivalry between the drivers. Initially Nuvolari, partnered by Guidotti (later Alfa Romeo racing manager) led, but at Florence he went off the road and hit a tree. Both Caracciola and Campari retired and Borzacchini/Bignami won at 68.28mph (109.86kph) from the *Scuderia Ferrari*-entered 8C 2300 of Trossi/Brivio. Alfa Romeos took the first eight places.

Six *Lungos*, including two works cars, ran in the Le Mans race and most of the drivers went flat-out from the start. Three of these cars crashed, but after six hours 8C 2300s were in the first three places in the order Cortese/Guidotti, Howe/Birkin and Sommer/Chinetti. Howe/Birkin retired because of cylinder head gasket failure, Cortese/Guidotti were worried about disqualification because their battered front wings bore little resemblance to the original shape and settled for second place behind Sommer/Chinetti. Brian Lewis/Tim Rose-

The first and second placed 8C 2300s after the 1932 Spa 24 Hours race. On the right is the winning car of Brivio/Siena and on the left the second-place car of Taruffi/d'Ippolito. Both are Zagato-bodied. They have been cleaned up and are about to be driven back to Scuderia Ferrari's premises at Modena. (Centro Documentazione Alfa Romeo)

Richards took third place with their Talbot 105.

The 8C 2300s completely dominated the Belgian 24 Hours race and the works-entered cars of Brivio/Siena and Taruffi/d'Ippolito took the first two places ahead of Howe/Birkin with their private car. Howe/Birkin ran an 8C 2300 in the JCC 1,000 Miles race at Brooklands held over two days, but the car was badly shaken by the bumpy surface and eventually retired on the second day because of a broken connecting rod. This car was repaired in time to run in the Tourist Trophy at Ards later in the month when Birkin and Howe had an 8C 2300 each. Howe set the fastest race average at 80.53mph (129.57kph) and finished fourth on handicap, with Birkin fifth.

Financial pressures caused Alfa Romeo to withdraw from racing in 1933, so *Scuderia Ferrari* represented the company instead of being a second-string affair. There was a vast number of *Scuderia Ferrari*-prepared Alfa Romeos in the Mille Miglia, mainly because the team offered a fixed price preparation service, and among them were four of Ferrari's own entries. The only opposition came from Manfred von Brauchitsch with a 7-litre Mercedes-Benz, but he retired. Alfa Romeo took the first ten places and Nuvolari/Compagnoni won from Cortese/Castelbarco. The second-place car, a private entry, only just made it to the start, as it caught fire overnight at the Portello factory and an hour before the 'off' a dozy mechanic had poured a can of water into the fuel tank.

Five 8C 2300s ran at Le Mans and Nuvolari/Sommer drove steadily and built up a comfortable lead over Chinetti/Varent, but towards the end of the race they were delayed by a badly leaking fuel tank. "At this stage it was seen that the entire pit crew of the Lewis/Rose-Richards car, under Arthur Fox, were chewing gum for dear life, which they secretly handed over to their Italian rivals to stop up the leaks in the tank." (Peter Hull, *Alfa Romeo: A History*, Cassell, 1964). Chinetti took the lead, but Nuvolari tore back into the race and went on to win by about ten seconds. Lewis/Rose-Richards finished third.

At the beginning of July Chiron/Chinetti with their 8C 2300 won the Belgian 24 Hours race from Sommer/Stoffel and Greeve/Thelusson with other eight-cylinder Alfa Romeos. A fortnight later the Mannin Moar race took place over 230 miles (370km) of a 4.6-mile (7.4km) road circuit on the Isle of Man. It was an event for racing cars over 1,500cc, but Kaye Don drove a stripped *Lungo* and finished fourth, a lap in arrears, behind a *Monza*, a Bugatti and another *Monza*. The 8C 2300s made their last appearance in a

Tourist Trophy race on 2 September, and although their handicap was very much against them, Rose-Richards and Howe finished third and fifth with their *Lungos*.

Scuderia Ferrari's entry in the 1934 Mille Miglia included four *Monzas* with sports equipment and 2,632cc (69×88mm) engines; they ran on racing fuel and developed about 180bhp at 5,400rpm. Nuvolari had left *Scuderia Ferrari* to drive for Maserati (who had no suitable car for the race) and he appeared with a 2.3-litre *Monza* prepared with the help of Vittorio Jano. The race now started at 4am so that it could be completed the same day and it was run in persistent rain. Varzi/Bignami with a 2.6-litre *Scuderia Ferrari* car running on the new Tecalemit *Pneugripp* crosscut tyres, which gave much better grip in the wet, won a race-long struggle with Nuvolari/Siena by a margin of eight minutes.

Four 8C 2300s ran at Le Mans and serious opposition was limited to two Bugattis, a 4.9-litre and a 2.3-litre. The race started in oppressively hot conditions and Sommer, co-driving with one Pierre Felix, soon took the lead only to be eliminated after 1½ hours when the car caught fire at Arnage. Chinetti/Etancelin built up a good lead, but in a repetition of what happened in 1933, the fuel tank developed a leak after five hours and their pit staff spent the next 19 hours masticating chewing gum. Quite where adequate supplies of this disgusting substance came from is unknown.

Clifford/Saunders-Davies retired their green-painted 8C 2300 because of a broken valve guide and because of the problems of Chinetti/Etancelin, Earl Howe/Rose-Richards were able to build up a good lead. They lost this just after 10pm when this Alfa's lights failed and by the time the problem had been solved, it had dropped to 11th place. This car retired when the clutch failed early on the Sunday morning. When the 4.9-litre Bugatti of Veyron/Labric retired early on the Sunday, Chinetti/Etancelin were unchallenged and won by a margin of 111 miles (179km) from the 1,500cc Riley of Sebilleau/Delaroche.

Seen during a pit stop when the mechanics were battling with a fuel leak is the winning 8C 2300 of Sommer/Nuvolari at Le Mans in 1933; this was a short-wheelbase car that had a larger fuel tank and could run another 20 minutes between refuelling stops – handy when you have a leaking tank. (Centro Documentazione Alfa Romeo)

The 8C 2300s were unable to compete in either the Belgian 24 Hours race or the Tourist Trophy because both events now banned superchargers. The 24-hour Targa Abruzzo race at Pescara in August attracted a strong entry of eight-cylinder Alfa Romeos, mainly in *Monza* form and with both 2.3-litre and 2.6-litre engines. They all ran into problems and a well-prepared team of the new 2.3-litre six-cylinder Alfa Romeos entered by *Scuderia Ferrari* took the first three places.

The 1935 Mille Miglia witnessed a battle between Pintacuda with a 2.6-litre Alfa Romeo *Monoposto* racing car and Varzi at the wheel of another racing car, a 3,725cc supercharged Tipo 34 Maserati. The Maserati retired, but Pintacuda won with the *Monoposto*. The bodywork of the Tipo B extended round the cockpit area so that co-driver, the Marquis della Stufa, could just about stuff himself in, without hanging too far into the airstream. *Monzas* took second and third places.

At Le Mans on 15–16 June four 8C 2300s battled for the lead with the 4½-litre Lagonda of Hindmarsh/Fontes. It was a long drawn-out battle with several changes of leader, three of the 8C 2300s were eliminated and the Lagonda won by just over five miles from Heldé/Stoffel with their Alfa Romeo. The Alfa Romeo pit manager became confused, thought his car was leading when it wasn't and failed to speed up his drivers. But whether it would have made any difference is academic. The appearance later in the year of the 8C 2900A (see Chapter 10) marked the end of the 8C 2300's serious racing career.

The 8C 2300 was in many ways the C-type Jaguar of its day, but rather more versatile. In all Alfa Romeo built 188 of the eight-cylinder cars and although Jaguar built only 53 C-types, owners of both often used them as road cars. Running a C-type on the road was simple, for all you had to do was make sure that it was well warmed-up (difficult in cold weather).

In contrast, instructions for the 8C 2300 included not running the engine on a lean mixture as this would cause cracks to develop in the alloy heads; to lubricate the front bearing of the supercharger with ⅕ of a litre of engine oil when this was changed; to change the cooling water once a month and every six months to flush the system out with a solution of distilled water and 10% soda.

Talbot 4-litre

1936–39

Chinetti/Mathieson drove this 4½-litre Talbot at Le Mans in 1939 and battled for the lead until Chinetti inverted it on the Sunday morning. Following are another Talbot and the 6C 2500 Alfa Romeo of Sommer/Bira. (LAT)

The later days of the French Talbot company were the remarkable story of a car manufacturer run by a charlatan; it staggered between bouts of insolvency, it was always lacking capital, but it achieved some fine successes with very fast cars. A 'fraudster' Antony Franco Lago may have been, but he was also a great racing enthusiast. In 1933 he negotiated a deal with the ailing Sunbeam-Talbot-Darracq group whereby he took over management of the Suresnes-based Darracq factory with an option to buy. He reorganised the factory, reduced the model-range and in 1934, by when S-T-D was heading towards liquidation, exercised his option.

For 1936 the *Automobile Club de France* announced a new sports car formula under which the French Grand Prix would be held. It was a protest against the overwhelming superiority in Grand Prix racing of the German Mercedes-Benz and Auto Union teams. Under the new formula, at least 20 cars of the type had to be built between 1 January–1 July 1936, engines had to be unsupercharged and there had to be at least two seats.

The line-up for the start of the rather peculiar Comminges Grand Prix in 1936. Heldé is at the wheel of the stripped 4-litre Talbot with which he finished second. Alongside is the unblown Type 59 Bugatti of Robert Benoist.

Talbot, Bugatti, Delage and Delahaye all responded to the challenge. Other organisers soon adopted the rules and the new formula gave French motor racing an immense boost.

Talbot's chief engineer Walter Becchia produced a redesign of the six-cylinder single overhead camshaft 3-litre T150 that the company had introduced at the 1934 Paris Salon. In competition form there was a new cast-iron cylinder block with a capacity of 3,989cc (90×104.5mm). The nitrogen-hardened crankshaft ran in seven instead of four main bearings, there was a new cylinder head with hemispherical combustion chambers and a reprofiled camshaft.

The most significant development was a new method of valve operation, a precursor of that of the BMW 328, with long and short rockers and supplementary crossover pushrods. Lubrication was dry sump. With three downdraught Stromberg carburettors, power output in tests just before the cars were raced was 165bhp, but this was soon increased. The transmission incorporated a clutchless Wilson four-speed pre-selector gearbox.

Becchia used a sturdier, narrower version of the T150 chassis with a shortened wheelbase of 8ft 8in (2,340mm). At the front there was independent suspension by a transverse leaf spring and parallel links, but at the rear Talbot relied on the familiar layout of a rigid rear axle, as on the production cars. The worm-and-nut steering and the Bendix brakes were also derived from the production cars. Talbot fitted a new two-seater body, often with teardrop wings, but sometimes these were very skimpy cycle wings. Maximum speed was around 125mph (201kph). Lago persuaded well-known driver René Dreyfus to act as team manager, as well as drive the new cars.

The first race for the new cars was the three-hour event on the Miramas, Marseille circuit in May 1936. Talbot led for almost 2½ hours, but both entries retired and Delahayes took the first three places. At this stage in their development, broken exhaust rocker arms and blown head gaskets plagued the Talbots. These problems were solved, but not as easily as the company's immediate financial difficulties. Widespread industrial unrest in France disrupted production, resulting in the cancellation of the Le Mans race and impacting on Talbot badly. Lago applied for the appointment of a receiver, confident that as the biggest creditor he could get a man who would do what he was told.

It came as little surprise that the receiver decided to continue Talbot production and racing under Lago's control. Four Talbots ran in the 621-mile (1,000km) French Grand Prix at Montlhéry on 28 June. In an effort to ensure reliability Walter Becchia used cast-iron cylinder heads (instead of the usual alloy heads) at this race and the rocker arms were drilled. Early in the race, the Talbots ran well, but a combination of rocker-arm failure and ignition problems delayed the Talbots and at the finish the highest-placed car of Heldé/Nime was a poor eighth.

A week later Talbot raced again in the 248-mile (400km) Marne Grand Prix at Reims. Dreyfus led initially and the Talbots lapped faster than the Bugatti 'tanks', despite a lower top speed. After setting a new record of 92.09mph (148.173kph) on his lap 23, he retired because of a broken crankshaft. Wimille and Benoist took the first two places with Bugattis, ahead of Heldé/Dreyfus (Talbot), Veyron (Bugatti) and Morel (Talbot).

Talbot missed the Belgian 24 Hours race in July and next ran in the Comminges Grand Prix on 9 August. This was held in two heats of 137 miles (220km) with the results decided on the aggregate. It was a race with peculiar regulations, for cars that were half and half sports and racing cars. Competing cars had to have a minimum cockpit width of 80cm, superchargers were banned, single-seater bodywork was permitted and wings, lighting and electrics were not required.

Talbot and Delahaye ran stripped sports cars and Bugatti, who was expected to face the handicap of racing the heavy, full-width 'tanks', caused a furore by arriving with two of their outdated, but still very potent, Type 59 Grand Prix cars fitted with unsupercharged Type 57G engines. It was widely considered that Jean Bugatti had broken the spirit of the race regulations. Jean-Pierre Wimille won on aggregate with his Type 59, while Benoist retired his Molsheim entry in the second heat with piston failure and Heldé and Raph took second and third places for Talbot.

Talbot entered three cars in the Tourist Trophy on the Ards circuit in Northern Ireland, but Lago scratched the entry after it became clear that the cars were not yet sufficiently reliable. Although the Talbots had performed increasingly better during the year, they had not yet won a race. That first victory came in the very short, 54-mile (87km) unlimited-capacity race forming part of the Grand Prix de l'Automobile Club de France at Montlhéry on 6 September. Raph, with a car loaned by the works, won from a Delahaye.

By 1937 Becchia and his team had the Talbots fully sorted and they were now both fast and reliable. The company's first race of the year was the 138-mile (222km) Pau Grand Prix on 21 February, held that year as a sports car race. Wimille (Bugatti) won, but Raymond Sommer brought his Talbot across the line in second place, with Dreyfus (Delahaye) third and veteran Albert Divo with another Talbot fourth. Pau had revealed that the Talbots were deficient in brakes, but this was soon remedied.

Talbot ran two cars in the Mille Miglia road race in April, but they were overgeared, slower on Italian roads than the six-cylinder Delahayes and both Comotti/Rosa and Cattaneo/Le Bègue crashed heavily. Sommer drove a Talbot with telescopic hydraulic dampers and much better ventilated 16-inch (406mm) brake drums in the 188-mile (302.5km) Tunis Grand Prix in May. The race was run in three heats and because of pressure from Bugatti, there was no refuelling between heats (only during the actual heats). The Talbots could complete all three heats without refuelling, but Wimille, hoisted by Molsheim's own petard could not. Sommer was second to Wimille in the first two heats, but the Bugatti ran out of fuel in the third heat and Sommer became the winner.

Next was the Marseille Grand Prix at Miramas on 6 June. Talbot fielded four cars, including two new examples with smoother bodies and deeper radiator grilles; the older 1936 cars had new and much lighter engines with alloy cylinder head and block developing a claimed 190bhp. The race was again run in three heats and after Wimille, in third place, retired in the third heat because of a cracked oil pipe that caused loss of pressure, Sommer, Comotti and Divo took the first three places with their Talbots.

Talbots withdrew their entries from Le Mans on 19–20 June to concentrate on preparation for the French Grand Prix on 27 June. Two private entries ran, but Raph (co-driving with Embiricos) was involved in the multi-car accident at *White House* which cost the lives of two drivers. Chiron retired the Talbot he was sharing with Chinetti because a sliver of metal from the accident holed a radiator hose and the car lost all its water.

Four Talbots ran in the 621-mile (1,000km) French Grand Prix at Montlhéry and they were the fastest cars in the race, following the withdrawal of the Bugatti 'tanks' and the early retirement of the new V12 Delahaye. It was a poorly supported race and after a duel between Chiron and Sommer – which ended when a valve touched a piston and bent a pushrod on

This 4-litre Talbot was one of four entered by the Suresnes works in the 1936 French Grand Prix held as a sports car race at Montlhéry. Ignition problems plagued all four and sole finishers, Heldé/Nime, were eighth. There was a wonderful stark brutality to the styling of these early 4-litre Talbots.

Sommer's car – Suresnes factory cars took the first three places in the order Chiron, Comotti and Divo.

There was a strong entry in the 306-mile (492km) Marne Grand Prix on 18 July, the race was run in very hot conditions and the cockpits of the Talbots became 'sweat-boxes'. Both V12 Delahayes retired and Wimille (Type 59 Bugatti) pulled steadily away from the Talbots, which, in turn, were chased by a horde of six-cylinder Delahayes. Confused in the heat, Comotti missed a gear-change on his Talbot, and broke one of the long exhaust rockers. Chinetti with his Talbot pressed the Bugatti hard, but retired because of cylinder head gasket failure. Divo, Le Bègue and Sommer took the next three places for Suresnes.

The 1937 313-mile (504km) handicap Tourist Trophy was held on the England's Donington Park circuit in September and Talbot sent an entry of three cars. A visit by the scrutineer to the *Usines Perfecta* (as the Suresnes factory had been known since early Darracq days) ruled out the alloy-block cars and Louis Chiron, influenced by the unsatisfactory state of his love life, quit the team. Because the Rootes Group, which had acquired the Sunbeam and Talbot names after the collapse of the S-T-D Group, held the exclusive right to the Talbot name in the British Empire, the entries at Donington had to be called Darracqs.

There was a panic for Lago in practice, for a piston seized on Sommer's car and there was a frantic rush to rebuild the engine in time for the race. Sommer had piston failure again in the race, but Comotti and Le Bègue, with a favourable handicap and able to run through the race non-stop, took the first two places ahead of Prince Bira (BMW 328). It was for Antony Lago a very satisfactory end to a good season, marred only by the performances of Wimille with the Bugatti 59, a car that Lago and others bitterly complained did not comply with sports car regulations.

Following the introduction of the new 3,000cc supercharged/4,500cc unsupercharged Grand Prix formula for 1938, some races in France were again held to Grand Prix rules, so less was seen of the sports cars. Becchia was designing a new V12 engine, but neither this nor a projected supercharged Grand Prix V16 engine left the drawing board. The V16 project so impressed the Automobile Club de France that it made a Ff600,000 grant to Talbot, which Lago promptly spent on a new factory to make Pratt & Whitney aero engines under licence. Talbot built a 4,483cc (93×110mm) version of the existing engine, strengthened throughout, but still with those fragile crossover rockers.

At Le Mans in June Talbot entered a car powered by the new 4.5-litre engine for Etancelin/Chinetti and two 4-litre cars for Carrière/Le Bègue and Trévoux/Levegh. There were also two production Lago SS *Spéciales* with coupé bodies for Louis Rosier/Maurice Huguet and Prenant/Morel (the latter's car had a very handsome Figoni & Falaschi body of the type known as *Goutte d'Eau*). The Etancelin/Chinetti car led, but retired because of the almost inevitable broken rocker, three of the other Talbot entries retired and the only small consolation was third place by Prenant/Morel behind two six-cylinder Delahayes.

Only one Talbot, driven by Levegh/Trévoux, ran in the Belgian 24 Hours race on 9–10 July, but it was eliminated by an accident during the night. Etancelin and Carrière drove 4½-litre Talbots running as Darracqs in the 314-mile (504km) Tourist Trophy at Donington Park on 3 September. Starting on scratch the Talbots ran well and Etancelin and Carrière finished third and fourth behind Gérard (3-litre Delage) and Horsfall (2-litre Aston Martin). Eight days later the latest 4½-litre Talbots driven by Le Bègue/Morel and Etancelin/Carrière ran in the Paris 12 Hours race at Montlhéry. Etancelin retired when the steering locked up, but Le Bègue/Morel rumbled on and won from a brace of Delahayes.

Talbot's main thrust in 1939 was Grand Prix racing and the company produced two offset single-seaters (the so-called *monoplace décalées*) as well as a pure *monoplace* that first appeared in the French Grand Prix. Two T150C Talbots ran in the 190-mile (306km) Antwerp Grand Prix held on 31 May in two heats. They were outclassed, Levegh finished fourth and Forestier took joint fifth place with B.H. Talbot (2-litre Aston Martin). Luigi Chinetti organised an entry of five Talbots on behalf of the works at Le Mans, but none of the entry that included two 4½-litre cars finished.

The last race for Talbot before the outbreak of war was the 273-mile (440km) Comminges Grand Prix, the first since 1936, on 6 August and Talbot entered the two *monoplace décalées* in sports trim for Raymond Sommer and René Le Bègue. There was a very strong entry and the race turned into a wonderful battle between the Talbot drivers and Wimille with the sports Type 59. Le Bègue beat the Bugatti driver by only 0.4sec and Sommer finished third.

Talbot survived the war years to resume limited production and in 1948 introduced a remarkably successful single-seater typed the 26C. Sports versions of this won Le Mans in 1950 and finished second in the Reims 12 Hours race in 1953. The last 4.5-litre Talbot appeared at Le Mans in 1955 and two new cars with detuned Maserati 250F engines ran in the 1956 race. Talbot was hopelessly insolvent throughout the whole time it was controlled by Antony Lago and in 1958 was absorbed by Simca. It had been exceedingly good while it lasted.

Bugatti 'Tank'

1936–39

Wimille at the wheel of the 3.3-litre 'Tank' that he shared with Benoist at Le Mans in 1937. Following the retirement of the Alfa Romeo driven by Sommer/Guidotti, this Bugatti scored an easy win, with six-cylinder Delahayes, once again, in second and third places.

That Ettore Bugatti was a perfectionist among automobile engineers is undoubted, but he was also very reactionary. It was only under the influence of his elder son, Jean, born in 1909, that the company modernised its policies during the 1930s and Jean became increasingly responsible for the running of the Molsheim factory, although his father retained control.

Bugatti had entered his new Type 59 2,821cc (67×100mm) twin overhead camshaft, straight-eight Grand Prix car in the 1933 Spanish Grand Prix and the following year he ran the cars in 3,257cc (72×100mm) form. They were uncompetitive, although there is little doubt that the Type 59 was one of the most beautifully styled and balanced racing cars of all time.

The 3,257cc engine in somewhat simplified form powered the Type 57 touring cars built in normally aspirated and supercharged forms from 1934 onwards. Despite the year in which they were introduced, Ettore Bugatti still retained a mind-set from the Vintage years and, although the 57 was a magnificent *Grand Routier* capable of 95mph (153kph) in standard form, it was of excessively heavy construction, had an unnecessarily long wheelbase and rigid axles front and rear.

A year after the appearance of the first model, Bugatti introduced the Type 57S with the wheelbase shortened from 10ft 10in (3,300mm) to 9ft 9in (2,980mm) and of much lower build so that the rear axle passed through the chassis frame. The engine was more highly tuned, it had dry-sump lubrication, an 8.5:1 compression ratio and the left-hand camshaft drove the Scintilla magneto mounted on the dashboard. The transmission had a twin-plate clutch to cope with the extra power. Maximum speed was around 110mph (177kph).

Mainly as the result of French manufacturers

Robert Benoist partnered by de Rothschild drove this Type 57G 'Tank' in the 1936 French Grand Prix at Montlhéry. On all three cars the rear valances caused the brakes to overheat and necessitated brake lining changes; this car also developed a misfire. They finished a poor 13th, but team-mates Wimille/Sommer won from two Delahayes.

(which, in reality, meant Bugatti) being unable to challenge German cars in Grand Prix racing, a French Sports Car Championship had been inaugurated for 1936 to gain support from more manufacturers. At Molsheim (while his father was in Paris enjoying himself with his mistress), Jean Bugatti devised and developed the 'tank' streamlined cars with the intention of running them at Le Mans. Industrial unrest in France resulted in the cancellation of the 24 hours' race, but there were still three events in 1936 in which these cars could compete, including the 621-mile (1,000km) French Grand Prix to be held at Montlhéry on 28 June.

The Bugattis, officially bearing the type number of the 57S, but known as the 57G at the factory, were in clear breach of the French Grand Prix rules which demanded that cars had to be of a type of which 20 had been constructed or laid down prior to June 1936. The other French manufacturers, Delahaye and Talbot, also broke the rules, but not so extremely. Bugatti built a car that was based on the Type 57S, but in reality it was technically more closely related to the Type 59 Grand Prix car less the supercharger. It was a big car, heavier than its rivals, but this was compensated for by its aerodynamics.

Molsheim used the 57S chassis, but the frame had new lighter-gauge side-members and was extensively drilled. The cross-members were fabricated in duralumin. The wheels and brakes, together with the oil cooler mounted between the dumb-irons were all Type 59. The front axle was damped by De Ram shock absorbers and as on both the Type 57 and the Type 59 the operating arms acted as brake torque rods. There was an 18-litre (4-gallon) oil tank for the dry sump lubrication system.

The weight of the engine was much reduced and there were straight-cut (instead of helical) gears to drive the camshafts. The camshafts had Type 59 profiles, together with an extra pinion to drive the gears for the magneto mounted at the back of the cylinder head. There was a single twin-choke updraught Zenith carburettor feeding into a long inlet manifold. The claimed power output was 160bhp, but some think that the real output was a little higher. The gearbox had close-ratio gears with synchromesh on the upper three ratios.

The streamlined, magnesium-alloy body had a large rear-hinged bonnet, simple horseshoe-shaped air intake and two vertical inlets either side of it for cooling the brakes; valances over the rear wheels were hinged at the top and the jacking points extended outside the body shell. A 30-gallon (130-litre) fuel tank was mounted in the streamlined tail. The 'tanks' were painted elegantly in two shades of blue and looked brutally potent, but their major weakness was the high weight, about 2,745lb (1,245kg), something over 440lb (200kg) heavier than its rivals from the Delahaye and Talbot stables.

Although the 'Tanks' ran well in the Grand Prix, the Bugatti pit work was slow and muddled, probably because of the absence of Jean Bugatti recovering in hospital from appendicitis. Wimille/Sommer won at 77.85mph (125.26kph), 50.2 seconds ahead of the Delahaye of Paris/Mongin. Because of plug and tyre troubles, the other 57G drivers did not fare so well: Pierre Veyron/'Williams' finished sixth and Benoist/Rothschild took 13th place, despite hard driving by Benoist to make up ground.

In July the 248-mile (400km) Marne Grand Prix took place on the fast Reims circuit. The Bugattis had superior straight-line speed, but the Talbots were faster through the corners. René Dreyfus's Talbot could have won if it had not broken its crankshaft. Wimille and Benoist with their Bugattis took first and second places ahead of Dreyfus who had taken over 'Heldé's' Talbot, with Veyron 57G finishing fourth.

The 1938 Le Mans race was cancelled because of strikes and political unrest in France. In 1939 Bugatti made only one entry at Le Mans: this 3.3-litre supercharged car with much neater bodywork and driven by Wimille/Veyron. It won, with a 3-litre Delage second and a 4.5-litre Lagonda third.

The AC du Midi held the Comminges Grand Prix on 8 August. It was an odd race, as it was for sports cars, but stripped of road equipment. There were two heats, each of 137 miles (220km). Because the 57Gs were at a disadvantage on slower courses, Bugatti entered two Type 59s, fitted with engines from the 57Gs and a small passenger seat over the oil tank mounted on the left side of the cockpit. The other competitors regarded this as very sharp practice and there was talk of a boycott, but it came to nothing. Wimille and Benoist took the first two places in the first heat, and in heat two Wimille again won, while Benoist retired because of engine maladies.

Bugatti did not race the sports cars again in 1936, but in September and October went record-breaking at Montlhéry with a 57G and broke a string of Class C records ranging from 100km (62 miles) to six hours. In September Benoist took the one-hour record at 134.84mph (217.00kph) and the speed of Benoist/Veyron when they took six-hour record in October was 126.80mph (204.05kph). Wimille, Veyron and 'Williams' went record-breaking again at Montlhéry on 19 November and with a 57G they broke Class C records from one hour to 24 hours. They averaged 123.83mph (199.27kph) for the 24 hours and fuel consumption was 13.4mpg.

Bugatti now raced 57Gs on faster circuits and the sports 59 on the slower ones. In its 1937 form the sports 59 had a new four-speed all-synchromesh gearbox, new body and chassis modifications. The 1937 Pau Grand Prix was held as a sports car race on 21 February, and Wimille easily won in the wet with his Type 59. On 16 May Wimille drove the 59 in the Tunisian Grand Prix at Carthage, won the first two heats, but ran out of fuel on the last lap of the third heat. A week later Wimille finished second to Carrière (Talbot) in the Algerian Grand Prix at Bône. Wimille and the 59 then ran in the Marseille Grand Prix on the Miramas circuit on 6 June, but a broken oil pipe caused his retirement.

Bugatti's main effort was concentrated on the Le Mans 24 Hours race and here the team entered two new cars with 4,433cc (84×100mm) alloy engines from the Type 50B single-seater and known as the T57S45. When Jean Bugatti realised that these cars would not be ready in time, two slightly modified 57Gs were substituted. Wimille/Benoist dominated the race after the retirement of the works-entered 8C 2900B Alfa of Sommer/Guidotti – Sommer over-revved the engine in avoiding the multi-car accident that cost the lives of Pat Fairfield and René Kippeurt.

They won at 85.125mph (136.97kph), despite Benoist sliding off into the bank at Arnage because of weakening brakes; it took ten minutes to extricate the car with the help of marshals and they avoided disqualification because outside help was permitted if the car was in a dangerous position. At the finish they were seven laps ahead of the Delahaye of Paul/Mongin. The Type 57G driven by Veyron/Labric retired because of clutch failure.

For the French Grand Prix at Montlhéry on 4 July Bugatti prepared two Type 57S45 cars and on this occasion one practised. Although the general shape was similar to that of the 57G, the wing-line swept down over the front wheels and up again over the rear wheels and, although such views are subjective, the writer considers it to be uglier than the 57G. Initially only one 57S45 arrived at the circuit and Wimille practised it, while Benoist went out in a production Type 57S *Atlante* coupé.

There was then a dispute as to whether Benoist had officially been allowed out on the course and he was disqualified. Eventually, Bugatti withdrew both cars because of engine problems. They never appeared again and were broken up at Molsheim. Wimille drove the sports Type 59 in the Marne Grand Prix on 18 July and won this 306-mile (492km) race from Divo and Le Bègue with Talbots. This elderly car, known at the works as *Grand-Mère*, was not raced again, and after it had been fitted with a more stylish radiator cowl, King Leopold of the Belgians bought it.

With the introduction of the new 3,000cc supercharged/4,500cc unsupercharged Grand Prix formula for 1938, many French GP races reverted to being single-seater events. But by 1938 Bugatti was in very serious financial trouble, when it appeared that the company's bankers would not sanction the 57Gs running at Le Mans, and after the French Grand Prix the team withdrew for the rest of the year.

In August 1939 Bugatti entered this sports Type 59 with 4.7-litre supercharged engine for Wimille in the Comminges Grand Prix. The Bugatti was plagued by overheating after the radiator had been holed and Le Bègue (Talbot) narrowly beat him into second place.

Bugatti returned to racing on a limited scale in 1939. Jean-Pierre Wimille drove a new sports car in the Grand Prix du Centenaire held over a distance of 140 miles (225km) on a circuit just outside the city of Luxembourg on 4 June. The event was held to celebrate the centenary of the founding of the Duchy. This latest car combined a Type 59 chassis with a Type 50B 4,433cc engine, a 57S45 gearbox and body resembling that of the 1938 single-seaters, incorporating a smooth, rounded nose cowling with horseshoe-shaped grille. Wimille drove another superb race to beat two Alfa Romeo 4.5-litre cars.

In 1939 Bugatti entered a single car at Le Mans, a version of the production, supercharged 57C. The chassis was much-modified, the supercharged 57C engine had been tuned to develop around 200bhp, the gearbox was 57S45 and the body was a smoother, cleaner version of the 57G. An unusual feature was a spotlight recessed in to the body on the right-hand side and directed at the verge. Wimille/Veyron drove a steady race, interrupted only when one of the Type 59 wheels started to break up, and came through to a fine win at 86.855mph (139.750kph) from the 3-litre Delage of Gérard/Monneret.

Wimille reappeared with the 59/50B at the 272-mile (437km) Comminges Grand Prix over the St. Gaudens circuit on 6 August. It was a very hard-fought race, between the Bugatti and two Talbots, and Wimille, with an overheated engine, was narrowly beaten into second place by René Le Bègue (Talbot). Shortly afterwards Bugatti's bankers notified father and son at a meeting in Paris that they were not prepared to fund the company any longer. Receivership was imminent and Ettore Bugatti immediately sought the support of King Leopold of the Belgians to move the factory to Belgium.

Two days before La Baule Grand Prix, a race for only drivers and cars that had competed in the 1939 Le Mans race, Jean Bugatti crashed with fatal results while testing the 57C that was to run there and with Jean, the future of Bugatti died. Ettore Bugatti died on 21 August 1947. Bugatti cars never re-entered production and in 1963 Hispano-Suiza bought the company. Bugatti had been in decline since the early 1930s and after that its only real contribution to motor racing history was the 'Tank' series which had a profound influence on the design of post-war sports-racing cars.

BMW 328

1936–40

Huschke von Hanstein, partnered by Bäumer drove the Le Mans class-winning 1939 328 coupé in the 1940 closed-circuit Mille Miglia. They led from start to finish, and set fastest lap, easily defeating the overweight six-cylinder Alfa Romeos.

In the immediate pre-war and wartime days BMW built what were probably the world's finest piston aero-engines, and in post-war days it recovered from a derelict and bomb-destroyed company to become a world leader in motor manufacture. The 328, its most famous model, was a car developed to appeal to sporting motorists, whose enthusiasm was inspired by German successes in Grand Prix racing. The first six-cylinder BMW was the 1,182cc (56×80mm) 303 of 1933–34, but the first model with a 1,971cc (66×96mm) engine was the much more shapely 326 built from 1936 onwards.

That year BMW also introduced the 328, an advanced car in many respects. An interesting aspect of the design was the expedient that provided additional engine power without resorting to twin overhead camshafts. The 328 retained a chain-driven camshaft mounted on the cylinder block, but while the inlet valves were operated in the conventional way by pushrods and rockers, bell-cranks actuated the supplementary crossover pushrods operating the exhaust valves. It was an ingenious, but very practical system that proved efficient and reliable, but it has to be

British concessionaires, AFN, borrowed four 328s from the works for the 1937 Tourist Trophy at Donington and here the drivers are A. P. F. Fane and H. J. Aldington. 'B. Bira' finished third on handicap with another AFN entry.

recognised that a not so very different system was adopted by the French Talbot company at around the same time.

With triple Solex carburettors topped by air cleaners, it was a very deep engine and so BMW/Bristol-powered cars have usually been characterised by a high bonnet line. In production form power output was 80bhp at 4,500rpm, but even the earliest competition cars had in excess of 90bhp on tap and by 1939 in racing form with larger Solex carburettors, power output was 105–110bhp. Running on alcohol fuel and with a 10.5:1 compression ratio the 328 engine developed 120bhp at 5,500rpm. BMW originally fitted a ZF gearbox, but the Series II cars built from about August 1938 had a much stronger Hirth 'box because of failures on hard-used competition cars.

The chassis was a twin-tubular structure with channel-section cross-bracing and underslung rear axle first seen on the 319 model introduced the previous year. At the front the suspension was independent by a transverse leaf spring and wishbones, while at the rear BMW retained the traditional layout of a rigid axle suspended on semi-elliptic leaf springs. There were hydraulic brakes and the wheels were four-stud, centre-lock disc with knock-off eared spinners, a system devised by the Kronprinz company to avoid infringing Rudge-Whitworth patents.

The body was a neat two-seater with what had become the 'trademark' BMW 'double-kidney' radiator grille, neat sweeping lines, forward-hinged bonnet, twin bonnet straps for racing, rear-hinged doors, with valances over the rear wheels and the spare wheel mounted horizontally on the sloping tail. BMW also supplied the 328 in chassis form and German coachbuilders constructed a wide range of special bodies. In its original form the 328 was a sports car that could be raced, but the later streamlined cars built by the factory were pure sports-racing cars.

The 328 first appeared in public when Ernst Henne drove one in the Eifel Trophy at the Nürburgring in June 1936. Together with two other cars, all factory-owned, the 328s competed regularly in 1936 and the first production examples did not appear until early 1937. Initially BMW race-prepared 328s, but did not enter works cars. In August, H.J. Aldington, managing director of British concessionaire AFN Limited (who also made Frazer Nash cars) drove a 328 to a win in the Munich Triangle race at 84.10mph (135.32kph). The works cars ran as Frazer Nash-BMWs in the handicap Tourist Trophy at Ards in September and A.F.P. Fane finished third, winning the 2-litre class.

In April 1937 S.C.H. Davis, Le Mans winner and Sports Editor of *The Autocar*, covered 102.12 miles (164.31kph) in the hour with a 328 at Brooklands, an outstanding performance for a 2-litre car, although it was a modified example. The 328s raced extensively during 1937 and dominated the 2-litre class. Three cars, nominally private entries, ran at Le Mans, but it was a disastrous outing, for two 328s were involved in the multi-car crash that cost the life of Pat Fairfield at the wheel of David Murray's 328, and the third car retired. In that year's Tourist Trophy at Donington Park, Prince Bira with an AFN-entered car took third place on handicap.

Four BMW 328s ran in the 1938 Mille Miglia and they took the first four places in the 2-litre sports class. First three places in the 2-litre class followed in the Belgian 24 Hours race. Following the banning of the Mille Miglia after a serious accident in 1938, it was replaced in 1939 by a 933-mile (1,500km) race between Tobruk and Tripoli in Libya, then an Italian

This is the 1940 Mille Miglia BMW 328 imported by the Aldingtons. It was converted to right-hand drive, shown to the press as the Frazer Nash Grand Prix, abandoned and then acquired by Gillie Tyrer. This very fast car is seen at Silverstone in May 1953 when Ernie McMillan was racing it. Later Michael Bowler raced it and it is now in the BMW Museum. (Guy Griffiths)

colony. Alfa Romeo 6C 2500s dominated the results, but works-owned 328s took the first three places in the 2-litre class. The BMWs had faced little in the way of opposition in their class and class-winners Briem/Holzschuh were little slower than the overall winner, averaging 87.10mph (140.14kph).

The 328s had missed Le Mans in 1938, but three cars ran there the following year. One of these was a new streamlined fixed head coupé developed at the factory, but built by Touring in Milan. The engines were modified and the cars ran with high-ratio, stronger rear axles. The complete team displayed excellent reliability. Schaumburg-Lippe/Wencher with the coupé won their class and finished fifth overall, covering 1,981.207 miles (3,187.762km) at 82.550mph (132.823kph) and the other 328s finished seventh and ninth.

Despite the outbreak of the Second World War, racing continued in Italy and a Mille Miglia substitute race over nine laps of a roughly triangular, 103-mile (166km) road circuit between Brescia-Cremona-Mantua-Brescia took place on 28 April 1940. The race was another event in which the BMWs and the 6C 2500 Alfa Romeos were the main contenders. BMW entered a team of five cars of three different types, all of them reckoned to develop 140bhp, and these were the only runners in the 2,000cc class.

The fastest car in the race was a works-developed 328 coupé, designed with the help of Professor Wunibald Kamm. It had the wheelbase lengthened by 7.9 inches (200mm) and although the factory claimed improved directional stability, Count 'Johnny' Lurani, who drove it with Franco Cortese, reckoned it was sensitive to crosswinds. They held fourth place, but retired because of ignition problems. The second coupé was the Le Mans car and von Hanstein/Bäumer drove this to a win at 103.62mph (166.72kph). These two cars were significantly more powerful, lighter and, thus, faster than the rival Alfa Romeos.

An open Alfa Romeo driven by Farina/Mambelli finished second. The other three BMWs were very handsome, aerodynamic two-seaters, two bodied by Touring in accordance with the factory design of Willie Meyerhuber, the other at the works, and reckoned to be good for 125mph (201kph). These took third, fifth and sixth places. Although BMW probably had little choice in the matter, the state-controlled *Nazionalsozialist Kraftfahrer-Korps* had been racing 328s since 1938 and was the entrant of the fifth and sixth-place cars in this race.

Subsequently in late 1940 three 328 chassis were delivered to Touring on behalf of the *NSKK* and they were fitted with platform-style, aerodynamic bodies. They were to have run in the 1941 Berlin-Rome race, alongside the works cars, but the race, of course, never took place. Development of the 328 had attained a state of excellence that the company never surpassed. Total production at Eisenach of 328s, including all prototypes, amounted to 464 cars, of which around half are known to survive. The ending of production because of World War Two marked only the first half of the 328 story.

Ordinary 328s were still widely raced in post-war days; BMW-powered specials proliferated throughout Europe. The post-war German Veritas was BMW-derived. Bristol put into production their 400 series of cars powered by their own version of the 328 engine with measurements changed from metric to Imperial. Bristol engines powered post-war Frazer Nash cars, many specialist competition cars and the AC Ace-Bristol built between 1956 and 1961. The engine was also used in the first post-war production BMW, the 501. It was a remarkable success story.

An interesting sports-racing 328: it carries the number 71, which was that of the sixth-place Nazionalsozialist Kraftfahrer-Korps entered car in the 1940 'substitute' Mille Miglia race. It is in fact one of this team's cars fitted with a Touring body to take part in the cancelled 1941 Berlin-Rome race.

Delage 3-litre

1936–39

Louis Gérard and his very elegant Figoni and Falaschi 3-litre Delage coupé at Le Mans in 1937; partnered by de Valence, he took fourth place. Following is a 3.6-litre six-cylinder Delahaye. (LAT)

Louis Delage was a very able engineer, with a love of motor racing, a good judge of what the public wanted and he was a man who enjoyed a sybaristic lifestyle. During the 1920s his company undertook two expensive Grand Prix programmes and at the same time had to finance Delage's château and exorbitant tastes. As the market hardened in the late years of the 1920s, survival for Delage became more and more difficult, and his company finally collapsed in 1935. In complicated circumstances the remains ultimately fell into the hands of Delahaye, controlled by Charles Weiffenbach.

Weiffenbach, whose staid conservatism had sustained Delahaye for many years, was to be fully involved in the French sports car renaissance and Delage was to be a leading contender. Initially, Weiffenbach contented himself with building Delage cars that were more staid, more luxurious than the new sporting six-cylinder Delahayes, but used the same basic mechanical components. Although penniless, and without any real influence, Louis Delage pestered and urged for the construction of a Delage competition sports car.

Walter Watney, Delage's main agent in Paris, had set up a deal whereby he and Weiffenbach worked in partnership in Delage, and it was in his works that the first sports-racing Delage based on a Delahaye chassis was built in 1936. The six-cylinder push-rod overhead valve Delahaye engine had a capacity of 2,973cc (83.5× 90.5mm), *Compétition Spéciale* modifications that included a six exhaust port cylinder head cast in bronze aluminium and triple Solex carburettors. Power output was a more than satisfactory 130bhp at 5,100rpm and it was an immensely strong engine with an exceptionally big valve overlap.

In Watney's workshops a Cotal electric gearbox was substituted for the usual Delahaye mechanical transmission and Watney then dispatched the chassis to Figoni and Falaschi who fitted an exceptionally beautiful and well-proportioned two/four-seater *berlinette* coupé body. It was proposed to run the car at Le Mans, but the race was cancelled because of the industrial situation in France. Instead it was the star of the *Concours d'Elégance* at Deauville that year and graced many similar events throughout France.

The first racing appearance of the 3-litre Delage *berlinette* was in the 1937 Le Mans race held on 19–20 June and at the Sarthe circuit Louis Gérard, the new owner, was partnered by Jacques de Valence. The Delage was completely trouble free and finished fourth behind a 'tank' Bugatti and two 3,580cc Delahayes and won the 3-litre class. It enjoyed a number of other successes that year, including a win in the Paris-Nice rally, third place behind two Delahayes in the *Coupe de Prince Rainier* at Monaco and third place and a class win in the *Coupe de l'Autumne* at Montlhéry.

For 1938 Louis Gérard had his beloved Delage rebodied by Figoni and Falaschi in open form and the original body was then fitted to a Delahaye. Gérard first raced the Delage that year on 23 April in the 201-mile (323km) Cork Grand Prix and he drove a good race to finish third. Gérard then drove the Delage in stripped form in the JCC International Trophy held on a special circuit at Brooklands on 7 May, but it was outclassed in a field in which many of the runners were driving pure racing cars.

His next appearance was in the 311-mile (500km) Antwerp Sports Car Grand Prix on 22 May. Although Gérard had come to racing quite late in life (he was married with a son), he drove with a forceful exuberance that upset his fellow competitors, but this did help to compensate for the power deficiency of the Delage. At Antwerp he fought his way to the front, but then dropped back to finish second, a lap behind Mazaud (Delahaye).

Another view of Louis Gérard's Figoni and Falaschi 3-litre Delage coupé at Le Mans in 1937.

Gérard entered the Delage and Jacques de Valence as co-driver in the Le Mans race. For once the 3-litre car failed its intrepid owner and retired without featuring on the leader board. In the Spa 24 Hour race in July Gérard was partnered by motorcycle-racing champion Georges Monneret and in atrocious weather – including a very violent hailstorm – they drove a hard race, leading briefly and going on to finish second, a mere lap behind Pintacuda/Severi (Alfa Romeo 8C 2900B).

The Tourist Trophy held on 3 September at Donington Park was as usual a handicap race. Although Gérard was the only starter in the 3-litre class and faced strong, larger-capacity opposition from Talbot for outright victory, he drove with cut-throat ferocity, spun four times at over 100mph (161kph) and went on to win from St John Horsfall (Aston Martin). In September the Paris 12 Hours race took place on the full combined banked track and road circuit at Montlhéry. Again the Delage failed to shine and Gérard retired because of a blown cylinder head gasket on the ninth lap, so co-driver de Valence never had a chance at the wheel.

It may be assumed that Gérard had a financial stake in *Écurie Walter S. Watney* formed to race two new 3-litre Delages during 1939. These cars were based on a production Delage chassis, known as the *Olympia*, with independent front suspension by a transverse leaf spring and a rigid rear axle suspended on semi-elliptic springs. The engines were similar to that used in Gérard's original car, save for aluminium-alloy (instead of bronze-alloy) cylinder heads. Cotal gearboxes were retained and the brakes were still mechanical. Watney commissioned coachbuilder Olivier Lecanus-Deschamps to design and build the bodies which looked both rakish and brutal.

The Antwerp Grand Prix was held for the second time on 31 May 1939 and *Écurie Watney*, as it was usually abbreviated, entered cars for Gérard and Monneret. The race was run in two heats and a final. In the first heat Gérard finished fourth, but in heat two he was rather carried away, overtook team-mate Monneret, spun, hit a kerb broadside, and impacted against a flag-pole. He carried on to the pits, but the steering was damaged and he retired. Monneret fin-

Lined up before they depart for the circuit are the two Écurie Watney entries in the 1939 Le Mans race, left to right, Georges Monneret/Louis Gérard and Roger Loyer/Armand Hug. Gérard/Monneret took second place to the Bugatti of Wimille/Veyron.

ished third in this heat and third in the final behind Farina and Sommer with much more powerful 4.5-litre unsupercharged Alfa Romeos.

At Le Mans *Écurie Watney* entered their two cars for Gérard/Monneret and Hug/Loyer. They faced more powerful, mainly French opposition, but also two V12 Lagondas. Gérard led initially and after the retirement of the fastest Delahaye, he and Monneret were still leading early on the Sunday morning. Then Wimille/Veyron with the supercharged Bugatti 57G gradually closed on the 3-litre car, as the Delage was delayed by exhaust manifold problems that necessitated a succession of pit stops. At the end of the race the Delage was defeated by a margin of just over 26 miles (42km). The V12 Lagondas took third and fourth places. The other Delage retired.

One of the last races before the Second World War was the 273-mile (449km) Comminges Grand Prix for sports cars on 6 August 1939. *Écurie Watney* entered Gérard and Monneret, but they were overwhelmed by the speed of Le Bègue (offset *monoplace* Talbot) and Wimille (4.5-litre unblown Type 59 Bugatti). Sommer finished second with another Talbot and Gérard took a distant third place. Monneret was an early retirement. Monneret was to drive a *Watney* Delage in the Liège Grand Prix on 27 August, but the race was cancelled because of Belgian mobilisation. *Écurie Watney* sent their cars to the 1940 closed-circuit Mille Miglia for Taruffi/Chinetti and Comotti, but both retired.

Although there had been three 3-litre Delages racing during the late 1930s, four were raced in early post-war days. One of the most successful drivers was Henri Louveau with an ex-*Watney* car and he ran his car in Grands Prix as well as sports car races. During 1947 he finished third in the Pau Grand Prix, fifth in the Jersey Road race, third at Marseille and sixth in the Italian Grand Prix.

In 1949 the four Delages ran at Le Mans and although a 2-litre Ferrari won the race, Louveau/Jover finished second and our old friend Louis Gérard partnered by Godia-Sales took fourth place behind the Bristol-powered Frazer Nash of Norman Culpan/H.J. Aldington. Shortly afterwards Louveau partnered by Mouche finished second to a Ferrari in the Belgian 24 Hour race at Spa-Francorchamps. The final appearance of Delage at Le Mans was in 1950 when Louveau partnered by Estager took seventh place.

The 3-Litre Delage was an understated successor to the great Delage racing cars of the Vintage years. It was underpowered compared to many of its contemporaries, but exceptional drivers could compensate for this by exploiting its excellent roadholding to the full and, in its prime, it was remarkably reliable, even when very hard-driven.

Alfa Romeo 8C 2900A/B

1936–39

One of the works 8C 2900B Alfa Romeos with Carrozzeria Touring body seen before the 1938 Mille Miglia. With its work on this chassis and the post-war Ferrari Barchetta body alone, Touring must rank as one of the greatest of all Italian coachbuilders. (Centro Documentazione Alfa Romeo)

In 1932 engineer Vittorio Jano completed work on the 8C 2600 *Monoposto* Grand Prix car. The specification included a straight-eight 2,654cc (65×100mm) engine with the cylinders cast in two blocks of four and between them a train of gears driving the twin overhead camshafts and the engine auxiliaries. The blocks were cast in alloy, with steel cylinder liners, and there were alloy cylinder heads. The general layout followed that of the 2,336cc straight-eight cars described in Chapter 5, but changes included fixed cylinder heads, and two small-capacity superchargers, each with a Weber carburettor and boosting at just less than 11psi.

Alfa Romeo claimed a power output of 198bhp at 5,400rpm and in 1934 introduced a larger-capacity, 2,905cc (68×100mm) engine claimed to develop 215bhp. Transmission was by a multi-plate clutch, four-speed gearbox and a unique final drive. There was a differential behind the gearbox with two propeller shafts enclosed in torque tubes, each leading to a bevel gear enclosed in a small light alloy housing under the chassis frame and only just inboard of each rear wheel. The virtue of the system was that it was lighter than a conventional transmission arrangement.

At the front, radius arms located the axle and there were semi-elliptic leaf springs. A similar suspension arrangement was used at the rear, but the semi-elliptic springs were longer, shackled at both ends and outrigged from the chassis. The *Monoposto* enjoyed a very fine racing record and was raced by the works throughout 1935, although success diminished after the appearance of the Mercedes-Benz and Auto Union cars in 1934.

Carlo Pintacuda, partnered by the Marquis della Stufa, won the 1935 Mille Miglia at the wheel of a *Monoposto* fitted with stark two-seater bodywork. At the end of 1935 Alfa Romeo announced the 8C 2900A, a purpose-built sports-racing car with a smoother two-seater body. Alfa Romeo claimed a power output of 220bhp at 5,300rpm for the 2,905cc engine. The new car was still based on the *Monoposto* chassis, but with the wheelbase lengthened from 8ft 8in (2,650mm) to 9ft 0.3in (2,750mm) and with independent suspension front and rear.

The front suspension was similar to that of the 8C 35 racing car of 1935 and was a Porsche-style trailing link system, with coil springs operating in engine oil and enclosed within telescopic shock absorbers, together with small Hartford friction-type shock absorbers. At the rear there were swing-axles, a transverse leaf spring that ran under the final drive casing and twin shock absorbers, telescopic and Hartford. Although the model was catalogued, only six of these cars were built.

Three Tipo As ran in the 1936 Mille Miglia driven by Farina/Meazza, Pintacuda/Stefani and Brivio/Ongaro and the 1935-winning *Monoposto* was entered for Biondetti/Cerasa. The 1,000-mile (621km) race was, again, an Alfa Romeo benefit and they took the first four places in the order listed above. The Tipo As ran again in the 1937 race but they now faced strong opposition from Delahaye and Talbot. Pintacuda partnered by Mambelli drove near-enough flat-out from start to finish in this wet race and won with his Tipo A at 71.30mph (114.72kph), 17min 39sec ahead of Farina/Meazza with another Tipo A. Schell/Carrière (3.6-litre Delahaye) took third place, but they were 38 minutes behind the winner.

In 1937 Alfa Romeo introduced the 8C 2900B, a series production version built in two chassis lengths, and there is evidence that the aim was to use up spare *Monoposto* engines. There were a number of minor changes to the engine and according to the factory the power output was lower, 180bhp at 5,200rpm. The *Corto* version had a 9ft 2in (2,800mm) wheelbase and the *Lungo* had a 10ft 10in (3,000mm) wheelbase and was primarily intended as a fast touring car rather than a competition model.

Alfa Romeo built 20 cars on the *Corto* chassis and ten on the *Lungo*. What made these cars so memorable was the combination of an outstanding performance on the road and the superb bodywork, built in most cases by Carrozzeria Touring. Useable maximum speed was about 115mph (185kph), but race-tuned examples were much faster, and fuel consumption worked out about 12mpg. The best-looking 2900Bs were undoubtedly the Touring two-seaters that ran in the 1938 Mille Miglia.

The 'in-house' team *Alfa Corse* now ran the works Alfa Romeos and they entered four 8C 2900Bs in the 1,000-mile race. Three of these had 2,905cc engines and Farina/Meazza, Pintacuda/Mambelli and Siena/Emilio Villoresi were the drivers. The fourth is reputed to have had a full Tipo 308 Grand Prix engine of 2,991cc (69×100mm) developing 295bhp at 6,000rpm and was driven by Biondetti/Stefani. Although this car was the fastest in the race, it required more refuelling stops. The opposition included the V12 4.5-litre Delahayes.

Pintacuda was leading at Rome at an average of 88.80mph (142.88kph), but he was delayed by brake problems that caused him to run off the road and at the finish Biondetti led from Pintacuda by 1min 52sec. Dusio finished third with his privately entered 8C 2900B. Farina crashed and Siena retired. Heavy tyre wear delayed the Delahayes and Dreyfus/Varet were fourth, over 40 minutes behind the winner, with a Talbot in fifth place.

Alfa Corse dispatched a single 8C 2900B with an exhilaratingly styled Touring coupé body to the Le Mans 24 Hours race held in June, and the drivers were Raymond Sommer and Clemente Biondetti. They had built up an enormous lead, 11 laps, over a 3,580cc Delahaye by 10am on the Sunday. Soon afterwards the Alfa Romeo had a front tyre burst at around 130mph

Clemente Biondetti and Raymond Sommer (in straw hat cleaning the windscreen) drove this 8C 2900B Touring coupé at Le Mans in 1938 and enjoyed a very substantial lead until it retired because of engine problems.

In torrential rain Clemente Biondetti corners his 8C 2900B Lungo at a junction on the autostrada at Milan in the 1947 Mille Miglia. He won the race from Nuvolari (Cisitalia).

(209kph) on the Mulsanne Straight and whirling tread shredded a streamlined wing. As it slid from side to side of the road, Sommer controlled it with great skill. After a wheel-change Biondetti took the wheel, but the 8C 2900B retired out on the circuit because of a broken valve.

Sommer/Biondetti and Pintacuda/Severi drove two 8C2900Bs entered by *Alfa Corse* in the Belgian 24 Hours race on 9–10 July. Sommer/Biondetti were leading when they retired on the Sunday morning because of gearbox failure. Pintacuda/Severi won from Gérard/Monneret with the 3-litre Delage. There were of course, many minor Italian events in which private owners competed successfully with these cars.

The 1939 Mille Miglia was cancelled and *Alfa Corse* did not race the 8C 2900Bs at all that year. At the 190-mile (305km) Antwerp Grand Prix in Belgium on 31 May two new *Alfa Corse* sports cars typed the 412 appeared. These were combined modified 8C 2900B chassis with 1937 2,996cc (72×92mm) Grand Prix engines with the superchargers removed. Three twin-choke Weber carburettors were fitted and power was 220bhp at 5,500rpm. The factory reckoned that the maximum speed was about 140mph (225kph). These cars were very fast and Farina and Sommer took the first two places, well ahead of a 3-litre Delage.

Five days later the 412s ran in the 140-mile (225km) Luxembourg Grand Prix, but here Wimille won with Bugatti and Biondetti having to settle for second place. Farina and Biondetti were due to drive the cars in a 180-mile (290km) race at Liége to be held in connection with an International Exhibition, but although they were fastest in practice, the race was cancelled because of the threat of war.

The works never raced the 8C 2900Bs or the 412s again, but they had also been racing six-cylinder cars closely related to Alfa Romeo production models, and they entered developments of these in both the 1940 'closed-circuit' Mille Miglia and post-war 1,000-mile races. The company sold one of the 412s to Swiss hill climb expert Willi Daetwyler who competed with it regularly. This car is now in the French National Motor Museum/Collection Schlumpf at Mulhouse.

Biondetti, partnered by Romano drove an 8C 2900B with *Lungo* chassis and Touring coupé body in the first post-war Mille Miglia; the 1947 event held over a distance of 1,139 miles (1,833km). This car was said to have a supercharged racing engine with the blowers removed and to develop a very modest 140bhp. He averaged 70.10mph (112.79kph) to win by a margin of just under 16 minutes from Nuvolari driving a 1,100cc Cisitalia.

Delahaye 145 V12 4½-litre

1937–39

Two type 145 biplaces ran in the 1938 Mille Miglia. Comotti, partnered by Roux, drove this car, but retired voluntarily when he learned that supplies of Dunlop tyres were running short and all available stock was needed by team-mate Dreyfus.

The French Delahaye company started to manufacture automobiles in 1894 and until the early 1930s they built dull, stodgy cars for the middle classes; cars that enabled the company to weather the Great Depression, albeit leaving it desperately impoverished. Charles Weiffenbach had been managing director since 1901, but he was not so entrenched in his ways that he did not realise that a change of direction was necessary. He made the calculated decision to build six-cylinder cars that would be lighter, faster, more elegant and feature independent front suspension.

Among the customers who approached Weiffenbach were the wealthy American Lucy Schell and her husband Laury. Other enthusiasts trekked the same path, and by 1935 Delahaye was competing at Le Mans. Then in 1936 the company introduced the very high-performance six-cylinder 135 *Compétition Spéciale*, a lighter, lower, faster sports version of the production car and developed for the French sports car Grand Prix series. Entrants included Lucy and Laury Schell, who ran their cars under the name *Écurie Bleue* and who worked very closely with the factory. On occasions as many as 14 of these cars ran in a race and they were consistent and successful performers.

Delahaye engineer Jean François, at the cost of Lucy

The type 145 V12 Delahaye was a very potent piece of machinery and one of the most enterprising sports-racing cars built during the 1930s. This photograph shows one of these cars stripped for a Grand Prix. If Écurie Bleue had committed itself only to sports car racing, the results would have been much better.

Schell, undertook the design of a very compact, unsupercharged 4.5-litre V12 engine, typed the 145, intended for sports car racing and also used in the 3,000cc supercharged/4,500cc unsupercharged Grand Prix formula of 1938 onwards. Although it was not the most advanced engine of its time, it was a major step forward by Delahaye. It had a capacity of 4,490cc (75×84.7mm) and the specification included aluminium-alloy cylinder heads, magnesium-alloy cylinder block, crankcase, timing and valve covers and the crankshaft ran in roller bearings. The two valves per cylinder, set an included angle of 65°, were push-rod operated.

There was twin-plug ignition fired by twin magnetos and three Zenith-Stromberg twin-choke downdraught carburettors. Lubrication was dry-sump. By early 1937 power output was 225–230bhp at 5,200rpm. The transmission incorporated a four-speed gearbox with electron alloy casing or a Cotal electric gearbox. The chassis was very similar to that of the six-cylinder 135, with 9ft 10in (3,000mm) wheelbase, channel-section chassis, independent front suspension by a transverse leaf spring and wishbones and a rigid rear axle suspended on semi-elliptic leaf springs. The bodies made no pretence at elegance, but were simple two-seaters with cycle wings.

Although the Tipo 145 lacked the sophisticated overhead camshafts of the V12 sports Alfa Romeo that appeared in 1939 (and there were practical, maintenance reasons for that), it was one of the finest and fastest sports-racing cars of the 1930s. *Écurie Bleue* appeared with the new V12 at the French Grand Prix at Montlhéry, but it was very new, untested, suffered a myriad of problems and René Dreyfus retired it early in the race, leaking oil everywhere and with no pressure showing on the gauge. A 4.5-litre V12 car from the related stable of Delage, the work of Albert Lory and with the once-great Louis Delage in attendance, also appeared at Montlhéry, but it failed to start and the career of this engine was dismal in the extreme.

The Schells had hoped to run three V12 cars in the Marne Grand Prix at Reims in July, but only two were ready and Carrière's car was barely finished in time for the race. One of the problems with the V12s was the failure of the Goodrich-Colombes tyres to cope with their power and Dreyfus was harassing Wimille (Bugatti Type 59) when his right front tyre deflated; after a series of spins he and the 145 came to rest in a field and out of the race. Carrière had worked his way up to second place when he too suffered a puncture; after a wheel-change, he rejoined the race and again worked his way back to second place before another puncture made him decide to retire.

After this debacle *Écurie Bleue* switched to Dunlop tyres and Dreyfus next drove the 145 in the contest for the million franc-prize, the *Fonds de Course*, a fund set up to revitalise French participation in Grand Prix racing. The sum was to be paid to the entrant of the French Grand Prix car, which complied in all respects with the 1938 Grand Prix regulations and which, by no later than 31 August 1937, exceeded by the greatest margin an average of 90.98mph (146.39kph) from a standing start at Montlhéry over a distance of 200km (124.30 miles).

The speed requirement was based on the winning speed of Chiron's Alfa Romeo in the 1934 French Grand Prix at Montlhéry, 85.08mph (136.90kph) plus a margin. In 1935 the Mercedes W25 cars took the first two places in the French Grand Prix and were much quicker than the *Monoposto*, but their lap speeds were slower because of chicanes introduced into the circuit. The 1936 race had been for sports cars and in the absence of chicanes Wimille/Sommer had averaged 77.85mph (125.26kph), slightly higher than that of the W25s, although this was over a longer distance and included pit stops.

Bugatti had already bagged an award of 400,000 francs earlier in the year, by arguing that he could not afford to build a car to contest the prize without funds. Wimille as sole contestant covered 200km at 91.13mph (146.63kph) with his outdated 3.3-litre Type 59 and to achieve this he had driven dangerously on the limit on a poorly surfaced, bumpy track. The contest was now between Dreyfus with the vastly improved 145 running in stripped form and Wimille with a 4,433cc Type 50B Bugatti.

After Wimille was involved in a road accident, Benoist took his place. Dreyfus with the Delahaye matched Wimille's speed of 91.13mph, but then Wimille arrived at the circuit late on 31 August. He started his attempt at 6.42pm and, under the agreed arrangements, Dreyfus started two minutes later. Wimille was forced to stop for a plug-change, but a plug failed again, and the contest was over. At the end

This streamlined type 145 was entered in the 1938 Tripoli Grand Prix for Dreyfus who was classified seventh. Despite its appearance it was a sports car. In post-war years the concept of streamlined body sections shielding the front wheels was tried by Maserati, adopted by Gordini and tried again by Brabham in 1972.

of Dreyfus's sixth lap, his team and supporters blocked the circuit, frantically waving to him to stop. Dreyfus had won the million francs for Delahaye. *Écurie Bleue* entered three 145s in the Tourist Trophy at Donington Park, but cars had to be production-based and the entry was rejected.

For the 1938 season *Écurie Bleue* had six 145 Delahaye V12 sports cars and the new 155 *monoplace* racing car. Although the 155 was a central-steering, single-seater, the chassis was little changed from that of the 145, save that it inclined upwards at the rear. The main changes were a conventional four-speed gearbox in unit with the final drive and a less than satisfactory de Dion rear axle located by a short Panhard rod and two radius arms and suspended on a transverse leaf spring. Front and rear there were hydraulic shock absorbers operated by long pushrods. The type 155 was not raced until the end of 1938.

Écurie Bleue's first race of 1938 was the Mille Miglia and the team fielded 145s for Dreyfus/Varet and Comotti/Roux. The Delahayes' consumption of tyres proved higher than expected and the Dunlops could not withstand the combination of high speeds on poor surfaces. Comotti withdrew to allow Dreyfus to use his stock of tyres and the surviving V12 finished fourth overall behind a trio of Alfa Romeo 8C 2900Bs.

A week later the team ran two stripped 145s driven by Dreyfus and Comotti in the 172-mile (277km) Pau Grand Prix. It was a remarkable race. *Alfa Corse* withdrew their entries after Nuvolari crashed in practice, Auto Union failed to enter and Mercedes-Benz sent only a single W154 for Caracciola. Dreyfus battled furiously with Caracciola, content in the knowledge that even in this short race, the German driver would have to stop to refuel. When Caracciola stopped, he imperiously waved at Lang to take over his car (the latter was, after all, only a 'jumped-up' mechanic) and by the time that the Mercedes was back in the race, Dreyfus was uncatchable. Comotti finished third.

In the 201-mile (323km) Cork Grand Prix in April, Schell non-started, Comotti retired but, despite a leak that was showering him with hot oil, Dreyfus won from Prince Bira with an ancient 8CM-3000 Maserati. *Écurie Bleue* ran three cars in the Tripoli Grand Prix in May, including a two-seater with streamlined body, but all retired. There was to be another *Fonds de Course*, to be allotted at the discretion of a committee; they, in their collective stupidity, awarded 600,000 francs of the one million available to Talbot, whose V16 engine consisted of nothing more than a few drawings. It was never built, of course.

Schell and Weiffenbach were aghast and the Schells moved the V12s to Monaco, declining to enter them in the French Grand Prix. *Écurie Bleue* ran two 145s at Le Mans. Comotti/Divo were out after seven laps because of gearbox failure and Dreyfus/Chiron also retired early with the engine boiling furiously. (Engine temperature was always a problem with these V12s.) Later the 145s ran mainly in stripped form in Grands Prix; Dreyfus was fifth at the Nürburgring and eighth at Bern. Two 145s ran in the Paris 12 Hours race in September, but again the V12s lacked endurance. Raph/Schell were victims of cylinder head gasket failure and Dreyfus/Divo were leading when a valve broke.

The 145s were largely unchanged for 1939 and it became clear that the type 155 single-seater was a failure because of handling deficiencies. *Écurie Bleue* appeared only occasionally. Two stripped sports cars ran in the 249-mile (400km) French Grand Prix in July, but they were outclassed and Dreyfus finished seventh, while Raph was ninth. In the German Grand Prix on 23 July the cars were entered in the name of *Écurie Lucy O'Reilly Schell* (O'Reilly was Lucy's maiden name). The single-seater had a new body, but it handled so badly that Dreyfus joined the team's other two entries at the wheel of a stripped *biplace* and he, Raph and Mazaud finished fourth, fifth and sixth.

At this point the Schells severed relations with Delahaye and bought the two works Maserati 8CTF Grand Prix cars. Lucy Schell entered two 145s in sports trim in the 273-mile (440km) Comminges Grand Prix on 6 August, but Dreyfus's car broke a piston during practice and non-started, while Raph retired because of rear axle failure. In October Laury Schell was killed in a road accident and Lucy Schell retired to the United States, taking the Maseratis along with Luigi Chinetti. Chinetti was 'trapped' in the United States for the duration once Italy joined the Second World War.

The single-seater Delahaye reappeared after the war fitted with a rigid rear axle. It made few appearances, just like the *biplace* cars. Two of these ran in the first post-war Le Mans race in 1949, but both retired. A single car ran again at Le Mans the following year, but it retired very early on because of a flat battery. In contrast the six-cylinders cars continued to be raced for some years and the best known in the UK was that of Rob Walker.

Delahaye, still with Charles Weiffenbach at the helm and Delage now a full subsidiary company, resumed production in post-war days and survived until 1954 when Hotchkiss absorbed them. The 145 was a significant car and if its backers had concentrated on sports-car racing and expended a little more money on development, it would have been an even greater success.

Veritas 2-litre

1947–50

The yellow-painted Veritas that came to Britain. Ken Hutchison competing at Prescott hill climb in May 1949 with this very promising car. (Guy Griffiths)

The story of Ernst Loof and the Veritas is that of the extreme efforts that enthusiasts will so often make to race, despite deprivation and hunger. Germany's defeat in the Second World War had left its industry in bomb-shattered ruins, its currency valueless and trade depending mainly on barter. The population was at near-starvation level and Karl Kling, later a member of the works Mercedes-Benz team, recounted how his family survived on a diet of raw potatoes and rhubarb jam. Many of the population were ill, not just because of a poor diet, but through the struggle to survive.

The country was divided into four zones, American, British, French and Russian and rules and regulations – many conflicting – governed almost every aspect of life. Even so, enthusiasts were thinking in terms of a revival of motor sport. They were affected by two rules in particular: no new cars could be produced (they could only be adapted from existing components) and Germany was banned from International motor sport. But these were no deterrent to the truly enthusiastic and ambitious.

Motor racing resumed in 1946 and a few short races were held. Kling had acquired a rather dilapidated BMW 328 and he drove it to second place in the first race at Karlsrühe. It was there that Kling met Ernst Loof whom he had not seen since pre-war days. Loof, slim, ascetic and regarded as something of an idealist, had been in charge of the BMW Competition Department in pre-war days.

Loof was building a BMW-based competition car in a rented shed at Kaufburen and he wanted Kling to join the project. The latter was too deeply involved in his work at Daimler-Benz and all he could do was to help in his very limited spare time. By early 1947 the prototype was nearly complete. Kling decided that he wanted a similar car and so he started work in the premises of a friend in Stuttgart, using his own BMW as a basis.

This left him without a car for the first post-war race at Hockenheim in May 1947, so Loof loaned him the 1940 Mille Miglia-winning BMW and Kling won. Subsequently he drove this car in a number of other events. When the first *Comet* was completed, Kling raced it and then delivered it to Toni Ulmen, a well-known racing motorcyclist and driver in pre-war days. Kling completed his own car later in 1947, but he crashed during testing and it was not rebuilt in time to be raced that season.

Loof entered into what was to prove a doomed partnership with Lorenz Dietrich who had managed the French Gnôme-Rhône aircraft engine plant during the war years. Dietrich reckoned that he had 'connections' and regarded himself as something of a 'Herr Fixit.' He wanted to build cars for purely commercial reasons, while Loof saw car production as a means of funding competition car racing and development.

A Veritas Comet competing in a German event on a badly surfaced road in 1949. The driver is Toni Ulmen.

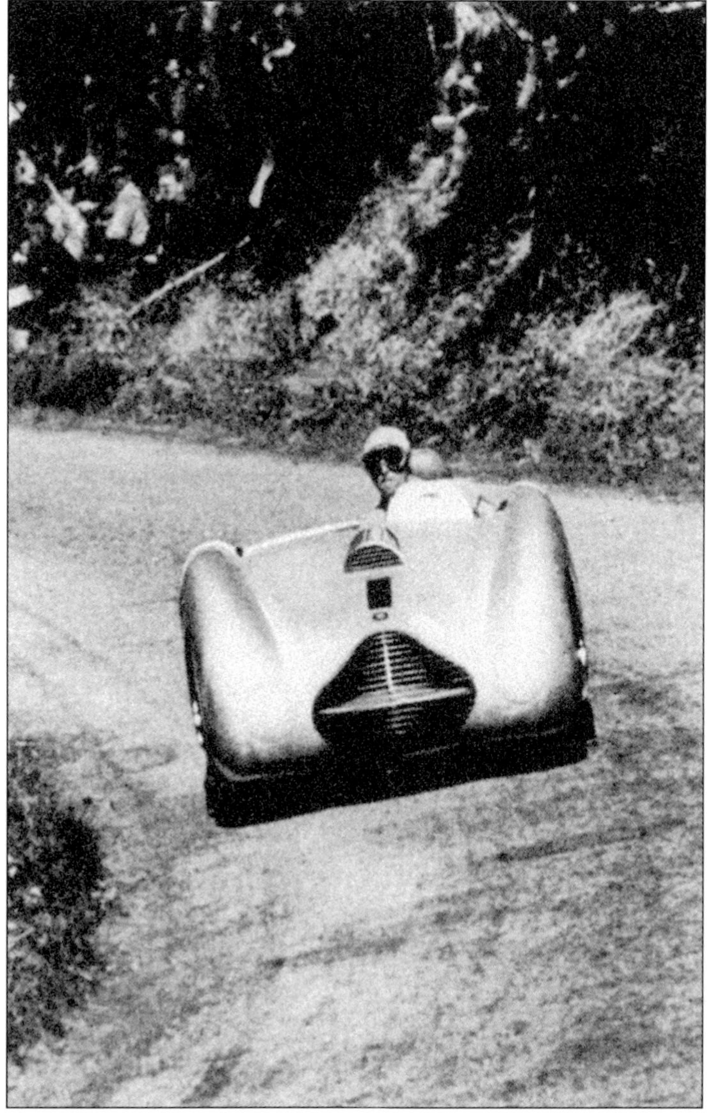

It was a conflict that has over the years affected many small companies in the motor industry. Dietrich needed Loof's technical input and he believed that he could convince Loof of the wisdom of building cars for sale, rather than merely racing them. Ultimately, the relationship failed, because the two had different ambitions and there was never enough money to fulfil even one.

They set up business in a former machine-tool factory in the village of Häusern in the French sector. This was because Dietrich had French contacts and he could 'buy' favours. According to Dietrich, the name 'Veritas' came about when a senior official in the French government supplies office asked him the name of the project. On the spur of the moment, he said 'Veritas', which happened to be the name of a French company that tested technical products.

The basis on which Loof and Dietrich worked was that the buyer provided the minimum of a BMW 328 engine, gearbox, chassis and axles, together with cash or goods of sufficient value and later Veritas delivered the 'new' car to the customer. On 1 March 1948 Veritas was reformed as Veritas GmbH and moved again to larger premises, a former labour camp at Messkirch, still in the French zone. At this time the total staff numbered about a hundred.

Kling developed and modified the BMW engine and raced his *Comet* throughout 1948; and he also helped Ulmen with the development of his BMW engine. With the approval of

Ken Hutchison's very aerodynamic Veritas Comet in Belgian racing colours at Goodwood on Easter Monday, 1949. Alongside is the same driver's magnificent Alfa Romeo Tipo B Monoposto. (Guy Griffiths)

Daimler-Benz he spent all his spare time either at Veritas or working on his car. He won races at Hockenheim and Cologne, where the event was run on part of the autobahn.

From Cologne he drove straight to Reims where well-known Talbot driver Eugène Chaboud drove the Comet in the 126-mile (203km) *Coupe des Petites Cylindrées*, a race for cars up to 2,000cc unsupercharged and 1,100cc supercharged that preceded the French Grand Prix – as a German National Kling was not allowed to race outside Germany. Chaboud drove well to finish third behind the V12 Ferraris of Raymond Sommer and Raoul Righetti. Later in 1948 Kling won races at Schotten and Eggburg (near Sacklingen) and finished third at the Grenzlandring after tyre trouble. He won the BMW-dominated 2,000cc class of the German Sports Car Championship.

Although rebuilds continued at Messkirch, Veritas built some 20 cars from scratch. No two Veritas cars were the same, but the description that follows is typical of streamlined *Comet* two-seaters delivered in 1948–49. Originally, the tubular chassis and the suspension remained almost pure BMW, although on some the side-members were cut short just ahead of the rear axle. The BMW gearbox was fitted with close ratios. There were two interconnecting fuel tanks, one on each side of the scuttle, with a total capacity of about 16 gallons and a quick-release filler with access through a flap in the bonnet.

Modifications to the engine included a special alloy cylinder head with oversize inlet and exhaust valves and a new camshaft. Some cars had roller main bearings, although Loof later admitted that this was not a successful modification. The compression ratio was raised to 8.0:1 and there were larger-choke Solex B32 carburettors. Veritas fitted two fuel pumps, one mechanical and one electric. At first power output was 115bhp, but later, with a mixture of one-third each of petrol, benzole and methanol, it was claimed as 135bhp at 5,500rpm – a figure challenged by some critics.

Some cars from late 1948 onwards had an improved space-frame designed by Loof and weighing a little over 80lb (36.3kg). It was still based on BMW main chassis members, but with the other members relocated to offer better support for the body and to install more conveniently the components that Loof had repositioned. Kling wrote that he believed this to be the very first frame with all the members in tension and compression. Franz Roller's design group at Mercedes-Benz, which built the space-frame 300SL, examined the Veritas, but the extent to which they were influenced remains speculative.

There was an aerodynamic, streamlined aluminium-alloy body and the bonnet, boot, metal tonneau over the passenger side of the cockpit and spats over the rear wheels were secured by spring catches. The weight of the *Comet* seems to have been around 1,350lb (612kg) dry. Veritas also completed cars in 1,498cc (66×73mm) form with a power output of 100bhp and preferred by some owners because it could be taken up to 6,500rpm safely. Helmut Glöckler raced a 1.5-litre Veritas with great success before he built his own Glöckler Specials that inspired the Porsche 550 *Spyder*.

Dennis Poore brought the only example of the *Comet* to come to Britain and showed it at the British Racing Drivers' Club exhibition in November 1948. At this time there was an ambitious plan by *Écurie Belge* to run a team of six of these cars, three with British drivers, one of whom was to be Poore. Although the plan was not fulfilled, *Écurie Belge* entered at least one *Comet* in European races.

Because of the publicity that the Veritas received, the Aldington brothers, whose company AFN Limited made BMW-derived Frazer Nash cars (and were British BMW concessionaires), were quick to put Fritz Fiedler on stage. Fiedler was the former BMW Technical Director and now worked for AFN. He announced in sonorous tones that, ". . . the new Frazer Nash is the genuine successor in every respect of design to the Type 328." He added that BMW in Munich gave no support to Veritas.

After Veritas cars were sold, tuning was a matter for the individual owner. Karl King firmly believed in durability rather than maximum power and always used plain, rather than, roller bearings. Kling shared all his tuning knowledge with Ulmen and their cars were the most reliable and most successful *Comets*. Other owners were more adventurous and Veritas had complaints from those who took their engines up to 6,200rpm or more and wondered why they broke. There were also overheating problems.

Kling enjoyed another good year in 1949 with wins at Hockenheim, Schotten, the Schauinsland hill climb, the Nürburgring (the first two post-war events were held there in 1949), the Grenzlandring and Solitude. After this Kling drove a single-seater Veritas, but he won the 2,000cc class of the German Sports Car Championship for the second successive year. Other drivers opting for single-seaters included motorcycle champion Georg Meier and American Alexander Orley, married to a German actress and said to have spent a fortune at Veritas – he took second place to Villoresi's Ferrari in the 1949 Brussels Grand Prix.

Erich Zippisch of Veritas had been working on an advanced derivative of the 328 engine. This was a 1,988cc (75×75mm) single overhead camshaft unit with hemispherical combustion chambers and the crankshaft running in seven main bearings. For road use this developed 100bhp at 5,000rpm, but the racing version had an output of 140bhp at 5,000rpm – it was claimed that some later engines developed as much as 170bhp. This engine was called the *Meteor* and Heinkel built it for Veritas. It had incurable piston and gasket problems caused by uneven cooling in the cylinder block, and another shortcoming was oil-pump seizure. Veritas also developed a five-speed gearbox.

Apart from proposed touring cars, Veritas increasingly concentrated on a single-seater also known, confusingly, as the *Meteor*. Some very aerodynamic versions were built, but once Germany was permitted to compete in International racing in 1950, it became evident that these cars were uncompetitive. Despite the company's inability to raise bank finance, Veritas at Dietrich's insistence moved in late 1949 to the much bigger, former Mauser works near Restart in Baden. Veritas launched a range of very expensive touring cars, but production never really got under way.

Dietrich then formed his own, unsuccessful company to build the Dyna-Veritas, using the Dyna-Panhard chassis with German-built bodies. As for Loof, Dietrich declared patronisingly about the man who had done so much to revive German motor racing success, "we still had the old Auto Union shops at the 'Ring. They were rented cheaply – so I told him that he could play up there." Loof set up his own Veritas company, built a few production cars with the Heinkel engine and an interesting very aerodynamic Formula 2 car that appeared at the 1950 Paris Salon.

As late as 1953 Wolfgang Seidel and Josef Peters drove the former's *Comet* to fifth place overall and a win in the 2,000cc class of the first Nürburgring 1,000Km race. Loof wound up his ailing business in September 1952 and rejoined BMW as a development engineer. There were probably only about ten cars built at the Nürburgring workshops. Loof died of a brain tumour on 3 March 1956.

Frazer Nash Le Mans Replica

1948–56

Bob Gerard with his Le Mans Replica Frazer Nash in the 1951 British Empire Trophy race in the Isle of Man. He finished second on handicap to Stirling Moss with a similar car. This Le Mans Replica had a straight-sided radiator grille instead of the more usual tapering type.

The Aldingtons, who ran AFN Limited, the makers of Frazer Nash cars, had an excellent claim to build the successor to the pre-war BMW 328. They were pre-war British BMW agents, they shipped to the UK one of the 1940 Mille Miglia 328s and H.J. Aldington had brought over all the information necessary for the new Car Division of the Bristol Aeroplane Company to manufacture BMW-derived cars. The original plan was a merger of Frazer Nash and Bristol Cars and to use their joint expertise to build Frazer Nash-Bristol cars.

When it became clear that this arrangement would not work, the two companies demerged in almost indecent haste. Bristol agreed to supply Frazer Nash with their version of the 328 engine and the Isleworth company used this with the Borg Warner-built Bristol four-speed gearbox. The first post-war Frazer Nash was the 1940 Mille Miglia BMW converted to right-hand drive and fitted with the latest Frazer Nash radiator grille. They called it the *Grand Prix* and as information about the 1940 Mille Miglia was sketchy, because the event took place after the start of the Second World War and there were no British witnesses to the event, AFN had little difficulty in duping the press.

A later Frazer Nash was the Sebring with full-width open body. Dickie Stoop/Tony Gaze drove this example at Le Mans in 1956, but they were eliminated in an accident. (LAT)

In 1947 Fritz Fiedler, former BMW chief engineer, joined AFN to develop a new car. The result was the *High Speed* (also known as the Competition two-seater) exhibited at Earls Court in 1948. Fiedler used a tubular chassis (almost A-shape in plan), BMW 328-style front suspension by a transverse leaf spring and lower wishbones and rear suspension derived from that of touring BMWs. The rigid rear axle was suspended on longitudinal torsion bars and located by an A-bracket that had its apex pivoted on the differential housing and its base on the chassis cross-member. There were BMW-type disc wheels, a cycle-wing two-seater body and the Bristol engine was in 120bhp form.

Despite a very high price, the competition potential of the *High Speed* was obvious and it attracted a steady stream of buyers. AFN lent one of these cars to Count 'Johnny' Lurani's *Scuderia Ambrosiana* for Dorino Serafini to drive in the 1949 Tour of Sicily. Serafini led for more than half-distance, but retired after hitting a kerb and deranging the steering. He also drove this car in the Mille Miglia, but retired. At Le Mans in 1949 former racing motorcyclist Norman Culpan entered his red car with H.J. Aldington as co-driver. A 2-litre Ferrari won the race, but Culpan/Aldington finished third overall and second in the 2-litre class, 110 miles (177km) behind the winner.

It was a good effort because the Frazer Nash was less powerful than the Ferrari and its traditional, stark lines presented far greater wind resistance than the smooth shape of the Touring-bodied Maranello entry. Frazer Nash changed the model name to *Le Mans Replica* and there followed a steady stream of orders. They were never going to beat competently driven Ferraris, but they were ideal cars for private owners who could drive them on the road to race meetings.

At the 1949 Earls Court Show AFN exhibited the *Mille Miglia* with full-width body derived from the 1940 works 328s and subsequently aped by MG for their MGA model. For 1950 Lurani took delivery of his own *Le Mans Replica* and again Serafini drove it; he was in second place in the Tour of Sicily when he retired because of a split fuel tank and he finished sixth overall and second in class, in the Mille Miglia. At Le Mans, Stoop and T.A.S.O. Mathieson drove the former's *Mille Miglia* to ninth place and a class win.

The Frazer Nashes met up with two works Ferraris in the one-hour Production Sports car race for cars up to 2,000cc at Silverstone in August 1950 and although the Tipo 166s finished first and second, *Le Mans Replicas* took the next three places. ERA driver Bob Gerard had taken delivery of a *Le Mans Replica* and in September finished third on handicap behind two Jaguar XK 120s in the Tourist Trophy at Dundrod. As production continued, AFN made minor changes to the specification and some owners had development work carried out on their Bristol engines.

The make's greatest season was 1951; Franco Cortese with Lurani's *Le Mans Replica* finished fourth in the Tour of Sicily, he took ninth place in the Mille Miglia (second in the 2-litre sports class), he won the parochial Enna Grand Prix and in September he won the first post-war Targa Florio held on the 44.7-mile

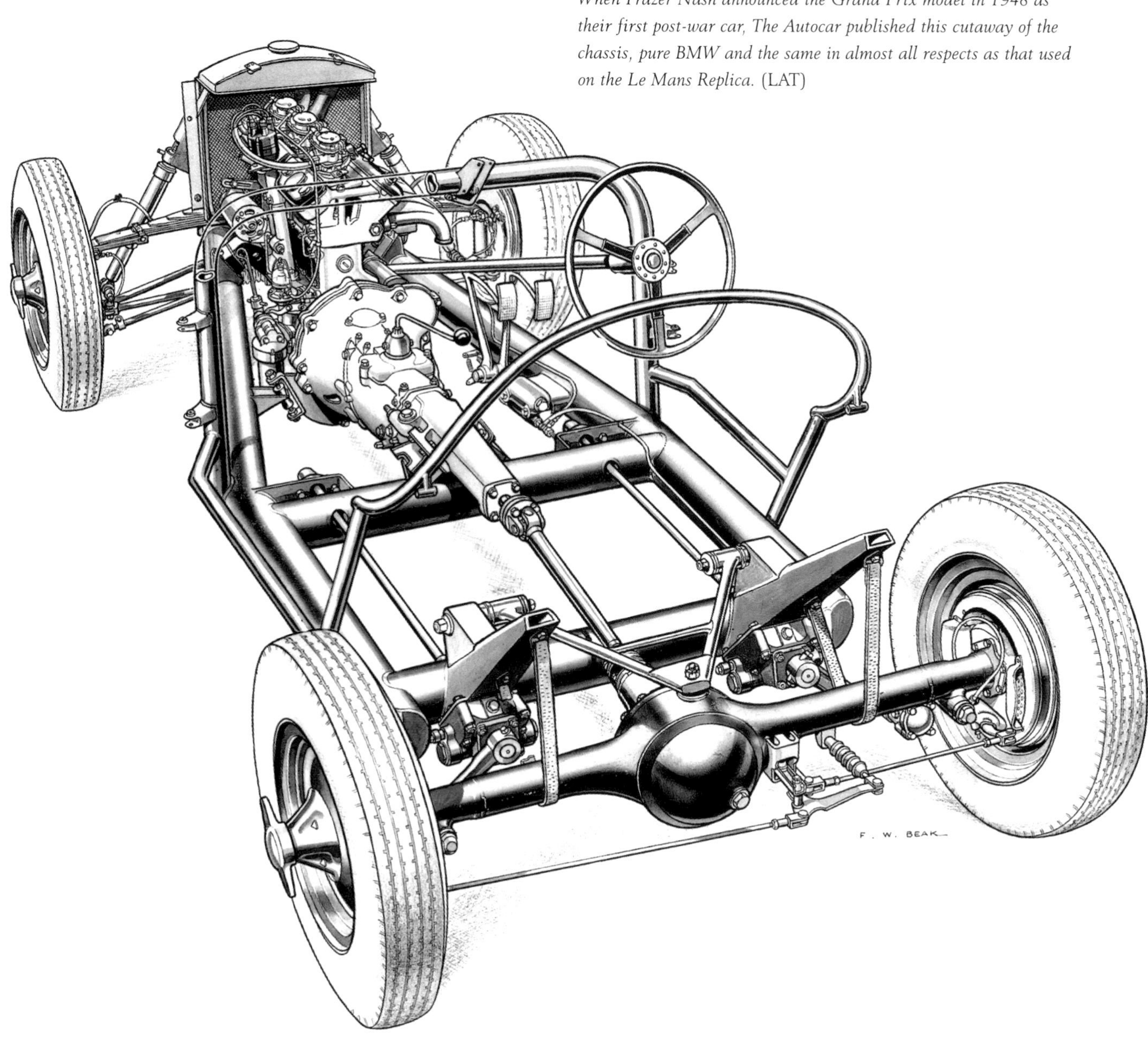

When Frazer Nash announced the Grand Prix model in 1948 as their first post-war car, The Autocar published this cutaway of the chassis, pure BMW and the same in almost all respects as that used on the Le Mans Replica. (LAT)

(72km) Little Madonie circuit. *Le Mans Replica* drivers took the first five places in the 2-litre class of the Production Sports Car race at Silverstone in May (Gillie Tyrer with the ex-Mille Miglia BMW 328 was sixth). Tony Crook with his Frazer Nash was third overall behind two Jaguar XK120s.

Another fine performance was in the British Empire Trophy in the Isle of Man in June where Moss and Gerard took the first two places with *Le Mans Replicas*. It was a handicap race and it has to be admitted that Pat Griffith with his 1,500cc Lester-MG had an uncatchable lead until his engine seized two laps from the finish. At Le Mans Winterbottom/Marshall finished 14th and second in class, and in the following month owner Winterbottom partnered by Duff drove the same car in the Alpine Rally, took second place overall and won a *Coupe des Alpes* for a penalty-free performance.

In September Gerard again took third place and a class win in the Tourist Trophy. Crook, who was a Bristol distributor and raced several Frazer Nashes took his *Le Mans Replica* to Montlhéry and in November covered 200 miles at 120.13mph (193.29kph). He took the Class E record for the distance, which had been held by Jack Dunfee (Sunbeam) since 1930. Crook's speed was very close to the maximum of the *Le Mans Replica*.

Grey/Kulok then won the 1952 Sebring 12 Hours race from a Jaguar and a Siata. During 1952 Frazer Nash brought out a Mark II version of the *Le Mans Replica* and this featured a simpler chassis, known as the series 200, formed by two parallel four-inch (101.6mm) main tubes with similar cross-tubes. These cars were lighter than their predecessors and had the minimum road equipment. Three Mark II cars were built as single-seaters for Formula 2 racing, but they were later converted to sports cars. Only now did the works run its own entry, a lightweight 'development' car usually driven by Ken Wharton.

In May 1952 Salvadori won the 2,000cc class in the Production Sports Car race at Silverstone and at the end of May, Mike Hawthorn (*Mille Miglia*) took third place behind two Lester-MGs in the handicap British Empire Trophy on the Isle of Man. Crook drove his new Mark II in the 127-mile (204km) Prix de Monaco in June and finished third behind a French Gordini and an OSCA. Wharton appeared with the works car in the Jersey road race on 10 July and finished second to Ian Stewart (C-type Jaguar) and he won the 2,000cc race at Boreham in August. In the Goodwood Nine Hours race Gerard/Clarke were fourth behind a works Aston Martin DB3 and two 2.7-litre Ferraris.

Alex von Falkenhausen in Germany fitted the works Mark II with a de Dion rear axle in 1953 and AFN later installed this axle arrangement on a few cars. Competition in the 2-litre class had been strengthened by the appearance of lightweight Bristol-powered cars built by Cooper, Kieft and Tojeiro and although the *Le Mans Replicas* continued to be raced, they gained few major successes. Cars with cycle wings were banned from international races in 1953, but *Le Mans Replica* owners circumvented this rule by fitting aluminium-alloy strips joining the wings to the body.

Frazer Nash delivered the last *Le Mans Replica* in January 1954 by when a total of 34 had been built. Following the *Mille Miglia* (eight 'off') the company had continued to build cars with full-width bodies; the *Targa Florio*, primarily a touring car of which there were 13 from 1952 onwards, and then the *Le Mans* fixed head coupé of which nine were completed between late 1953 and 1956. In 1953 Wharton/Mitchell drove a works fixed head coupé to 13th place and a class win in the Le Mans 24 Hours' race.

Le Mans Replica successes in 1953 included a second place by Wharton in the British Empire Trophy in June, sixth place and a class win by Gerard/Clarke in the Goodwood Nine Hours and third place on handicap by Wharton/Robb in the Tourist Trophy at Dundrod, now a race in the World Sports Car Championship, although sadly lacking overseas entries. Marcel Becquart/Maurice Gatsonides (the latter a rally driver who will remain notorious for his invention of the 'Gatso' radar speed camera) drove the 1953 class-winning fixed-head coupé at Le Mans in 1954, but after a fairly slow race they finished fourth in class behind the Bristol 450s.

Another new Frazer Nash model was the *Sebring* open two-seater and Dickie Stoop ran one of these cars, of which only three were built. Stoop's car had new front suspension by double wishbones and coil springs, as well as a de Dion rear axle. Partnered by Marcel Becquart, Stoop finished tenth overall at Le Mans in 1955, again behind the trio of Bristol 450s. This was the last appearance of a Frazer Nash at Le Mans and the make's international racing career came to an end when Wharton was involved in a multi-car crash in the Tourist Trophy that wrote off the works car.

Post-war Frazer Nash cars were like high-quality bespoke suits, made to order at high cost and to the individual buyer's requirements. Likewise, they were durable and the very nature of their construction made them easy to maintain and, if necessary, rebuild. *Le Mans Replicas* ran in British events throughout the 1950s and continued to appear in club racing into the 1960s. By 1965–6, when Historic Sports Car racing started, they were able to embark on a new career.

Ferrari Tipo 166

1948–53

Clemente Biondetti drove this Ferrari Tipo 166 Mille Miglia with Superleggera Touring Barchetta body to a win at record speed in the 1949 Mille Miglia. It was his fourth win in the race, a record unmatched by any other driver.

In post-war days Enzo Ferrari was free of all restraints to build cars under his own name, a restriction that had originally been imposed on him when he left the works Alfa Romeo team, *Alfa Corse*, in 1938. Despite whatever romantic tosh Ferrari claimed for his choice of the V12 engine layout, his experience in pre-war days with V12 units convinced him that this was the layout to adopt and Alfa Romeo's technology was there for the taking.

Giaocchino Colombo was still working at Alfa Romeo when he designed the first Ferrari engine on a consultancy basis. It was an engine that embraced the original design of Vittorio Jano, the development work of Colombo himself and the refinements Wifredo Ricart made when he built the unsuccessful Tipo 512 rear-engined *Voiturette* (and whatever else may have been wrong with the 512, it was not the engine). Colombo did not join Ferrari on a full-time basis until August 1947.

The first Ferrari V12 had a 1,497cc (55×52.5mm) engine with the cylinders set at an angle of 60° and a 20mm offset between the banks to enable side-by-side connecting rods to be used. The cylinder heads, block and crankcase were cast in aluminium-alloy, with shrunk-in cast iron liners. A train of gears from the

Tazio Nuvolari's drive in the 1948 Mille Miglia

Tazio Nuvolari before the start of the 1949 Mille Miglia, with what appears to be a bottle of brandy slung round his neck. His co-driver looks a might subdued. In Italy Nuvolari was held in god-like awe.

Nuvolari spent the winter quietly, submitting to the care of his doctors in order to regain his health . . . In the spring of 1948 he made his way to Modena, where Enzo Ferrari greeted him with delight. The wizard of Maranello was preparing his latest 2-litre cars for the forthcoming Mille Miglia, which he was determined to win for the first time. Enzo understood immediately why Nuvolari had come, and offered him one of the 2-litre cars. As usual the runners included most of the stars, youngsters and veterans from Biondetti to Ascari and Villoresi to Sanesi.

The aces covered the stage from Brescia to Padua at a spectacular speed, with the young Ascari (Maserati) in the lead. Then Nuvolari attacked the Adriatic straights with surprising vigour. From fourth place he overhauled the leaders one by one, and while crossing the Appenines took the lead with Biondetti (2-litre Ferrari coupé) tailing him. The hot pace set by Nuvolari soon began to tell, and caused the retirement of several fancied drivers. At Rome, only 12 seconds separated the leader from his nearest rival, Ascari, who had made up ground magnificently and was followed by Cortese and Sanesi, while Biondetti had dropped back to fifth place.

The second phase of the race took place after leaving Rome on the return journey, over the Futa and Raticosa passes. Ascari's efforts caused him to retire soon after leaving Rome, and the same thing happened to Cortese and Sanesi, Sanesi finding himself automatically in second place, a reward for his judicious waiting game.

Nuvolari was absolutely unrestrained, he was flying, with his engine answering perfectly, but the coachwork was beginning to cause trouble. While speeding along the bonnet somehow became unfastened, and a gust of wind blew it over Nuvolari's head and down the mountainside.

'That's better,' shouted Tazio to his mechanic, 'The engine will cool more easily.'

Running at reduced speed was not one of Tazio's habits; if he had 30 minutes' advantage, he would do his utmost to conserve them to the finishing line, especially as on the stretch from Bologna to Brescia, along the Via Emilia, Biondetti would be able to take advantage of his engine's greater power. The tremendous jousting on the bends of the Futa and Raticosa caused other mishaps – not to the engine, which Nuvolari knew how to take care of, in spite of what many still like to insinuate.

His seat began to come adrift, through shocks and counter-shocks sustained on the tortuous passes, twisting the chassis, proving again that the coachwork was not first-class. Nuvolari could feel himself sliding, bringing on a feeling of seasickness, and he did not hesitate to jettison the seat. He continued the race seated practically on the frame, using a bag of lemons and oranges as a cushion. The machine was beginning to give way, but not so Tazio, much to the discomfort of his white-faced mechanic who swore to himself that never again would he sit beside this devil incarnate.

A big hole taken at over 100mph broke a spring shackle. With car reduced to almost a bare chassis, Tazio arrived at Bologna with an advantage of more than 35 minutes over Biondetti. In Bologna they saw the broken-down condition in which the car arrived, reminiscent of the very earliest of machines; it was folly to continue under such circumstances.

Nuvolari answered with a derisive gesture, putting his foot down hard as he shot away along the Via Emilia. At Modena, Enzo Ferrari saw him fly past; he wept as he realised that the machine could not possibly hold out.

Between Modena and Regio came the final breakdown, when the rear brakes ceased to function and the car skidded off the road at several corners. The driver finally decided to retire. The engine was still purring beautifully, as evidence of the driver's excellent treatment, but the chassis was a wreck. The retirement took place at Villa Ospizio.

(Adapted from *Nuvolari* by Count Giovanni Lurani, published by Cassell & Co., 1949)

crankshaft drove the single overhead camshaft per bank of cylinders and ignition was by two Marelli magnetos driven from the rear of the camshafts. There were aluminium-alloy pistons, forged H-section steel connecting rods and the crankshaft ran in seven main bearings. With three Weber 30DCF carburettors the power output was 118bhp at 7,000rpm.

The transmission consisted of a single dry-plate clutch and a five-speed gearbox without synchromesh. The chassis was constructed from deep oval-section main tubes that swept over the rear axle, but, later, were underslung, with a fabricated box-section at the front, tubular cruciform central bracing and a raised tubular rear, triangular-shaped structure that mounted the rear suspension. Front suspension was independent by a transverse leaf spring, with double wishbones and hydraulic shock absorbers.

At the rear Ferrari used a rigid rear axle suspended on semi-elliptic leaf springs, hydraulic shock absorbers and, on the earliest cars, an anti-roll bar mounted inside the rear tubular cross-member. Steering was originally by worm and peg and the hydraulic brakes had large cast aluminium-alloy drums with shrunk-in steel liners. The first cars, typed the 125C *Competizione*, had bodywork by Superleggera Touring, two with rather ugly, full-width bodies and the third a neat, cycle-wing design.

Two cars appeared at the 62-mile (100km) race at Piacenza on 11 May 1947, but one crashed in practice and the other retired. The 1.5-litre cars ran in another eight races in Italy that year and won four. The main opposition came from Maserati's A6G 6-cylinder, 1.5-litre cars, but Maserati produced a 2-litre version. Because of this and the proposed 2-litre Formula B for 1948, Ferrari re-linered the V12 engines and fitted new crankshafts so that capacity became 1,929cc (59×58.8mm). This model was known as the Tipo 159 and had an output of 125bhp at 7,000rpm. They ran in four races, one of which, the 313-mile (503km) Circuit of Valentino, Raymond Sommer won with the open car.

Over the winter of 1947–48 Ferrari enlarged the engine size again, by increasing the bore to 60mm and lengthening the stroke to 58.8mm, and the latter became the classic stroke for all Colombo V12 engines. Engine capacity was now 1,995cc, larger-choke Weber 32DCF carburettors were fitted, the power output was 140bhp at 6,600rpm and the model was typed the 166. Two of the 1947 cars were fitted with new cycle-wing bodies, with the headlamps nacelled neatly either side of the large air intake and in this form they were known as the 166 *Spider Corsa*.

Ferrari built another six or so of these cars during the year and they were raced in both Formula B and sports car events. Allemano fitted the third 1947 car with a full-width open body. For the Mille Miglia this car had a hard top fitted. Potentially, Ferrari's main opposition came from Maserati, but industrial problems mounted at the Maserati works and these cars became less of a threat. By 1948 the Ferrari V12 was showing a high degree of reliability, and it achieved a good level of success.

The Targa Florio in early April was held as a 671-mile (1,080km) circuit of Sicily. Prince Igor Troubetzkoy, husband of Woolworth heiress Barbara Hutton, had bought a new 166 *Corsa* and entered it for Clemente Biondetti, while he went along as co-driver/riding mechanic. After the retirement of the works Maseratis and Cortese (works Ferrari), Biondetti won at 55.50mph (89.30kph) from Taruffi (Fiat). In the Mille Miglia on 1 May Ferrari entered *Spyder Corsas* for Cortese/Marchetti and Nuvolari/Scapinelli and the Allemano-bodied car for Biondetti/Navone. The two 2,500cc short-chassis works Alfa Romeos retired and Biondetti won by a margin of almost 1½ hours.

In May Luigi Chinetti entered his new 2-litre Ferrari for Louis Chiron and himself in the first post-war Belgian 24 Hours Touring Car race at Spa-Francorchamps. Although it was the fastest car in the race, Chinetti retired the Ferrari before Chiron had a drive. What in pre-war days was known as the Coppa Acerbo was run at Pescara on 15 August as a 316-mile (508km) sports car race. Sommer retired his works Ferrari and Ascari went on to win with the Maserati that he had taken over from Bracco. Sterzi took second place with his Ferrari. The Paris 12 Hours race was held in September on a short, banked track and road circuit at Montlhéry and Chinetti, driving single-handed, won from a 3-litre Delage.

For 1949 Ferrari introduced the Tipo 166 *Mille Miglia*, unchanged mechanically from the 1948 cars, but usually fitted with new and striking full-width bodywork by Superleggera Touring known as the *Barchetta* ('little boat'). A few cars had fixed head *berlinetta* bodywork. Maximum speed was around 130mph; they proved both very fast and exceptionally reliable and they enjoyed an excellent run of success during the 1949 season. Subsequently this body style was adopted on larger-capacity Ferraris and copies of it were fitted to a number of British cars including Cooper-MG and Tojeiro-Bristol.

On 20 March Biondetti, partnered by Benedetti, with a Tipo 166MM won the class for sports cars over 1,100cc in the combined Targa Florio and Tour of Sicily. There was no outright winner as such, but Biondetti was fastest overall at 51.35mph (82.62kph). It was a very arduous race as the low average speed indicates.

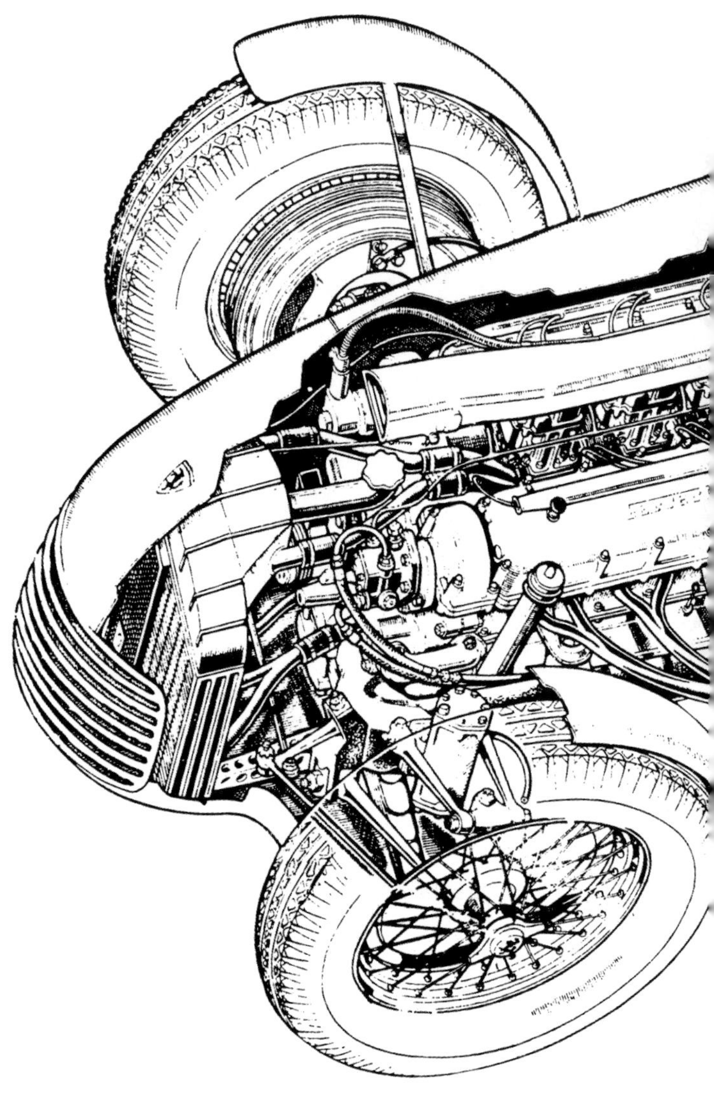

Second fastest was Franco Rol, partnered by Richiero, with a works short-chassis, 2,500cc Alfa Romeo.

It was this Alfa Romeo that provided the strongest opposition to the three works 166MMs in the Mille Miglia on 24 April. The Italian road race was over a distance of 996 miles (1,603km) run anti-clockwise. Biondetti, partnered by Salani, set a searing pace in superb weather conditions and he won at a record 81.53mph (131.18kph) from Bonetto/Carpani with another works Ferrari and Rol/Richiero (Alfa Romeo).

Later in 1947 Ferrari increased engine capacity to 1,903cc. Ferrari built only three cars that year and this was the sole example with cycle-wing bodywork.

It was Biondetti's fourth win in the race, an unmatched record.

Another Italian race of some importance was the three-hour *Coppa Inter-Europa* held at Monza at the end of May, again run on a class basis, and Sterzi, who averaged 81.37mph (130,92kph), Bianchetti and Cornacchia took the first three places in their class with their 166s and were the first three finishers on the road.

The first post-war Le Mans 24 Hours race was held on 25–26 June and after the 4½-litre Delahaye of Chaboud/Pozzi caught fire during the fifth hour, Chinetti went ahead with Lord Selsdon's 166MM, and stayed in front for the remainder of the race despite a slipping clutch. Selsdon took the wheel for a couple of hours during the night. They averaged 82.28mph (132.39kph) and finished nearly ten miles ahead of the second-place Delage of Louveau/Jover. They also won the Index of Performance, which was worth the equivalent of £10,000.

Chinetti next appeared with the Selsdon car in the Belgian 24 Hours race on 9–10 July and here he was partnered by Jean Lucas, who drove for a couple of hours while Chinetti had a meal and a rest. Again there was no outright winner, but a series of class awards. Chinetti took the lead at the three-hour mark and the Ferrari stayed in front for the rest of the race. There was a hiccup half an hour from the finish when Chinetti slid off on oil dropped by Louveau's Delage and hit the side of a house. After the rather crumpled Ferrari was checked in the pits, Chinetti resumed, finishing first on the road at 78.70mph (126.63kph). Louveau/Mouche were second with their 3-litre Delage.

On 8 August Chinetti drove the Selsdon Ferrari in the French Grand Prix at Comminges, held in 1949 as

Ferrari's race debut with a car bearing his own name was at Piacenza in May 1947. Franco Cortese was the driver of this Touring-bodied 125S 1.5-litre car, but he retired because of mechanical problems.

a 311-mile (500km) sports car race. Crowd control was abysmal and the race was run in exceptionally hot conditions. Pozzi was leading with his 4½-litre Delahaye and Chinetti was second, hard-pressed by John Heath (HW-Alta). Chinetti spun off to avoid spectators on the track and stalled; he was push-started and although he finished first on the road, a penalty discounted every lap after his spin and dropped him to eighth place. Apart from Comminges, Ferrari had won every major sports car race in 1949, something that is now long forgotten.

Early in 1950 Stagnoli and Cornacchia with 166MMs finished second and third behind Sanesi's 2,500cc Alfa Romeo in the *Coppa Inter-Europa* at Monza. Bernabei and Le Motta with 166s were second and third behind Bornigia's Alfa Romeo in the Targa Florio (again combined with Tour of Sicily). Eleven 166MMs ran in the Mille Miglia and Bracco/Maglioli drove their car into fourth place overall and won their class. Three 166MMs ran at Le Mans, but all retired. On 26 August Ferrari entered two 166MMs for Ascari and Serafini in the up to 2,000cc one-hour Production Sports Car race at Silverstone and they won. It was the only opportunity for the British public to see these cars in action.

Over the next two years the *Mille Miglias* performed well in the 2,000cc class and later cars had a number of mechanical changes. Ferrari adopted coil ignition with two distributors horizontally and driven from the front of the camshafts. On later cars twin torque rods located the rear axle and at the front the shock absorbers were mounted separately from the upper suspension arms. Certain 166MMs that ran in the 1953 Mille Miglia had three four-choke Weber 36IF4C carburettors and these were fitted to the last cars built. The 166MMs were no match for the latest A6GCS Maseratis and by 1954 the model had been superseded by the four-cylinder Tipo 500 *Mondial*.

In 1950 Ferrari had introduced the 2,341cc Tipo 195 *Sport*, the early versions of which were identical in all other respects to the 166 *Mille Miglia*. Further developments of the Colombo V12 line were the Tipo 212 2,562cc *Export* of late 1950 onwards and the 2,715cc Tipo 225 *Sport*. Bracco won the 1952 Mille Miglia with a 2,953cc (73×58.8mm) Tipo 250 *Sport*, and the following year Ferrari introduced the 250 *Mille Miglia* with Vignale open two-seater or Pinin Farina *berlinetta* body and this proved one of the best-balanced sports-racing Ferraris of all time. This, the last, of the original Colombo-based designs, enjoyed a formidable record, mainly in the hands of private owners.

Jaguar C-type

1951–53

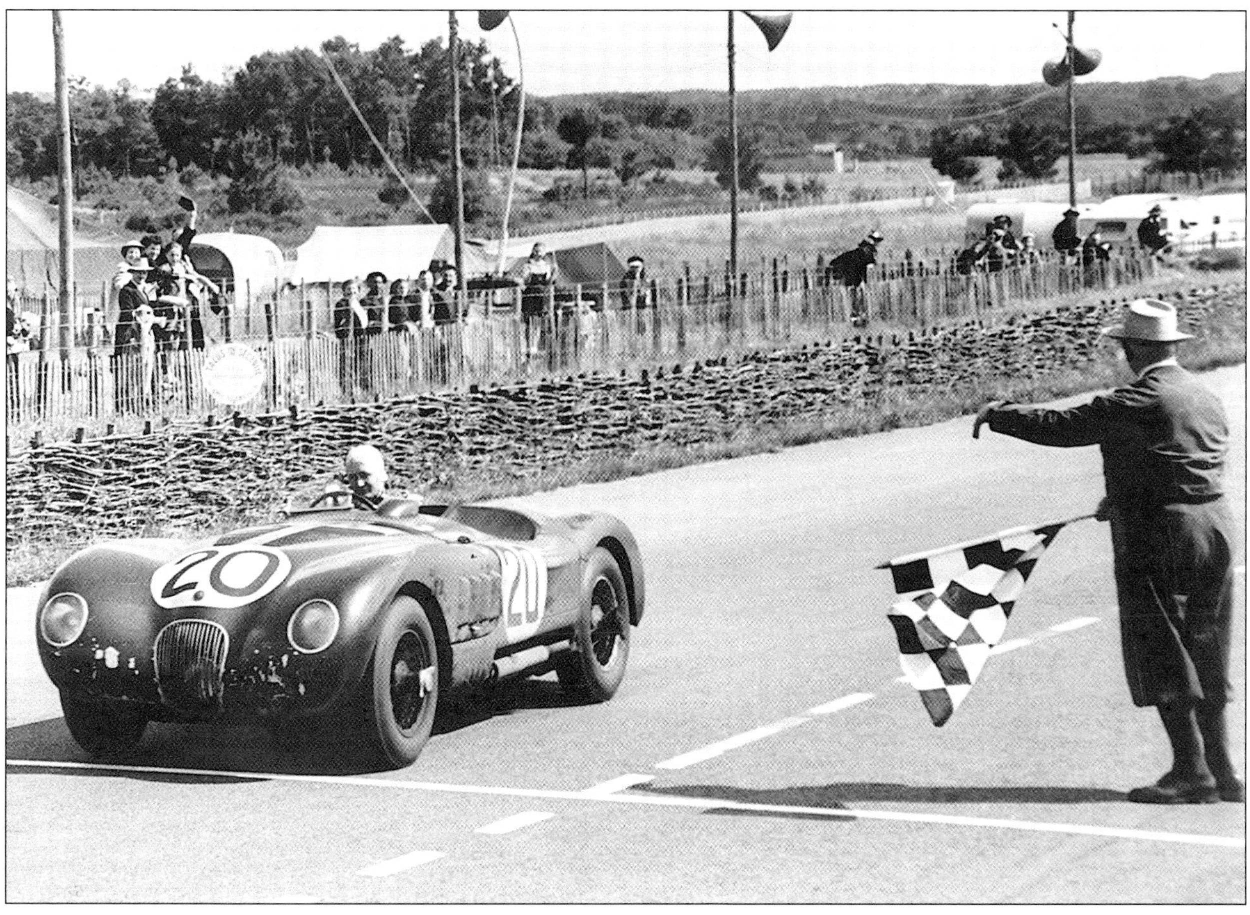

Peter Whitehead crosses the finishing line at Le Mans in 1951 at the wheel of the C-type that he and Peter Walker drove to a win on the model's first appearance in the 24 Hours race. The nose of the car is badly battered by stones and chips thrown up during the race. Facilities remained Spartan and spectators were thin on the ground.

When the team at Jaguar developed the C- and D-types, they produced not only highly successful competition cars, but cars that could be put into limited production for sale to private owners and raced by them with confidence. In the writer's opinion, the C-type was not just more powerful than the rival Aston Martin DB3S, but its braking was superior and its handling gave the driver great confidence and was more forgiving than that of the DB3S. The engine was also much more flexible than that of its Feltham rival.

William Lyons held the strong and undoubtedly correct view that the only sports car race worth winning was Le Mans, as it was the one race that boosted sales of production cars. Motor racing 50 years ago, even Le Mans, attracted far less public interest than it does today. The one exception, in Britain at least, was the 1953 Le Mans race when Jaguar's overwhelming victory was achieved less than a fortnight after the coronation of Queen Elizabeth II.

Jaguar's first appearance at Le Mans was in 1950 when the works supported the entry of three slightly modified XK120s. Johnson/Hadley rose as high as second by half-distance, dropped back to third; they were forced to rely heavily on the gearbox to slow the car, which resulted in too much strain on the clutch and the centre pulled out. The other XK120s driven by Clark/Haines and Peter Whitehead/Marshall finished

12th and 15th. Jaguar's Chairman and Chief Engineer William Heynes had learned all they wanted to know.

Some ten years later Heynes told Andrew Whyte, "This race [Le Mans], as far as I was concerned, debunked the tradition of a tuning wizard with a lifetime's experience on the track and a special gimmick in his tool box. I realised that a car could be built of standard production units from the factory, and that such a car could win the race given the luck." In the autumn of 1950 Jaguar design staff set to work on a competition car based on the XK120 engine, gearbox and rear axle that emerged as the XK120C (more usually known as the C-type). The main aims were to reduce weight and to improve both the handling at high speeds and the braking.

The chassis was a welded, multi-tubular structure, fully triangulated and with drilled channel-section members as the base. There were two-inch main and lower tubes, 1.5-inch upper tubes and 1-inch connecting struts, the diameter of the tubes varying according to loading. Additional rigidity was provided by a welded panel scuttle and at the rear of the main chassis by a further bulkhead. A subsidiary channel-section frame at the rear mounted the rear of the body, the 40-gallon fuel tank and carried the spare wheel. The wheelbase was 8ft 0in (2,440mm), with a track front and rear of 4ft 3in (1,295mm).

One of the 1952 Le Mans C-types seen outside Jaguar's Browns Lane factory. The hastily devised, more aerodynamic nose and tail proved a disaster and all three cars retired early in the 24 Hour race. Ian Stewart/Peter Whitehead drove this car.

At the front Jaguar used many XK120 components in the independent suspension by unequal-length wishbones and longitudinal torsion bars. The design team devised completely new rear suspension with a rigid axle suspended on a single transverse torsion bar and anchored at the centre. From each end of the torsion bar a trailing link ran to a hanger bracket attached under the rear axle casing.

Just inside the right rear wheel an A-bracket located the axle laterally and reduced the tendency for the right wheel to lift by working in reaction to the torque resulting from hard acceleration. Other design features were rack-and-pinion steering, 16-inch alloy-rimmed wire wheels with knock-off hubs and Lockheed self-adjusting brakes with 12-inch drums. The body was a very stylish, low-drag full-width design, with a nose section that hinged forwards, and there is little doubt that designer Malcolm Sayer derived inspiration from the bodywork of the Bugatti 'tanks'.

Part of the genius of Jaguar was the six-cylinder 3,442cc (83×106mm) engine with twin overhead camshafts driven from the nose of the crankshaft by a two-stage duplex chain and with the crankshaft running in seven main bearings. There were elements in the design of both Ettore Bugatti and Georges Ruesch of Talbot. As fitted to the C-type, with a compression ratio of 8:1, two SU horizontal carburettors and a twin exhaust system power, output of the XK engine was about 200bhp at 5,800rpm.

Transmission was by a Borg & Beck single dry-plate clutch and a modified version of the Moss four-speed gearbox used on production cars, with slow, crunchy

The C-types in revised 'Lightweight' form dominated the 1953 Le Mans race. Here, in the opening laps of the race, Moss leads Rolt, but the cars are rather closer together than racing manager 'Lofty' England would have liked. The 'Lightweight' cars were identifiable by the air scoop on the right-hand side of the bonnet.

changes despite supposedly having synchromesh on the upper ratios. What the Moss Gear Co. Ltd meant by synchromesh was that you changed gear as quickly and as hard as you could, the next gear was selected with a crunch and you wouldn't have jarred your wrist if you'd been sensible enough to change gear slowly in the first place. From the gearbox the drive was taken by a Hardy Spicer prop-shaft to a hypoid bevel final drive. The weight distribution was approximately 50/50 front and rear and the dry weight was 2,070lb (939kg).

The C-types appeared in the 1951 Le Mans race and although there had been very limited time for development, they ran perfectly. After initial skirmishes with 4.5-litre Talbots, the C-types settled into the first three places in the order Moss/Fairman, Peter Whitehead/Walker and Johnson/Biondetti. Two of the cars retired because of a broken oil pipe and thus loss of pressure. Whitehead/Walker won at a record speed of 93.495mph (150.433kph), 77 miles (124km) ahead of the second-place Talbot of Meyrat/Mairesse. Moss also set a new lap record of 105.232mph (169.318kph).

In September the C-types ran in the handicap 319-mile (513km) Tourist Trophy and Moss and Walker took the first two places on scratch and handicap. Later that month Moss won a couple of minor races with a C-type at Goodwood. By 1952 power output of the works cars was 210bhp at 5,800rpm on a reduced compression ratio of 9:1. The company also started building production cars for sale to selected owners.

Jaguar was conducting disc brake development with Dunlop and Moss drove a disc-braked car twice. He finished fourth in a sports car handicap at Goodwood on Easter Monday and then partnered by chief tester Norman Dewis raced the same car in the Mille Miglia. There was no properly organised back-up, little practice over the course, but despite a leaking fuel tank and tyre problems he was in third place after Rome when he went off-course, damaged the steering and had to pull out of the race.

Moss won the over 2-litre Production Sports Car race at Silverstone from Parnell and Abecassis (Aston Martin DB3s). 'Production' was very loosely interpreted in these races. He then drove in the 195-mile (314km) Monaco Grand Prix held as a sports car race that year and was in second place behind Manzon (2.3-litre Gordini) when they both ran into a multi-car crash at Ste Devote. Moss rejoined the race with a very battered C-type, but was disqualified for receiving outside assistance at the scene of the accident.

After the Mille Miglia, Moss had telegrammed William Lyons to say "Must have more speed at Le Mans." Jaguar held Moss in such esteem that at the very last moment they built new lower and more aerodynamic nose and tail sections. The new noses necessitated the use of smaller radiators. In practice the cars overheated badly and two of them were fitted with standard radiators that made ugly bulges in the bonnet. All three retired early in the race, two of them boiling furiously. In fact the works Mercedes-Benz 300SLs were slower than the C-types and won through good luck – a major part of that was Jaguar's misfortune.

Jaguar returned to the fray in the Goodwood Nine Hours in August and the main opposition came from a works team of sluggish Aston Martin DB3s and a couple of 2.7-litre Ferraris. The C-types reigned supreme in first three places, but, one by one, fell by the wayside. Whitehead crashed the car he was sharing with Ian Stewart, the Rolt/Hamilton C-type lost a wheel when a drive-shaft broke and the Moss/Fairman car crawled into the pits with a broken A-bracket. This was repaired and Moss rejoined the race to finish fifth. Collins/Griffith (DB3) won the race from Cole/Graham Whitehead and Baird/Salvadori with Ferraris.

Private owners Duncan Hamilton and *Écurie Ecosse* won many minor events in 1952, Peter Walker with a works car set sports car records at Shelsley Walsh and Prescott hill climbs, while Rolt won a short race at Goodwood. In October *The Motor* published its road test of a C-type. A mean maximum speed of 143.711mph (231.231kph) was set with only the driver on board. Maximum speed in third gear was 119mph (191kph). During acceleration testing the C-type achieved 0–60mph (96.5kph) in 8.1 seconds and 0–100mph (161kph) in 20.1 seconds. Overall fuel consumption was 16mpg, compared with the 11.4mpg averaged by the winning C-type at Le Mans in 1951.

In 1953 the first World Sports Car Championship was held and although Jaguar did not contest this seriously, it found itself vying with Ferrari for the lead, mainly because of the efforts of private owners. At Sebring in March, Johnston/Wilder and Gray/Gegen finished third and fourth. Three C-types, one a works car for Moss, ran in the Mille Miglia on 26 April, but all retired. Moss crashed his C-type in practice for the Production Sports Car race at Silverstone in May, when the whole team was off-form and the highest placed driver was Peter Walker in fifth place. On 24 May private entrants Peter Whitehead/Cole and Roboly/Simone took first two places in the Hyères 12 Hours race on the French Riviera.

For Le Mans Jaguar produced three improved 'Lightweight' cars; these had lighter chassis tubing, the flimsiest of aluminium-alloy bodywork and a new rear suspension arrangement whereby a Panhard rod and a second pair of trailing links ran forward from above the axle casing. Aircraft-type flexible rubber fuel tanks were fitted and, perhaps most important of all, the cars had Dunlop disc brakes. The engines now had triple Weber twin-choke 40DCF carburettors and power output rose to about 220bhp.

Despite the strongest Le Mans entry ever, Jaguar dominated the results; Rolt/Hamilton won at 105.841mph (170.298kph), Moss/Walker were second after delays in the pits to resolve fuel-feed problems, Peter Whitehead/Ian Stewart took fourth place and the works-prepared private C-type of Laurent/de Tornaco finished ninth. The pace, braking and reliability of the C-types wore the Alfa Romeos, Ferraris and Lancias into the ground. Shortly afterwards Moss/Peter Whitehead with the latter's private car won the Reims

The C-type in its original form as raced at Le Mans in 1951. Although the XK 120 engine was retained in much-modified form, there was a completely new tubular chassis. (LAT)

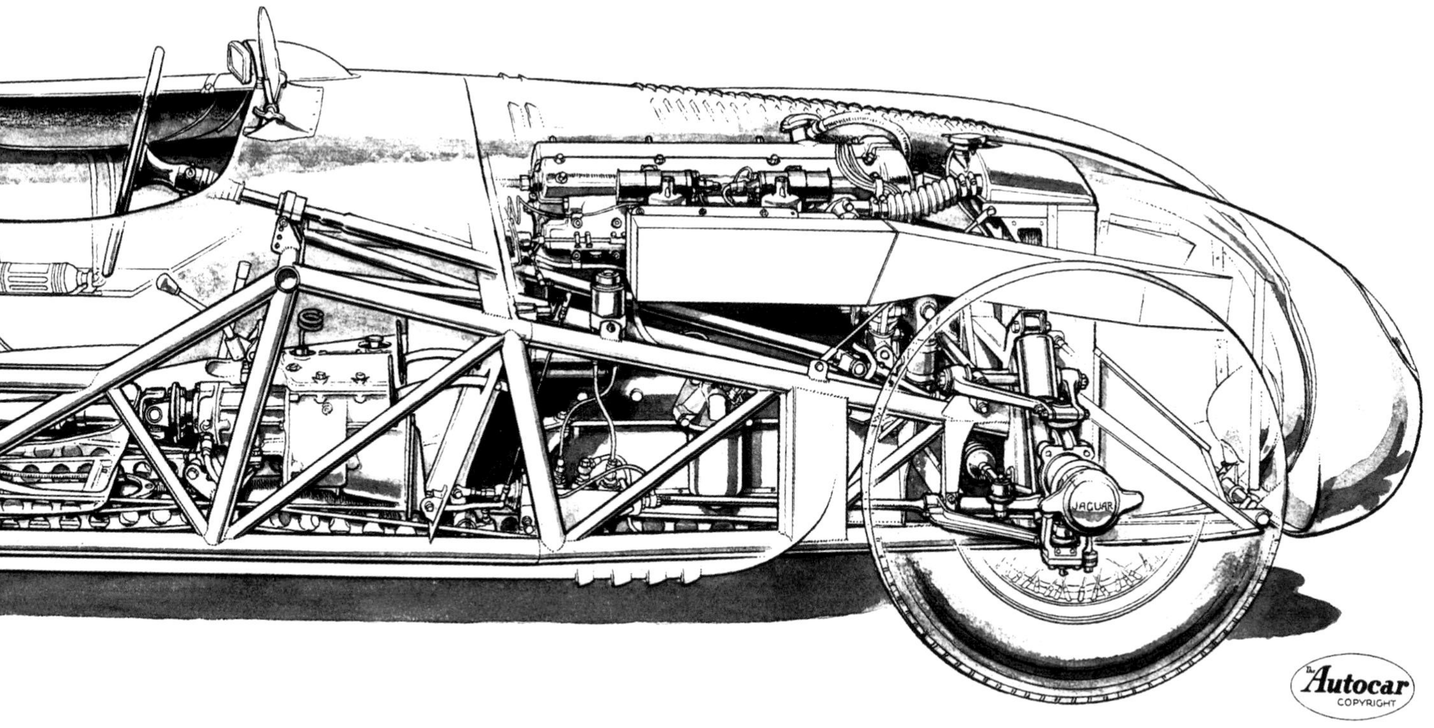

12 Hours race with the *Écurie Ecosse* entry of Scott-Douglas/Sanderson fourth.

The next round of the Championship was the Belgian 24 Hours race on 25–26 July. Hawthorn/Farina won with a 4.5-litre Ferrari, but Scott-Douglas/Gale drove their *Écurie Ecosse* C-type into second place and six points. The Goodwood Nine Hours race on 22 August was another Jaguar shambles. Moss/Walker and Rolt/Hamilton ran away from the latest Aston Martin DB3S cars, but Walker and Hamilton started a private battle, ignored racing manager 'Lofty' England's signals to ease off and both cars retired with overheated oil and low pressure. Whitehead/Stewart finished fourth despite their low oil pressure and the discs of their Dunlop brakes glowing cherry-red in the dark.

The newly inaugurated Nürburgring 1,000Km race on 30 August was next on the Championship calendar and Roy Salvadori/Ian Stewart finished second with an *Écurie Ecosse* C-type to the 4.5-litre Ferrari of Ascari/Villoresi. Although Jaguar had prepared XKC 039 to Le Mans specification (apart from less flimsy bodywork) with a view to running it in the Mexican road race, the idea was abandoned just prior to the Tourist Trophy. The outcome of the Championship now depended on how Jaguar performed in the Tourist Trophy (which Ferrari did not enter) and how Ferrari behaved in Mexico.

Jaguar lost the handicap TT on a newly resurfaced Dundrod before the race started. The 3.4-litre C-types had to cover 107 laps compared with the 106 of the 3-litre Aston Martin entries. Aston's Avon tyres lasted longer than the Jaguar's Dunlops and on this circuit the DB3S entries were just about as quick as the Jaguars. Heavy braking and wheel-locking caused the constant pinion shafts in the gearbox to fail on all three cars. Moss stopped short of the finishing line and at the flag struggled across the line to finish fourth on handicap and third on scratch. On net points Ferrari led Jaguar by 26 points to 24 and clinched the Championship when Mancini finished fourth in Mexico.

By 1954 Jaguar was racing the D-types; the three Le Mans cars were sold to *Écurie Ecosse* and Duncan Hamilton bought XKC 039. During the year they both scored many wins in less important events, Dan Margulies acquired XKC 039 in 1955 and ran it in a number of overseas races with a modicum of success and private owners were still campaigning C-types in minor events until the end of the decade.

Cunningham
1951–55

Cunningham made their only appearance in Britain when they entered two C-4Rs in the sports car race at Silverstone in July 1953. Both retired. The driver of this car is Briggs Cunningham, who retired because of suspected piston failure. (Guy Griffiths)

Before Ford won at Le Mans in 1966–67, several other American teams had tried to win the 24 Hours race. In 1928 a 5-litre Stutz had finished second behind the surviving Bentley, with Chryslers in third and fourth places. Chrysler tried again in 1929, but could manage no higher than sixth and seventh places. American efforts lapsed until 1950 when wealthy sportsman Briggs Swift Cunningham and brothers Sam and Miles Collier entered the race with 5½-litre Cadillacs, to which the French gave appropriate nicknames, *La Petite Pitaud* ('Little Elephant') for the Colliers' near-enough standard 61 sedan and *Le Monstre* for Cunningham's rebodied car with aerodynamics by Grumman Aircraft.

The Colliers took tenth place at 81.533mph (131.19kph) and Cunningham, partnered by Phil Walters, was 11th after an excursion into a sandbank and the usual slow extrication. What was interesting was that both finished ahead of the formidably quick, streamlined ex-Embiricos 1938 4½-litre Bentley of Soltan Hays/Ian Hunter that took 14th place at 78.605mph (126.475kph). In pre-war days this Bentley had lapped Brooklands at 114mph (183kph).

Cunningham was captivated by the magic of Le Mans and returned to the circuit the following year with a team of his own Cunningham sports-racing cars. Bill Frick and Phil Walters did much of the design and construction work in a factory at West Palm Beach, Florida. After building a first prototype, the C-1, the team constructed a team of three, improved C-2R cars for the 1951 race. It needs to be said immediately that Cunningham did not appreciate just how swift and sophisticated European sports-racing cars were becoming. Cunningham always lagged behind European developments.

The C-2R was a large car with a simple tubular 8ft 9in (2,670mm) chassis. Front suspension was by coil springs and wishbones and there was a de Dion rear axle suspended on coil springs. The engine was a modified Chrylser 'Hemi' V8 push-rod ohv, cast iron-block engine with the crankshaft running in five main bearings. This had a capacity of 5,425cc (96.83×92.1mm) and with a four-choke Zenith carburettor and other modifications developed around 270bhp at 5,200rpm. Neat open two-seater bodywork was fitted. Dry weight was a porky 3,450lb (1,565kg).

Cunningham/Huntoon and Rand/Wacker crashed at Le Mans, but Walters/Fitch drove a good race and were holding second place behind the ultimate winner, the C-type Jaguar of Peter Whitehead and Walker at half-distance. As the race progressed the Chrysler engine protested at the low-grade fuel supplied at Le Mans; it began to overheat, burnt valves were suspected and they had to reduce speed to crawl to the finish. They took 18th place at 78.139mph (125.725kph). Cunningham also raced his cars in the United States and after Le Mans the C-2s won at both Elkhart Lake and Watkins Glen.

In 1952 Cunningham put a touring car into limited production and built new sports-racers for Le Mans. The production car was the C-3 *Continental*, similar in many respects to the 1951 sports-racers, but with a less highly tuned engine developing 220bhp at 4,000rpm, a live rear axle and the option of a three-speed manual or Chrysler Fluid-Torque semi-automatic transmission. The body was a beautifully styled coupé designed by Michelotti for Vignale and a cabriolet became available. About 26 of these cars were built and they were available up to 1954.

The 1952 competition car was the C-4R with shorter 8ft 4in (2,540mm) wheelbase, new five-speed gearbox, rigid rear axle and weight reduced to 2,410lb (1,093kg). Two cars had open bodies, but the third, the C-4RK, was a coupé with chopped-off tail in accordance

Under the Dunlop Bridge at Le Mans in 1954 come the Cunningham C-4R of Spear/Johnston, the Lagonda of Thompson/Poore and the 1,100cc Gordini of Thirion/Pilette. Spear/Johnston finished third, although they were never in contention for the lead.

with the theories of German aerodynamicist Wunibald Kamm. In practice at Le Mans the new gearboxes gave problems, so three-speed gearboxes were substituted. Another problem was the cracking of brake drums. The ratios of the three-speed gearboxes were too low for the lighter 1952 cars and Fitch/Rice and Walters/Carter (coupé) retired because of valve problems caused by over-revved engines.

Cunningham, who drove for 20 hours of the race, and Spear were much more cautious and finished fourth at 88.002mph (141.595kph) behind two works Mercedes-Benz 300SLs and a Nash-Healey. Cunningham and his crew still had to learn the necessity of development testing and in both 1951 and 1952 the cars had barely turned a wheel before being shipped to the circuit. On its return to the United States the team had a very successful season in Sports Car Club of America racing, in which the opposition came mainly from private Ferrari and Cadillac-Allard owners and there was little well-organised competition.

It was obvious that Cunningham would not win at Le Mans, unless the team trimmed weight substantially and undertook a serious development programme. The results in 1953 were better and Cunningham ran in more European races. The Sebring 12 Hours race on 8 March was a round in the newly inaugurated World Sports Car Championship and Cunningham entered a single C-4R for Fitch/Walters. The only other team to contest the race was Aston Martin with a brace of 2.9-litre DB3s. Fitch/Walters drove a steady race and won at 74.96mph (120.61kph), a lap clear of the DB3 of Parnell/Abecassis.

For Le Mans Cunningham developed the C-5R with smoother body and unconventional front suspension that bucked the trend, a rigid axle suspended on torsion bars. The Chrysler engine was now said to develop 310bhp at 5,200rpm and the team used a modified Siata four-speed gearbox. There were 16-inch (406mm) Halibrand magnesium-alloy wheels and enormous Al-fin radially finned brake drums. Cunningham gave the weight as 2,590lb (1,175kg). The team entered three cars in the 24 Hours race, the C-5R for Walters/Fitch, a C-4R for Cunningham/Spear and the C-4RK driven by Moran/Bennet.

At no time in its history has there been such a strong entry at Le Mans and the works Jaguar C-types annihilated the opposition with, arguably, the exception of the Cunninghams. The cars were timed for the first time over a flying kilometre of the *Mulsanne Straight* at *Hunaudières* and Walters/Fitch were fastest at 154.838mph (249.135kph) and they also split the Jaguars by finishing third. But the suggestion that Cunningham could have won the race if all its horses had been unleashed is illusory.

Once the fastest opposition had fallen by the wayside the leading Jaguar of Rolt/Hamilton eased its speed. The second-place Jaguar of Moss/Walker had stopped at the pits just before the end of the second hour because of a blocked oil filter. Moss/Walker resumed the race in 23rd place, regained second place from the Cunningham at about 11am on the Sunday morning and built up a lead of over a lap by the chequered flag at 4pm. They set a pace that the Cunningham could not conceivably have matched.

Cunningham then ran two cars in the Reims 12 Hours race starting at 12 midnight on 4 July. Fitch, co-driving with Shermann lost control of the C-5R through the fast curves at *Garenne* and crashed heavily, *possibly* because of a steering defect. Peter Whitehead and Moss with the former's private C-type Jaguar won

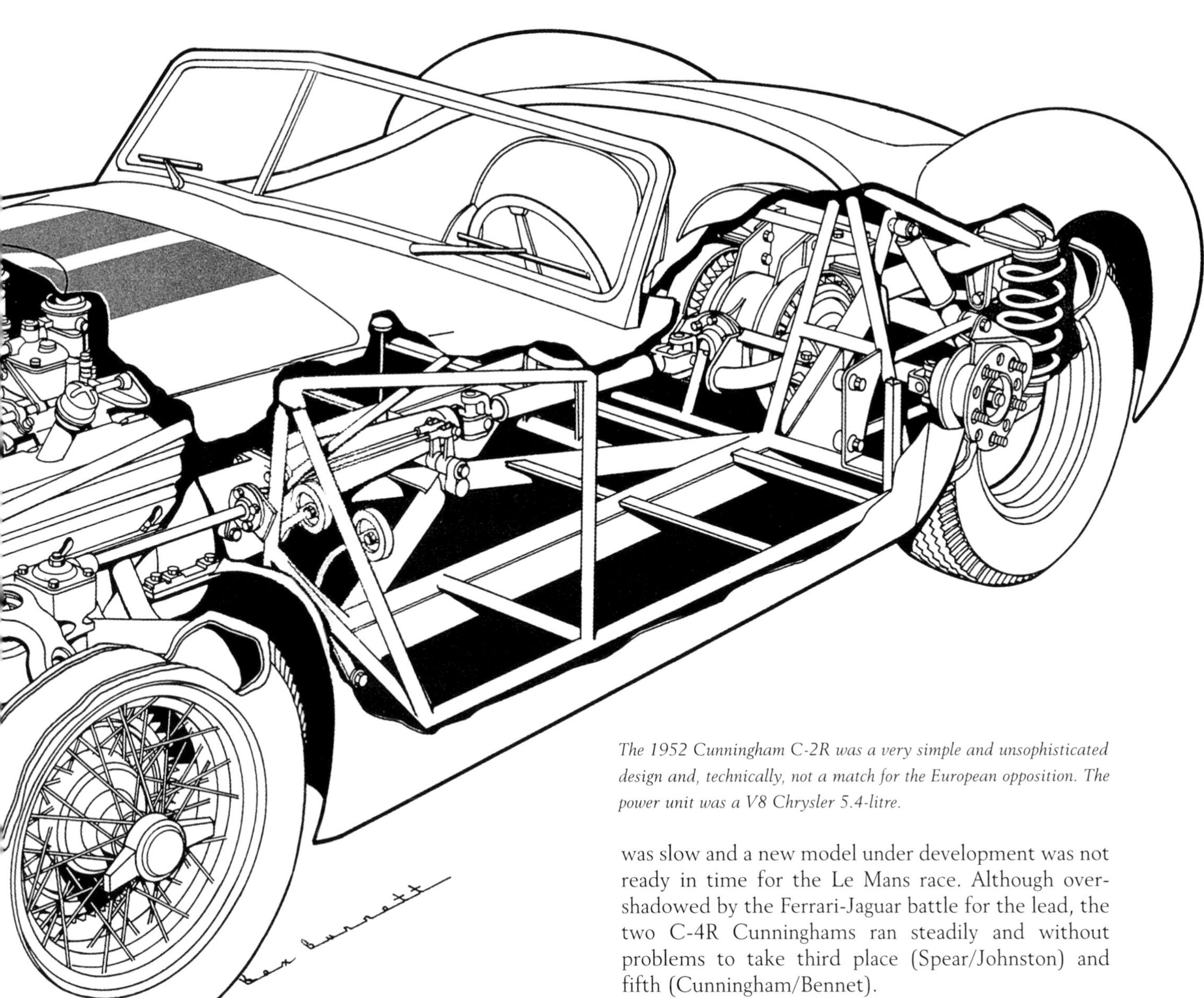

The 1952 Cunningham C-2R was a very simple and unsophisticated design and, technically, not a match for the European opposition. The power unit was a V8 Chrysler 5.4-litre.

from Rosier/Giraud-Cabantous (Talbot) and Cunningham/ Sherwood Johnston finished third. Before cutting short their European season Cunningham ran the two C-4Rs in the 102-mile (164km) sports car race at Silverstone on 18 July, the day of the British Grand Prix, but both cars retired.

Johnston/Cunningham drove the sole Cunningham, entry, a C-4R in the 1954 Sebring 12 Hours on 7 March and although it went well initially, it dropped back after its exhaust caught fire during its first routine pit stop. It was in fifth place when it retired because of engine problems. Development work at Cunningham was slow and a new model under development was not ready in time for the Le Mans race. Although overshadowed by the Ferrari-Jaguar battle for the lead, the two C-4R Cunninghams ran steadily and without problems to take third place (Spear/Johnston) and fifth (Cunningham/Bennet).

Cunningham had hoped to fit Dunlop disc brakes, but he was thwarted by a long-term development agreement between Dunlop and Jaguar. At Le Mans he also ran a 1953 340 Ferrari with 4.5-litre engine and, experimentally, water-cooled brakes made by a company in Connecticut. Water leaks developed in the system and operation of the pumps threw a strain on the Ferrari's timing gears; and Walters/Fitch retired the car because of engine trouble during the 13th hour.

The team ran the two C-4Rs in the Reims 12 Hours race on 4 July, but the Jaguar D-types and Masten Gregory/Biondetti (Ferrari Tipo 375) outpaced them; they finished fifth, Cunningham/Johnston, and sixth, Fitch/Walters. On 28 September Cunningham scored a good victory on home territory when Phil Walters and Sherwood Johnston finished first and third in the 101-mile (163km) Watkins Glen Grand Prix.

By 1955 the team had completed the C-6R model

The Meyer-Drake-powered 3-litre Cunningham C-6R at Le Mans in 1955. Driven by Cunningham/Johnston, it ran badly and retired because of a burnt piston in the 14th hour of the race. (T.C. March/FotoVantage)

and it was lower and lighter than earlier Cunninghams. It had the usual tubular chassis, with front suspension by double wishbones, coil springs and twin dampers (a telescopic and a lever-type) and at the rear a de Dion axle with trailing arms and coil springs. The power unit was the four-cylinder push-rod overhead valve, cast-iron block 2,942cc Meyer-Drake engine, as used at Indianapolis.

With the supercharger removed and two Weber twin-choke carburettors substituted, Cunningham claimed a power output of 270bhp at 6,000rpm. Transmission was by a multi-plate clutch, four-speed gearbox and a final drive incorporating a Hi-Tork limited slip differential. A very stylish body with a single Jaguar-style tail fin was fitted and Cunningham claimed a dry weight of 1,850lb (839kg).

Cunningham/Bennet drove the car at Sebring in 1955, but it was slow and retired because of a broken flywheel (it was steel and should have been duralumin alloy). It reappeared at Le Mans with Cunningham/Johnston at the wheel and survived until the 19th hour when it succumbed to a burnt piston while holding 13th place. By this time it had only the use of top gear. The car then ran in a few American events without success.

By now Cunningham was an East Coast Jaguar distributor. He had been the entrant of the winning D-type at Sebring in 1955 and he ran a 'long-nose' D-type at Le Mans that year. Although he captained the winning US yacht *Columbia* in the 1958 America's Cup, he continued to enter Jaguars, Maseratis and Chevrolet Corvettes through to the 1960s. His last drive in a race was with a Porsche 904 in the 1966 Sebring race at the age of 59. After an expensive divorce, he had remarried in 1963 and his wife Laura was with him when he died from complications of Alzheimer's disease, aged 96, on 2 July 2003.

Mercedes-Benz 300SL

1952

Regenmeister Rudolf Caracciola sweeps through the wet, slippery roads between Florence and Bologna in the 1952 Mille Miglia. He finished fourth.

By the time of Germany's unconditional surrender on 7 May 1945 the Daimler-Benz works at Untertürkheim, Stuttgart, a main target of Allied bombing, were tangled ruins of fallen, twisted girders and collapsed masonry. The country's greatest manufacturer of quality cars, commercial vehicles, aero engines and armoured vehicles, and the leading Grand Prix contender in the 1930s, appeared to have been completely destroyed. Slowly, painfully, the company resumed car and commercial vehicle production, but what the directors wanted was a successful return to motor racing so that Mercedes-Benz cars could recover the esteem and regard that the marque had possessed in pre-war days.

Germany was banned from international motor racing until 1950 and when German drivers ran in overseas events that year they were met with undisguised hostility. In 1951 the company dispatched three 1939 W154 3-litre supercharged Grand Prix cars to compete in the two Formule Libre races at Buenos Aires in February. Argentina was a country with strong German sympathies, undiminished by the war because of its isolation from Nazi oppression and brutality. In these short races, in hot weather and on a slow circuit, the

The 300SLs took first and second places at Le Mans in 1952, but only after the retirement of Levegh with his Talbot-Lago in the 23rd hour. Here the winning car of Lang/Riess sweeps through the Esses.

W154 drivers, Hermann Lang, Karl Kling and Juan Fangio were unable to match the performance of Froilan Gonzalez with a 2-litre supercharged Ferrari.

Success had not been the main aim of the exercise. Mercedes-Benz wanted to re-familiarise the technical staff and mechanics with the disciplines, practice and routines of motor racing. They returned to Stuttgart with a 'hands-on' feel for post-war motor racing. The technical team, headed by Rudolf Uhlenhaut, now initiated the design of a new Grand Prix car that would be raced when the 2,500cc formula came into force in 1954 and a sports-racing car that would be relatively cheap and easy to build and would be ready for the 1952 season.

The new sports car, designated the W194 (but known publicly as the 300SL or *SportLeicht*) was powered by a modified version of the six-cylinder 2,996cc (85×88mm) single overhead camshaft engine that powered the luxurious 300 saloon. This engine had a cast iron block, double-roller chain-drive to the camshaft and a crankshaft running in seven main bearings. In standard form, it developed 115bhp, but as modified for use in the 300SL, with competition camshaft and three Solex downdraught carburettors, power output was 171bhp at 5,800rpm.

To reduce overall height the engine was canted in the chassis at an angle of 50 degrees to the left. This made it virtually impossible to change the sparking plugs mount-

The 1952 300SL racing coupé. This view shows clearly the space-frame chassis construction that necessitated the adoption of gull-wing doors. Rather less obvious is the canted engine with the exhausts emerging high up under the bonnet. (Mercedes-Benz Fotodienst)

ed in the block and during the year Mercedes cast new cylinder heads in which the plugs were now mounted. Originally Mercedes used the original wet-sump lubrication, but dry-sump was adopted before the cars were raced. Transmission was by the standard 300 model's four-speed synchromesh gearbox with cast iron casing.

The 300SL retained suspension almost identical to that of the production car, with wishbones and coil springs at the front, and with the same swing-axle and torsion bar suspension at the rear, save that the supplementary torsion bars of the saloon – necessary because of its considerable weight – were deleted and the shock absorbers were behind instead of in front of the axle-line. Uhlenhaut knew that with such components the 300SL would be a heavy car and so the chassis and body were built as light as possible.

Uhlenhaut and his colleagues designed a multi-tubular space-frame constructed from small-gauge tubing, apart from large tubes running across the front at the suspension attachment points, and at the rear above the differential and providing the coil spring and shock absorber mountings. Much of the torsional stiffness of the frame was derived from the latticework of side tubes. It was a frame that was very advanced, but whether it was fully stressed in tension and compression, the hallmark of a true space-frame, is doubtful.

The wheels were 15-inch (380mm) disc-type with BMW-style centre-lock knock-off hubcaps. Fuel capacity was 45 gallons and there was just enough room in the tail for the tank, together with two spare wheels. The wheelbase was 7ft 10½in (2,400mm), front track 4ft 6½in (1,380mm) and rear track 4ft 9in (1,445mm).

The decision had been made to fit a coupé body, but the space-frame construction would not permit the use of standard doors, so the bodybuilders adopted the famous gull-wing doors cut into the roof.

The power output was low for a car weighing 1,914lb (868kg) – the target weight had been 1,760lb (798kg) and compared unfavourably with other sports-racing cars, notably the Jaguar C-type that was also derived from production components. The C-type was heavier at 2,072lb (940kg), but was 30bhp more powerful. Racing Manager Alfred Neubauer thought that the 300SL was underpowered, wanted a five-speed gearbox and had doubts about the 15-inch wheels. He reported, "The German press and public await the overall victories by Mercedes-Benz sports cars, with which I am entrusted, but without the means to deliver them."

Mercedes-Benz ran in five races in 1952, three of them of major International status, and won four, but their performances were less satisfactory than the results suggest. The defeat suffered in the team's first race, the Mille Miglia held on 3–4 May, was not – with the benefit of hindsight – surprising. Giovanni Bracco won after 12 hours' racing, much of it on wet roads, by a margin of 4min 32sec. His 250 *Sport* Ferrari 3-litre coupé developed about 220bhp at 7,000rpm, it weighed much the same as a 300SL, it was one of the better handling of its breed and Bracco knew the course intimately.

Although the Mercedes drivers had practised extensively over the course, they could not match home knowledge. Kling drove well with his 300SL to finish second. Caracciola had an engine less powerful than those of his team-mates and was beaten into fourth place by Fagioli with a Lancia Aurelia GT, a modified production car. Hermann Lang retired early in the race after hitting a large stone which put the rear axle out of alignment.

On 18 May, the day of the Swiss Grand Prix, the same drivers with the same cars, plus Fritz Riess with the spare car, ran in the 81-mile (130km) Preis von Bern at Bremgarten. The spare car had doors that continued down into the sides of the body, a modification adopted for Le Mans to ensure that there would be no difficulties with the hostile scrutineers.

Bremgarten proved a 300SL demonstration. The only serious opposition came from local champion Willi Daetwyler (4.1-litre Ferrari) who retired after three laps. Kling, Lang and Riess took the first three places, ahead of Geoff Duke and Reg Parnell (works Aston Martin DB2s). Sadly, 51-year-old Caracciola crashed his 300SL into a tree because of locking rear brakes, suffered serious injuries and was never to race again.

Mercedes built three new 300SLs for Le Mans on 14–15 June. The engines were detuned to 166bhp at 5,100rpm for reliability and in practice the team tried out a rooftop mounted air brake on an experimental spare car. During the race Neubauer ran the cars to pre-determined lap times, at which they averaged 11.7 miles per gallon, but they lost more time in the pits than expected because of the heavy wear of their Continental tyres. Jaguar, panicked by a telegram from Stirling Moss about the speed of the 300SLs in the Mille Miglia, ran their C-types with untested streamlined noses and tails and all three retired early in the race.

Behra/Manzon with their 2.3-litre Gordini led for many hours, but retired because of brake problems. Then Pierre 'Levegh' (real name Pierre Bouillon) took the lead with his 4.5-litre Talbot-Lago and despite entreaties from his wife, 'co-driver' Marchand and his pit crew, insisted on driving single-handed. It was obsessive and irrational, but Levegh led by four laps until the 23rd hour when the Talbot broke its crankshaft – possibly because of a missed gear-change.

Lang/Riess won for Mercedes-Benz from team-mates Helfrich/Niedermayr. Early in the race Kling/Klenk had held second place behind the Gordini before their dynamo failed. The German victory was highly unpopular with the French crowd, many of whom lived in the areas where *Das Reich SS* Panzer Division had committed so many atrocities in the weeks following the D-day landings.

The 300SLs next appeared in the 142-mile (228km) Rheinland Cup race that preceded the German Grand Prix at the Nürburgring on 2 August. Mercedes-Benz had made substantial changes to the cars for this race and four were entered, all with the coupé top removed, neat metal decking and metal tonneau cover. The team had entered two supercharged cars, one a new version with shorter 7ft 2½in (2,200mm) wheelbase.

In supercharged form these cars developed 230bhp at 6,400rpm, but they were no quicker round the Nürburgring than the unblown version and were scratched from the race. The only serious opposition came from Manzon with a 2.3-litre Gordini, a car that looked diminutive alongside the bulky 300SLs, and after his retirement the Mercedes entries took the first four places in the order Lang, Kling, Riess and Helfrich. Fifth place went to Piero Carini who drove a 4.1-litre Ferrari.

Mercedes-Benz had not intended to race the 300SLs again, but under pressure from their agent in Mexico City they relented and entered a three-car team in the Carrera Panamericana Mexico Road Race. Kling/Klenk and Lang/Grupp had coupés, while American John Fitch/Geiger drove a roadster. Because there was no 3,000cc class in this race the 300SLs had engine capa-

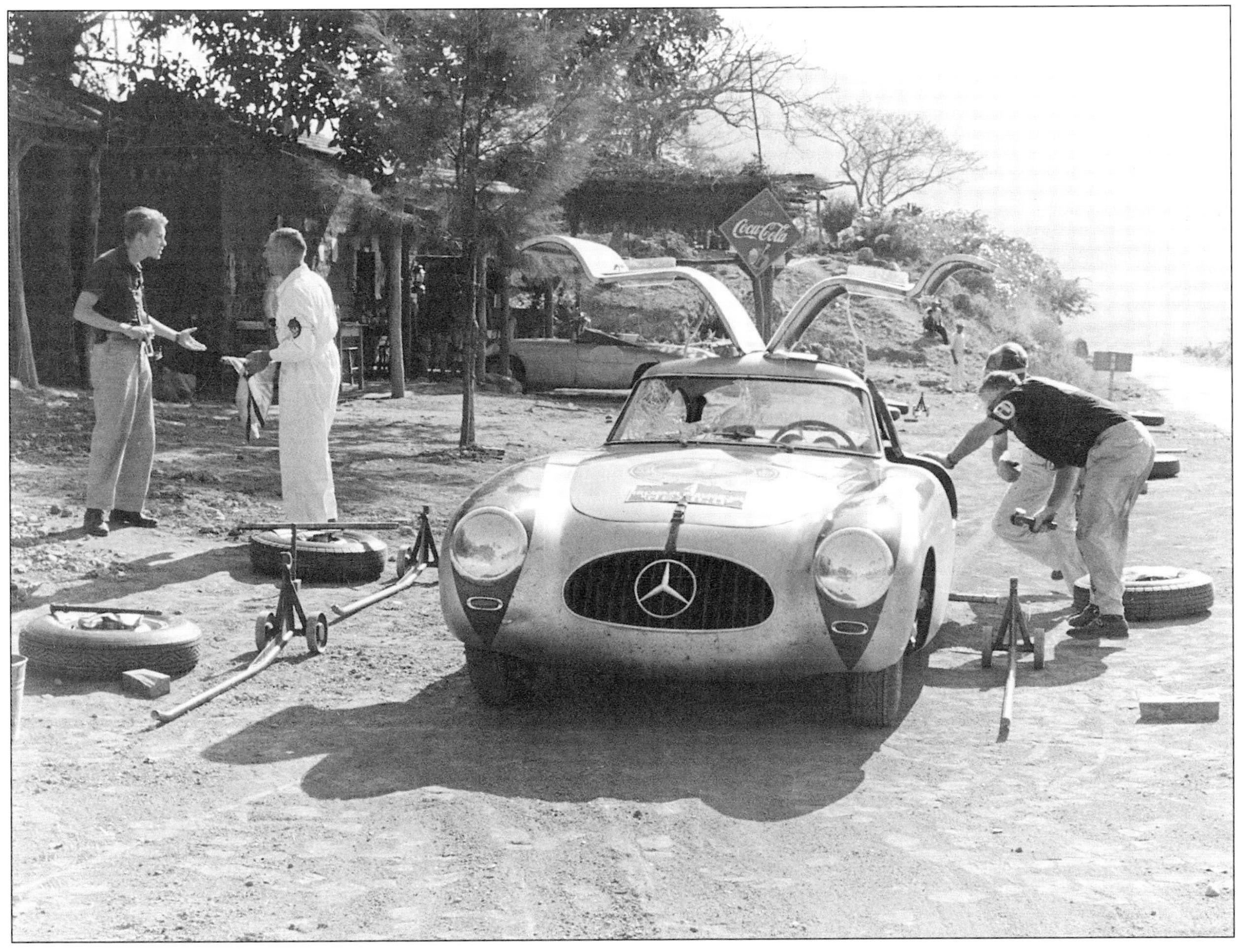

The 300SL of Kling/Klenk stops for a tyre change during the third stage of the 1952 Carrera Panamericana Mexico road race. A buzzard shattered the windscreen earlier on the stage. Kling/Klenk won at 102.59mph (165.07kph). (Mercedes-Benz Fotodienst)

city increased to 3,067cc (86×88mm) and this increased power to 177bhp at 5,200rpm.

Opposition came from a trio of 4.1-litre Ferrari *Mexico* coupés driven by Ascari, Villoresi and Bracco and although they were faster than the 300SLs, all retired; Ascari crashed and the other two Ferrari drivers were eliminated by transmission problems – Bracco while leading on the seventh of the eight stages. The vastly hyped sensation of the race was Kling's collision on the third stage while travelling at around 135mph (217kph) with a buzzard which smashed the windscreen and stunned co-driver Hans Klenk. By the next stage Mercedes-Benz had fitted 'buzzard bars', eight metal bars vertically across the windscreen attached top and bottom to the bodywork.

Fitch was disqualified at the end of the race for receiving outside assistance in adjusting the tracking of the front wheels during the seventh stage. Kling/Klenk and Lang/Riess took the first two places ahead of Chinetti/Jean Lucas with a 4.1-litre Ferrari. Of the 300SLs Fitch wrote, "The cars themselves looked disreputable, the paint literally sand-blasted away to the base metal, the bodies battered by stones, dented by birds, and torn and bent by the flying treads, which had become whips at speed." In the earlier stages of this race the 300SLs had been plagued by tyre problems.

For Mercedes-Benz, the 300SLs had achieved all that was wanted and they now went into graceful semi-retirement. From the competition 300SLs, Mercedes-Benz developed the slightly restyled production car that appeared in 1954. Apart from a small number of lightweight cars, the production 300SLs had steel main body panels, with aluminium-alloy bonnet, boot and doors, and all had Bosch fuel-injection engines that gave an official 219bhp at 5,800rpm. Maximum speed was 140mph. Mercedes-Benz built 1,400 gull-wing coupés between 1954 and 1957 and between 1957 and 1963 there followed a further 1,858 roadsters.

Alfa Romeo Disco Volante

1952–53

The 6C 34 of Sanesi/Carini seen before the 1953 Le Mans race, surrounded by its drivers and crew. Note the large bug screen in front of the wipers. All three 6C 34s retired in the race. The styling of these very potent, but largely unsuccessful cars, exuded machismo. (LAT)

At the end of 1951 Alfa Romeo withdrew from Grand Prix racing after an era of domination with the Tipo 158 and 159 *Alfettas* that had started racing in 1946. By 1951 the latest 159s were overdeveloped, less than reliable but, despite a strong challenge from Ferrari, Juan Fangio won his first World Championship for the Milan company. Alfa Romeo was still on top, but only marginally so, and another season would have resulted in humiliating defeat.

The company had been building competition cars for over 30 years and the decision was made to build a sports-racing car based on 1900 production saloon components. But, in effect, the project ran away with itself and the outcome was the development of stylish bodies of unique shape and very high performance cars that could battle for supremacy in major endurance races.

Giaocchino Colombo, who had returned from Ferrari and was soon to join Maserati, was very much involved in the development of the *Disco Volante* and the car was the result of close collaboration between the Alfa Romeo engineering department and coachbuilder Carrozzeria Touring. The chassis was a multi-tubular structure of different-dimension tubing, to which a lighter tubular superstructure was welded and this carried the Touring body. The wheelbase was 7ft 3.4in (2,220mm).

Suspension was independent at the front by unequal-length double wishbones, coil springs and separate dampers; at the rear Alfa Romeo used a rigid rear axle suspended on coil springs. The four-cylinder engine had a capacity of 1,997cc (85×88mm) with one-piece alloy cylinder block and crankcase, detachable liners and twin overhead camshafts chain-driven from the nose of the crankshaft. With two Weber twin-choke carburettors the power output was 158bhp at 6,500rpm. Transmission was by a multi-plate clutch and a four-speed gearbox in unit with the final drive.

The bodies of the first two cars were dramatically curved spiders and these became known as the *Disco Volante* or 'Flying saucer'. One of these cars was subsequently fitted with a six-cylinder 2,960cc (87×83mm) engine developing 230bhp at 6,000rpm. After Colombo left, Rodolfo Hruska took control of the project, as a sort of adjunct to his responsibility for the production 1900.

Hruska commissioned two further cars with body by Touring. One was the so-called ogival coupé that looks like an E-type designed by Malcolm Sayer when he had a bad day and mislaid his slide rule, while the other was a very neat open 'narrow-sided' two-seater that was to make quite a good hill-climb car. One of the original open *Disco Volantes* and the coupé are in the Alfa Romeo museum.

Consalvo Sanesi, Alfa Romeo's chief tester and occasional racing driver, tested the 3-litre *Disco Volantes* extensively at Monza; thanks to their low weight of about 1,620lb dry (735kg) and good power output, they were not short of straight-line speed, but they handled badly and suffered from aerodynamic lift. Plans to race the cars in their existing form were abandoned and work started on a much-revised design. The basic chassis frame was largely unchanged, but gone was the integral body framework that was part of the original design and the track was wider. At the rear there was now a de Dion axle suspended on coil springs.

The engine capacity had been increased to 3,495cc (87×98mm) and by the time of the 1953 Mille Miglia power output was reckoned to be 275bhp at 6,500rpm.

The dramatically styled Alfa Romeo Disco Volante with bodywork by Touring. These 1952 cars were never raced, but the style influenced Malcolm Sayer of Jaguar when he designed the D-type body. (Centro Documentazione Alfa Romeo)

Built in early 1953, the 'ogival' Disco Volante 2-litre coupé was ugly enough to transcend most barriers of good taste. This and one of the open 1952 cars survive and are in the Alfa Romeo museum. (Centro Documentazione Alfa Romeo)

There was now a five-speed gearbox. The aluminium-alloy body on the four cars built was the work of coach-builder Colli and although the frontal treatment resembled that of the *Disco Volante*, the overall effect was of a very pugnacious racing coupé with a full-width 'bug-screen' across the bonnet, large scoops on the rear wings and, as tested, valances over the rear wheels. These cars are properly (if inaccurately) known as 3000CMs and also as 6C 34s.

Three 3000CMs ran in the Mille Miglia in April and the drivers were Juan Fangio, Sanesi and Karl Kling. Goffredo Zehender also drove the 2-litre 'narrow-sided' car, but retired early in the race. From the start Sanesi set a cracking pace, averaging 113.8mph (183.1kph) to Verona, around 107mph (172.kph) at Ravenna and 110mph (177kph) at Pescara. It was a pace that the 4.1-litre Ferraris could not match and it was the finest drive in his career, but he retired because of transmission trouble.

Kling then took the lead and he and Fangio were 1–2 at Rome before the German driver retired because of a cracked transmission housing. Fangio, still not at the peak of his form following a bad crash at Monza in June 1952, led until a track rod broke, resulting in only one front wheel responding to the steering. He plugged on to the finish, taking second place, just under 12 minutes behind Giannino Marzotto with a semi-works 4.1-litre Ferrari. It was a great performance by Alfa Romeo, even though they didn't win.

Le Mans attracted an immensely strong entry with works teams from Ferrari, Jaguar, Cunningham, Lancia and Alfa Romeo. The Alfas displayed excellent speed, but poor reliability. It was a race that started fast and the Jaguars dominated it almost throughout. None of the Alfa Romeos survived and the first retirement was the car of Fangio/Marimon with piston failure after two hours. Sanesi/Carini rose to second place at the end of the sixth hour, but after another five hours dropped out with gearbox problems. Kling/Riess also held second place briefly, but were eliminated by engine maladies.

Alfa Romeo fielded a single car for Fangio/Sanesi in the Belgian 24 Hours race. Fangio started and was holding third place after two hours and then handed over to Sanesi who promptly spun off on a wet track

This 1940 ex-Mille Miglia BMW 328 had a long and chequered history. It was brought to Britain shortly after the end of the Second World War and Frazer Nash announced it as their new 'Grand Prix' model. They sold it to 'Gillie' Tyrer, seen here at Goodwood in 1949, and he raced it for many years. (Guy Griffiths)

In early post-war days E.J. Newton (of Notwen Oil, well-known at the time) was a stalwart Frazer Nash driver. Here he is competing with his Le Mans Replica at the long-forgotten Gamston circuit near Nottingham in 1951. (T.C. March/FotoVantage)

Ferrari sent two 2-litre Tipo 166 Mille Miglia cars to compete in the one-hour up to 2,000cc Production Sports Car race at Silverstone in August 1950. This is Ferrari tester, Dorino Serafini, who finished second behind team-mate Alberto Ascari. (Guy Griffiths)

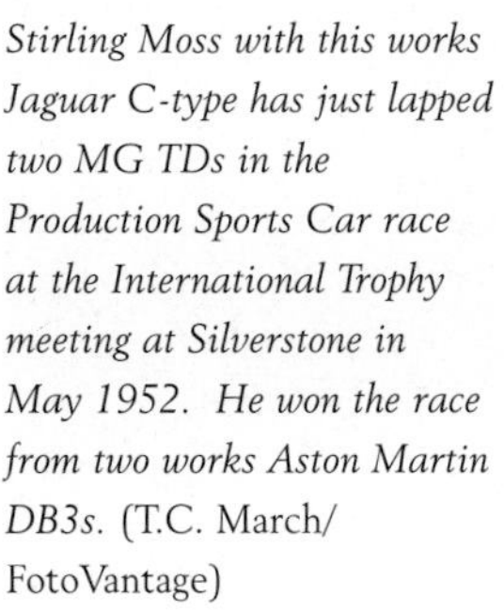

Stirling Moss with this works Jaguar C-type has just lapped two MG TDs in the Production Sports Car race at the International Trophy meeting at Silverstone in May 1952. He won the race from two works Aston Martin DB3s. (T.C. March/FotoVantage)

In 1953 the Ferrari 4.1-litre Mille Miglias dominated the Production Sports Car race at Silverstone. Tom Cole with his Vignale-bodied car finished second to Mike Hawthorn with a works car. A month after the photograph was taken, Cole crashed at Le Mans with fatal results. (T.C. March/FotoVantage)

Jocelyn Stevens at the wheel of an ex-works DB3S Aston Martin at the International Easter Monday meeting at Goodwood in 1955. During 1954 Carroll Shelby of Cobra fame had raced the car in a deal with the works in American white and blue colours. (LAT)

While Écurie Ecosse was awaiting delivery of their new D-types in 1955, they continued to race the ex-works Le Mans C-types. This is Ninian Sanderson at the wheel in the 1955 British Empire Trophy at Oulton Park. The handicap final favoured smaller-capacity cars and Sanderson finished a poor 16th. (FotoVantage)

Tony Rolt drove this works, ex-Le Mans D-type Jaguar in the sports car race at the International meeting at Silverstone in May 1955. He took third place behind two works DB3S Aston Martins. (T.C. March/FotoVantage)

Porsche's 550 Spyder was a brilliantly successful contender in the 1,500cc class. Here Hans Herrmann is at the wheel of the 550 he co-drove with Wolfgang von Trips in the 1956 Sebring 12 Hours race. They finished sixth overall and won their class. (Porsche Werkfoto)

In 1959 David Brown's Aston Martin team achieved its peak with wins at Le Mans and in the World Sports Car Championship. This is the winning DBR1 of Roy Salvadori and Carroll Shelby at Le Mans. Roy Salvadori is at the wheel.

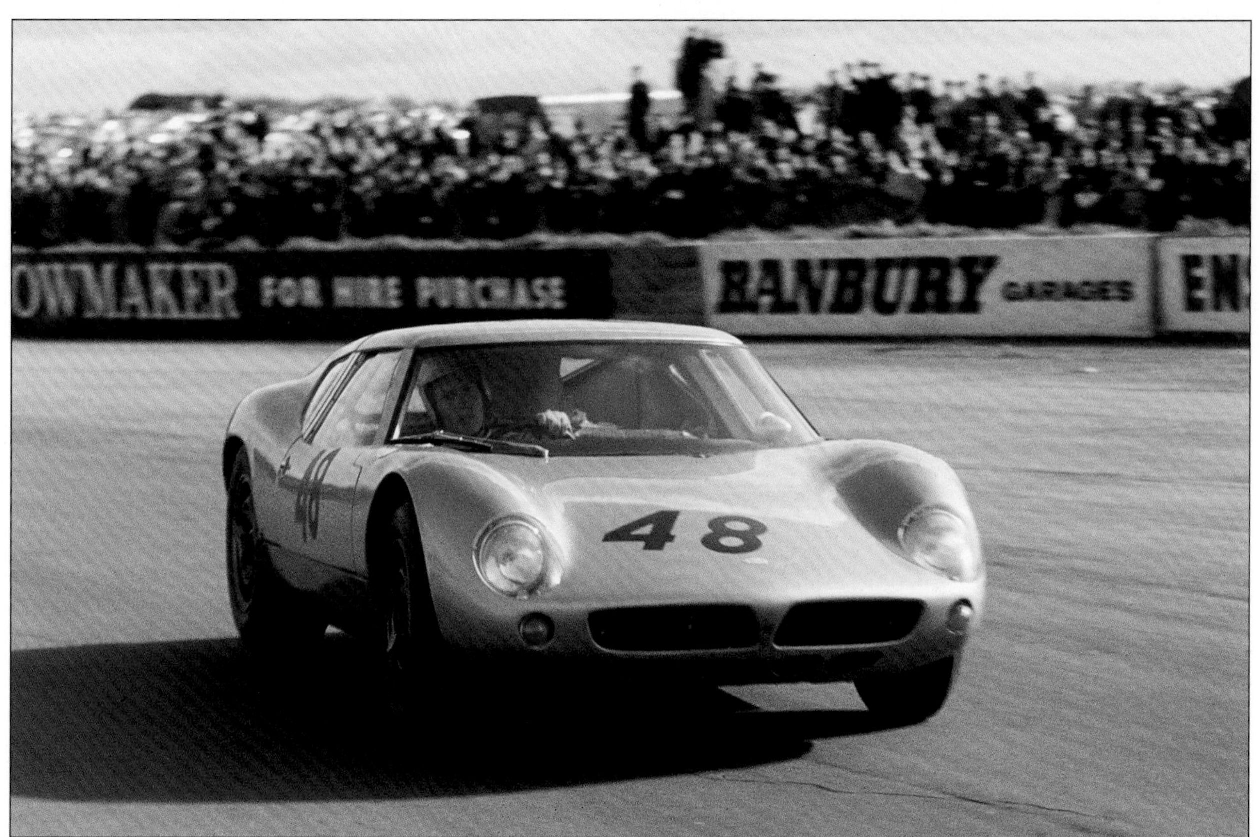

The Lola Mark 6 GT was a technically advanced and sensational car when it appeared in 1963. Here South African Tony Maggs is at the wheel on the racing debut of the GT at the International meeting at Silverstone in May of that year. (FotoVantage)

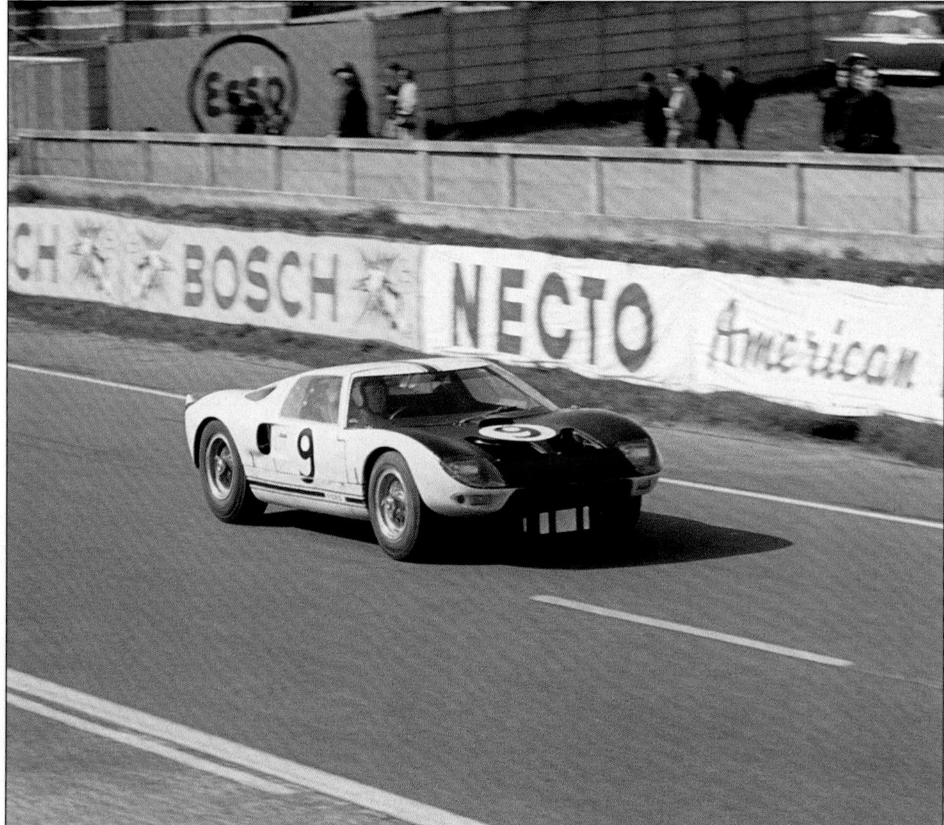

One of the Ford GT40s on its first public appearance at the 1964 Le Mans Test Weekend. It is believed that this is the car that Jo Schlesser crashed on the Saturday because of aerodynamic instability. (Ford Motor Company)

The Lola T70-Chevrolet was the most successful of the British Group 7 sports cars. Denis Hulme drove this car belonging to Irishman Sid Taylor to a win in the 1966 Tourist Trophy race at Oulton Park. (T.C. March/ FotoVantage

The Lola T70 Mk III-Chevrolet coupé was homologated in 5-litre form as a Competition Sports Car in 1968. In that year's round of the RAC Group 4 Championship at Oulton Park in August Mike de Udy with his Lola-Chevrolet, the race-winner, leads Joakim Bonnier with a similar car through Lodge Corner. Bonnier's car is fitted with a borrowed nose after the original had been damaged by Pedro Rodriguez at Karlskoga the previous weekend. (T.C. March/FotoVantage)

This Ford Mark II is seen in practice at Le Mans in 1965. It is a late practice photograph showing the car as modified prior to the race by spoilers on the front wings and tail fins. The drivers were Bruce McLaren/Ken Miles and although they led early in the race, they retired because of gearbox trouble. (Ford Motor Company)

American Jim Hall was the pioneer of advanced aerodynamics. This is his Chaparral 2F in the 1967 Targa Florio road race in Sicily. It was a completely unsuitable car for the circuit, but drivers Phil Hill and Hap Sharp were holding an almost certain fourth place, when they were forced to retire because of a puncture. (LAT)

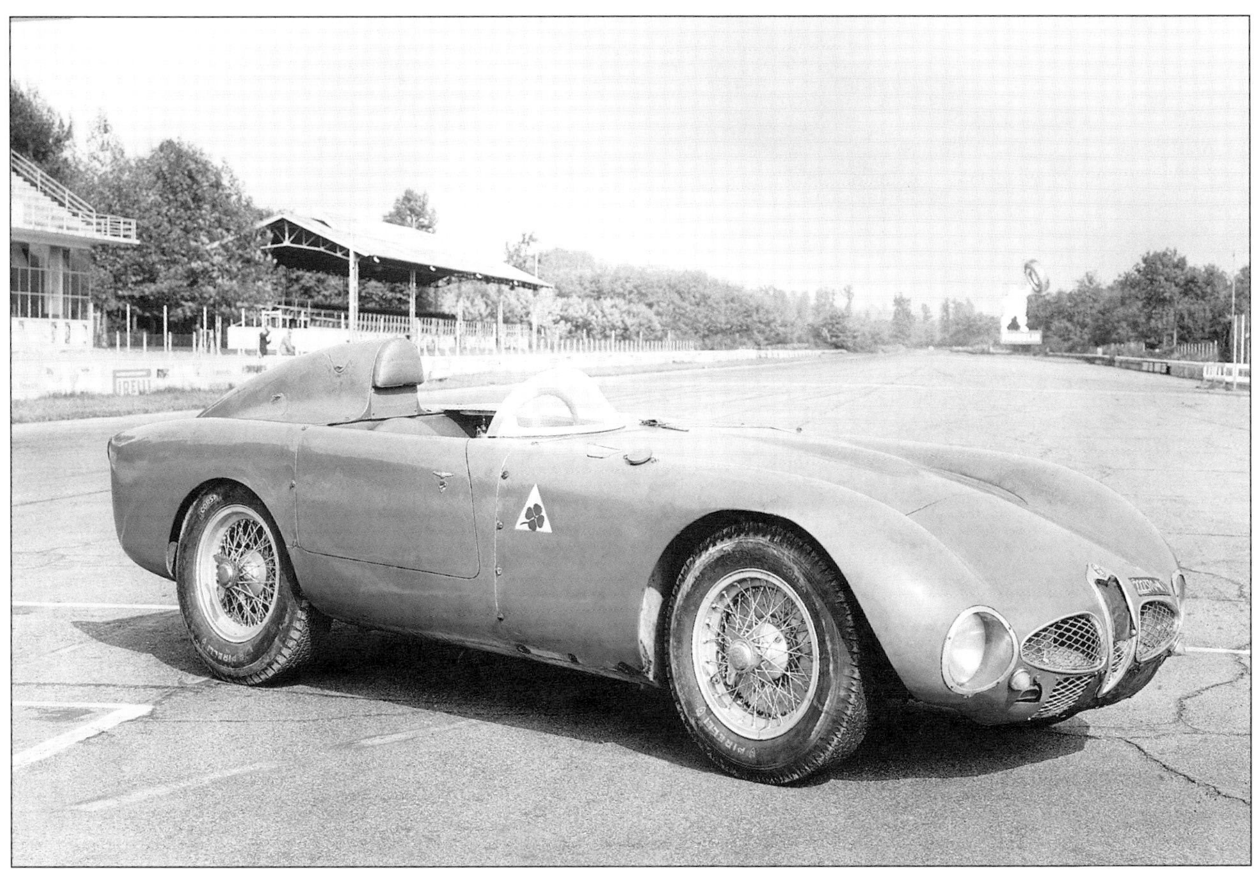

and out of the race. The factory planned a full works entry in the first Nürburgring 1,000Km race at the end of August, but during a pre-race practice session, Kling crashed when the steering failed. So, as any entrant would wish to satisfy himself that the cars were safe to drive before running in a race, Alfa Romeo withdrew.

The works sent a single car for Fangio to drive in the *Supercortemaggiore* Grand Prix, a 168-mile (270km) race held at Merano in the foothills of the Italian Alps in September. The car was a new version with a development of the 2,943cc engine now giving 260bhp. Strong Lancia opposition faded and Fangio won the race from Mantovani (2-litre Maserati). This car is also in the Alfa Romeo museum.

It was not quite the end of the story. In 1954 Alfa Romeo developed a further 3-litre car known as the 6C 3000PR, with a shorter 7ft 2.6in (2,200mm) wheelbase and lighter open bodywork by Touring. Sanesi was to drive it in the *Supercortemaggiore* Grand Prix, now held in June at Monza. Alfa Romeo booked the track for a test session on 24 May and initially the new car went well, but Sanesi went off the road and crashed heavily. He suffered severe injuries and burns and the new car was a write-off.

The 6CM 3000 photographed during a testing session at Monza. Like the other 1953 sports-racing cars, it had brutal, aggressive styling. Fangio drove this car to a win in a minor race at Merano in September 1953. (Centro Documentazione Alfa Romeo)

Development came to a halt, as the Alfa Romeo board had decided that racing was peripheral to the company's main aim of mass-producing high quality sporting cars. The 6Cs handled well, were more than adequately powerful and had a potential that was not fully exploited. Swiss driver Jean Ducrey had bought the 'narrow-sided' 2-litre car and ran it in a number of hill climbs in 1954–55. The Schlumpf brothers later acquired this car and it is in the French National Motor Museum/Collection Schlumpf at Mulhouse.

One of the 3.5-litre cars was sold to Joakim Bonnier, then an Alfa Romeo dealer in Sweden, and he had it rebodied in rather ugly open form by Zagato. Bonnier drove it in minor Swedish races in 1955, but it appeared more frequently in 1956, occasionally in British races with Ken Wharton at the wheel. The factory did not compete in sports car racing again until 1967 when its Autodelta racing department introduced the first of the long series of Tipo 33 cars, a 2-litre V8 Prototype.

Gordini

1952–56

For 1954 Gordini sold a 3-litre straight-eight sports car to Italian pilot and successful amateur driver Franco Bordoni. He is seen at the wheel of his red-painted car at a control in that year's Mille Miglia. Bordoni retired in this race, but he scored a large number of successes in other Italian races.

It is an odd fact that three of the most significant French racing marques were the work of men of Italian birth, Ettore Bugatti, Antony Lago and Amédée Gordini. Born in Modena on 23 June 1899 and christened Amadeo, Gordini emigrated to France in 1925 and after working with engineer Guido Cattaneo for two years, he set up his own engineering business in a former stable near the Talbot works at Suresnes.

Gordini specialised very successfully in the development and modification of production Fiats for competition purposes. He had such an intimate and skilful knowledge of Fiat engines that he made these rather pedestrian cars perform in a manner that was truly *formidable* and he became known as *le sorcier* (the wizard). Such was his reputation that at one time enthusiasts in Britain, who modified their production cars, talked about 'Gordinising' them.

The French Simca company (which built Fiats under licence) was battling to gain a market share and in January 1936 they entered into a contract with Gordini whereby he became the official factory competition representative. In pre-war days it was a very successful and, in the main, contented relationship. With 1,100cc and 1,500cc cars the Gordini équipe scored class successes in both French and International events and later cars had very attractive and effective 'tank' bodywork. When the first post-war motor race meeting was organised in the Bois de Boulogne in Paris on 9 September 1945, Gordini won the 62-mile (100km) 1,500cc race with the 1939 'tank'.

Over the next six seasons Gordini continued to race under the Simca name and entered both single-seaters and sports cars. Although some fine successes were gained and famous drivers, including 'B. Bira', Juan Fangio and Jean-Pierre Wimille, appeared at the wheel of Gordini-entered cars, failures were disproportionately high to the large number of races entered. Simca was keen to maintain a close connection between the competition cars and its production models, while Gordini was determined to compete in the top echelons of racing. Relations became very strained.

For 1951 Gordini was allowed to build a four-cylinder twin-cam 1,500cc engine, but at the end of the year Simca severed links with him. Gordini lost substantial financial support and had extensive workshops and a staff of about 50 employees to support, but he now had freedom and raced under his own name. He had many friends in Italy, especially the Maserati brothers, with whom he could collaborate on design work. He secured adequate, if not generous financial support in France and there is reason to believe that he received some financial assistance from a major Italian industrial concern.

Work was put in hand on a new design that would be built in both Formula 2 and sports car forms. The power unit was a six-cylinder, twin overhead camshaft design, with the camshafts driven by a train of gears from the front of the engine. There was dry-sump lubrication. With a capacity of 1,988cc (75×75mm), cylinder dimensions apart, it had much in common with the Formula 2 OSCA that appeared later. There were three Weber twin-choke 38mm carburettors and Gordini claimed 175bhp at 6,000rpm, and if it had been an accurate figure that would have matched the new four-cylinder Ferrari. The true output was around 155bhp.

Transmission was by a five-speed gearbox with synchromesh on the upper four ratios and a final drive that incorporated a ZF limited slip differential. The design of the chassis followed earlier Gordini practice and was a very light twin-tubular structure with a wheelbase of 7ft 4.8in (2,250mm). Suspension front and rear was by torsion bars, independent at the front by wishbones and with a rigid rear axle. The Gordinis' best quality was their very low weight, but they were also exceptionally fragile.

During 1952 the Formula 2 cars showed dashes of speed, achieved some reasonable places and their drivers turned in some gutsy performances, especially Jean Behra, who scored a remarkable victory in the three-hour Reims Grand Prix, defeating the works Ferraris. There remains the suspicion that Behra drove a car powered by the 2.3-litre engine used in the Monaco and Le Mans sports car races. Gordini could be confident that the organisers of a French race would not check the cylinder dimensions of his cars.

In sports car racing the cars showed considerable potential, but achieved little success. The Monaco Grand Prix in early June was held as a sports car meeting. Robert Manzon with a 1,500cc Gordini won the Prix de Monte Carlo for cars up to 2,000cc. In the Grand Prix itself Manzon was at the wheel of Gordini's latest six-cylinder 2,262cc sports car. He drove a stirring race, catching and passing Moss's leading C-type Jaguar, but along with several other drivers, including Moss, he crashed after hitting oil dropped on the road by an Allard. Vittorio Marzotto won the race with a 2.7-litre Ferrari.

At Le Mans Gordini entered the 2,262cc 'six' for Behra/Manzon. They were a formidable combination; they took the lead during the third hour and by midnight were a lap ahead of 'Levegh' who was driving his Talbot-Lago solo and the Mercedes-Benz 300SLs that ultimately took the first two places. Early on the Sunday morning a brake-shoe anchor pin broke, jamming the drum; although the drivers wanted to carry on. Gordini insisted that the car be withdrawn for safety reasons.

In the 224-mile (360km) Reims sports car race held a fortnight later Manzon with the 2.3 again led convincingly until it shed a wheel at *Garenne* and he crashed into a telegraph pole. Manzon was back at the wheel of this car in the 62-mile (100km) Coupe du Salon at Montlhéry in October and won easily from Blanc's Talbot. Behra drove the 2.3-litre car in the Carrera Panamericana Mexico road race in November; he won the first 329-mile (529km) stage and was leading in the second stage when, apparently blinded by the sun, he went off the road at a tight corner and crashed heavily into a ditch, suffering severe injuries.

Throughout 1953 Gordini was beset by financial problems, the biggest of which was paying his staff. There was little scope for development work, although one new model appeared, and standards of preparation and reliability fell badly. Part of the reliability problem was that Gordini was so financially embarrassed that he

Gordinis rarely performed well in endurance racing because of poor reliability. There was an exception in 1953 when Maurice Trintignant/Harry Schell drove this very stylish six-cylinder 2.5-litre car to sixth place and a class win at Le Mans.

used components that should have long been scrapped. Although the Formula 2 cars performed abysmally, the sports cars achieved a measure of success.

At Le Mans, Trintignant/Schell drove a car with 2,473cc (80×82mm) engine developing 190/200bhp and very neat 'platform' body. They finished sixth and won the 3,000cc class at 102.150mph (164.360kph). Another new sports-racing car appeared in the Reims 12 Hours race. This was powered by a straight-eight 2,982cc (78×78mm) engine, in effect a 'doubled-up' version of the old Simca-financed four-cylinder engine. Four twin-choke Weber carburettors were fitted and power output was said to be 235bhp. There was a five-speed gearbox and a central driving-position, as on the 1948 cars. All-up weight was 1,400lb (635kg) and the power-to-weight ratio was exceptionally good.

Behra/Manzon drove the 3-litre and Behra initially led from a 4.5-litre Ferrari, but he fell back and then stopped for a wheel-change. After rejoining the race, the Gordini went off the road, perhaps because of structural failure. Trintignant/Schell with the 2.5-litre car held on to second place, but retired after six hours' racing. In September Behra drove the 3-litre in the Tour de France high-speed rally and won eight out of the nine special stages, as well as the speed section of the event.

Gordini had been selling off sports cars to raise money. Italian pilot Franco Bordoni bought a 2.3-litre, which was painted red. He scored wins in the Coupe de Vitesse at Montlhéry, the Tuscany Cup and the Trullo d'Oro and finished second at Senigállia and in the Sicilian Gold Cup.

In 1954 the new 2,500cc Grand Prix formula came into force and, against the odds, Gordini struggled to compete in both this and sports car racing. In the non-Championship Pau Grand Prix early in the season, Behra scored a remarkable victory against works Ferrari opposition, but it was a poor year for the two-seaters. At the end of February Jean Behra raced the 3-litre car in the 75-mile (120km) Circuit of Agadir in Morocco and finished second to Farina with a works Ferrari.

Local driver André Guelfi with his private Gordini finished second in the 2,000cc class behind Picard (Ferrari) at Agadir and Mme Annie Bousquet was at the wheel of a new 1,100cc car that combined an old body/chassis with a new four-cylinder, over-square 1,060cc (75×60mm) engine. It was on the heavy side and the chassis was three years' old, but it ran well before retiring. This car subsequently appeared in the Mille Miglia (drivers Mme. Bousquet/Mme Thirion) and Le Mans (Mme. Thirion/André Pilette), but retired in both events. In the Reims 12 Hours race Mme. Thirion/Olivier Gendebien drove it into third place in the 1,600cc class behind two Porsche 550s.

By Le Mans the works 3-litre car had been fitted with Messier disc brakes, but it lacked a servo, apparently through an oversight caused by pressure of work. Behra/Simon had the 3-litre in sixth place at the end of the sixth hour, but gradually slipped further and further down the field. Behra stopped out at *Arnage* in the 11th hour because of ignition problems, but pushed the car back to the pits. Magneto failure was diagnosed and the 3-litre was retired. Guelfi/Jacques Pollet drove a good race with a 2.5-litre car, finishing sixth overall and winning the 3,000cc class.

Behra/Bordoni next drove the 3-litre car in the Reims 12 Hours race, but Behra, confused by the glare of lighting from the spectator enclosure at *Thillois Corner*, ran up the back of the Rolt/Hamilton Jaguar D-type and wrecked the radiator. Subsequently Pollet, partnered by Gauthier, won the Tour de France outright with this car and Behra won the 94-mile (151km) Coupe du Salon at Montlhéry from Masten Gregory's 4.5-litre Ferrari. Interestingly, it was Gordini's third successive win in this race.

In October Behra, driving his last race for the team before joining Maserati, was fastest in practice for the 157-mile (253km) Barcelona Cup race on the *Pedralbes* circuit at Barcelona and led the race until he retired with the inevitable mechanical problems. Picard (Ferrari *Monza*) won from Roy Salvadori (*Écurie Ecosse*-entered C-type Jaguar). Salvadori had been harrying Behra and struggling to get by. After the race Behra said to Roy, "When you know the Gordini better, you will have patience. The Gordini is fast, but never lasts. So do remember that." In 1954, Bordoni took delivery of a 3-litre Gordini and with it won six Italian events.

Little was seen of Gordini sports cars in major European events in 1955–56, but at Le Mans in the latter year the team entered two eight-cylinder cars with 2,474cc engines complying with the capacity limit on prototypes in the 24 Hours race that year. In the early stages Manzon/Jean Guichet ran strongly, holding fifth place for the first three hours, but retired in the eighth hour because of engine problems, while de Silva Ramos/Guelfi lasted for more than 11 hours before their car succumbed to clutch failure.

Gordini had received an offer to join Renault, but because of his experiences with Simca he procrastinated over his decision. He ran Formula 1 cars at Pau and Naples in 1957, but then, with very great reluctance, withdrew from racing. Gordini became the high-performance engine development subsidiary of Renault and apart from working on hotter versions of Renault's *Dauphine* and other production cars, subsequently produced the V6 engine that was developed in turbocharged form for Grand Prix racing.

Bristol 450

1953–55

Le Mans 1955: on the Sunday morning the dusty, grime-covered 450 of Keene/Line accelerates out of Mulsanne Corner. They finished third in the 2,000cc class. (T.C. March/FotoVantage)

Over a three-year period the Bristol Aeroplane Company stunned the sports car world with the aerodynamics of its 2,000cc sports-racing cars. The 450's success in sports car endurance races was consistent and there is little doubt that but for the application of aeroplane-developed aerodynamics to Bristol competition cars in 1953, the appearance of such advanced designs as the Lotus Mark VIII would have been considerably delayed.

In the early 1950s the Bristol Aeroplane Company based at Filton was keen to develop its car division formed immediately after the Second World War and anxious to increase sales of its rather specialist and very expensive BMW-derived touring cars. The design dated back to pre-war days and the six-cylinder 1,971cc (66×96mm) engine was identical to that of the BMW 328 cars discussed earlier, apart from Imperial instead of the original metric tooling.

In 1952 Mike Hawthorn demonstrated the potential of the Bristol engine in his Formula 2 Cooper and while the company derived publicity from this, the directors could see much greater benefit if they entered their own cars. An opportunity at reasonable cost came when racing driver Leslie Johnson suffered a heart attack and decided to sell the ERA company. In pre-war days ERA had been controlled by Humphrey Cook and built very successful *Voiturette* racing cars. Johnson ran ERA, now in Dunstable, Bedfordshire, as an engineering consultancy, but it also raced a Bristol-powered car in Formula 2 during 1952.

This car, the G-type, was an unusual design, the work of young engineer David Hodkin, and featured a chassis with very large, oval-section, twin-tubular, magnesium-alloy side-members and smaller dimension cross-members of the same material. At the front there was coil spring and unequal-length double wishbone independent suspension. An A-bracket with the apex ball-jointed to the chassis at the base of the final drive located the de Dion rear axle. Sheet-steel trailing arms were connected to a chassis-mounted, anti-roll torsion bar and were designed to flex in accordance with the roll of the car. The locating points of the trailing arms could be adjusted to change the handling characteristics.

The magnesium-alloy wheels consisted of a rim with

lugs by which it was bolted to five spider arms that were integral with the hubs. Hodkin had built the ERA with the prop-shaft alongside the driver, which made the car wider than necessary for a single-seater and increased the frontal area. Despite all the thought that had gone into the design, the G-type was too heavy and the handling was unsatisfactory. Bristol saw it as an ideal basis for a sports car, although it was really a little too narrow for a two-seater. They bought the car and drawings and appointed Vivian Selby, who had some experience of pre-war racing, to head the newly formed racing division.

Bristol rebuilt the G-type with an aerodynamic coupé body of startling configuration and after extensive testing, it built three cars, but with significant differences from the prototype. The basic layout was unchanged, but the chassis was of steel construction and the rear suspension was redesigned so that the trailing arms could no longer alter the handling. The Bristol engine and gearbox were used with a short, universally-jointed prop-shaft and a Ford commercial vehicle final drive. The wheelbase was 8ft 0in (2,440mm), and the track was 4ft 3in (1,295mm).

The steering was rack-and-pinion and Bristol used Lockheed hydraulic brakes with 12-inch (305mm) Al-fin drums front and rear and retained the ERA magnesium-alloy wheels. Filton carried out extensive development work on the engine. With three Solex carburettors, power output was 150bhp at 6,000rpm. A new crankshaft had been developed and when designer Stuart Tresilian saw one of engines on test, he concluded that the crankshaft balance weights were attached in such a way that they would come adrift under racing conditions. He mentioned this to the Bristol engineers, but they failed to heed his warning because there had been no problems in bench-tests.

Engineers in the main Bristol aviation section designed the distinctive coupé body based on steel and aluminium-alloy panelling. There was a long, sloping nose and two dorsal fins extended down to the tail. In original form the body was very smooth and uncluttered, but the racing department made their own changes, adding twin spot-lights in protruding cowlings, protruding quick-release fuel fillers on the front wings, bonnet straps, an oil cooler mounted in the shallow air intake at the base of the nose and a slatted air intake above it.

The original purity of line was lost, but there was something endearing about the looks of these first cars, much in the same way that a warthog can seem a very attractive animal, especially after a few pints. When the cars practised at Le Mans, they were over-geared and this may have been because the alterations made to the original body shape had damaged the airflow. Bristol planned to enter only two races in 1953, the Le Mans 24 Hours and the Reims 12 Hours, together with a record attempt later in the year.

'Sammy' Davis joined Bristol as part-time consultant to Vivian Selby. Le Mans was an unhappy debut as Tresilian's prediction proved correct. After about 3½ hours, Graham Whitehead was out of the race because a crankshaft balance weight fell off, pierced the sump and started a fire – this was the first Bristol to go because of co-driver Lance Macklin's very forceful style. Then Tommy Wisdom crashed the car he was sharing with Jack Fairman, because of the difficulty he had in controlling the car following the engine failure and fire.

By the Reims race that started at midnight on 4 July, Bristol had sorted out the engine problem and to a certain extent had cleaned up the frontal appearance of the cars. Peter Wilson/Fairman held second place in the 2,000cc class behind the Gordini of Loyer/Rinen, but this succumbed to gearbox problems on the Sunday morning and the Bristol went ahead to win the class at 92.67mph (149.11kph) from a Ferrari and a Frazer Nash. Graham Whitehead/Macklin retired their car because of a sheared key in the final drive, the result of Macklin letting-in the clutch at the start with such a tremendous jerk that it overstrained the transmission.

On 6–7 October Fairman, partnered by Macklin for the longer distances, drove a 450 with new and much smoother body in record attempts on the 1.606-mile banked track at Montlhéry. The team took six Class E records ranging from 200 miles (321.8km) at 125.87mph (202.52kph) to six hours at 115.43mph (185.73kph) and rounded off the successful attempt with a lap at 126.11mph (202.91kph). Bristol then exhibited this car at the Paris Salon and the London Motor Show.

There were a number of changes made to the cars for 1954. Three Solex twin-choke carburettors were adopted and there were six separate inlet pipes. A new exhaust system had six individual pipes feeding into three and then into a single tail-pipe. The roofline had been raised slightly to reduce drag and this marginally increased maximum speed. Once again Bristol adopted a two-race policy and entered three cars at both Le Mans and Reims.

The 450s enjoyed a successful Le Mans. There was little serious opposition in the 2,000cc class and, regardless of engine size, Bristol was the only team to finish the race intact. It was a very wet race and one problem was windscreen wiper failure on the car driven by Peter Wilson/Jim Mayers. Wisdom/Fairman were leading the class when Fairman lost concentration, slid into a barrier and crumpled the nose of the 450. A pit stop for metal-bashing dropped them to second in class.

In 1954 the 450s had much smoother lines. Here at Le Mans they are lined up in the order, Wisdom/Fairman, Keene/Line and Wilson/Mayers. They took the first three places in the poorly supported 2,000cc class. (FotoVantage)

At the end of the 24 hours, the Bristols took the first three places in the 2,000cc class and crossed the finishing line in order of their race numbers, 33 (Tommy Wisdom/Jack Fairman) eighth overall at 89.713mph (144.348kph): 34 (Mike Keene/Trevor Line), ninth overall at 88.989mph (143.183kph) and 35 (Wilson/Jim Mayers), seventh overall at 90.760mph (146.033kph).

Bristol then fielded three cars in the Reims 12 Hours race. Picard/Pozzi won the 2,000cc class with a 2-litre Ferrari *Testa Rossa* and there were two reasons for Bristol's defeat. Heavy rain fell during the early hours of the race and the Bristols were sucking spray from cars that they were following into the air intakes and the water then worked its way to the ignition leads and plugs – it was odd that the heavy rain at Le Mans had not affected the cars in the same way.

The Bristol pit was also over-confident that the Ferrari would break and failed to speed up the 450s as the weather improved. Keene/Line, Wilson/Mayers and Wisdom/Fairman finished tenth, 11th and 12th overall, taking second, third and fourth places in the classes, but none of the 2,000cc cars could match the pace of the class-winning 1,500cc Porsche 550 *Spyder*. This averaged 95.35mph (153.42kph) compared with the 94.87mph (152.65kph) of Picard/Pozzi and 93.80mph (150.92kph) of Keen/Line.

Bristol proposed running in the same two races again in 1955, but the 450s now appeared in open form, with a metal tonneau over the passenger seat and a single, more modest, tail fin. The team had come to the inevitable conclusion that a coupé was not the best configuration for a competition car. The interior was very noisy; in wet weather it steamed up and the driver was dependent on the not always reliable windscreen wipers. With just an aero-screen, the frontal area was reduced and the cars were faster.

Le Mans was marred by the most terrible accident in the history of motor racing, but the race went on and the Bristols of Wilson/Mayers, Keene/Line and Wisdom/Fairman took seventh, eighth and ninth places overall and the first three places in the 2,000cc class. Well ahead of them was a trio of Porsche 550s that dominated the results of the 1,500cc class. The fastest Bristol was timed on the *Mulsanne Straight* at 138.43mph (222.73kph) compared with the 139.45mph (224.38kph) achieved by the fastest Porsche *Spyder*.

As a result of the Le Mans disaster many races in 1955 were cancelled, including the Reims 12 Hours race, and the Bristols did not race again. The directors at Filton were becoming disenchanted with motor racing and were horrified by the death toll of the disaster. They concluded that the goals of the racing programme – increased sales of the 403 and 405 saloons – had been met. Bristol had sold over 500 cars in three years and this was more than satisfactory when the basic price without purchase tax in 1955 was over £2,000.

Development was abandoned of a new competition Bristol with space-frame chassis and the very deep six-cylinder engine canted 45° to the left. The 450s had served their intended working life and with one exception they were scrapped. What in 1956 became Bristol Cars Ltd, an independent company, kept the surviving 450 until a few years ago, when it was sold to a private enthusiast.

Lancia D20 & D24

1953–54

This view of a D20 Lancia outside the Turin factory shows to good advantage the smooth well balanced lines of the Pinin Farina coupé body. These cars raced for only three months before being replaced by an open version.

Vincenzo Lancia was a leading works Fiat driver, but when he and Claudio Fogolin set up the Lancia company in 1906, they avoided competition work, with the exception of a few special cars built to compete in the Mille Miglia. Vincenzo died in April 1937 and shortly afterwards Vittorio Jano, one of the greatest automobile engineers of all time joined the company. Much of Jano's early work at the Turin factory was devoted to V6 engine development, a layout that previous designers had eschewed because of theoretical balancing problems – but when Lancia's V6 1,754cc Aurelia B10 appeared in 1950, it proved to be an engine of remarkable smoothness and balance.

The Aurelia also had superb handling, largely attributable to the excellent weight distribution resulting from having the clutch and gearbox in unit with the final drive. A year later Lancia introduced the B20 Aurelia GT with 1,991cc engine and Pinin Farina coupé body with remarkable purity of line. Many, including the writer, rate the Aurelia GT, later with a 2,451cc version of the six-cylinder engine, as one of the finest fast touring cars of all time.

Giani Lancia had taken control of the company founded by his father and against the wishes of his mother Adele and managing director Panagadi, embarked on a competition programme. They wanted the company to expend money on improved factory production methods and new and easier to build cars. Ultimately, they were to be proved right, but for a short while Giani and Lancia had their moments of glory on the world's racetracks. In 1951, Giani set up *Scuderia Lancia* managed by Attilio Pasquarelli. The works Aurelia GTs enjoyed phenomenal success in races and rallies and, perhaps, the most outstanding was Giovanni Bracco's second place in the 1951 Mille Miglia road race.

Jano and his colleagues started work on a sports-racing car that followed the general lines of the B20 and even the designation, D20, stressed its relationship with the production car. Ettore Zaccone was responsible for the design of the all-alloy 60° staggered V6 engine of 2,962cc (86×85mm). The twin overhead camshafts were chain-driven from the nose of the crankshaft, there were wet cylinder liners and the crankshaft ran in four main bearings. With twin distributors, twin plugs per cylinder and three twin-choke Weber 42DCF4 carburettors, initial power output was 217bhp, but with development this soon rose to a competitive 245bhp.

The D20 had an Aurelia gearbox mounted ahead of the final drive, but there was a much stronger multi-plate clutch. The chassis was a very rigid multi-tubular structure with an 8ft 4.5in (2,540mm) wheelbase [different sources can disagree by a ½in or so], independent front and rear suspension by transverse leaf spring, trailing arms and telescopic shock absorbers; at the rear there were additional shock absorbers controlled from the cockpit by levers and chains. Both front and rear brakes were mounted inboard, those at the front connected to the wheels by universally jointed shafts. As with most early inboard brakes (which positioning reduced unsprung weight) they were not sufficiently exposed to the airstream for adequate cooling.

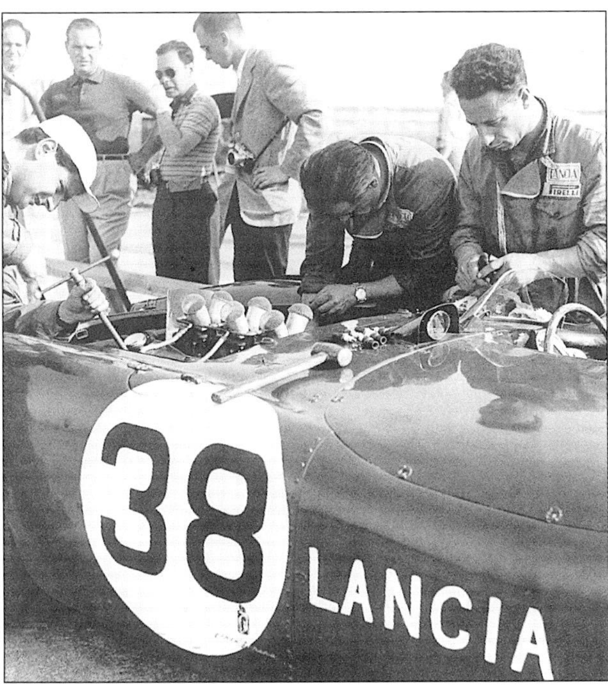

The Lancia mechanics work on the D24 of Taruffi/Manzon during practice before the 1954 Sebring 12 Hours race. Taruffi pushed this D24 back to the pits after the engine had seized, and then Manzon pushed it across the finishing line and into disqualification because it had not crossed the line under its own power.

Lancia commissioned a very neat and stylish aluminium-alloy Pinin Farina coupé body for good aerodynamics, driver comfort and to retain a family resemblance to the B20. As on the production cars, there was a shield-shaped air intake, but without grille, and a long bonnet-top air scoop. The D20s were painted blue and white, the colours of the Lancia badge. It was a potentially very formidable competition car, but far more development work than Lancia anticipated was necessary.

Five D20s appeared in the 1953 Mille Miglia. Piero Taruffi with his Lancia held second place at one stage, but retired because of engine problems. Veteran Felice Bonetto finished third with his D20 behind Giannino Marzotto (4.1-litre Ferrari) and Fangio (crippled 3.6-litre Alfa Romeo) and another veteran, Clemente Biondetti, took eighth place.

Then came the D20's only race win in the 357-mile (575km) Targa Florio in Sicily on 14 May. The race started in heavy rain, the windscreens and rear windows of the D20s misted up, water poured through the almost non-existent seals and their Michelin 'X' radial tyres lacked grip in the wet. As the circuit dried out, Taruffi went ahead with his Lancia but crashed on the last lap through trying too hard – in a masterpiece of mismanagement the Lancia pit displayed a signal indicating that he was in second place when he was comfortably in front. Umberto Maglioli won the race for Lancia from two 2-litre Maseratis.

At Le Mans Jano ran the D20s with engine capacity reduced to 2,693cc, belt-driven Roots-type superchargers and lower compression ratio. Power output was 240bhp at 6,500rpm. He was testing his theory that in this form the engines would be less stressed. It seemed crackpot at the time and it still does. The D20s were uncompetitive, some 15mph (24kph) slower than the C-type Jaguars on the *Mulsanne Straight* and all four retired – three with engine failure and one refused to start after a pit stop.

The coupé body was obviously a failure and Jano was dissatisfied with the rear suspension. Two D20s were fitted with new rear suspension that retained the transverse spring, but incorporated a de Dion axle located by radius rods and a vertical guide. Lancia then dispatched them to Pinin Farina for the bodies to be rebuilt in open form and they were now typed the D23. All open competition Lancias were painted a striking shade of dark red.

Taruffi and Bonetto drove D20s in the Oporto

Alberto Ascari on the ramp at Brescia for the start of the 1954 Mille Miglia, as the seconds are counted off. Lancia chief engineer Commendatore Vittorio Jano, wearing his usual raincoat and trilby hat, looks over Ascari's shoulder. One of the race founders, Rezo Castagneto in his famous grey bowler hat, watches over the starter's shoulder. The World Champion scored a superb victory.

Grand Prix, but retired. The D23s, along with two D20s next ran in the Autodrome Grand Prix, a race limited to cars of up to 3,000cc and held at Monza at the end of June. The race was decided on the aggregate of two heats, one held on the Saturday and the other on the Sunday. Bonetto with his D23 finished second to Villoresi (Ferrari).

The team then contested the 186-mile (300km) Dolomite Grand Prix at Belluno and Taruffi (D23) finished second to Paolo Marzotto (Ferrari). Lancia returned to Portugal to compete in the 169-mile (272km) Lisbon Grand Prix. Bonetto (D23) won from Stirling Moss whose works C-type Jaguar handled very badly on the bumpy Monsanto circuit.

By the first Nürburgring 1,000Km race on 30 August, a round in the newly inaugurated World Sports Car Championship, Lancia had ready their much-modified D24. This had an enlarged 3,284cc (88×90mm) engine developing 260bhp at 6,500rpm. The wheelbase had been reduced to 7ft 10½in (2,400mm) and this, coupled with modified rear suspension, vastly improved the handling. The engine was mounted lower in the chassis, the de Dion tube now ran in front of the final drive and was suspended on quarter-elliptic springs. A new four-speed gearbox was mounted behind the differential and in unit with it. The open Pinin Farina body was much neater and more stylish.

Lancia tested at the Nürburgring in early August and the D24's engine and chassis characteristics proved well suited to this very difficult circuit. Three cars were entered and although the Lancias dominated the race in the early laps, the race proved another dismal failure for the Turin team. Fangio retired the D24 he was sharing with Bonetto because of fuel pump failure and, at the first pit stops the D24 of Taruffi/Robert Manzon and the D23 of Bracco/Eugenio Castellotti failed to restart because of battery failure caused by the bumpy circuit. Ascari/Farina won with a works 4.5-litre Ferrari.

A week later Lancia fielded four cars in the 168-mile (270km) *Supercortemaggiore* Grand Prix held at Merano in the Italian Alps. It proved another failure for Lancia and all the cars retired. Fangio with the latest 6CM 3000 Alfa Romeo *Spyder* won after a long battle with Bonetto until the Lancia driver's gearbox failed.

Taruffi's D24 is already scarred after practice for the 1954 Targa Florio road race in Sicily. He scored a fine win from Luigi Musso's 2-litre Maserati A6GCS.

At this late stage in 1953 it looked as though Lancia could get nothing right. The team rounded off the European season with a win by Castellotti in the long and fast Catania-Etna hill climb and first and second places by Bonetto and Castellotti in the Bologna-Raticosa event.

The last round in the World Sports Car Championship was the Carrera Panamericana Mexico road race held in eight stages totalling 1,833 miles (2,950km) between Tuxtla Gutierrez in the south and Ciudad Juarez near the United States border at El Paso. Lancia entered five cars and had a full backup that included an aircraft to fly the mechanics and support crew between stages. Taruffi and Bonetto drove D24s with engines reduced in capacity, for no clear reason, to 3,102cc (88×85mm) and Bracco and Castellotti were entered with D23s.

The results exceeded expectation, although the opposition was weak apart from a team of Ferraris privately entered by *Scuderia Guastalla*. Tragedy struck the Lancia team on the fourth stage when veteran Felice Bonetto crashed with fatal results. Giani Lancia insisted that for the remaining stages his drivers were accompanied by riding mechanics. Bracco retired, but Fangio, Taruffi and Castellotti took the first three places ahead of Mancini (*Guastalla* Ferrari).

In January 1954 Lancia announced the most expensive venture that they could least afford, the V8 D50 Grand Prix cars to be driven by World Champion Alberto Ascari and Luigi Villoresi. These were not ready until the end of the season and Lancia continued with the sports car programme. The team first appeared in the Sebring 12 Hours race, the second round in the Championship on 7 March. Lancia fielded four D24s and the only other works teams were Aston Martin and Cunningham.

The Lancias dominated the race in the early stages and after the Fangio/Castellotti car retired because of rear axle failure, Taruffi/Manzon and Ascari/Villoresi held the first two places, while Piero Valenzano partnered by Dominican Republic playboy and diplomat presumptive, Porfirio Rubirosa trailed seventh. Valenzano was so incensed by Rubirosa's incompetent driving that he literally kicked him out of the car. Ascari/Villoresi retired because of gearbox failure and Taruffi/Manzon then led until the D24's engine seized up an hour before the finish. Taruffi pushed the car 1½ miles back to the pits where the mechanics tried unsuccessfully to free the engine by pouring oil down the plug holes.

Unexpectedly, Stirling Moss/Bill Lloyd won with a 1,500cc OSCA entered by Briggs Cunningham, five laps ahead of the surviving Lancia of Valenzano/Rubirosa. Manzon pushed the seized D24 across the line, but was disqualified from third place, as the car had not crossed the line under its own power. It was a very disappointing result for Lancia, but they still had good prospects of winning the Championship. In April Taruffi with a D24 won the 671-mile (1,080km) Tour of Sicily and the following weekend Villoresi and Castellotti retired their D24s in the 472-mile (760km) Tuscany Cup. Sicilian mineral water-bottler Piero Scotti won with his private 4.5-litre Ferrari.

The Mille Miglia at the beginning of May was excluded from Ascari's contract. He had always disliked the race and after an accident in 1951, which had cost the life of a spectator, he had refused to take part. When Villoresi was injured in a practice crash, he relented. Lancia entered four D24s for Ascari, Taruffi, Castellotti and Valenzano. They were new cars built for the race with detuned engines developing 245bhp. Ferrari entered two of his new 4.9-litre 375 *Plus* cars for Farina and Maglioli, but Maranello's entry was weakened because of driver problems.

Much of this arduous race was run in the wet and on roads that were in poor condition after a hard winter. Taruffi set a searing pace, leading at Pescara at a record average of 110.6mph (177.96kph). Already Farina and Valenzano had crashed. By Rome Taruffi had averaged 98.75mph (158.89kph) and led Ascari comfortably. At Vetralla, not far out of Rome, Taruffi crashed when a much slower competitor crossed his line. Ascari was now unchallenged and despite a misfiring engine, he crossed the line at Brescia, looking worn and haggard, to win at 86.77mph (139.61kph). He was half-an-hour ahead of the second place 2-litre Ferrari of Vittorio Marzotto.

Lancia and Ferrari jointly led the Championship with 14 points each. Lancia decided to miss the next round, the Le Mans 24 Hours race, and concentrate on the Nürburgring 1,000Km event at the end of August. Their new and more powerful D25 was not yet ready and Lancia, rightly, believed that the D24s would be outpaced at Le Mans. Taruffi won the 358-mile (576km) Targa Florio from Musso (2-litre Maserati), but young Castellotti, having a high testosterone day, drove too hard and crashed.

In the 207-mile (330km) Oporto Grand Prix, Villoresi and Castellotti took the first two places from Peter Whitehead (Cooper-Jaguar); Ascari had led until a pit stop and spun out of the race when the steering failed. In July Castellotti with a D24 won two Italian hill climbs, the 15.5-mile (25km) Bolzano-Mendola event and the Aosta-Grand St Bernard. The Nürburgring race was cancelled and with it serious hopes of winning the Championship evaporated. Lancia next appeared in the Tourist Trophy on the 7.2-mile (11.6km) Dundrod road course near Belfast. It was a handicap race, but Championship points were awarded on a scratch basis.

Lancia entered two new D25 cars with 3,750cc (93×92mm) engine developing 295bhp at 6,200rpm. These cars had an even shorter 7ft 6in (2,290mm) wheelbase, outboard brakes and a weight reduced to 1,350lb (612kg). Ascari/Villoresi and Fangio/Castellotti drove the D25s and Taruffi/Piodi and Valenzano/Manzon had D24s. Both Aston Martin and Jaguar contested the race, but neither was competitive, while the 3-litre Ferrari *Monza* of Hawthorn/Trintignant was unbeatable, finishing first on scratch and second on handicap.

Fangio retired his D25 early in the race and switched to share Taruffi's D24. With his D25 Ascari performed rather better, leading the over 3,000cc class, but fell back after hitting a bank and retired because of a broken prop-shaft. On scratch the D24s of Fangio/Taruffi and Manzon/Valenzano took second and third places (fourth and sixth on handicap). Lancia had lost the World Sports Car Championship to Ferrari and missed the Carrera Panamericana Mexico race, partly because of the impending debut of the D50.

Lancia rounded off their sports car year by appearing in a number of minor Italian events. Over the weekend following the Tourist Trophy, Taruffi with a D24 won the 19.75-mile (31.8km) Catania-Etna event that ran up to and round the crater of the active volcano and Castellotti, also with a D24, was the winner in the Bologna-Raticosa. Taruffi drove a D24 in the Sicilian Gold Cup at Siracusa on 17 October, won his heat, but became unwell and missed the final. The following day Lancia withdrew from sports car racing.

The D50 Grand Prix cars appeared in the Spanish Grand Prix on 26 October 1954, but failed to win a major race before Ascari was killed at the wheel of a sports Ferrari in late June 1955 and they then withdrew from racing altogether. By this time Lancia was insolvent and Giani Lancia was ousted from the company. Lancia handed over the Grand Prix cars to Ferrari and struggled on, losing its independence later in 1955. Lancia was a tragic case of misapplied enthusiasm for motor sport by a company that was not in the best financial health at the outset. The legacy that the sports car programme left was the V6 engine, the concept of which was later adopted for many mass-production saloons.

Ferrari Tipo 375 Le Mans/Plus

1953–54

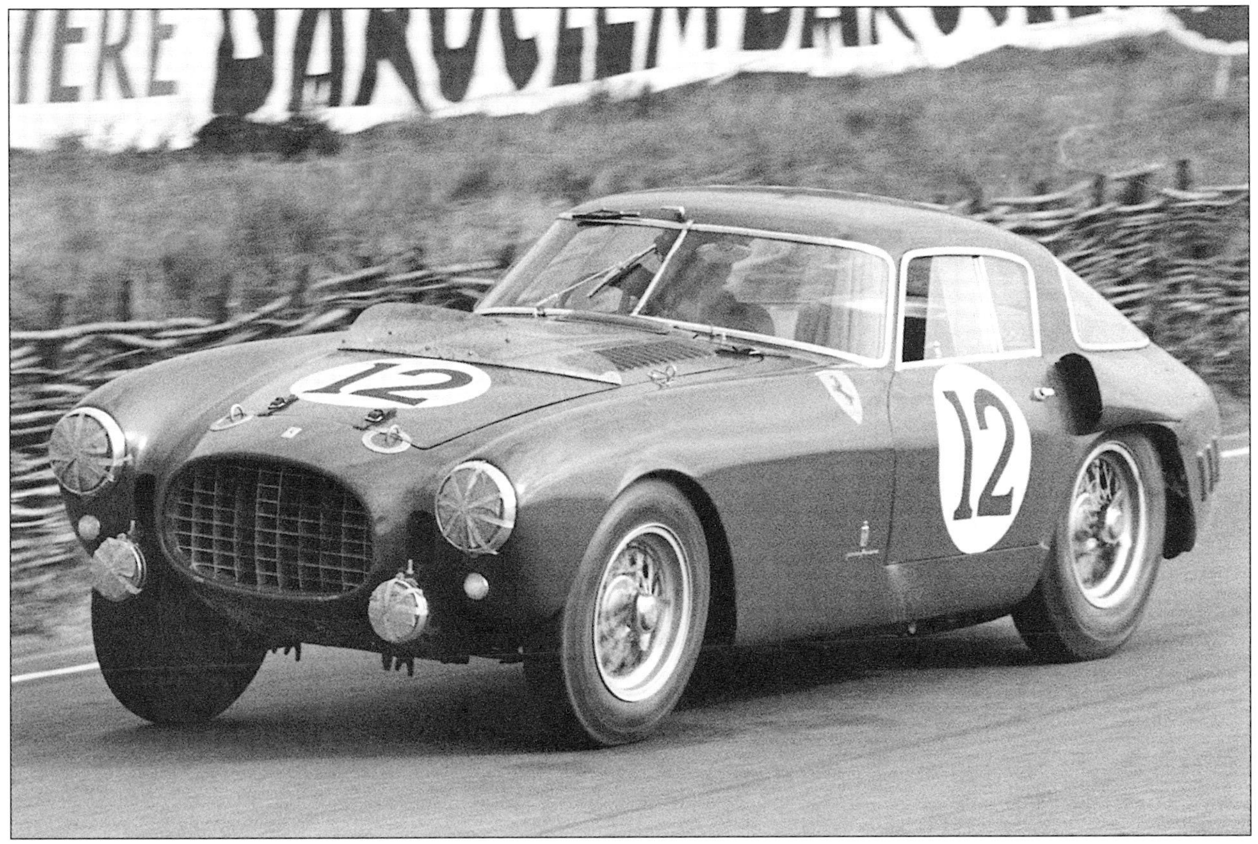

Ascari and Villoresi with this Pinin Farina-bodied Tipo 375 Le Mans were the only drivers in the race to offer any sort of challenge to the Jaguar team. Although they retired, they held second place for many hours and led briefly. Ascari also set a new lap record. (LAT)

Between 1950 and 1954 Ferrari built a series of large-capacity sports-racing cars that had the 'long-block' V12 engines developed from the original designs of Giaocchino Colombo. These Aurelio Lampredi-designed engines are known as 'long-block' because the larger bore necessitated new, longer cylinder block and head castings. The water jackets were cast integrally with the cylinder heads and the steel cylinder liners had threaded upper ends passing through the bottoms of the water jackets and screwed into threaded bosses surrounding the valve and combustion areas. This solved a weakness of the Colombo engines: the seal between the cylinder heads and the block. The lower ends of the liners seated in matching bores in the crankcase.

Lampredi conceived the 'long-block' engine at the time Ferrari decided to challenge the supremacy of the supercharged Alfa Romeos in Grand Prix racing with unblown cars. The first Lampredi V12 was the 3,322cc (72×68mm) Tipo 275 that appeared early in 1950 and later that year was increased to 4,102cc (80×68mm) and then 4,494cc (80×74.5mm). The 4.1-litre sports version first appeared in chassis form at the 1950 Paris Salon and the following year Villoresi drove a 4.1-litre coupé to a win in the Mille Miglia. Although the 4.5-litre Grand Prix cars had twin-plug ignition in 1951, the sports cars retained a single plug per cylinder.

Ferrari sold a number of these cars to private owners, and Taruffi drove one in the 1952 Mille Miglia, but the first serious works interest was the entry of three Tipo 340 *Mexico* 4.1-litre cars with an engine developing a claimed 280bhp at 6,600rpm, five-speed gearbox and Ghia coupé body in the 1952 Mexican road race.

Luigi Villoresi, partnered by Cassani, drove this 340 Mexico with Vignale coupé body to a win in the 1951 Mille Miglia. It had been a hard race, as the battered state of the body clearly indicates.

These cars had a rather long 8ft 6in (2,600mm) wheelbase. They were not successful and the best performance was third place by Luigi Chinetti.

For 1953 Ferrari developed an improved 4.1-litre car with shorter 8ft 2½in (2,500m) wheelbase, an engine that with three Weber four-choke 40IF/4C carburettors developing a claimed 300bhp at 6,600rpm and a four-speed gearbox. There were probably only six of these 340 *Mille Miglia* cars, two with Superleggera Touring body and four with Vignale bodies. Early successes were a win by Villoresi in the Tour of Sicily and by Giannino Marzotto with a works-prepared Vignale-bodied car in the Mille Miglia. Giannino Marzotto was one of four sons of a wealthy textile family, all of whom raced Ferraris, and in the 1950s they must have poured vast sums into the Ferrari coffers.

Except in the most skilful of hands the 340 *Mille Miglia* was lethal and three private owners were killed at the wheel of these cars. Pierre Pagnibon was leading the Hyères 12 Hours race when he overturned his *Mexico* and suffered fatal injuries; Anglo-American Tom Cole, who had finished fourth in the Mille Miglia, crashed his car with fatal results at Le Mans; and Bobby Baird was killed when he crashed his *Mille Miglia* in practice at Snetterton in July 1953.

At Le Mans in 1953 the works entered three new cars with the longer 8ft 6in (2,600mm) wheelbase, four-speed gearbox and strikingly beautiful Pinin Farina coupé bodywork. These and the 3-litre V12 250 *Mille Miglia* exhibited at the Geneva Salon earlier in the year were the first Ferraris to be bodied by Pinin Farina. Two of these cars had 4.1-litre engines and were driven by Farina/Hawthorn and Marzotto brothers, Giannino and Paolo. Ascari/Villoresi had a new version known as the Tipo 375 *Le Mans* with 4,494cc engine developing 340bhp at 7,000rpm. Villoresi first drove a car with the 4,494cc engine a little earlier at Senigállia.

Farina/Hawthorn retired early in the race because the car had boiled away all its brake fluid, but the Marzotto brothers, despite problems, finished fifth. Ascari/Villoresi showed impressive form with the 375, holding second place for many hours and they led briefly, but their Ferrari lacked the stamina of the Jaguar C-types and retired because of overheating and clutch failure in the 21st hour, by when it had dropped well down the field. While the car was running well, Ascari set a new lap record of 112.866mph (181.601kph).

After Le Mans Ferrari fitted the other two cars with 4.5-litre engines and Pinin Farina reprofiled the front of the body with the headlamps under Plexiglas covers. Maranello sent a single car to compete in the Reims 12 Hours race and it was leading when it switched its lights off before the permitted time because of battery trouble. Ferrari sins doubled when the car was pushed in the pits road and disqualification followed. Team manager Ugolini threatened to withdraw the Ferraris from the French Grand Prix later in the day, an unfulfilled threat, and Ferrari wasted everyone's time by pursuing his protest to appeal.

Three cars ran in the Spa 24 Hours and although two retired because of rear axle failure, Farina/Hawthorn with the survivor scored an easy win. Subsequently Paolo Marzotto drove one of these *berlinettas* to a win in a race at Senigállia and Hawthorn/Maglioli won the Pescara 12 Hours race. In the first Nürburgring 1,000Km race on 30 August the only Ferrari to start was a 375MM with Vignale open two-seater body and driven by Ascari/Farina it scored another easy win – but only after the retirement of the Lancias.

No works Ferraris ran in the Carrera Mexico Road Race, but Franco Cornacchia's *Scuderia Guastalla* entered a team of 375MMs, two of which were ex-works cars. They had an unsuccessful race in the face of strong Lancia opposition, but Mancini's fourth place was enough to clinch Ferrari's win in the first World Sports Car Championship.

In 1954 Ferrari sold a number of these cars with Pinin Farina open two-seater bodies and revised cylinder dimensions of 84×68mm (4,522cc) and buyers who performed well with these cars included Sicilian mineral water-bottler Piero Scotti, Portuguese driver Casimiro de Oliveira and Kansan Masten Gregory. Gregory brought his white and blue car to Britain where he drove a feisty race at Aintree in September and with great caution at the wet Prescott hill climb the same month.

The latest Ferrari sports-racing car was not ready in

time for the first round of the Championship, the Buenos Aires 1,000Km race on 24 January. Farina/ Maglioli drove a Tipo 375MM with Pinin Farina open two-seater body and they won by a margin of three laps from a private 3-litre Ferrari. Apart from its sheer power, one of the qualities of the 375MM was its balanced, predictable handling (a complete contrast to the earlier shorter-wheelbase 4.1-litre model) and it was a safe car for reasonably competent amateurs.

Ferrari's 1954 works car was the monstrous 375 *Plus* with 4,954cc (84×74.5mm) engine, three twin-choke Weber 46DCF3 carburettors and a claimed 330bhp at 6,000rpm. There was now a de Dion rear axle and the four-speed gearbox was in unit with the final drive. The open two-seater body was similar to that of the customer 375MMs, but with a hump on the tail to clear the fuel tank and spare wheel. These were purely works cars, with a high axle ratio they were said to be capable of 186mph (300kph), and when tested on the roads around Maranello, they looked and sounded fearsome.

In February Farina drove the 375 *Plus* in the 76-mile (122km) Circuit of Agadir in Morocco and scored an easy win from Behra (Gordini) and Scotti (Ferrari 375MM). Umberto Maglioli drove a 375 *Plus* in the 621-mile (1,000km) Circuit of Sicily, but crashed at Enna. The 375 *Plus* was too powerful and too much of a handful for both the Sicilian race and the Mille Miglia. Both Farina and Maglioli crashed their 4.9s in the 1,000-mile race and Ascari won for Lancia. Ferrari sent along a 375 *Plus* for Gonzalez to drive in the 73-mile (117km) sports car race at Silverstone in May. On a streaming wet track he drove a masterly race to win from Abecassis (HWM-Jaguar).

The Le Mans 24 Hours race was the highlight of the sports car season and in 1954 witnessed an epic battle between Ferrari and Jaguar that completely overshadowed the rest of the entry. Two of the 375 *Plus* entries driven by Maglioli/Paolo Marzotto and Rosier/Manzon retired because of rear axle failure, but Gonzalez/ Trintignant with their 375 *Plus* battled for the lead with Rolt/Hamilton at the wheel of the only surviving Jaguar D-type. Just over 1½ hours before the finish the Ferrari led by close to two laps, but when Trintignant came in to refuel and hand over to Gonzalez at 2.22pm, the Ferrari refused to fire up because of a rain-soaked magneto.

Six minutes were lost while the mechanics – more than the permitted number – worked on the car. A mechanic eventually fired it up from under the bonnet and another held the accelerator down, while Gonzalez clambered into the Ferrari. This was another breach of the regulations and as *Maestro* Nello Ugolini, a vastly experienced team manager, was in charge of the Ferrari pit, there was no excuse for these lapses. Gonzalez rejoined the race with a two-minute lead and won from the Jaguar by a margin of 2½ miles, the closest-ever finish up until that time. Jaguar did not protest the Ferrari.

Lined up before the start of the 1954 Le Mans race are two of the monstrous 4.9-litre 375 Plus spyders and the 375 Mille Miglia coupé of Baggio/Rubirosa.

Umberto Maglioli won the Carrera Panamericana Mexico held between 19–23 November with a 375 *Plus*, loaned back to the works by Ernie Goldschmidt, and Phil Hill partnered by Richie Ginther finished second with the 375MM that won the 1953 Nürburgring race. Argentinian Enrique Valiente bought another of these cars and drove it with José Ibanez in the Buenos Aires 1,000Km race on 23 January 1955. They won at 93.75mph (150.84kph). In 1955 Ferrari supplied American property developer Tony Parravano with a similar car powered by the *SuperAmerica* 4,963cc (88×68mm) V12 production engine installed in a 9ft 2in (2,795mm) wheelbase chassis, with rigid rear axle.

When Ferrari needed an interim car to run in the 1956 Buenos Aires 1,000Km race, he revived the concept of the Parravano car. The 1956 works cars had the same engine capacity, but twin-plug ignition and a claimed 380bhp power output; the wheelbase was reduced to 7ft 8½in (2,350mm), Scaglietti built the bodies, there was a de Dion rear axle and a four-speed gearbox in unit with the final drive. These cars were very fast and ran well in the Argentine, but both retired. After this race Ferrari sold them on to private owners.

The gradual increase of engine capacity of the V12 cars led to overpowered monsters that were too fast for their chassis – and for many drivers. The new V12 sports-racing cars developed for 1956 by former Lancia engineer Andrea Fraschetti were much improved and combined a good power output with satisfactory roadholding. Above all, they were balanced, manageable cars.

Aston Martin DB3S

1953–56

When Peter Collins and Paul Frère drove this DB3S into second place at Le Mans in 1955, it was the make's best performance ever at the circuit. This photograph, with Collins at the wheel at Mulsanne Corner on the Sunday morning, shows off the lines of Frank Feeley's 'Gothic arch' body to good effect. (T.C. March/FotoVantage)

After David Brown's acquisition of Aston Martin and then Lagonda in 1947, Aston Martin was based in what was little more than an aircraft hangar at Hanworth Air Park, Feltham in Middlesex. The earliest post-war cars had a rectangular tubular chassis designed by Claude Hill, who had been with the company since the late 1920s, and a four-cylinder 1,970cc engine. From these beginnings Aston Martin developed the DB2 which combined the tubular chassis, the six-cylinder twin overhead camshaft Lagonda engine and a new and very stylish fixed head coupé body designed by Frank Feeley who had been with Lagonda since pre-war days.

The Lagonda engine was designed by 'Willie' Watson, working under the general supervision of W.O. Bentley and with capacity increased from the original 2.3 litres to 2,580cc (78×90mm) it developed 105bhp at 5,000rpm. Aston Martin redeveloped this engine substantially and while it provided the company's salvation, it was retained too long and throughout the years 1951–56 the company's sports-racing cars were always underpowered.

The DB2s performed well in racing, especially at Le Mans. In 1950 Macklin/Abecassis and Brackenbury/Parnell finished fifth and sixth (first and second in the 3,000cc class). The following year Macklin/Thompson and Abecassis/Shawe-Taylor took third and fifth places overall, first and second in the 3,000cc class and the third-place car won the Index of Performance. The DB2 remained in production in various forms until mid-1959.

Former Auto Union engineer, Professor Robert Eberan von Eberhorst had joined the company. He was a slim, austere man, who preferred his slide rule to common sense, and appeared to have little grasp of the realities of motor racing. He was responsible for the DB3 that first ran in the Tourist Trophy at Dundrod in September 1951. This had a heavy, substantially braced, ladder-type chassis, with 7ft 9in (2,360mm) wheelbase. Front suspension was by trailing links and transverse torsion bars and at the rear there was a de Dion axle and similar suspension. The 2.6-litre engine developed 140bhp and there was a David Brown four-speed gearbox (although it was first raced with a five-speed gearbox).

In the Tourist Trophy the DB3's engine ran its bearings and during 1952 these cars achieved success only in minor British events. The three cars that ran in the 1952 Monaco Grand Prix, held that year as a sports car race, had the engines enlarged to 2,922cc (83×90mm). All three cars retired because of an engine design fault for which von Eberhorst was responsible. The only success of any significance during the year was the win by Collins/Griffith with a 2.6-litre car in the Goodwood Nine Hours race in August. The 2.9-litre DB3 of Parnell/Thompson caught fire in the pits and team manager John Wyer suffered injuries that included temporary blindness.

Over the winter of 1952–53 'Willie' Watson redesigned the chassis in much shorter, 7ft 3in (2,210mm) wheelbase form and built in lighter tubing. Watson reduced the track to 4ft 3in (1,300mm) and redesigned the rear suspension, so that instead of a Panhard rod providing transverse location of the axle, there was a central sliding block operating in mild steel guide-plates bolted to the light alloy final drive casing. Brown and Wyer approved the design and von Eberhorst left. The new car was typed the DB3S and Feeley designed a stylish body. Development work boosted power output with three Weber twin-choke 35DCO carburettors to 182bhp at 5,500rpm.

The team continued to race the DB3s early in 1953 and Reg Parnell's fifth place in the Mille Miglia accompanied by photographer Louis Klementaski, was the best performance ever by a British car in the race. Parnell drove a DB3S in a minor British race and then a full team ran at Le Mans where they were outclassed and all retired. The team ran in six more races that year, all in Britain and won them all. In four of these races Jaguar had entered works C-types. Aston Martin's main strengths were John Wyer's superb team management and a crew of drivers of high ability who enjoyed racing for the team.

Four days after Le Mans, Parnell won the handicap British Empire Trophy on the Isle of Man and in July Parnell, Salvadori and Collins took the first three places in the sports car race at the British Grand Prix meeting at Silverstone. The most significant defeats of Jaguar were in two endurance races. In the Goodwood Nine Hours race in August, Parnell/Thompson and Collins/Griffith took the first two places after the Jaguars had been sidelined by oil pressure problems. The DB3S entries were as fast as the Jaguars in the World Championship Tourist Trophy at Dundrod in September and Collins/Griffith and Parnell/Thompson finished first and second.

Aston Martin had a disappointing 1954 season. It started well enough with third place by Collins/Griffith in the Buenos Aires 1,000Km race, but all three entries retired in the Sebring 12 Hours race and both Parnell and Collins crashed in the Mille Miglia. Much of the race was run in rain and the Astons' Avon tyres, specially requested by Wyer to be of sufficiently hard compound to last the race without a wheel-change, made the cars virtually uncontrollable in the wet.

At the International Trophy meeting at Silverstone in May the team entered the new Lagonda, a car with the makings, on paper at least, of being a Ferrari-beater. The engine was again the work of 'Willie' Watson and his brief was to follow the design principles of the six-cylinder unit. The Lagonda had a V12 4,486cc (82.5×69.8mm) engine with a barrel-type crankcase similar to that of the Aston Martin, but cast in aluminium alloy,

The DB3S in its early 1954 form with single-plug cylinder head and outboard rear brakes. In their early racing days these cars were under-powered compared to most of the opposition in the 3-litre class. (LAT)

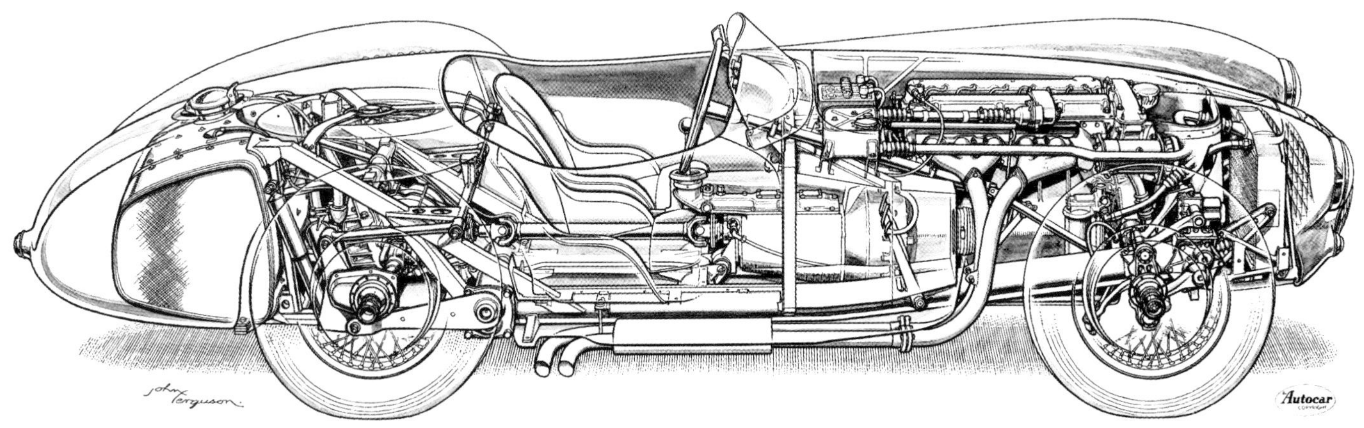

Roy Salvadori and racing the DB3S

In 1953, the year that Aston Martin brought out the DB3S, I became a works driver and I was still driving for the team as late as 1963; I was the longest-serving works driver. I drove the DB3S for four seasons, during which it was steadily developed and became increasingly competitive in the 3-litre class. During that time power increased by about a third and the braking was transformed by fitting Girling disc brakes.

These brakes had no servo and so needed quite a lot of effort to operate. In my opinion this gave much greater braking control than the Dunlop discs fitted to the C-type Jaguar, which I also raced on a few occasions. Jaguar brakes had a powerful servo, they required only the lightest of touches and I thought that they were far too sensitive. The DB3S was always underpowered compared to some of its rivals, such as the Ferrari *Monza*, but it handled far better than the Ferrari or, for that matter, contemporary C and D-type Jaguars.

Although the DB3S had a short wheelbase and could be skittish in the wet, its handling suited

Roy Salvadori leads the Sports Car race at the International Trophy meeting at Silverstone in 1956 when he scored a controversial win. (T.C. March/FotoVantage)

my style of driving perfectly – through corners I could push it past its limit, and then control the rear end so that I could do a near-enough perfect four-wheel drift. I had many successes with the DB3S and in eleven years with the team I never had a serious accident.

One of my more notorious successes was at Silverstone in May 1956 when there was the usual Aston Martin versus Jaguar battle. To beat the Jaguars at Silverstone, it was necessary to build up a lead on the first lap, otherwise we had insufficient power to pass them on the straights and were held up through the corners where we could not get past.

That year Stirling Moss was in the team and at Silverstone he led away in an enormous power slide. I was right behind him and behind me was a Jaguar driven, I thought, by Mike Hawthorn. On the approach to *Stowe* corner, Stirling waved me past, but I did not have enough speed, so I waited until we were almost into the corner and passed him as we lined up for it. Unfortunately two of the works Jaguars followed me through.

I had to stay in front through *Club* corner, for if the Jaguars passed me, they would build up a good lead on the straight leading into *Abbey* curve. I had this D-type right behind me as I went into *Club* and I was convinced that it was Mike Hawthorn, a really hard driver and not prepared to give an inch. I moved over to the right, leaving it up to the Jaguar driver to pass me on the left if he could. If he did, I could dive through on the inside and outbrake him before the corner.

The Jaguar was still trying to pass me as we went deeper into the braking area and I realised that it was not going to make it. Then all I could see in my mirror was a puff of smoke. The driver was, in fact, Desmond Titterington. I saw none of this, but Stirling and Mike with his D-type slipped past the spinning Jaguar; Peter Collins hit it amidships with his DB3S, Reg Parnell took to the ditch with his DB3S and Ninian Sanderson (*Écurie Ecosse* D-type) spun up the bank.

I went on to score a good win ahead of Stirling. There was quite a lot of discussion within the Aston Martin team about the accident, but I took no part in it. Because of a mechanical fault, I crashed my Maserati 250F in the Formula 1 International Trophy and was taken unconscious to Northampton hospital.

twin overhead camshafts per bank of cylinders, wet cylinder liners, twin-plug ignition and dry-sump lubrication. It proved a failure.

Instead of the anticipated 350bhp, when it first appeared, it developed only 280bhp at 6,000rpm and the maximum ever achieved was 312bhp. Because of a design fault, the crankcase and the main bearing diaphragms were of the same alloy and they expanded at the same rate. Clearances remained constant through the heat range, the engine failed to seal properly and the oil pressure dropped rapidly. The chassis was a strengthened and lengthened, 8ft 4in (2,540mm) version of that of the DB3S. The new car raced three times in 1954 without success and after a final appearance at Le Mans in 1955, by when it had a multi-tubular, backbone-type chassis, it was abandoned.

At the Silverstone meeting in May 1954 two new DB3S cars had coupé bodywork developed in the Vickers Aircraft wind tunnel, but they were another failure and both crashed at Le Mans in 1954 because of aerodynamic lift. More important was a new cylinder head with the valves at an included angle of 60°, twin-plug ignition, three Weber twin-choke 45DCO carburettors and a power output of 225bhp at 6,000rpm. The DB3S was now reasonably competitive in the 3,000cc class. One car was fitted with Lockheed disc brakes, but it would not be until 1956 that all DB3S works cars had Girling discs without servo assistance.

The David Brown team completely overreached itself at Le Mans with a five-car entry. Early in the race Eric Thompson spun the Lagonda in the Esses, wrecking the tail, the coupés crashed and the other two DB3S entries retired. One of these had a Wade supercharger, single-plug ignition, a single Weber twin-choke carburettor and developed 240bhp at 6,000rpm. In the hands of Parnell/Salvadori it was holding sixth place when it succumbed to cylinder head gasket failure at Sunday lunchtime. The team ran only in British events for the remainder of the season and the sole success was first three places in the sports car race at the British Grand Prix meeting at Silverstone in July.

Aston Martin introduced a production version of the DB3S at the 1954 Earls Court Show, but with single-plug cylinder head, three Solex twin-choke carburettors, a power output of 180bhp at 5,500rpm, it represented poor value for money at a basic price of £2,600. Triple Weber twin-choke carburettors were soon adopted, giving a claimed, but rather optimistic 210bhp; it was a very delectable 140mph road car. However, it was hopeless for racing.

For 1955 Aston Martin built two new DB3S cars with Frank Feeley's so-called 'Gothic arch' distinctive, curvaceous bodies and other team cars were rebodied in this style. Peter Collins drove the sole DB3S entry in the Mille Miglia, but retired because of engine problems. At the May Silverstone meeting Parnell and Collins took the first two places, defeating the works Jaguar D-types. The following day Paul Frère with a DB3S won the 175-mile (282km) Spa Grand Prix for production sports cars from a brace of new and more powerful Ferrari *Monzas*. This DB3S was a works car, but fitted with single-plug 200bhp engine and drum brakes.

On 29 May three production DB3S cars entered by the *Kangaroo Stable* and driven by Gaze/McKay, Cosh/Cobden and Sulman/Brabham took second, third and fourth places behind a Ferrari in the Hyères 12 Hours race, an event primarily for private owners. It was the only occasion on which production DB3S cars turned in a decent performance. Aston Martin entered three DB3S cars at Le Mans on 11–12 June; the terrible accident overshadowed the race, but Aston Martin turned in their best performance ever at the circuit and Collins/Frère finished second behind Hawthorn/Bueb (Jaguar D-type).

Aston Martin took first four places in the 50-mile sports car race at the British Grand Prix meeting at Aintree and in August Walker/Poore and Collins/Brooks were first and third in the Goodwood Nine Hours race, split by the *Écurie Ecosse* Jaguar D-type of Titterington/Sanderson that came close to winning. The following weekend Parnell with a works DB3S won the 221-mile *Daily Herald* Trophy at Oulton Park. The team rounded off the season with fourth place by Walker/Poore in the strongly contested Tourist Trophy at Dundrod. It had been Aston Martin's best ever season, despite the fact that the DB3S was obsolescent, and this was mainly due to improved reliability.

Although proved at Le Mans to be aerodynamically unstable, the DB3S coupés were very handsome cars. In the very wet sports car race at Silverstone in May 1954 Graham Whitehead drove this example into a poor 12th place. (T.C. March/FotoVantage)

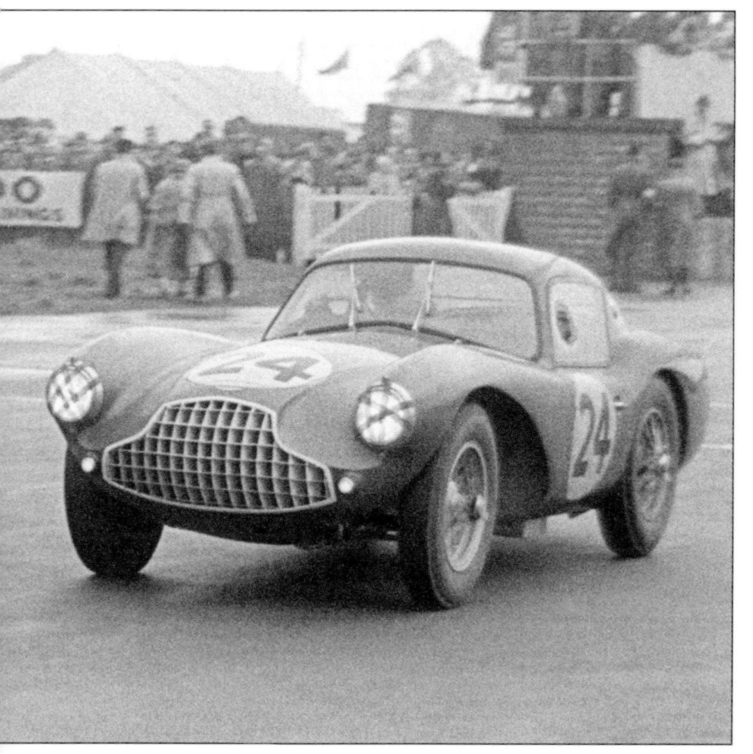

The team struggled through another season before its successor was raceworthy and again the results were satisfactory. A major Aston Martin asset was that Stirling Moss had joined the team. In the 1956 Sebring 12 Hours race two of the DB3S entries retired, but despite the loss of second and top gears Salvadori/Shelby finished fourth and won the 3,000cc class. Salvadori with his DB3S led away at the start of the 73-mile (117km) sports car race at Silverstone in May, behind him Titterington (works D-type) triggered off a multi-car accident that eliminated two of the Aston Martins, and Salvadori and Moss took the first two places.

Parnell drove a DB3S in full works tune in the 105-mile (169km) Production Sports Car race at Spa-Francorchamps on 13 May, but finished second to Ninian Sanderson with an *Écurie Ecosse* D-type. The DB3S entries in the Nürburgring 1,000Km race on 27 May were uncompetitive but Collins/Brooks drove a steady race to finish fifth. The 203-mile (327km) Rouen Grand Prix on 8 July was limited to cars of 3,000cc and was a straight fight between Aston Martin, Maserati and Ferrari. Aston Martin produced two new cars with smoother frontal treatment and streamlined headrests. Castellotti (works Ferrari *Monza*) won from Moss, Behra (Maserati 300S), Brooks and Salvadori.

At Le Mans the DB3S was accepted as a production car and although one of the two entries crashed, Moss/Collins with a car that was desperately tight on fuel finished second, despite having to coast in neutral before the end of the *Mulsanne Straight*. Two wins in minor races followed. The works Aston Martins took the first four places in the 110-mile (177km) *Daily Herald* Trophy at Oulton Park on 18 August and first two places in a 50-mile (80km) race at Goodwood in September.

It had been a good year for a car in its fourth racing year and its successor, the DBR1, had already appeared in Prototype form at Le Mans. The team entered the DB3S in a couple of minor races in 1957 before the DBR1s took over completely. It was still not the end of the racing career of the DB3S and as late as 1958 Peter Whitehead and half-brother Graham drove their private car into second place at Le Mans.

Porsche 550 *Spyder*

1953–57

One of the first appearances of the 550 with four overhead camshaft engine was in the 1954 Mille Miglia. Hans Herrmann, partnered by Herbert Linge, drove a brilliant race to finish sixth overall and win the 1,500cc sports class. (Porsche Werkfoto)

After the first production Porsche 356 with a rear-mounted, horizontally-opposed four-cylinder air-cooled engine was rolled out from the original small works at Gmünd in Austria in 1948, the marque flourished. The company then returned to its roots, in the Zuffenhausen suburb of Stuttgart in 1950, and the following year it made its International racing debut at the Le Mans 24 Hours race where a 1,100cc coupé won its class.

Already one enthusiast, Walter Glöckler, a VW dealer in Frankfurt, had seen the potential of the Porsche as a competition sports car and built what became known as the Glöckler-Porsche. He drove the 1952 version with 1,500cc engine developing 98bhp on methanol to a class win in that year's German Sports Car Championship. Porsche were well aware of what Glöckler was doing and in 1952 they started developing their own sports-racing car, typed the 550. Because the existing push-rod engine would not be powerful enough, Porsche developed a new engine to power it.

Porsche designed a ladder-type tubular frame with 6ft 10½in (2,100mm) wheelbase; there was independent front suspension by trailing arms and torsion bars and independent rear suspension by swing-axles and torsion bars, as on the production cars. Transmission was by a hydraulically operated clutch and a four-speed all-synchromesh gearbox. The body was constructed in one piece from aluminium-alloy sheet. The four-cam engine, typed the 547, was not available initially, so the earliest cars had the push-rod 1,488cc (80×74mm) engine tuned to develop about 82bhp.

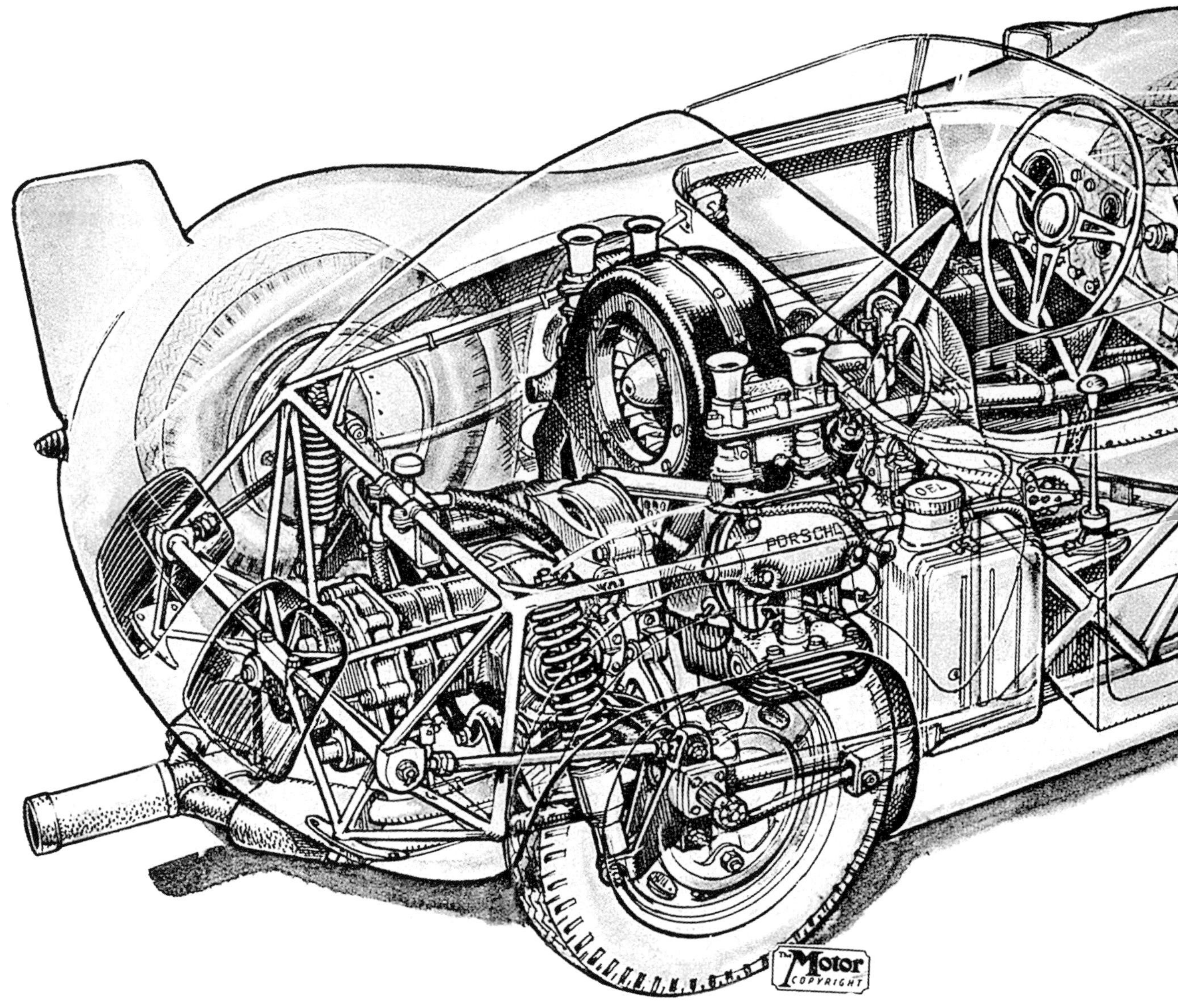

By 1958 the sports-racing Porsche in its latest 1,587.5cc form was a very formidable competition car and capable of chasing an outright victory. One of these cars finished third overall at Le Mans and they won their class in every round of the Sports Car Championship. (LAT)

Glöckler drove the prototype to a win in a minor race at the Nürburgring in 1953 and then two cars with coupé tops were entered in the Le Mans 24 Hours race. In this form the 550s were noisy, hot and claustrophobic, but as had become expected of Porsche they were completely reliable. Von Frankenberg/Frère, 15th, and Herrmann/Glöckler, 16th, took the first two places in the 1,500cc class. The cars ran topless in the Rheinland Cup race preceding the German Grand Prix and Herrmann won at 75.81mph (121.98kph).

Herrmann drove a third car in practice, the first 550 fitted with the *Typ* 547 engine. This flat-four had a capacity of 1,498cc (85×66mm), aluminium-alloy crankcase, separate cylinders and cylinder heads. The overhead camshafts were driven by shaft, there were two plugs per cylinder and a Hirth-type built-up crankshaft running in four main bearings. With four Solex downdraught twin-choke carburettors, power output was 110bhp at 6,200rpm.

The four-cam 550 (the full designation was 550-1500RS *Rennsport*) was exhibited at the Paris Salon in October and the first racing appearance was in the Carrera Panamericana Mexico road race in November. Although Herrmann led his class at the end of the first stage, both 550s retired. The works started the 1954 season by entering a 550 for Hans Herrmann/Herbert Linge in the Mille Miglia. Despite 20 minutes lost sorting out wet electrics, they finished sixth overall at 78.74mph (126.70kph) and won the 1,500cc class.

At Le Mans Porsche entered four cars, three 1,500cc 550s and one powered by a 1,089cc engine. The 1500s suffered from burnt pistons caused by incorrect ignition settings; two retired, while Claes/Stasse struggled

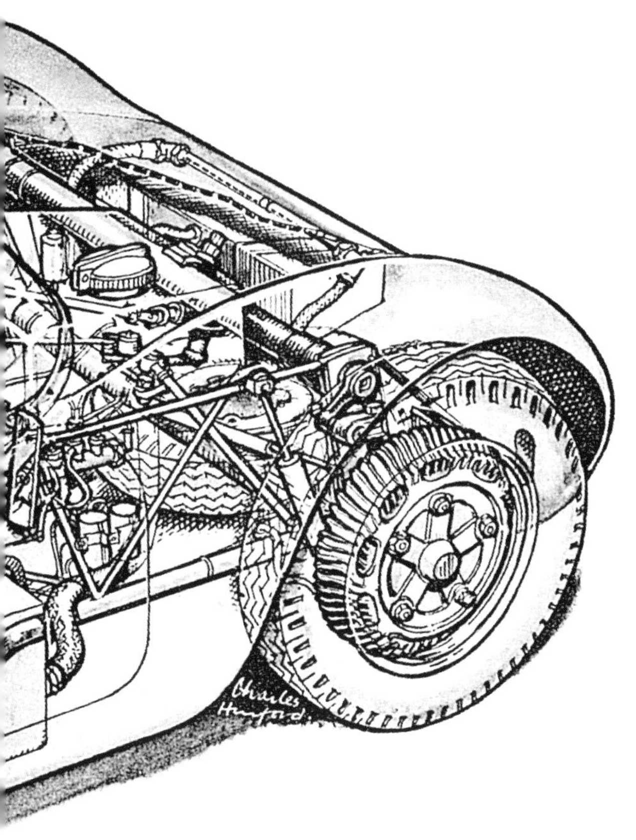

on three cylinders for the last five hours of the race to finish 12th and win the 1,500cc class at 79.303mph (127.60kph). Despite gearbox problems, Arkus Duntov/Olivier took 14th place at 75.140mph (120.900kph) and won the 1,100cc category.

In July Polensky/von Frankenberg drove a 550 into eighth place overall and a class win in the Reims 12 Hours race. The cars performed well in minor German races, but they made a mistake when they entered a 1,500cc car for Herrmann and a 1,100cc for von Hanstein in the 1,500cc sports car race at the British Grand Prix meeting at Silverstone in July. The 550s were wrongly geared for the circuit and Colin Chapman (streamlined Lotus Mark VIII-MG) and Peter Gammon ('square-rigged' Lotus Mark VI-MG) beat Herrmann into third place. Von Hanstein finished fifth overall and won the 1,100cc class.

In November Porsche contested the Carrera Panamericana Mexico road race held in eight stages totalling 1,908 miles (3,070km). Herrmann and Guatemalan Jaroslav Juhan were the drivers and they took the first two places in the 1,500cc class after class-leader Walter Bechem (Borgward) collided with a Spanish Pegaso. Juhan bought his car after the race.

Towards the end of 1954 Porsche put the 550 into production and Porsche sold more than 100, mainly in the United States and buyers included *Rebel Without a Cause* star James Dean who was killed at the wheel of his 550 in 1955. The good sales were partly attributable to excellent marketing, but there was little opposition in the 1,500cc class, for the Maserati brothers built their OSCA cars in only limited numbers and Borgward built only works cars, not selling any to private owners.

In January Juhan drove his 550 from Guatemala to Buenos Aires and in the 1,000Km race he finished, driving solo, fourth overall behind two Ferraris and a 2-litre Maserati. In the Sebring 12 Hours race in March von Hanstein/Linge took eighth place and won the 1,500cc class. Wolfgang Seidel drove a 550 solo in the Mille Miglia, finished eighth and won the 1,500cc class – but only after Cabianca, leading the class with his OSCA, retired because of gearbox failure.

Veuillet/Olivier and Jeser/Mme. Bousquet with private 550s took first two places in the Paris 24 Hours race for cars of up to 2,000cc held at Montlhéry in May on the 3.9-mile (6.28km) combined road and banked track circuit. Porsche was out in force at Le Mans; with Teutonic efficiency four cars started and four finished. Polensky/von Frankenberg, Seidel/Gendebien and Glöckler/Juhan were fourth, fifth and sixth overall, taking first three places in the 1,500cc class. Olivier/Jeser finished 13th and won the 1,100cc class.

Porsche sent two 550s to compete in the Goodwood Nine Hours race in August, an event that attracted a mainly, rather parochial British entry. Stirling Moss drove one of the cars, partnered by Porsche team manager Huschke von Hanstein, who was around ten seconds a lap slower. During the hours of darkness (the race started at 3pm) Moss collided with Tony Crooks's Cooper-Bristol that had spun on oil dropped by the other works car driven by Seidel/Dickie Steed. This second Porsche finished tenth overall and third in the 1,500cc class behind a Connaught and a Cooper.

On 28 August the 550s, works and private, suffered a humiliating defeat when Jean Behra drove the new Maserati 150S to victory in the Nürburgring 500Km for sports cars up to 1,500cc. Von Frankenberg (Porsche) and Rosenhammer/Barth (East German EMW) followed him across the line, some distance behind. Ironically, it was one of the few occasions when the 'baby' Maserati went really well.

In the Tourist Trophy at Dundrod the works 550s

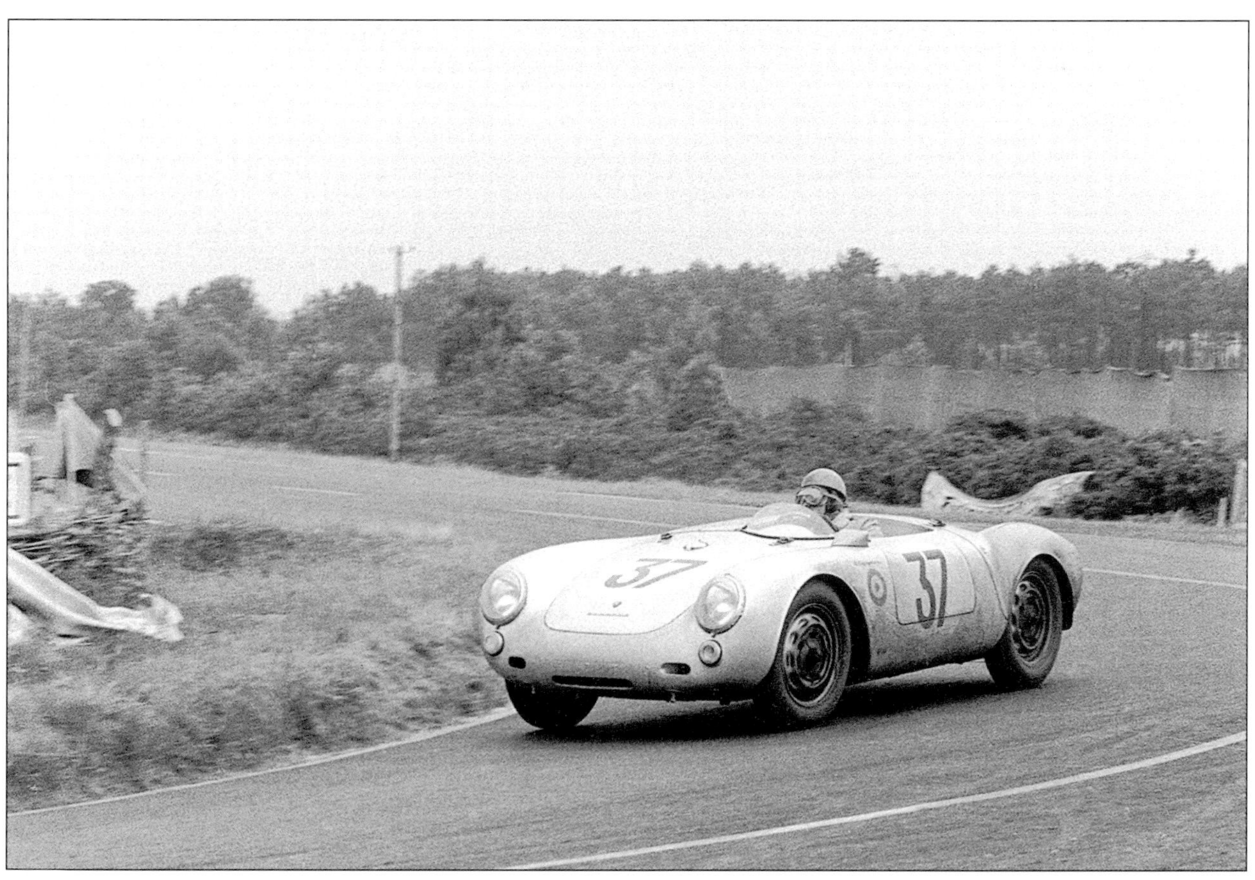

The 1955 Le Mans event was disastrous, but Porsche had a very good race. This 550 driven by Polensky/von Frankenberg finished fourth overall, winning the 1,500cc class and the very lucrative Index of Performance. (T.C. March/FotoVantage)

were faster and more reliable than the British opposition and took first three places in the 1,500cc class, ahead of the 2-litre class-winning Maserati in the order, Shelby/Gregory (ninth overall), Glöckler/Seidel (12th overall) and von Frankenberg/Linge. Eight days later von Frankenberg won the 155-mile *Avusrennen* at 122.78mph (197.55kph) from the East German EMWs of Rosenhammer and Thiel.

Over the winter of 1955–56 Porsche developed an improved version, the 550A, with a lighter and stiffer steel tubular space-frame, a much lighter body (with the space-frame much of the former body framework was no longer required). There was new low-pivot swing-axle rear suspension and with two Weber twin-choke 40DCM carburettors maximum power was boosted to 135bhp at 7,200rpm. Porsche used a new five-speed gearbox with unsynchronised first gear and with accidental engagement of first gear prevented by a safety catch.

At the beginning of the 1956 season Porsche continued to race the existing 550. In the Sebring 12 Hours race, held on 8 April, Herrmann/von Trips and McAfee/Lovely finished sixth and seventh overall, taking first two places in the 1,500cc class. Both works 550s retired in the Mille Miglia and the team next ran in the Nürburgring 1,000Km race. The 550As made their race debut in the hands of von Trips/Maglioli and Herrmann/von Frankenberg and they performed superbly, taking fourth and sixth places overall and the first two places in the 1,500cc class.

Porsche sent a single car to compete in the 447-mile (719km) Targa Florio on Sicily on 10 June. It had been intended that Maglioli/von Hanstein should share the driving, but the team manager found his hands full, including repainting the car white from Porsche's usual silver to comply with the pernickety requirements of the organisers. So Maglioli drove single-handed and won at 56.37mph (90.70kph) from Maserati and Ferrari opposition. At the end of June von Frankenberg/Storez with a 550A won a 12-hour race at Reims for cars up to 1,500cc.

In the Le Mans race, postponed until the end of July, Porsche decided to make the best of the very special regulations that included full-width windscreens and ran two 550As with coupé tops. Von Trips/von

Frankenberg drove a superb, troublefree race to finish fifth overall at 98.182mph (157.97kph) and a win in the 1,500cc class. The other 550A, driven by Herrmann/Maglioli, retired because of valve trouble, probably the result of a third gear jumping out during practice, causing the engine to soar up to 9,800rpm.

Porsche put the 550A into production in late 1956 and sold around 30 cars to private owners. Already, the company was working on a new model, the RSK, a much-improved, lower and lighter car, and this first appeared in practice at the Nürburgring in June 1957. The first entry by the works that year was in the Mille Miglia and in this race Maglioli drove his 550A into fifth place and a class win – despite running out of fuel between controls. Maglioli/Barth finished fourth overall at the Nürburgring and yet again won their class. All the Porsche works entries at Le Mans that year retired.

By 1958 Porsche relied for most of the year on the RSK model, but sent 550As to the first two rounds of the Sports Car Championship. After their Maserati had been damaged in practice, Moss/Behra drove a 550A with 1,587cc (87.5×66mm) engine into third place behind two 3-litre Ferraris. Another third place by Schell/Seidel followed at Sebring.

From then onwards Porsche raced the RSKs and became increasingly a serious contender in the World Sports Car Champion, partly because the 3-litre capacity limit proved a great leveller. Porsche raced for outright wins, especially on the slower circuits, and after finishing third in the Championship in 1958 and 1959, the marque was second in 1960 and third again in 1961. Zuffenhausen was entering a new phase in its racing history.

The chassis of the RSK was lower and lighter and an interesting feature was a centrally mounted steering box so that the car could easily be adapted for single-seater Formula 2 racing. The front brakes were of a new turbo-finned type and at the rear there was a new low-pivot swing-axle mounted on coil springs. The body was distinguished by twin tailfins. The RSK was known as such because the carrier tubes of the front suspension formed roughly the shape of the letter K.

During 1958 these cars proved exceptionally successful and their performances included second place in the Targa Florio, third and fourth places overall at Le Mans and fourth overall in the Tourist Trophy at Goodwood; at each of these races the RSKs also won their class. Porsche was rapidly becoming a contender for outright victory in Championship races and in 1959 won the Targa Florio outright, won their class in every race in the Championship series and took third place in the Championship behind Aston Martin and Ferrari.

It was much the same in 1960, although the new and faster RS60 cars performed badly at Le Mans. That year they took second place in the Championship behind Ferrari and they were third again in 1961. By 1962 and the first year of the new Prototype racing category the team from Zuffenhausen was racing 2-litre cars. Porsche had embarked on a new era that was to lead to major Prototype successes recounted later.

Umberto Maglioli after his winning solo drive with a 550A in the 1956 Targa Florio. Huschke von Hanstein was to combine the roles of racing manager and co-driver, but he became preoccupied with other problems, including painting the car white to satisfy the organisers' requirements. (Porsche Werkfoto)

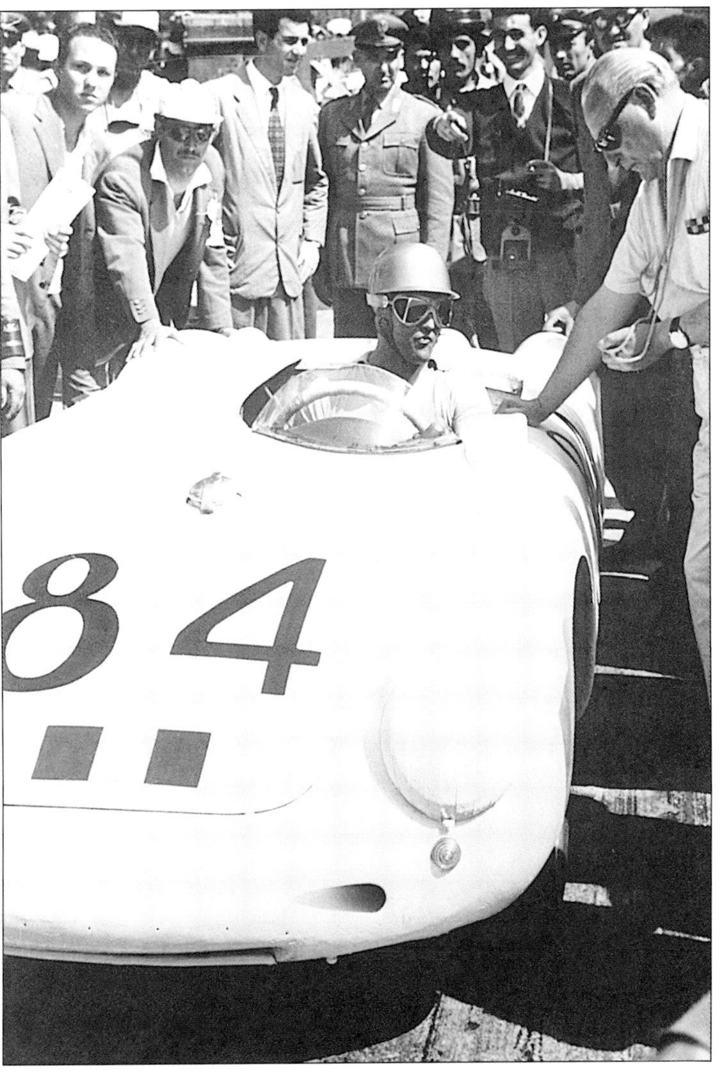

Jaguar D-type
1954–57

Early in the 1955 Le Mans race Mike Hawthorn with the winning long-nose D-type leads Juan Fangio (Mercedes-Benz 300SLR) through the Esses. Note that the air brake of the 300SLR is in the raised position. (T.C. March/FotoVantage)

In 1953 Jaguar built a new sports-racing car with a very advanced magnesium-alloy tubular chassis and much sleeker body designed by Malcolm Sayer, clearly influenced by the design of the 1952 Alfa Romeo *Disco Volante*. This interim car was variously known as the 'XK120C Mark II', the light-alloy car and the C/D-type. At the wheel of this car fitted with a Plexiglas 'bubble' canopy, test driver Norman Dewis covered the flying mile at a mean 178.383mph (287.018kph) on the motorway at Jabbeke in Belgium in October 1953 and it was later used for side-by-side testing with the more radical 1954 D-type (originally known as the XK120D).

Jaguar retained a rigid rear axle, but otherwise the D-type was a very advanced car. The central section of the chassis was a stressed magnesium-alloy elliptical monocoque, with longitudinal pontoon or sill structures to provide additional rigidity. The front bulkhead was a box-member that ran the full width of the body and another bulkhead at the rear added further stiffening and formed the firewall between driver and fuel tank. At the front there was a trident-shaped, fully welded frame constructed in square-section aluminium-alloy tubing and the central 'prong' extended through the monocoque to the rear bulkhead. Two channel-section members ran across and were riveted to the rear bulkhead and these located the rear suspension and mounted the tail-section.

The front suspension was by double wishbones and torsion bars, while the rigid rear axle was suspended on a transverse torsion bar and telescopic shock absorbers and located by parallel upper trailing arms. Steering was by rack-and-pinion and the great glory of the D-type was the Dunlop disc brake system, part of a pioneer programme run jointly by Dunlop and Jaguar and, probably, one of the most important automotive developments since the Second World War. The wheels were 16-inch Dunlop alloy with centre-lock hubs and these were lighter than the wire-spoked wheels used previously.

The fuel was carried in a rubber bag tank with a capacity of 36½ gallons (166 litres) and contained within a spot-welded aluminium-alloy skin. The aluminium-alloy body was distinguished by the single and very prominent tail fin that made a significant contribution to high-speed stability. The driver was enclosed behind a Plexiglas wrap-round screen and there was a metal tonneau cover on the passenger side. The wheelbase was 7ft 6in (2,290mm), front track 4ft 2in (1,270mm) and rear track 4ft 0in (1,220mm). At 1,900lb (862kg), the D-type was about 170lb (77kg) lighter than its predecessor.

Although the engine was the familiar 3,442cc XK unit, it had been strengthened and was inclined to the left at an angle of 8½° from the vertical to provide sufficient room for the long inlet trumpets of the three Weber 45DCO3 twin-choke carburettors. By modifying the cylinder head and fitting larger inlet ports and valves, engine breathing was improved and power output was now 245bhp at 5,750rpm. A significant change was the adoption of dry-sump lubrication.

There was no flywheel as such, but only an 8¾-inch adapter plate for mounting the triple-plate clutch. Jaguar had adopted a four-speed all-synchromesh gearbox, based on the C-type iron main casing and with an aluminium-alloy cover. The Salisbury rear axle incorporated their Powr-Lok limited-slip differential.

A team of three D-types first raced at the 1954 Le Mans race in June. The only real opposition came from the three works Ferrari 375 *Plus* 4.9-litre cars. Gonzalez/Trintignant with their 4.9 led throughout – Maranello brute force was that year more than a match for Coventry sophistication. Initially Moss, partnered by Peter Walker, tigered with the Ferraris, but fell back because of an engine misfire and the car was retired after Moss found himself without brakes at the end of the *Mulsanne Straight* and made a high-speed and frightening exit up the escape road. The Whitehead/Wharton car retired because of a rough-running engine in the early hours of the Sunday morning.

Two of the Ferraris also retired and Gonzalez/Trintignant led Rolt/Hamilton with the surviving D-type. Throughout the Sunday the circuit was treacherous, with intermittent rain, and this intensified as the race drew to a close. When a slow Talbot crossed his line, Rolt hit the bank at Arnage and around two minutes were spent in the pits while the wing was bashed back into shape. This cost Jaguar the race. At 2.22pm the Ferrari made its final pit stop, but failed to fire up, and rejoined the race after six minutes of frantic work and the breach of at least two of the race regulations. Jaguar then replaced Rolt with Hamilton, who was usually faster in the wet, but to no avail.

"We were quite happy with the outcome, really," Bob Berry reflects, "although we were very disappointed to lose by a minute and a half, about the narrowest margin possible, particularly when at the last pit stop they couldn't get the Ferrari to start; we were in the next pit and there's no doubt that they had two or three times the number of mechanics working on the car to get it started than they were allowed under the regulations.

"One of the organising officials came down to our pit afterwards and said, 'You saw what went on, quite clearly they were in breach of the regulations, you're entitled to make a protest.' Lofty England said, 'It's not my decision, you will have to talk to William Lyons.' They went over to Lyons and he said, 'No, if we can't win the race on the road, we don't win it at all.'"

Jaguar next ran in the Reims 12 Hours race. The D-types had their problems, but Whitehead/Wharton won the race from Rolt/Hamilton, whose car had been shunted by Behra's Gordini while leading and finished the race with an oil-less, holed differential caused by a deranged sub-frame member eroding the casing. In September Jaguar ran three cars in the Tourist Trophy at Dundrod and although it was a round in the World Sports Car Championship, it was still run as a handicap event.

The classes were rather odd and Jaguar entered a 3.4-litre D-type for Rolt/Hamilton and two cars with 2,482cc engines driven by Moss/Walker and Whitehead/Wharton. The capacity limit in the class for the smaller cars was 2,483cc and the reduced capacity was achieved by using a 76.5mm stroke crankshaft in a 3.4 block. Power output in this form was 190bhp at 6,000rpm. Rolt/Hamilton retired because of loss of oil

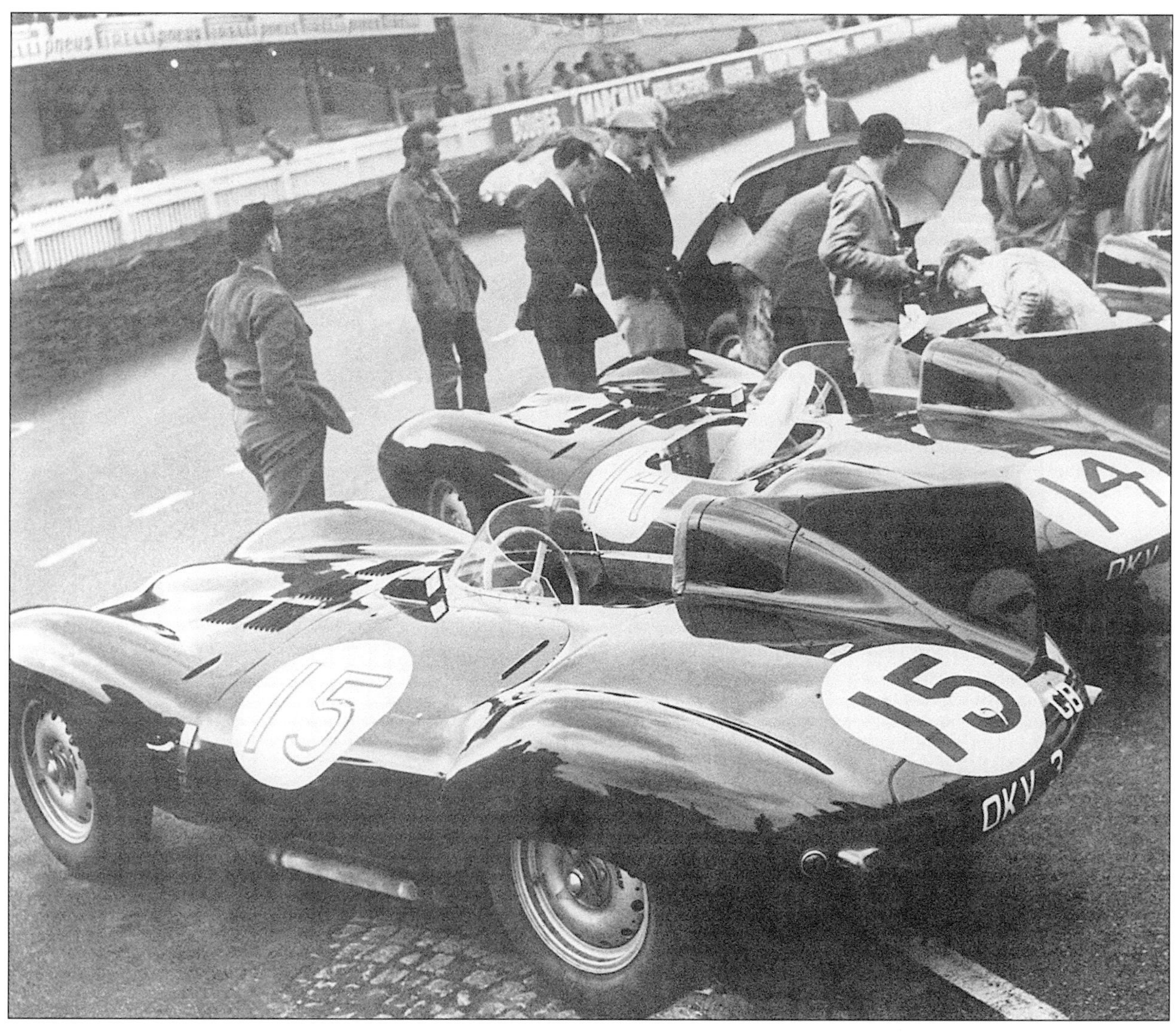

The line-up of works Jaguar D-types during practice for the 1954 Le Mans race. Number 14 is the car driven by Tony Rolt and Duncan Hamilton into second place behind the winning 4.9-litre Ferrari of Froilan Gonzalez and Maurice Trintignant.

pressure and Whitehead/Wharton took fifth place on handicap; the Moss/Walker car had a piston fail an hour before the finish and Moss waited at the start/finish line to drive into 18th place. It was not a Jaguar race or a Jaguar circuit.

At the Earls Court Show Jaguar announced the D-type as a production car with a basic price of £1,895 (it soon rose to £2,585, but still remained an incredible bargain). The tail fin was optional on production cars and, if fitted, was smaller than that used by the works.

Jaguar loaned a 1954 works D-type to Briggs Cunningham for the Sebring 12 Hours race in March and it was driven by Mike Hawthorn, who had joined the Jaguar team for 1955, and Phil Walters. They led for much of the race, but during the last hour made a number of pit stops, because (according to Mike Hawthorn) the cylinder head had warped, the engine was losing oil and water and developed a misfire. After the D-type took the chequered flag to win the race, Allen Guiberson protested that his Ferrari *Monza* driven by Phil Hill/Carroll Shelby was a lap ahead and was the real winner. After eight days, the protest was rejected, but Jaguar lost a lot of publicity.

All production D-types and the latest long-nose works cars had a new tubular structure at the front, with a separate, detachable round-tube frame ahead of it to carry the oil and water radiators and act as a pivot for the one-piece bonnet and wings, both constructed in high tensile steel. Some bottom-end engine performance was sacrificed for more power in the higher ranges. The cylinder head was redesigned and this included increasing the valve size and also increasing the inclination of the exhaust valves from 35° to 40° to ensure clearance from the larger inlet valves.

Other changes included a modified exhaust system, with two separate tail-pipes from each three-branch exhaust manifolding emerging from under the tail and there were also modifications to the inlet system. Power output was around 270bhp at 5,750rpm. As the result of tests carried out at the Royal Aircraft Establishment at Farnborough, Sayer introduced a new 7½-inch (190mm) longer nose with better air penetration and a new wrap-round windscreen with higher sides that merged into the headrest.

At Le Mans the very swift Ferraris faded after Castellotti had led with one of the Maranello straight-six 4.4-litre cars in the early stages in the race. There was a superb, closely fought duel for the lead between Hawthorn and Fangio (Mercedes-Benz 300SLR shared with Moss) until the terrible accident involving Macklin (Austin-Healey 100S) and Levegh (300SLR) at 6.27pm. Although Hawthorn was initially blamed for the accident by cutting sharply across Macklin immediately before he pulled into the Jaguar pit, close examination, frame by frame, of film footage exonerated him completely.

By the time that Mercedes-Benz withdrew from the race at 1.45am, the Jaguar was in second place, two laps behind the leading 300SLR. What would have happened if Mercedes-Benz had stayed in the race is a matter of speculation, but Hawthorn/Bueb went on to win this tragic, gloomy race at 107.67mph (173.241kph) with the works-prepared *Équipe Nationale Belge* car of Claes/Swaters in third place. The other two works D-types retired.

Jaguar entered a single long-nose D-type for Hawthorn in the 51-mile (82km) sports car race at the British Grand Prix meeting at Aintree and although he led initially, he was off-form and the four-car works Aston Martin team pushed him back into fifth place. One of the two works Jaguars at the 623-mile (1002.4km) Tourist Trophy at Dundrod on 17 September had a de Dion rear axle, but this was not raced and Hawthorn/Titterington drove a car with the usual rear suspension. They put up a terrific fight against a full Mercedes-Benz team and seemed assured of second place when the crankshaft broke two laps from the finish.

The Jaguar entry in the 1956 Sebring 12 Hours race ran in American white and blue colours and was a joint works/Briggs Cunningham effort. Hawthorn/ Titterington (car with Lucas 'sliding throttle' fuel injection) and Hamilton/Bueb retired because of brake seizure caused by the temperature at which the race was run. Johnston/Spear were eliminated by engine problems and the surviving car of Cunningham/Bennet took 12th place, after Cunningham ran out of fuel and pushed the car three miles to the pits.

Jaguar ran three cars in the 73-mile (117km) sports car race at the International meeting at Silverstone in

The D-type in 1954 short-nose works form as drawn by Vic Berris for The Autocar in the autumn of 1954. (LAT)

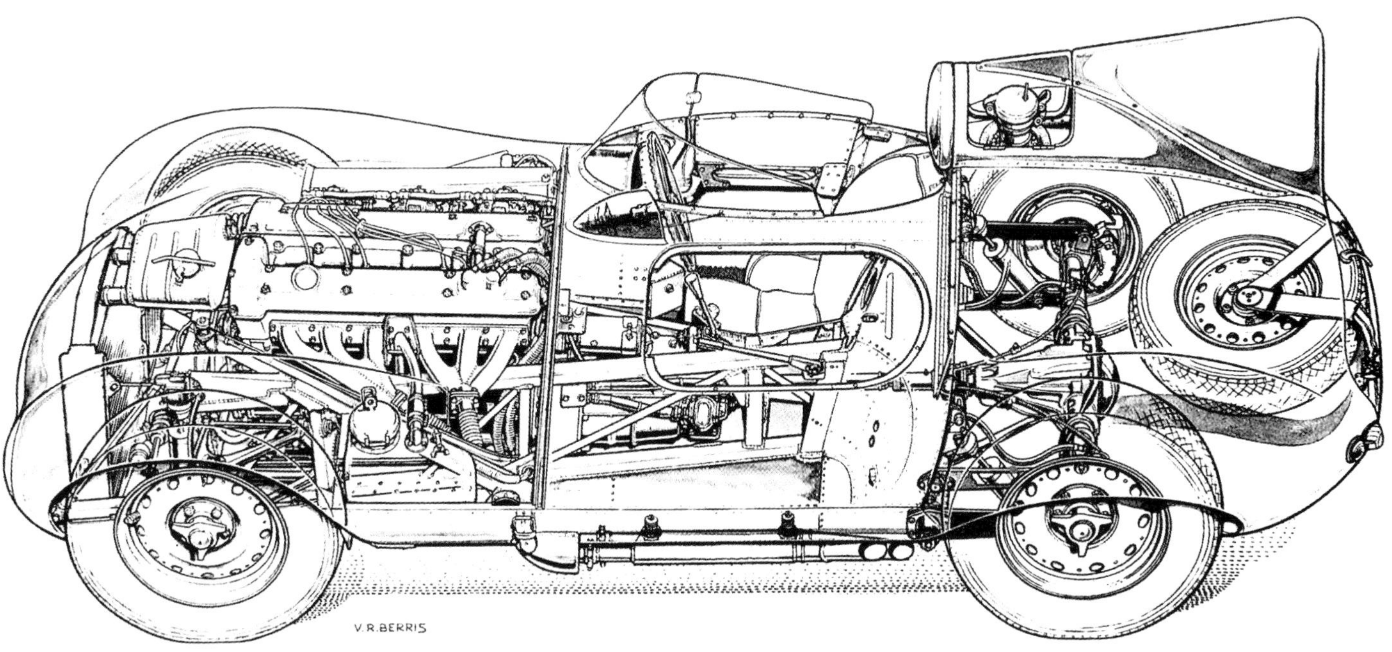

Driving the Jaguar D-type

Bob Berry was employed in the Public Relations Department of Jaguar and later became Marketing Director. Between 1955 and early 1957 he raced an ex-works D-type for Jack Broadhead. He frequently drove works D-types to races and shows and he was reserve driver at Le Mans in 1955.

You had to drive it very smoothly and with great precision. Some drivers put the cars into lurid four-wheel drifts at every opportunity, but it wasn't the way to get the best out of a D-type. You had to drive it with great care, it wasn't a car that you could bully. The D-type was built for two races only, Le Mans and Reims, and the whole of the design of the car was aimed at those two races.

Driving at other circuits was taking it out of the environment for which it was designed. It had a very high straight-line speed, particularly in relation to the power output. It was also a very safe car to drive. It was entirely predictable, it never bit you back in extreme circumstances and it warned you what it was going to do before it did it.

The handling characteristics were interesting because the design was aimed at straight-line stability. When I drove a works long-nose car in practice at Le Mans in 1955, I was amazed that I could be doing 170mph (273kph) or so down the *Mulsanne Straight* and able to hold the steering wheel with the tips of my fingers; you got down in the cockpit, just sitting there in a pool of almost completely calm air, and the D-type ran absolutely straight, unaffected by crosswinds. You knew that you were getting near the maximum speed of the car because the nose would rise slightly, you didn't need to look at the speedo, you knew that you were doing 170mph and it would stay there in that attitude.

The D-type was basically a safe understeerer, but the understeer could be reduced by incorporating an anti-roll bar between the lower trailing links of the rear suspension. I adopted this modification on the car I drove for Jack Broadhead. I discovered the best way to set up the D-type was playing with the tyres. If I ran the tyres almost as slicks, I got a lot more grip than I would do even running them with a reasonable amount of tread. Without almost all the tread off, you got a bigger contact patch.

I also used to run at low tyre pressures, around 32–33lb psi, 35lb rear, but a lot of people used 35–40lb front and rear. My car's cornering speed was higher than that of the other D-types mainly because of those two factors, but tyres in this state were never very popular with scrutineers and frequently I had to call on the Dunlop technicians to

Bob Berry in the cockpit of Jack Broadhead's ex-works D-type at Silverstone in May 1955. Broadhead, in peaked cap, is standing behind the car. (T.C. March/FotoVantage)

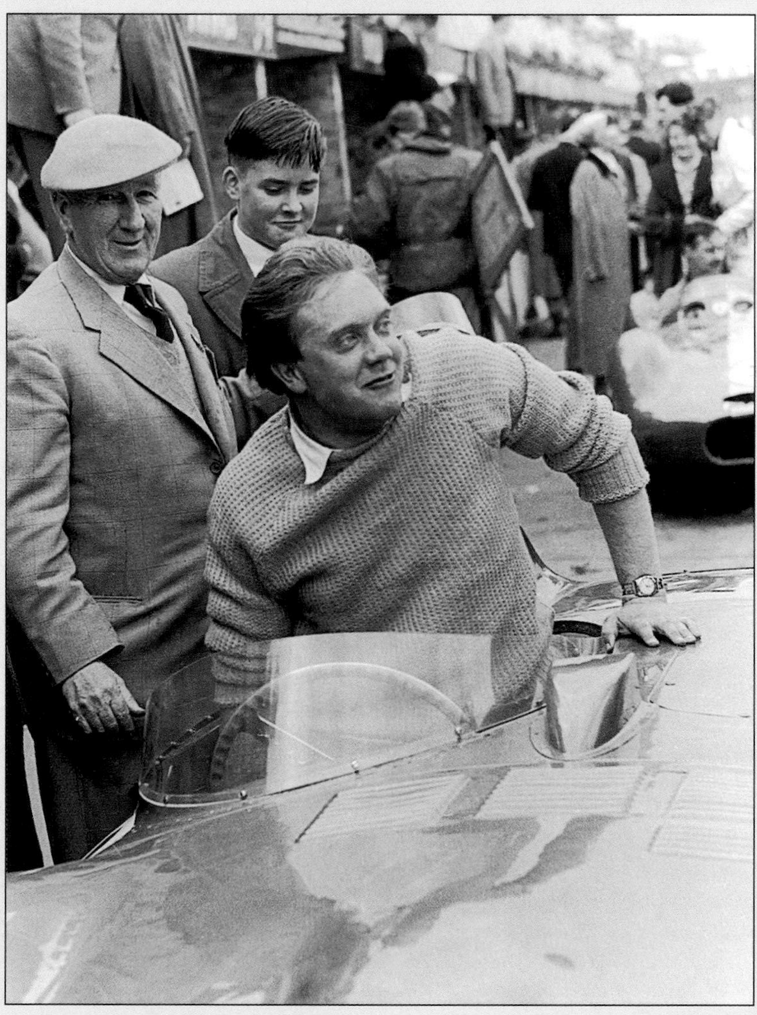

vouch for their safety.

The gearbox had synchromesh on all four gears and because of a tendency to drop out of gear on the over-run at high speeds, Jaguar introduced an interlock and I had this on my car. This was linked to the clutch and as you dipped the clutch, it freed the gear-lever. It was a very basic device. It was a fast gearbox and it might have been crude, but it was robust and totally reliable. When you selected the next gear, you could feel when it engaged.

The disc brakes were superb and you could use them to kill what was left of the understeer. You had always to take a slightly wide line into a corner with a D-type and the technique was to go into a corner slightly more quickly than you would envisage, but trailing the brakes slightly; that would unstick the rear wheels – you could feel the back end go light – and the moment the rear wheels came unstuck, you could then use the throttle to hold it right the way through the corner – it took a lot of practice to do that, but it was very effective.

The brakes were fantastic; there were two systems. The production system was a powered front brake set-up with a 'normal' brake pressure rear system. The works cars had a full power system with a pump driven off the back of the gearbox – by moving the pedal you opened the valves. The brake pedal was so very light that on a bumpy road the brake pressure could change because your foot was being moved by the vibration of the car.

This was later modified so that you had to press the pedal more firmly to get the valves open. I preferred it in its original state, it was almost feather-light, and on a wet road it was fantastic, you almost could just waggle your toes and change the braking effect. You could rely on these brakes time after time after time and I don't recall a single occasion when I felt that they weren't going to do the job. Confidence became total.

The D-type was so very well engineered, there were no excessive vibrations, no huge amount of noise, it was screwed together properly and it all worked as a unit. It was rock solid, you got into it and knew that you were as safe as you could be.

May, but it proved another debacle. Titterington tried to pass Salvadori (DB3S) for the lead on the inside of Club Corner on the first lap and triggered off a multi-car crash. Hawthorn retired because of steering problems and Jack Fairman's car broke a drive-shaft.

For some illogical reason Jaguar decided to compete in the Nürburgring 1,000Km race, an event for which the D-types were totally unsuitable. In practice Paul Frère crashed very heavily with the car that he was to drive with Duncan Hamilton, so a replacement had to be driven out from Coventry. This lasted only six laps in the race before the gearbox broke. Hawthorn/Titterington (still with the fuel injection car) went well and at one stage were in fourth place, but the stewards who were still harbouring grudges about the 1955 Le Mans race, black-flagged Hawthorn for overtaking slow-moving Porsche entries on the wrong side.

Another pit stop was necessary to knock out the bodywork after Hawthorn collided with one of these mobile chicanes, the car developed a fuel leak and a drive-shaft broke on the last lap. Not for the first time Jaguar suffered from the folly of no transporter and three undriveable cars. Jaguar's racing department was small, but it appears that the notion of having a transporter simply never occurred to the team.

In the poorly supported Reims 12 Hours race, Hamilton/Bueb, Hawthorn/Frère (with the fuel injection car) and Titterington/Fairman took the first three places, with the production *Écurie Ecosse* D-type driven by Flockhart/Sanderson fourth. After the race team manager 'Lofty' England sacked Hamilton for ignoring instructions to 'maintain position' by overtaking the Hawthorn/Frère car and breaking the lap record.

Following the 1955 disaster, modifications to the circuit necessitated postponement of the 1956 Le Mans race until the end of July. The 1956 race had its own special regulations and the D-types were accepted as production cars. Modifications included a proper two-seater cockpit, a full-width windscreen and a flexible, clear plastic Vybak tonneau running from the top of the windscreen to the tail decking. Jaguar entered cars for Hawthorn/Bueb (fuel injection), Frère/Titterington and Fairman/Wharton. The track was very slippery following a rain shower and on the second lap Frère spun in the *Esses*, Fairman spun in trying to avoid him and, in modern parlance, was T-boned by de Portago's Ferrari.

Hawthorn had been leading, but was soon in and out of the pits because of a misfiring engine. Eventually, chief engineer 'Bill' Heynes said, "We've changed everything, that leaves only the injection pipes, so we'll change those." One of the pipes was discovered to have an invisible hairline crack. Hawthorn rejoined the race 26 laps in arrears, back in 42nd place, and he and Bueb had an exhilarating drive through the field to finish sixth, about 170 miles behind the winner. The winner, fortunately for Jaguar, was the *Écurie Ecosse* D-type of Sanderson/Flockhart.

Le Mans in 1956 was the last works entry by the original Jaguar team, for the company announced their withdrawal from racing at the end of the year. Although the racing department occupied a small part of the service area, the design and development work was carried out in the experimental department, which was devoting more and more time to competition cars at the expense of development of new production models. Private owners, notably *Écurie Ecosse*, Briggs Cunningham and Duncan Hamilton raced ex-works cars and there were 42 production cars, many raced by private owners.

In 1957 Hawthorn/Bueb drove a works-loaned Cunningham-entered car with the new 3,781cc (87×106mm) engine at Sebring, but were delayed and finished third. That year's Le Mans race provided Jaguar's fifth Le Mans win and the greatest racing success in the company's history. Bueb/Flockhart and Lawrence/Sanderson with *Écurie Ecosse*-entered ex-works long-nose cars took the first two places, Lucas/Brussin (*Los Amigos*) and Frère/Rousselle (*Équipe Nationale Belge*) were third and fourth with production cars, while Hamilton/Gregory, delayed by electrical and exhaust problems, finished sixth. The introduction of a 3,000cc capacity limit for Sports Car Championship events in 1958 brought an end to the D-type's serious successes, for the 3-litre version of the XK engine proved unreliable. The one occasion when the engine did not fail was in the Duncan Hamilton/Ivor Bueb entry in 1958. With less than six hours to the finish and firmly ensconced in second place, Hamilton crashed heavily while avoiding a small French car that had stopped in the middle of the track during a rainstorm.

In late 1956 Jaguar had introduced the XK SS, a D-type for the road, by converting unsold D-types, but they were planning to build more cars when the disastrous fire at the Browns Lane, Coventry factory destroyed not only 16 completed and semi-completed cars, but also the jigs and tooling. At Le Mans in 1960 Briggs Cunningham entered Jaguar E2A, a works prototype with new aluminium-alloy monocoque, independent rear suspension and 2,996cc (85×88mm) petrol-injected engine giving 295bhp. It did not run well and retired because of piston failure. E2A was a link in the evolution of D-type to E-type and the brilliant E-type appeared in March 1961 at Geneva.

Jaguar's most successful year at Le Mans was in 1957 after the works team had withdrawn from racing. Ivor Bueb (seen here) and Ron Flockhart won with this ex-works car entered by Écurie Ecosse and other D-types finished second, third, fourth and sixth. (LAT)

Ferrari *Monza*

1954–56

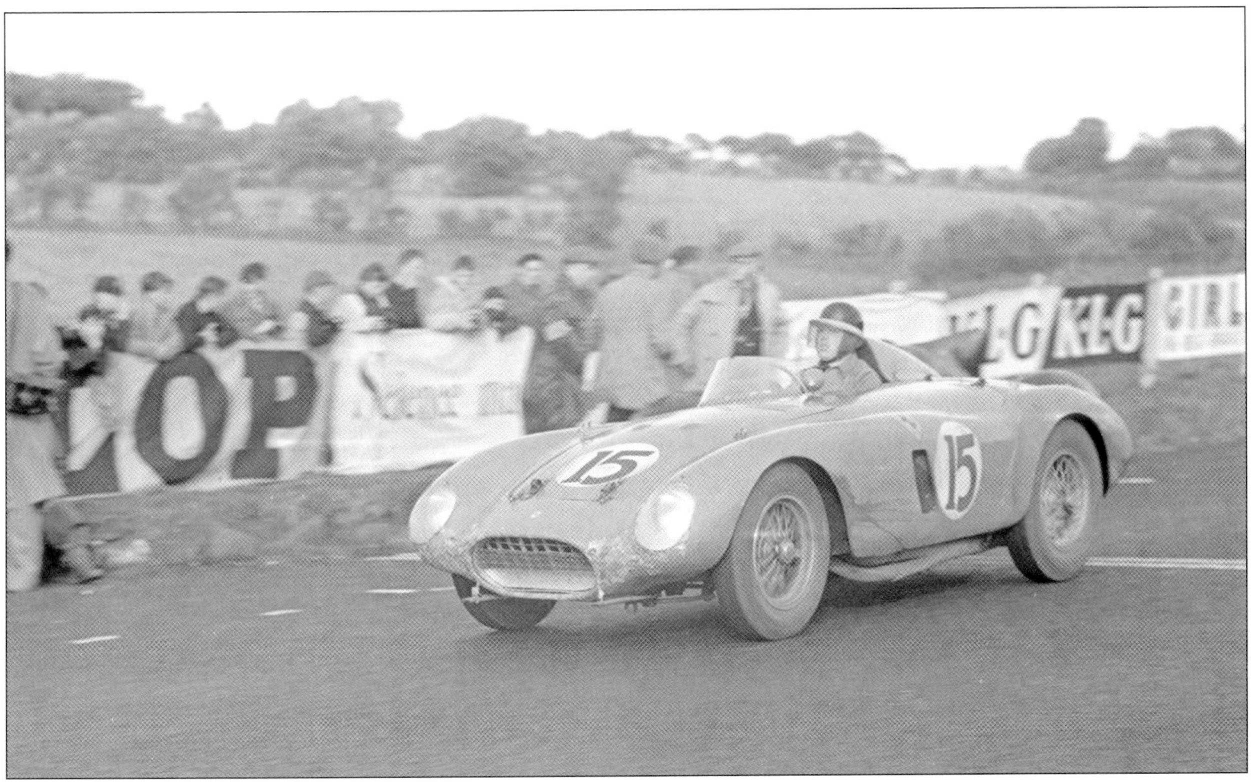

Mike Hawthorn co-drove this Tipo 750 Monza with Maurice Trintignant in the 1954 Tourist Trophy. They finished second on handicap and first on scratch. Note the gravel-battered nose. Although these cars had difficult, near-lethal handling, they were highly successful and popular with private owners. Ferrari built 33 of them. (LAT)

During the period, 1952–56, Ferrari successes, and failures, were closely linked to the brilliant four-cylinder designs of Aurelio Lampredi. Initially he designed the Tipo 500 Formula 2 car of 1,985cc (90×78mm) and the Tipo 625 of 2,498cc (90×94mm) with a view to use in the proposed 2,500cc Grand Prix formula of 1954 onwards. Lampredi was particularly anxious to ensure a satisfactory compression seal, so he used a one-piece alloy block, with no cylinder head as such, but with cylinder barrels that screwed into the block casting. A train of gears from the nose of the crankshaft drove the twin overhead camshafts.

In accordance with Ferrari's usual practice the short crankshaft was machined from a steel billet and it ran in five aluminium-bronze Vandervell Thin Wall bearings. There were twin plugs per cylinder fired by two Marelli magnetos and two twin-choke Weber carburettors. Transmission was by a multi-plate clutch and a four-speed gearbox in unit with the final drive. Ferrari raced both the Tipo 500 and the Tipo 625 in late 1951 and with the Tipo 500 the team – and more particularly Alberto Ascari – dominated World Championship races held to Formula 2 rules in 1952–53.

Throughout 1952 Ferrari tested four-cylinder sports cars, but these were not raced until the Coppa Inter-Europa at Monza on 28 June 1953. At least two cars were built combining the existing Tipo 166 *MM* chassis (see Chapter 14) with the Tipo 625 engine and Vignale bodywork. In 1953 sports form the 2,498cc engine had two twin-choke Weber 40DCO carburettors and developed 225bhp at 6,800rpm. The first 2,942cc (102×90mm) cars had a four-speed gearbox in unit with the engine and a rigid rear axle. Lampredi sketched out the body for the 3-litre car, known as the 735 *Sport*, and had it built by the Autodromo concern

John Bolster tries a 750S Ferrari (*Autosport,* 13 January 1956)

I set off in the darkness and the rain on a single operative headlamp. As is usual with racing clutches, this one is of the in-or-out type, and the 'extreme' valve timing causes the engine to hunt and misfire below 2,000rpm. It is thus not particularly easy to move off smoothly, but the drama follows as the revs rise and the motor suddenly hits on all four. Then wheelspin occurs with the peculiar abruptness that is typical of the ZF differential. The same thing is apt to happen again after the change into second gear. Of course, one gets used to all this, but it certainly added excitement to that first ride through the night.

Even if one were content to put up with such inflexibility, plus the plug-changing business, there is another characteristic of the 750S that renders it virtually undriveable on the public road: it makes more noise than the average Grand Prix car! I admit that I have used it for a few selected journeys, and if one can cruise continuously at a fairly high speed, the noise is almost within reason . . .

Although Mackay Fraser's car has a new engine, the chassis and transmission are of a slightly earlier type. Thus, the gearbox has four speeds, instead of five, and there are some detail differences in the suspension. I have only driven the car with a fairly 'low' final drive ratio, such as one would use for British circuits. Thus equipped, the four-speed box meets all requirements . . . The gearbox is carried very low in the chassis, and has no synchronising mechanism, the change being by a short, central remote control lever . . .

The two-seater body by Pinin Farina gives a superb driving position and excellent visibility, allied with surprisingly good protection. Provided that soft plugs are employed, the engine starts immediately from cold. Once it is warm, the racing plugs may be fitted, after which the unit must not be allowed to idle.

The engine develops 260bhp at around 6,000rpm and the weight is a fraction under 15cwt (762kg). It is a short, compact car, the wheelbase and track being only 7ft 4½-in (2,250mm) and 4ft 2½-in (1,390mm) respectively.

Although the engine is so lumpy at the bottom end, once it has taken hold, it has an exceptionally wide effective revolution range. Its punch when accelerating from medium speeds is quite a new experience, and it is this phenomenal acceleration that has earned this model many of its victories. The gear-change is excellent, the ultra-close ratios being easy to select as fast as the hand can move. The de Dion axle, reinforced by the limited-slip differential, gives remarkable freedom from wheelspin when accelerating away strongly from corners.

The general handling characteristic is an understeering one, but this can at once be converted to oversteer by a slight increase of pressure on the accelerator pedal. Nevertheless, if too much power is applied, it is not easy to retain full control. The suspension, particularly at the rear, is surprisingly hard, and the rear wheels sometimes tend to lose adhesion over bumps . . . With a suitable final drive fitted, I would expect to exceed 160mph (257kph) ... Suffice it to say that even among supercharged racing cars, I have never felt such a sensation of sheer power as when I gave the 'big four' full throttle. On a road circuit, where there is no restriction on noise, this is a most delectable car to drive.

Although it is not smooth, the engine has an effortless feel about it that has always been a feature of big four-cylinder units. Above all, there is that certainty of always having a bit more power under your foot, in fact the car seems to accelerate just a violently on top gear as it does on the lower ratios.

The 750S is not the perfect sports car; indeed I am doubtful whether these competition machines are really sports cars at all. Nevertheless, it is one of the most exciting cars that I have ever driven.

John Bolster at the wheel of Herbert Mackay Fraser's Tipo 735 Ferrari during testing at the end of 1955. He collected the car after the race meeting at Brands Hatch on Boxing Day and the left-hand headlamp had been smashed in a collision during the Ferrari's race.

in Modena (which survives as a builder of bus bodies).

Umberto Maglioli first drove the 3-litre car at Senigallia, but a con-rod broke. Two 3-litre cars then appeared at the 3,000cc Monza Sports Car Grand Prix in June 1953. Ascari drove the Autodromo-bodied car, but the engine broke in practice and so the 3-litre unit was transferred from Hawthorn's car. In the race, decided on the aggregate of two 137-mile (220km) heats, Ascari collided with a woman driver who cut across his line and Hawthorn, with a 2.5-litre engine, finished fourth. Ferrari then entered two 2.5-litre cars in the first Nürburgring 1,000Km race on 30 August. On hearing of the speed of the 3.3-litre Lancias from team manager Ugolini, Ferrari ordered them to be withdrawn.

The two Vignale-bodied cars were sold to South American owners who raced them successfully with 3-litre engines. Work had also been proceeding on a 2-litre sports-racing Ferrari that became known as the *Mondial* and this first appeared in the Casablanca 12 Hour race in December 1953 when Ascari/Villoresi drove it into second place overall. Ferrari built the *Mondial* and developments of it in small numbers through to late 1957.

The factory had been developing the Tipo 750 *Monza,* which was to become the definitive 3-litre sports-racing car. This had a 2,999.6cc (103×90mm) engine based on that of the 1954 short-stroke Tipo 553 *Squalo* Formula 1 car. With two Weber twin-choke 50DCOA/3 carburettors, the power output was 260bhp at 6,400rpm. Scaglietti, who was increasingly becoming a Ferrari favourite, built the body.

Ferrari entered two of these cars in the 1,000km (621-mile) *Supercortemaggiore* Grand Prix, sponsored by the fuel company of that name, at Monza in June 1954 with a 3,000cc capacity limit. During practice veteran driver Giuseppe Farina crashed heavily with the car that he was to share with Maglioli. Ferrari substituted a 2,942cc Tipo 735 *Sport* with de Dion rear axle and Pinin Farina body and Mike Hawthorn took his place. Hawthorn/Maglioli won at 100.63mph (161.91kph) from Gonzalez/Trintignant with a *Monza* that had Scaglietti bodywork of the style that was to become standard.

In early August Luigi Piotti drove the Farina-bodied 735 *Sport* to a win in the short Reggia Calabria race. Soon afterwards Ferrari sold this car in South America and it was bought by 28-year-old Herbert McKay-Fraser, who was born in Connecticut and was the son of the owner of a Brazilian coffee plantation owner. In 1955 McKay-Fraser brought the 735 *Sport* to Europe to race and when he blew up the engine, he had a 2,999.6cc *Monza* engine fitted. After he raced the car at the Brands Hatch Boxing Day meeting in 1955, he loaned it to John Bolster of *Autosport* whose impressions were published in the issue of 13 January 1956 (see sidebar).

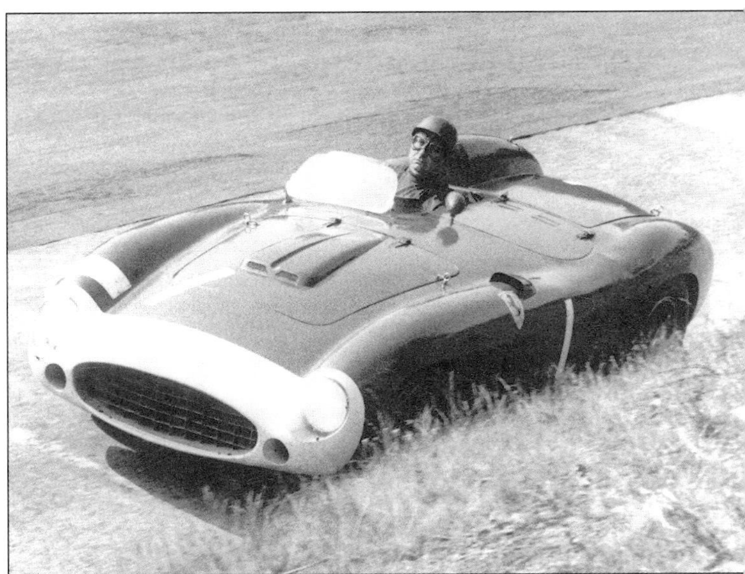

In the 1956 Nürburgring 1,000Km race Fangio, partnered by Castellotti, drove this 3.4-litre Tipo 860 Monza into second place behind Moss/Behra (Maserati 300S).

Maglioli/Manzon drove a *Monza* in the Reims 12 Hours race. It was well up with the works Jaguars in the early stages, but retired because of a broken gearbox. The works entered two *Monzas* in the Tourist Trophy in September. Gonzalez crashed heavily during the first practice session and suffered spinal injuries, while Maglioli learned that his mother had died and returned home. Trintignant teamed up with Hawthorn and they finished second on handicap and first on scratch. De Portago and Bracco drove *Monzas* in the Carrera Panamericana Mexico road race in November, but they both retired.

The last of the first batch of 2-litre *Mondials* delivered in late 1954 had new bodywork by Scaglietti and this style was adopted for both *Monzas* and *Mondials* in 1955. It had a more vertical air intake, reshaped nose and the bodywork on the left side cut away to clear the exhaust pipes. Later *Monzas* also had coil spring front suspension. By 1955 Ferrari was delivering *Monzas* in considerable numbers to amateur drivers in both Europe and the United States and well over 20 were built.

During 1955 the works Ferrari team used six-cylinder cars, Lampredi's last throw at Maranello, and these amounted to little more than the four-cylinder engine with two cylinders added and mounted in a slightly modified *Monza* chassis. These cars were built in Tipo 118 *Le Mans* 3,747.6cc (94×90mm) and Tipo 121 *Le*

Mans 4,412.5cc (102×90mm) forms. They were very fast, very unreliable and, certainly, underdeveloped.

Their best performances were Taruffi's win in the Tour of Sicily and third places by Maglioli in the Mille Miglia and by Castellotti in the short, non-Championship Swedish Grand Prix. Once the Lancia D50 grand prix cars had passed to Ferrari, he dispensed with Lampredi's services and this talented engineer went to Fiat where he carried out significant work on production twin overhead camshaft engines.

In the meanwhile private owners were running *Monzas* successfully in less important events, despite their inherently lethal handling. One of the best performances was in the 1955 Sebring 12 Hours race in which Phil Hill/Carroll Shelby with a *Monza* entered by Allen Guiberson contested a disputed victory with Mike Hawthorn/Phil Walters at the wheel of a works-prepared, Briggs Cunningham-entered Jaguar D-type. After protests, it was decided that the Jaguar had won by less than a lap.

The works entered *Monzas* in the 1,000km (621-mile) *Supercortemaggiore* Grand Prix, a race limited to 3,000cc cars at the Monza circuit on 29 May. Alberto Ascari, the 1952–53 World Champion, had barely recovered from his ducking the previous weekend when his Lancia D50 locked a brake and plunged into Monte Carlo harbour. In practice he took out a *Monza*, lost control at the *Lesmo* Curves, the car rolled and he was killed. Unsuitable tyres caused the crash. It was a terrible blow, especially in Italy where he was a national hero, and even British newspaper sellers had posters reading 'ASCARI KILLED'. Hawthorn/Maglioli finished second to Behra/Musso (works Maserati 300S).

After Enzo Ferrari decided that the six-cylinder cars should be abandoned, the team was left with nothing competitive to race in the last rounds of the 1955 World Sports Car Championship. A design team headed by ex-Lancia engineer Andrea Fraschetti had started work on a new V12 car, but this would not be ready until 1956. So Ferrari resurrected a larger-capacity version of the *Monza* that had previously been under consideration. Typed the 860, it had a 3,431.93cc (102×105mm) engine, lengthened in stroke, but with the original bore. With two Weber twin-choke 58DCOA/3 carburettors the power output was 280bhp at 6,000rpm.

Castellotti/Taruffi drove the new car in the Tourist Trophy in September, but it was neither fast enough nor handled well enough to be competitive. They finished sixth, while a standard works-entered *Monza* driven by Maglioli/Trintignant was eighth. A year previously, a *Monza* had dominated the scratch division of this race, but now the opposition had become very much stronger.

Ferrari built production four-cylinder sports-racing cars in two sizes, the 3-litre Monza and the 2-litre Mondial. Engine dimensions apart, there were few substantial differences between the two models. This is the 2-litre Mondial seen in the form in which it was raced in 1954. (LAT)

The last round of the Championship was the 581-mile (935km) Targa Florio held in October. Ferrari entered an 860 *Monza* for Castellotti/Manzon and a standard *Monza* for Maglioli partnered by test driver Sergio Sighinolfi. The 3-litre car lost a wheel, but Castelloti and Manzon put up a fierce challenge to the three Mercedes-Benz 300SLRs. They were in second place behind the very battered 300SLR of Moss/Collins, but had to stop for a wheel-change and dropped back to finish third. If they had been able to hold on to second place, Ferrari would have won that year's Championship. The final results were Mercedes-Benz 24 points, Ferrari, 22 points.

In 1956 Ferrari raced the Tipo 860 in improved form developing 310 bhp at 6,200rpm and the new single-cam per bank V12 Tipo 290*MM* 3,490cc car. They had similar Scaglietti bodies and with the bonnet shut the only way to identify them was that the 860 had two long bonnet-top blisters to clear the cam covers (these were subsequently opened up at the front to form scoops), while there was a single scoop on the bonnet of the 290*MM*. Both types performed well in 1956 and although the V12s were faster on some cir-

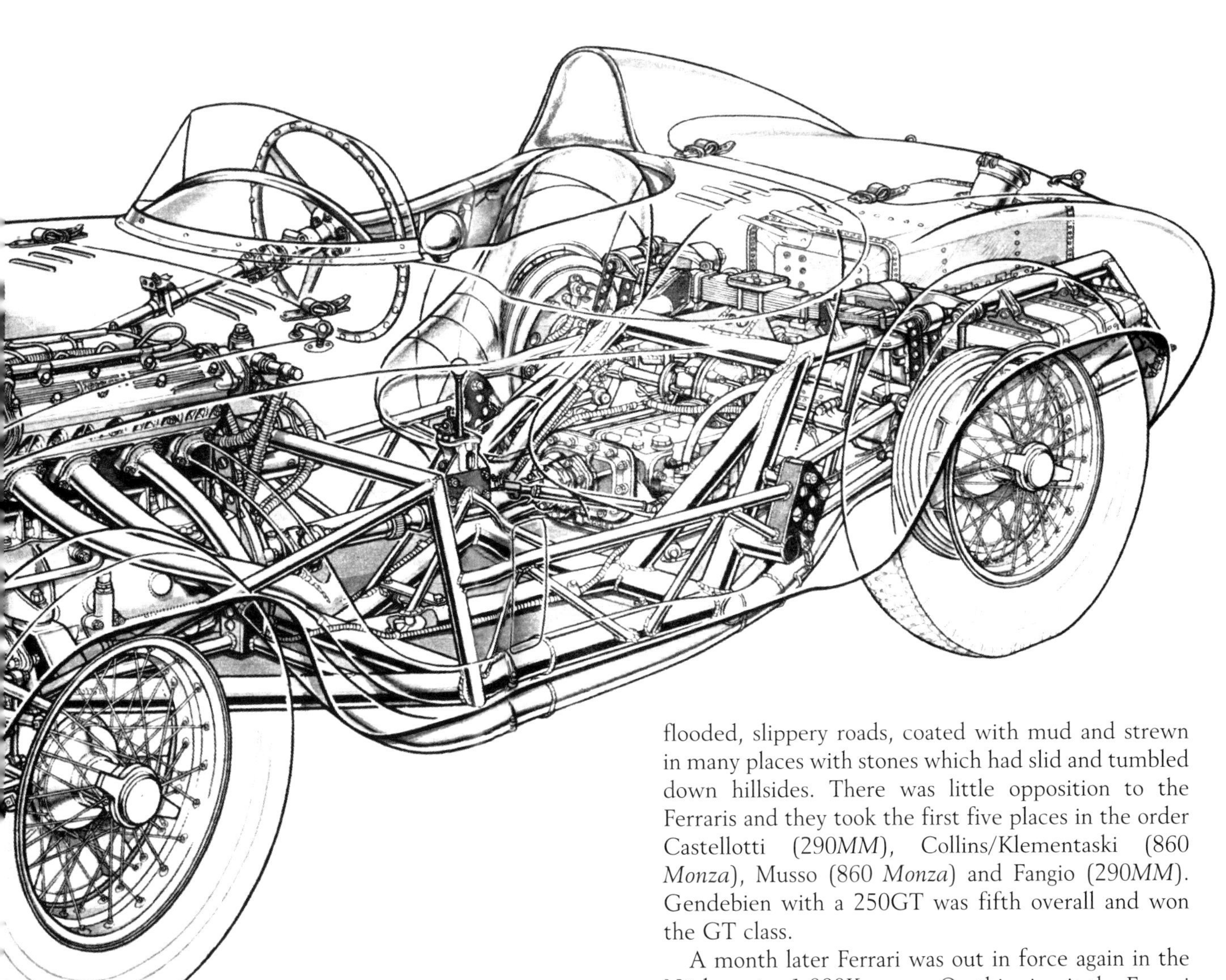

cuits, there was little to choose between the performances of the two types.

The Ferrari entries in the first round of the 1956 World Sports Car Championship, the Buenos Aires 1,000Km race in January consisted of two 4.9-litre cars, together with a Tipo 860. Both the larger Ferraris retired, but Olivier Gendebien/Phil Hill brought the *Monza* across the line in second place behind the Maserati 300S of Moss/Menditeguy. At Sebring on 25 March the Tipo 860s performed magnificently in the hands of Fangio/Castellotti and Musso/Schell and they took the first two places.

Back in Europe Peter Collins, partnered by photographer Louis Klementaski, won the 671-mile (1,000km) Tour of Sicily in April with an older 1955-type 860. Taruffi finished second with a Maserati 300S. The Mille Miglia at the end of April was run for much of its distance in torrential rain and high winds and on flooded, slippery roads, coated with mud and strewn in many places with stones which had slid and tumbled down hillsides. There was little opposition to the Ferraris and they took the first five places in the order Castellotti (290*MM*), Collins/Klementaski (860 *Monza*), Musso (860 *Monza*) and Fangio (290*MM*). Gendebien with a 250GT was fifth overall and won the GT class.

A month later Ferrari was out in force again in the Nürburgring 1,000Km race. On this circuit the Ferrari drivers could not match the pace of the fastest of their opponents in the Maserati team; Moss/Behra won with the 300S that they had taken over from Taruffi/Schell, Fangio/Castellotti with an 860 finished second and in third place came de Portago/Gendebien with a 290*MM*. Maranello sent only a single 860 *Monza* to the Targa Florio for Castellotti, but it retired early in the race when the rear axle broke. Maglioli won the race with a works 1,500cc Porsche.

The final round of the Championship in 1956 was the 621-mile (1,000km) Swedish Grand Prix at Kristianstâd in August. Despite a strong challenge from Maserati, Trintignant/Phil Hill won with a 290*MM* (just to confuse matters, it had a twin-blister *Monza* bonnet), Collins/von Trips took second place with a Tipo 860 and Hawthorn/Duncan Hamilton/de Portago shared the third-place 290*MM*. This was the last occasion on which the works raced the 'big fours' and Ferrari used only V12 cars in 1957. Private owners in both Europe and the United States continued to race 3-litre *Monzas* with success in relatively minor races.

Osca 1,100 and 1,500cc
1954–59

At Le Mans in 1957 this 750cc OSCA (left) was driven by Laroche/ Radix and although it finished in 19th place, it was over 200 miles behind the class and Index of Performance-winning 750cc Lotus. Mike Hawthorn with a 4,023cc Ferrari is lapping the OSCA. (LAT)

On 1 January 1937 Adolfo Orsi bought Maserati from the surviving brothers and they remained with the company that their brother Alfieri had founded on a ten-year contract. At its expiry Bindo, Ernesto and Ettore founded their own company in their hometown of Bologna, Officina Specializzata per la Costruzione de Automobili-Fratelli Maserati SpA (OSCA). Ernesto was the development engineer, just as he had been at the old company, Ettore was tooling-up engineer and Bindo was the plant manager.

Over the next 11 years they built successful sports-racing cars, following the general design principles of their former employees at Modena, but, in the main, without competing with them directly. They also built relatively unsuccessful single-seaters, a V12 4½-litre Formula 1 car in 1951 and a six-cylinder 2-litre Formula 2 car in 1952–53.

The first OSCA was the MT4 1100 with the company's own four-cylinder, single overhead camshaft 1,093cc (70×71mm) engine. This had a cast-iron cylinder block, aluminium-alloy cylinder head, hemispherical combustion chambers, two inclined valves per cylinder and Maserati-style 'finger' cam followers. With two Weber carburettors, the claimed power output was 72bhp at 6,000rpm. They installed this engine, together with a single-plate clutch and four-speed Fiat gearbox with synchromesh on third and top ratios, in a simple tubular chassis with cruciform bracing.

Front suspension was by coil springs and unequal-length wishbones and at the rear, an underslung rigid axle was suspended on quarter-elliptic springs and located by radius arms. Like all early OSCAS, it had a distinct oval air intake and early cars had cycle wings. The wheelbase was 7ft 6.5in (2,300mm), front track 3ft 11.25in (1,200mm) and rear track 3ft 9.25in (1,150mm). In 1949 the MT4 1350 with 1,343cc (75×76mm) engine was introduced.

In the right hands, these cars performed well, but the Maseratis were not achieving the level of sales or success that they had hoped for. By 1950 Ernesto had developed a gear and chain-driven twin overhead camshaft cylinder head, which was installed in both models, and these usually had slab-sided fuel-width bodies. In this form the cars were typed MT4 2AD (*due albi di distribuzione*). The 1,350cc model was available until only 1953, but the 1,100cc version, with modifications, lasted until 1956. Fagioli finished eighth overall in the 1951 Mille Miglia and headed OSCA's first three places in the 1,100cc class. Giulio Cabianca won the 1,100cc class in six Italian races in 1951.

Stirling Moss and Bill Lloyd drove this 1,453cc, brakeless OSCA to a surprise win in the 1954 Sebring 12 Hours. Here, a cautious Lloyd laps a Jaguar XK120. (LAT)

OSCA introduced the MT2 2AD 1450 in 1953. This had a larger-capacity, 1,453cc (76×78mm) alloy-block engine and with two Weber twin-choke 36DC03 carburettors, the power output was around 110bhp at 6,200rpm. The body was a much neater and more stylish, full-width-bodied two-seater. Stirling Moss, partnered by Briggs Cunningham's brother-in-law, Bill Lloyd, drove a Cunningham-entered 1450 to a surprise win in the 1954 Sebring 12 Hours race after the retirement of most of the faster opposition.

Moss wrote (*My Cars, My Career*), "[The] OSCA was quite amazing ... You could drive it as hard as you liked, slinging it sideways was no trouble, and that was a good thing because as the race progressed we found it had little or no brakes and we had to put into a slide to slow it down. Typical Italian, it was designed to go, not stop." In the Mille Miglia Cabianca drove one of these cars to tenth overall, second in class to the new Porsche 550 *Spyder*.

In May 1954 OSCA produced a full 1,491cc (78×78mm) model, the MT2 AD 1500, developing 120bhp at 6,300rpm. Maximum speed was around 120mph (194kph). OSCA also introduced the Tipo 2000S, a sports car powered by the six-cylinder, twin overhead camshaft, 1,987cc (76×73mm) Formula 2 engine, but only a couple were built. The business was expanding and profitable, even though OSCA only built about 20 competition cars a year. They never employed more than 50 staff, among them, at one time, a young lady mechanic. In late 1954 OSCA moved to new and more spacious premises in San Lazzaro di Savena, eight kilometres from central Bologna.

The following year OSCA introduced a twin-plug 1,500cc car, typed the TN-1500 (*Tipo Nuovo*). In 1955 OSCAs took the first three places in the 1,100cc sports class of the Mille Miglia and a 1,500cc class second. By 1956 Ernesto was 60, but still keen on introducing new developments. That year OSCA added the Tipo 187, 749cc (62×62mm) model to the range and the body was much lower and sleeker. Capelli drove one of these cars to a class win in the 1956 Mille Miglia and Cabianca won the 1,500cc sports class. At Le Mans the 750cc car was eliminated in an accident.

At the Rome Grand Prix in October Grand Prix drivers Musso and Castellotti drove OSCAs in the one-hour, 1,500cc race. The opposition included the latest 1,460cc Lotus Elevens driven by Allison and Flockhart and Salvadori with a works Cooper. These retired and

Musso won from Naylor (Lotus-Maserati) and Cabianca with another OSCA. Another new model in 1956 was the Tipo S-950, but this was only tested and not raced.

In 1942 Ernesto Maserati had prepared drawings of a desmodromic-valve engine (that is, mechanically operated valves without springs). Originally, only 1,500cc OSCAS had desmodromic valves and these were actuated by two cam lobes, opening and one closing. This valve-operation system and independent rear suspension were adopted for 1957 and the model was known, confusingly, as the Tipo S-273. Alessandro de Tomaso was now deeply involved in racing OSCAs, together with fiancée Isabelle Haskell, daughter of a United States newspaper magnate.

De Tomaso and Haskell co-drove a very low, slippery 1,500cc car with streamlined headrest and tailfin in the 1957 Buenos Aires 1,000Km race, finishing sixth overall and winning their class. By the Sebring race in March they were husband and wife and drove a 750cc OSCA, only to retire because of mechanical problems. In the last Mille Miglia OSCAs had a clean sweep in the 750cc and 1,100cc classes, taking first three places in both categories. Laroche/Radix drove a 750cc car at Le Mans, but finished a poor fourth in their class.

On the day of the French Grand Prix at Rouen there was a close battle in the 75-mile (120km) Coupe Delamere-Debouteville between de Tomaso with the desmodromic OSCA and Colin Chapman with a twin-cam Climax-powered Lotus. The OSCA was more powerful, but the Lotus was lighter and handled better. De Tomaso was no mean driver, but not in Chapman's class, and he won after Chapman made a pit stop to top up the radiator of his overheating engine. That the two cars were closely matched was obvious, but, unfortunately, the 'desmo' OSCA was only seen once in Britain.

The de Tomasos ran a 'desmo' in the Swedish Grand Prix in August, but retired. In the three-hour Belgian sports car Grand Prix at Spa-Francorchamps on 25 August de Tomaso led the 1,500cc class and set a class record of 115.37mph (185.66kph), but retired because of engine problems. Isabelle took third place in the class behind a Lotus and a Porsche. De Tomaso then drove the 'desmo' OSCA in the 1,500cc sports car race at Silverstone in September, but fell right back after being involved in a multi-car accident. He was pumping his wife's money into OSCA and the brothers saw him as a saviour. Without a works team, OSCA came to rely on the de Tomasos more and more.

In the Sebring 12 Hours race in March 1958, the de Tomasos finished eighth overall with a 750cc car, winning their class and the Index of Performance. Two 1,500cc OSCAs ran in the Targa Florio in May and

The MT4 OSCA had a jewel-like twin overhead camshaft engine and a simple, but sturdy twin-tubular chassis. (LAT)

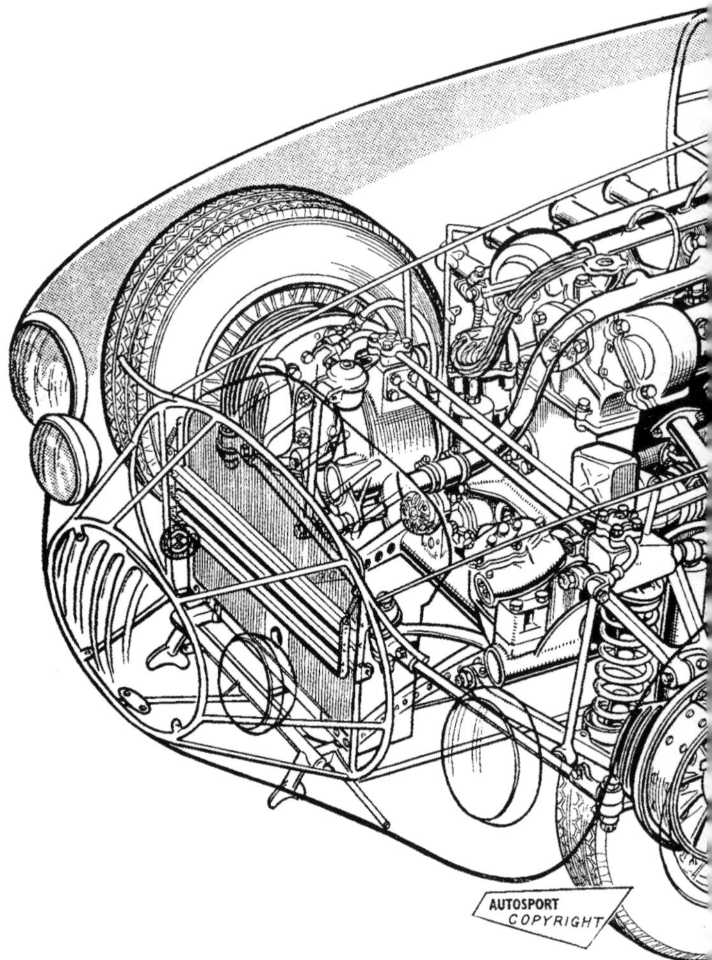

although each held third place at different times early in the race, Colins Davis/de Tomaso retired after two laps and Cabianca/Bordoni fell back to finish fifth, beaten in their class by the works Porsche of Behra/Scarlatti. A superb performance followed at Le Mans in June when de Tomaso/Davis with a 750cc car finished 11th overall at 87.659mph (141.043kph), won their class and the Index of Performance, trouncing the DB-Panhards.

Although de Tomaso had a new 1,100cc car with desmodromic valves for 1959, he gave up racing that year to start his own car construction business (using OSCA engines in some of his early cars). The Maserati brothers increasingly concentrated on the 750cc category and the 1959 car was claimed to develop 70bhp at 7,500rpm. Apart from a class win in the Targa Florio nothing much was achieved at an International level. Two cars ran at Le Mans, one driven by the Mexican Rodriguez brothers, but both retired. OSCA continued development of the desmodromic engines on a half-hearted basis, but the brothers were getting old and the fire had fled their bellies.

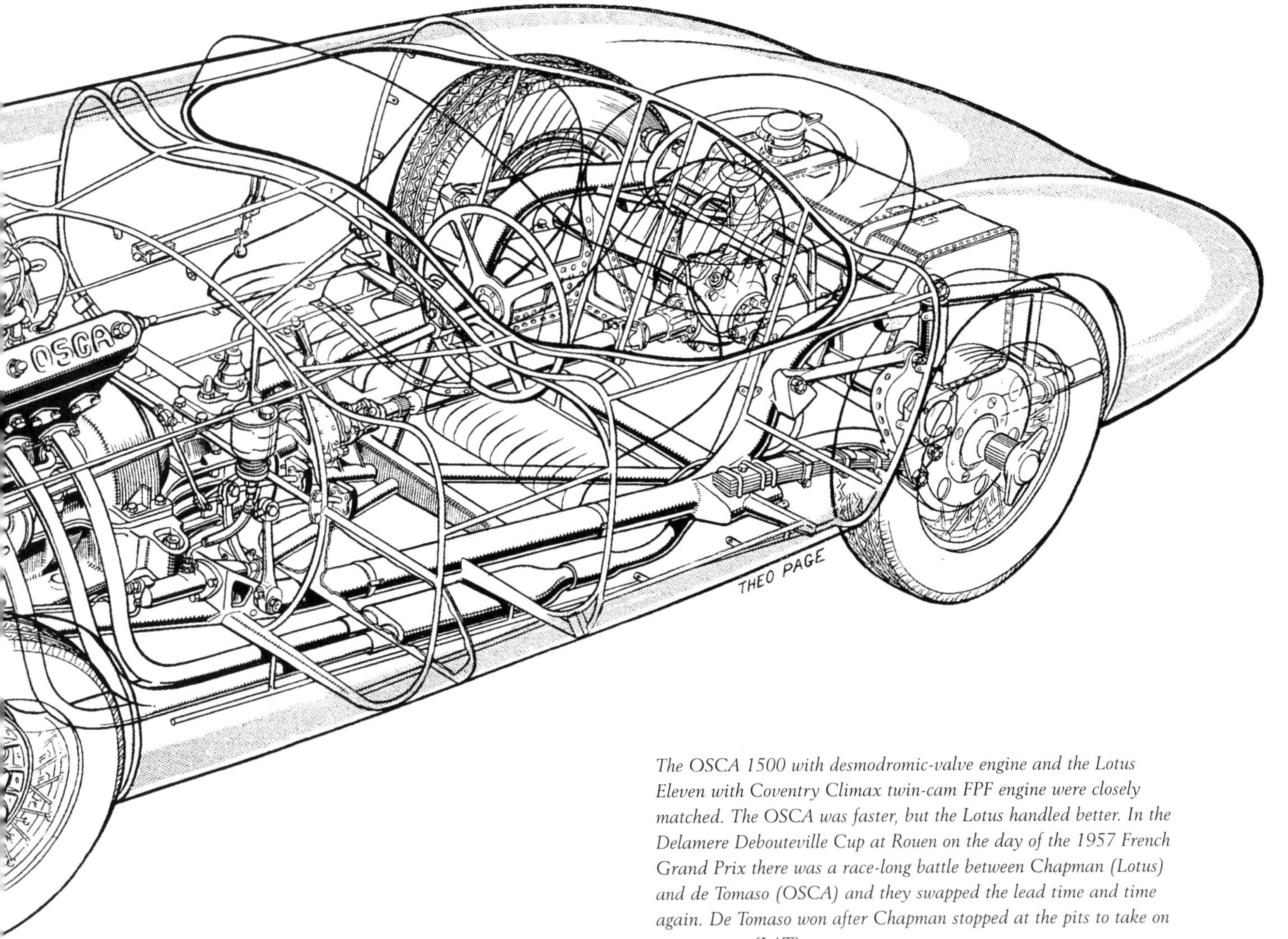

From 1959 Fiat offered their 1500S sporting car with Fiat-built, OSCA-designed twin-cam engine. OSCA also built 118 GT cars powered by this engine, with coachwork by Fissore, Touring and Zagato. During 1958–60 OSCA constructed relatively successful, front-engined, Fiat-powered Formula Junior cars. The Maserati brothers sold out to MV Agusta in 1963 and the last OSCA, the 1600GT, had a Ford V4 engine. The marque finally disappeared in 1966.

During the 1950s the OSCA was a jewel-like car with a beautifully built twin-cam engine and a superbly rugged, if somewhat basic chassis. They were delightful traditional sports cars of the very best kind, but their appeal was always, despite the very powerful desmodromic emgines of later years, to only a limited number of private owners.

The OSCA 1500 with desmodromic-valve engine and the Lotus Eleven with Coventry Climax twin-cam FPF engine were closely matched. The OSCA was faster, but the Lotus handled better. In the Delamere Debouteville Cup at Rouen on the day of the 1957 French Grand Prix there was a race-long battle between Chapman (Lotus) and de Tomaso (OSCA) and they swapped the lead time and time again. De Tomaso won after Chapman stopped at the pits to take on extra water. (LAT)

Mercedes-Benz 300SLR

1955

Early in the Le Mans race the ill-fated Pierre 'Levegh' leads Karl Kling, both drivers at the wheel of immaculately turned-out 300SLRs. (T.C. March/FotoVantage)

In 1954 the plans laid down in 1951–52 by Rudi Uhlenhaut, Director of the Mercedes-Benz research and development department, came to fruition. The Mercedes-Benz W196 Grand Prix car made its debut in the French Grand Prix at the beginning of July and Juan Fangio scored an easy win on the very fast Reims circuit. After a failure in the British Grand Prix at Silverstone a fortnight later, Fangio and the W196 won the German, Swiss and Italian Grands Prix.

Mercedes-Benz continued to race the W196 in 1955, now with Stirling Moss in the team alongside Fangio, and also entered sports car racing with the 300SLR (the company used this name to retain links with the 300SL, now in production, but the official name was W196S for the car and M196S for the engine). In 1955 the W196 won every race entered except one and, likewise, the 300SLRs won every race except one – and it is arguable that the team could have won that race.

In many respects the two models were identical, apart from two-seater Elketron alloy bodywork with left-hand drive on the 300SLR. The sports car's straight-eight engine had a capacity of 2,979cc (78×78mm) and it was inclined 30 degress to the right from the vertical. The advanced specification included Bosch high-pressure fuel injection, desmodromic valves operated by cams and rockers without springs, twin-plug ignition and dry-sump lubrication.

The Hirth built-up crankshaft ran in roller main and big end bearings. From the centre this provided the

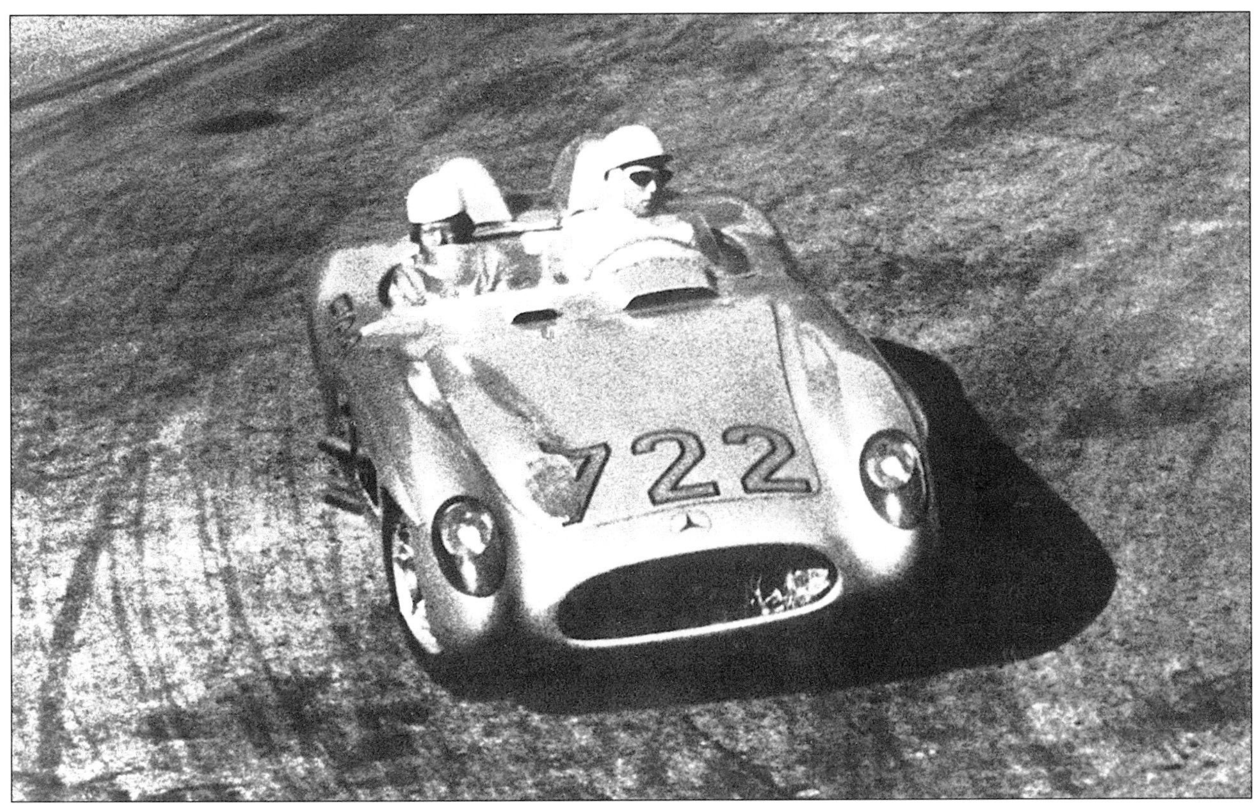

One of the greatest drives in Stirling Moss's career was his win partnered by Denis Jenkinson in the 1955 Mille Miglia. Here Jenkinson concentrates on his roll of route notes, while Moss swings the 300SLR through a well-travelled slippery bend.

drive for the twin overhead camshafts. The main difference from the W196 was that the Grand Prix car had welded cylinder jackets made from sheet steel, a traditional Mercedes feature, but the 300SLR had aluminium-alloy cylinder blocks with an integral fixed cylinder head. Power output was 300bhp at 7,500rpm.

Transmission was by a single-plate clutch, with a divided prop-shaft taking the power to the ZF five-speed gearbox with synchromesh on the upper ratios and in unit with the final drive that incorporated a limited slip differential. The multi-tubular space-frame chassis had independent suspension front and rear and massive inboard brakes. The front suspension was by double wishbones, longitudinal torsion bars and telescopic shock absorbers. At the rear there were low-pivot swing axles with a central pivot below the differential housing, a Watts linkage located the hubs fore and aft, and there were longitudinal torsion bars and telescopic shock absorbers.

The 300SLR had a 7ft 9½in (2,370mm) wheelbase, front track of 4ft 2⅓in (1,330mm) and rear track of 4ft 6⅓in (1,380mm). Dry weight was 1,830 pounds (830kg). According to the gearing, maximum speed was 174–180mph (280–290kph). Originally Mercedes-Benz planned to fit coupé bodywork, but used an open two-seater to suit the preferences of the drivers. When assessing the achievements of Mercedes-Benz in 1954–55, it must be remembered that their resources vastly exceeded those of other entrants. Over 200 people were employed in the racing department and the racing budget would have made many of today's Formula 1 teams green with envy.

For the 1955 sports car programme Mercedes-Benz built ten cars: two development and Mille Miglia practice cars, four regular team cars, two unraced coupés, plus an uncompleted car and a lightweight car for development work. Although 3-litre engines running on alcohol fuel powered the W196 cars that finished in first and second places in the Formule Libre Buenos Aires City Grand Prix in January 1955, the team did not race the 300SLRs until the Mille Miglia at the end of April.

In 1955 the Italian opposition was enormous in numbers, but weak in quality. The Italians' advantage was that their drivers knew the course intimately and so Mercedes provided the first two 300SLRs for their drivers to use to learn the circuit. Untertürkheim entered cars for Fangio, Stirling Moss partnered by Denis Jenkinson, Karl Kling and Hans Herrmann partnered by Mercedes mechanic Hermann Eger. Fangio was to be partnered by his former Alfa Romeo mechanic, Giulio Sala, but he found the wind buffeting with full-width windscreen caused neck pains and Fangio decided to drive solo.

Moss and Jenkinson devised a roller on which they entered route notes and Jenkinson unwound this as they raced and indicated to Moss the road ahead by hand signals. The full length of the roll was 15ft 6in (4,115mm). It played a critical roll in Moss's win, as he trusted Jenkinson absolutely and had the confidence to take blind brows flat out. Jenkinson's account of the race was published in *Motor Sport* for June 1955.

The race proved humiliating for the Italian teams. Moss won at the staggering record speed of 97.95mph (157.60kph) and was frequently attaining 170/175mph (274/282kph). Fangio took second place, delayed while a fuel injection pipe was changed. Karl Kling crashed heavily and Herrmann retired at about three-quarters' race distance because of a split fuel tank.

At the end of May Mercedes-Benz entered three 300SLRs in the 142-mile (228km) Eifelrennen, a minor sports car race at the Nürburgring to give German spectators the opportunity to see the 300SLRs in action. Fangio and Moss took the first two places, but Masten Gregory finished third with his private Ferrari *Monza*, ahead of Karl Kling.

Mercedes-Benz's main concern about the Le Mans race on 11–12 June was the speed and reliability of the D-type Jaguars, coupled with their Dunlop disc brakes that were vastly superior to the very sophisticated drum brakes of the 300SLR. For this race the team adopted an airbrake formed by a large flap that extended across the tail and incorporating the single head fairing. Mercedes had first tried this sort of device in 1952, but not persevered with it. The aim was to use it for braking at the end of the *Mulsanne Straight*. In addition it increased the adhesion of the rear tyres.

A lever on the scuttle operated the hydraulic rams that raised the airbrake and a linkage ensured that it was lowered automatically when second gear was selected at *Mulsanne Corner*. During practice Moss discovered that the airbrake could be used at most corners to reduce speed thereby saving the brakes, and he was faster through some corners with the airbrake in the halfway position. So the system was modified so that the drivers could raise or lower the airbrake at will. Another device consisted of four plungers on the scuttle that could be pushed if a brake was grabbing and this squirted oil into the brake drum, rendering it inoperative.

The reasoning was that an inoperative brake was safer than a grabbing brake. In fact the drivers did not need to use this device during the race. The driver pairings were Fangio/Moss, Kling/Simon (Hans Herrmann had injured himself in a practice crash at Monaco) and Pierre 'Levegh'/John Fitch. 'Levegh' was included in the team as a misguided appreciation of respect for his drive in the 1952 Le Mans race and team manager Alfred Neubauer had been very impressed by Fitch's driving in the 1952 Mexican road race.

Castellotti led at the end of the first hour with his 4.4-litre Ferrari, but then Hawthorn (works Jaguar D-type) and Fangio forged ahead, battling furiously, and at the end of the second hour Hawthorn headed the Argentinian by four-fifths of a second. Just before 6.30pm, two-and-a-half hours after the start Hawthorn, who had slightly extended his lead, pulled into the pits to refuel. Hawthorn had pulled across the front of the much slower Austin-Healey 100S driven by Macklin; Macklin pulled his car to the left, 'Levegh', who had just been lapped for the second time by Hawthorn and was about to be lapped again by Fangio, collided with the Austin-Healey and went over its tail.

The sixth-place 300SLR then veered into a concrete upright at the side of a tunnel entrance and the engine and the front suspension, torn off by the impact, scythed through the spectator area opposite the pits. 'Levegh' and more than 80 spectators were killed. After Neubauer had consulted the Daimler-Benz directors, he called the remaining two cars into the pits at 1.45am and the team withdrew from the race. Hawthorn/Bueb went on to win and what would have happened if the 300SLRs had continued racing is a matter of speculation.

Nearly two months elapsed before the 300SLRs raced again and Fangio and Moss drove two of these cars fitted with airbrakes into first and second places in the 130-mile (209km) Swedish Grand Prix at Kristianstâd. The 623-mile (1,002km) Tourist Trophy, now held as a scratch race at Dundrod. Moss/Fitch, Fangio/Kling and von Trips/Simon were the drivers and they took the first three places in that order. The winning car was missing much of its right rear wing after a flailing tyre tread started the damage and Moss's ensuing slide into a bank completed the work. Hawthorn/Titterington put up a strong fight with the only works Jaguar D-type entered, but retired because of a broken crankshaft.

In 1955 the Targa Florio was a round in the World Sports Car Championship and was held over a distance of 581 miles (935km) on 16 October. By this time it was known that the Mexican road race had been cancelled and so the Sicilian race was the last round. Mercedes-Benz entered three cars and brought in new drivers by whom Neubauer had been impressed with a view to possibly including them in the 1955 sports car team. Aston Martin driver Peter Collins partnered

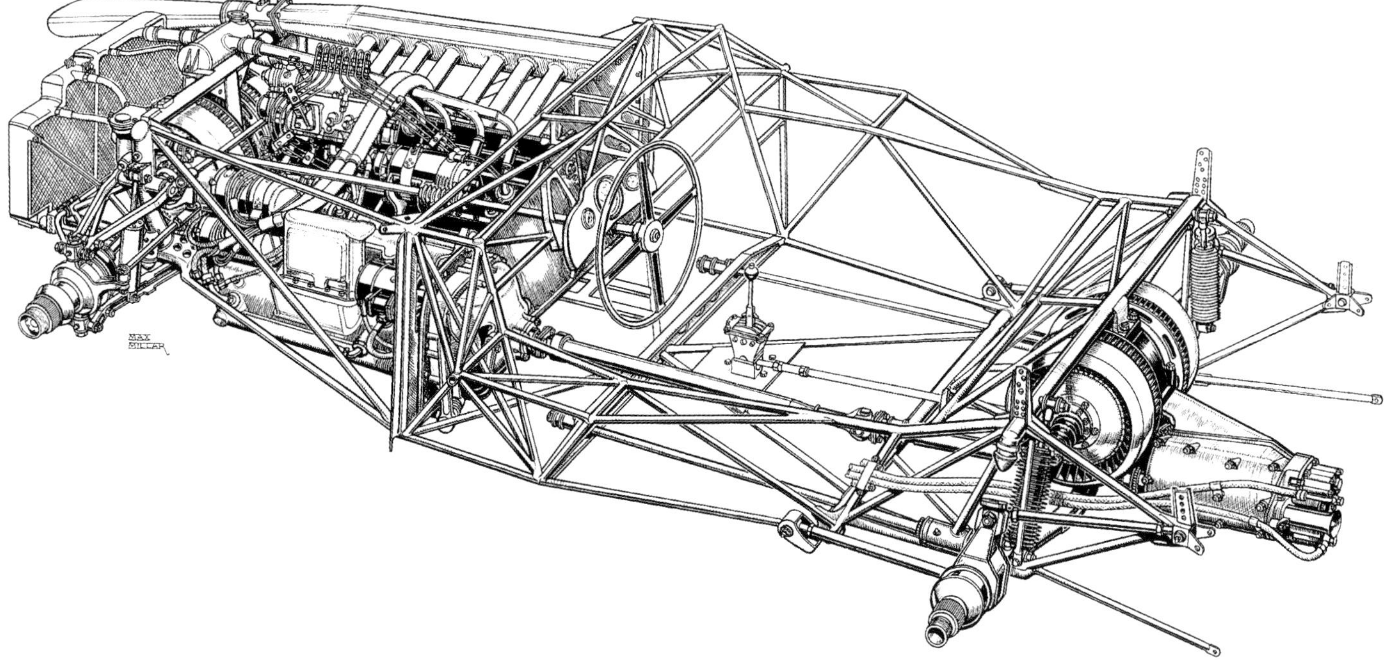

An interesting view of the 300SLR with body, wheels and tanks removed. This view shows very clearly the extreme angle at which the engine was canted to reduce frontal area, the very wide inboard brakes front and rear and the swing-axles with a Watts linkage. (LAT)

Moss and after a race interrupted by off-course excursions they brought their car across the line in first place.

Second came Fangio and Kling, a Ferrari finished third and John Fitch partnered by works Jaguar driver Desmond Titterington took fourth place. The team had planned to run two of the very fast coupé 300SLRs in the Carrera Panamericana Mexico road race, together with two open cars. The race was cancelled, partly because of the backlash from Le Mans and partly for financial reasons. As a result the coupés were never raced, but the Swiss magazine *Automobile Revue* tested the first built and attained a maximum speed of 180mph (300km) and 0–100mph (62km) in 13.5 seconds.

Although everyone involved with the Mercedes-Benz racing programme knew that Mercedes-Benz was withdrawing from Formula 1 at the end of 1955, it came as something of a shock when Daimler-Benz Managing Director Dr Könecke announced that the 300SLR racing programme was at an end, despite the fact that plans for a 1956 lightweight car were well advanced.

The 300SLR's racing record was immaculate, and the question mark as to whether they would have won at Le Mans, added a certain *je ne sait quoi* to Mercedes-Benz's reputation. The 300SLR was just about as perfect a sports-racing car as it was possible to build at the time, but the company would have done well to have abandoned national pride and adopted disc brakes.

As Peter Collins, co-winner of the Targa Florio with Moss, motors through a typical setting, the 300SLR is already becoming battered. In the background is a Lancia Aurelia GT coupé that has already given up the struggle. Crowd control remained just as lax until the last race in 1973.

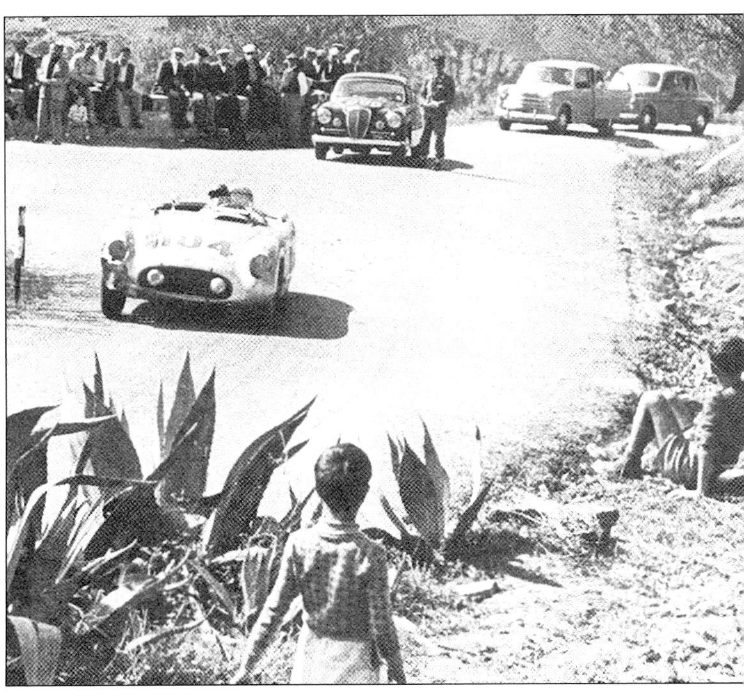

Maserati 300S & 450S

1955–57

Luigi Musso, partnered by Valenzano, drove this works 300S at Le Mans in 1955. The 300S ran exceptionally well and held second place for a long time, but retired because of transmission failure in the 20th hour. (T.C. March/FotoVantage)

Between the years 1952 and 1955 Maserati, controlled by the Orsi family, underwent a transformation. After racing the six-cylinder 2-litre A6GCM cars in the Formula 2 World Championship of 1952–53, the company developed the 250F car for the new 2,500cc Grand Prix formula of 1954 onwards. It was one of the most successful cars of the new formula: it was raced by the works team, it brought Juan Fangio his fifth Drivers' World Championship and provided the mainstay for private owners who wanted to compete in Grand Prix racing.

Maserati had been building the A6GCS six-cylinder 2-litre sports-racing car in considerable numbers since early 1953 and they had proved highly competitive in their class. The company wanted to build cars that had the potential to be outright winners and engineer Giulio Alfieri developed a version of the 250F for sports-car racing and this car, the 300S, was first revealed to the public in December 1954. Later in 1955 Alfieri developed four-cylinder cars with 1,484cc and 1,994cc engines (the 150S and the 200S).

The 300S had a version of the 2,493cc 250F engine with stroke increased to 90mm, which gave a capacity of 2,992.5cc. The six-cylinder engine, with twin overhead camshafts gear-driven from the nose of the crankshaft, twin-plug ignition and triple Weber twin-choke carburettors, developed 245bhp at 6,200rpm. Transmission was by a four-speed gearbox in unit with the final drive. The multi-tubular chassis of the 250F was widened to take two-seater aluminium-alloy bodywork. At the front suspension was by upper and lower wishbones with coil springs and Houdaille hydraulic dampers.

There was a de Dion axle suspended on a transverse leaf spring and Houdaille dampers at the rear. The wheelbase was 7ft 7in (2,310mm) and dry weight was 1,720 pounds (780kg). Maserati's in-house coachbuilder Menardo Fantuzzi designed a neat and well-balanced body. Maximum speed was around 180mph (290kph). During its life, power output of the 300S rose, but only slightly, and cars built in 1958 had a five-speed gearbox. Although the 300S handled superbly and was very tractable, it was only just a match for the Ferrari *Monza* and was outclassed by the Mercedes-Benz 300SLR. It did, however, achieve many wins in the hands of both factory drivers and private owners.

Racing debut for the 300S came in two events on the same day, 13 March 1955. In the 228-mile (367km) Dakar Grand Prix in Sénégal the works car of Jean Behra led until transmission problems brought its fast run to an end, and at Sebring the Briggs Cunningham entry for Spear/Johnston took third place. Later Musso with a works car took third place in the 671-mile (1,080km) Tour of Sicily and in the Mille Miglia Perdisa was holding third place, worrying the 300SLR Mercedes-Benz of Fangio on time when the engine failed.

The first 300S victory was in the 172-mile (277km) Bari night race when Musso was again the driver. Shortly afterwards Behra/Musso and Mieres/Perdisa took first and third places in the 626-mile (1,000km) *Supercortemaggiore* Grand Prix at Monza. Both works entries retired at Le Mans and the only satisfying results later in the year were the wins by Behra in the 253-mile (407km) Portuguese Grand Prix and by Fangio in the 213-mile (343km) Venezuelan Grand

Stirling Moss and Denis Jenkinson with their 350SL Maserati on the starting ramp for the 1956 Mille Miglia. The car suffered from serious handling deficiencies, and Moss crashed late in the race. The 350S was an unsuccessful interim model which was soon abandoned.

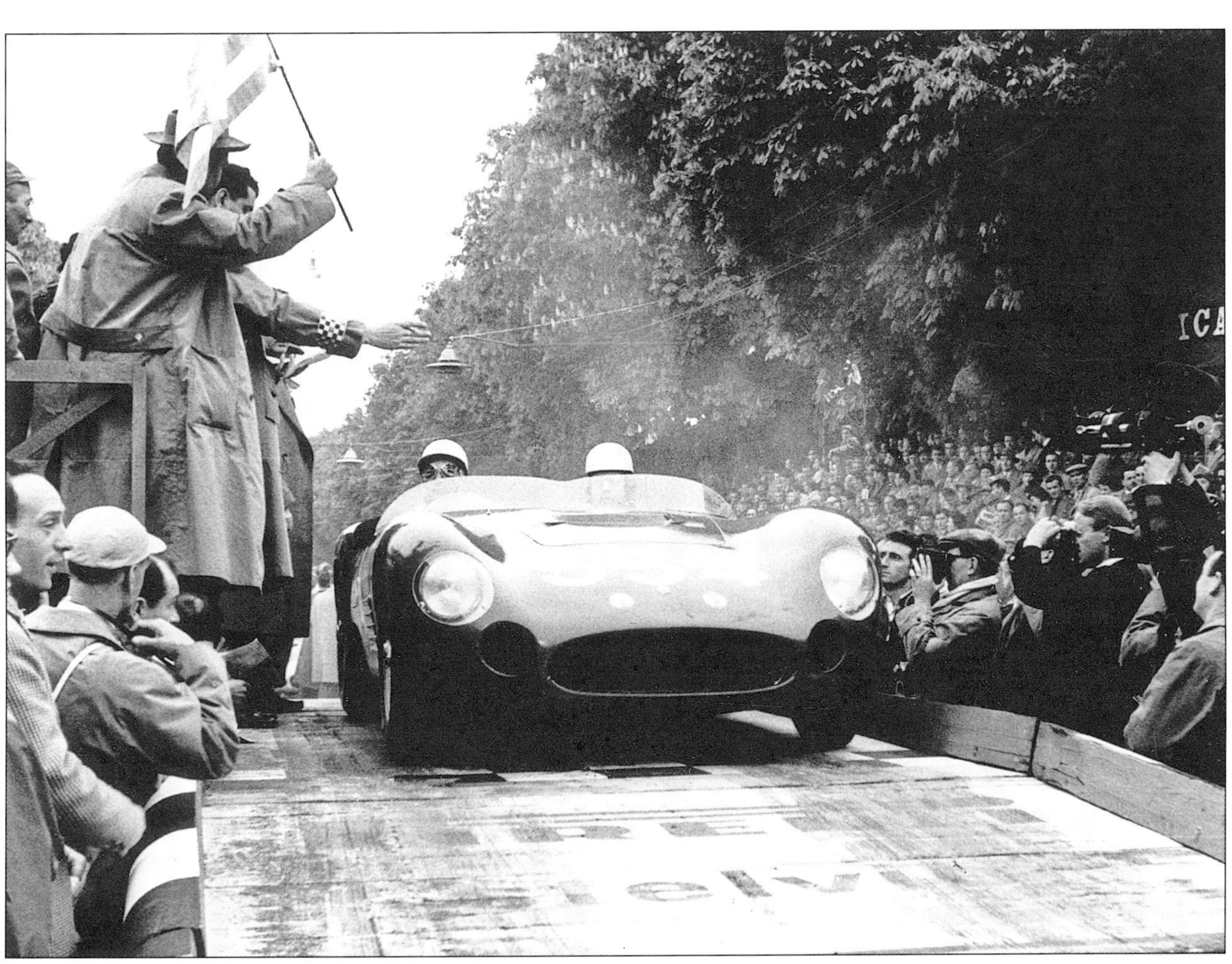

Prix. During the year Maserati had sold eight of these cars to private owners – Maseratis were always popular with private owners because the company gave excellent service and often granted extended credit.

All came good in 1956 when Stirling Moss became team-leader and the whole of the racing department was rejuvenated. Changes to the 300S included the adoption of larger Weber 45DCO3 carburettors and a more aerodynamic front end. The year started well with a win by Moss/Menditeguy and third place by Behra/Gonzalez in the Buenos Aires 1,000Km race on 29 January. It was Maserati's first win in a Sports Car Championship race. Early in the European season Taruffi finished second to Peter Collins (Ferrari) in the Tour of Sicily.

That year's Mille Miglia proved a disaster for Maserati. Moss, partnered by Denis Jenkinson, was cajoled into driving a new version, the Tipo 350S, with 3,485cc (86×100mm) engine developing 270bhp and completely redesigned de Dion rear axle. It suffered front-end lift at speed and handled atrociously and Moss was in second place when the 350S lost front-end adhesion in heavy rain and crashed. Piero Taruffi also crashed his works 300S as the result of brake failure. The Maserati racing department had been hopelessly overstretched and all the factory-prepared cars – the majority for private owners – displayed signs of sloppy workmanship.

Then it all came right again in the Nürburgring 1,000Km race on 27 May. Moss/Behra with their works 300S led the race until the rear transverse leaf spring broke away from its mounting. They then took over the third-place 300S of Taruffi/Schell and brought it through to win from two works Ferraris headed by Fangio/Castellotti. Maserati sent a 300S for Taruffi to the 447-mile (720km) Targa Florio in June, but he was delayed by a broken fuel tank mounting, finished third and was elevated to second place by the disqualification of Cabianca (1.5-litre OSCA).

During the remainder of the season the 300S performed well in minor events. On the same day as the Targa Florio, works driver Jean Behra partnered Louis Rosier at the wheel of his private 300S in the Paris 1,000Km race at Montlhéry. Although they won from a quartet of private Ferraris, it was a close-run thing, as the Maserati ran out of fuel on its lap of honour. With works cars Moss won the 73-mile (117km) race at Silverstone in July and the 124-mile (200km) Bari Grand Prix later that month. The complete team retired in the Championship Swedish Grand Prix at Kristianstâd in August.

In October Behra and Harry Schell with works cars took the first two places in the one-hour Rome Grand Prix, while Moss won the Venezuelan Grand Prix, the Australian Tourist Trophy and the Nassau Tourist Trophy. Another four new cars were sold to private buyers and six were sold in 1957. Ex-works cars also found their way into private ownership. Maserati had more ambitious plans for 1957 and introduced the 4.5-litre 450S, first seen in prototype form at the 1956 Swedish race and with more than enough power to beat the works Ferraris.

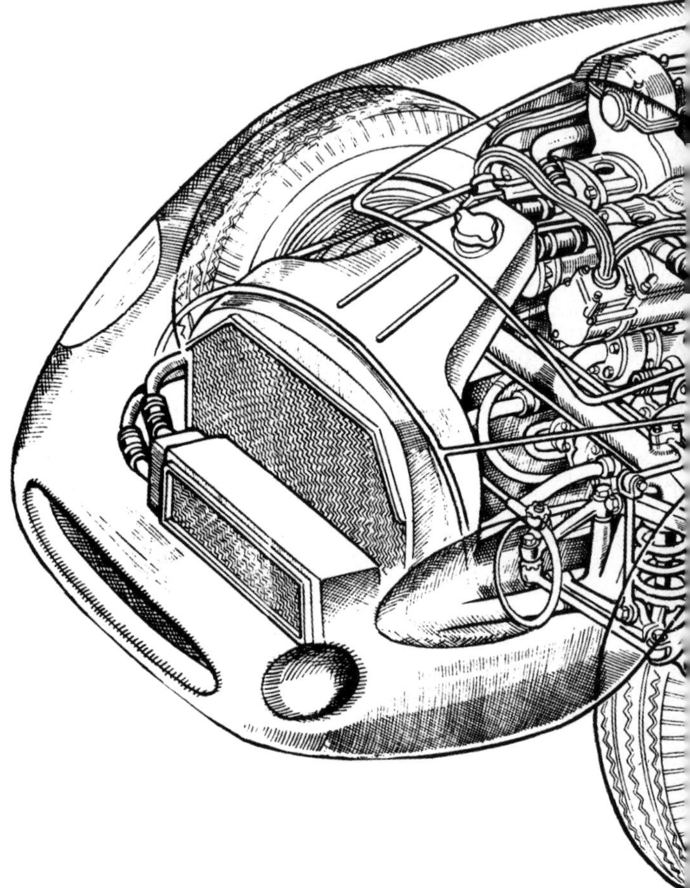

The new car had a 90-degree V8 engine of light-alloy construction throughout with a capacity of 4,477cc (93.8×81mm). A train of gears from the nose of the crankshaft drove the twin overhead camshafts per bank of cylinders, the inlet ports were in the centre of the vee of the cylinders and there were twin

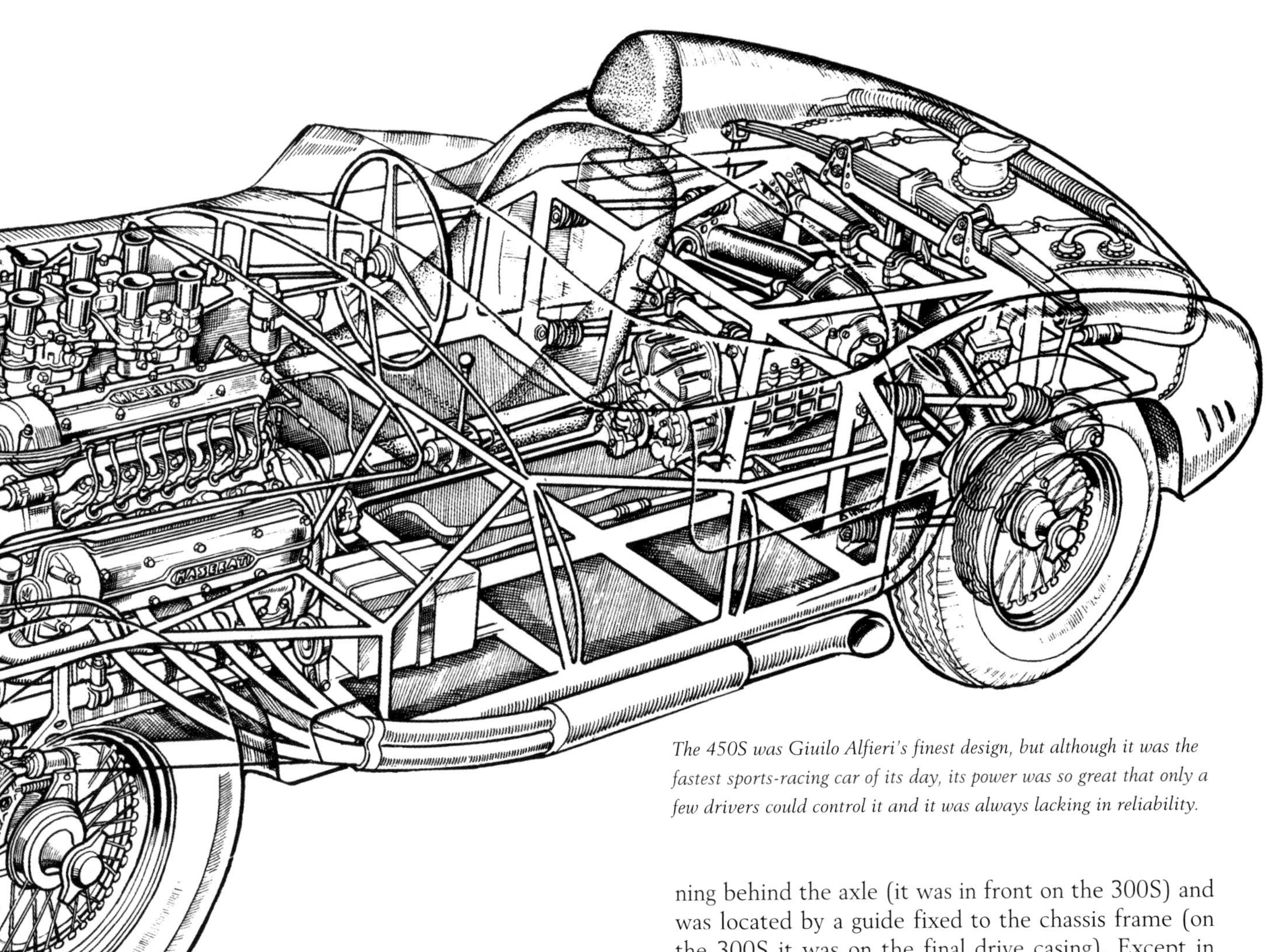

The 450S was Giuilo Alfieri's finest design, but although it was the fastest sports-racing car of its day, its power was so great that only a few drivers could control it and it was always lacking in reliability.

plugs per cylinder in accordance with normal Maserati practice. There were twin ignition systems, a magneto driven by the gear-train for the left bank of cylinders and a pair of coils with the distributor driven from the gear-train of the right bank of cylinders. With four Weber twin-choke 45IDM carburettors, power output was 400bhp plus at 7,500rpm.

The chassis resembled that of the 300S, but was of beefier construction and with the wheelbase lengthened to 7ft 10.5in (2,400mm). Maserati had completely redesigned the rear end, with a new five-speed gearbox that had its shafts in line with the axis of the car and this was mounted in front of and in unit with the final drive (on the 300S the gearbox was behind the final drive). The new de Dion axle-layout had the tube running behind the axle (it was in front on the 300S) and was located by a guide fixed to the chassis frame (on the 300S it was on the final drive casing). Except in very skilful hands, the 450S was an overpowered brute, difficult to drive in the dry and impossible in the wet.

Juan Fangio/Stirling Moss drove the 450S on its race debut in the 1957 Buenos Aires 1,000Km race and the car steadily drew away from the Ferrari opposition, despite failure of the clutch-operating mechanism, but it was withdrawn after clutchless gear-changes proved too much for the gearbox. Moss took over with the 300S entered for Behra/Menditeguy and brought it across the line second, a minute behind the winning Ferrari. At Sebring in March the 450S was driven by Fangio/Behra, held together and scored an easy win from the 300S of Moss/Harry Schell.

For the Mille Miglia the 450S was fitted with a supplemental two-speed gearbox mounted between the clutch and the normal gearbox. It provided two sets of gears, high (maximum speed 185mph/297kph) for the plains and low (maximum 165mph/265kph) for the mountains. When he tested the car, Moss discovered that he could use the low setting to accelerate up to

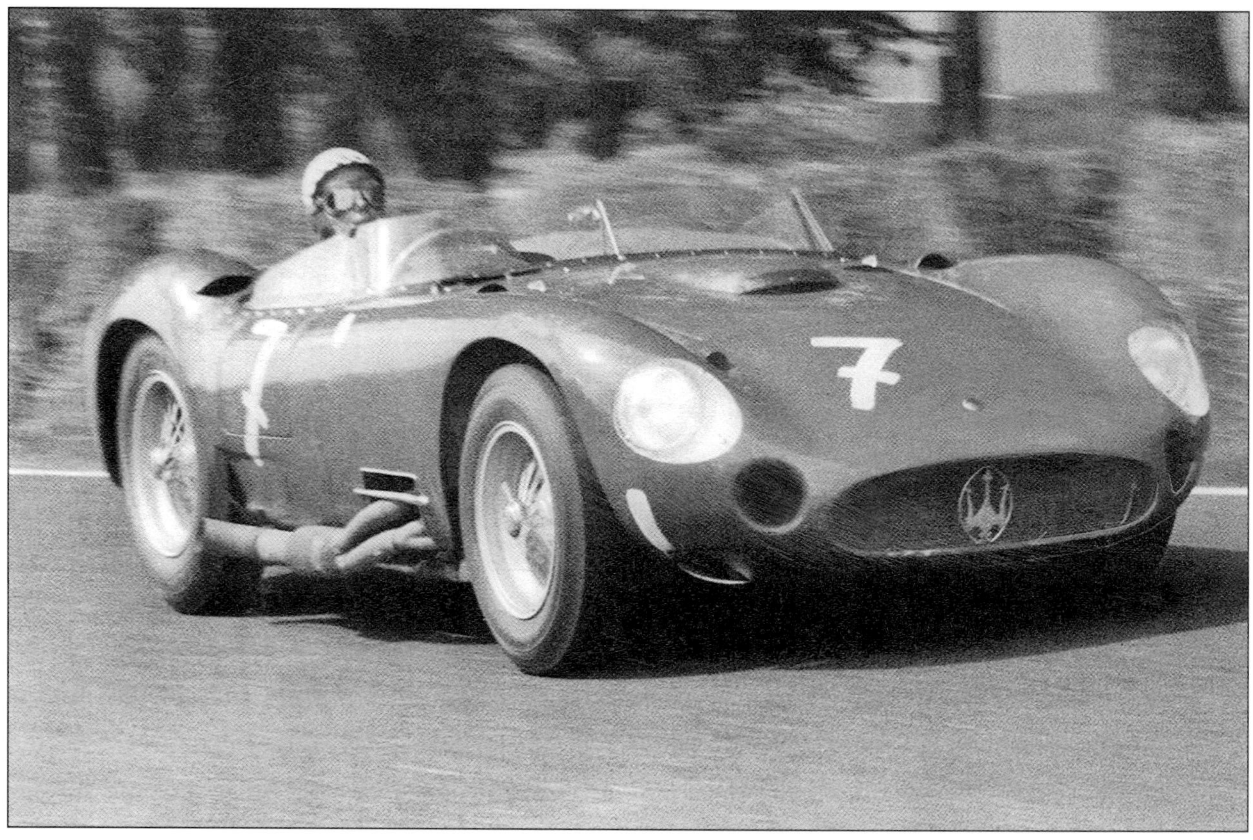

Maserati entered two 450S 4.5-litre cars in the 1957 Swedish Grand Prix. During the race Moss swapped 450S cars and won with Jean Behra, seen here at the wheel. This was one of only two Championship races that Maserati won with the 450S. (LAT)

160mph and then change into the higher ratio of the two-speed gearbox to continue acceleration up to 180mph (289kph).

Behra was injured in a practice crash, so his 450S non-started, and only minutes after the start Moss/Jenkinson were out because the brake pedal broke. Scarlatti with a 300S finished fourth and Herrmann drove an experimental V12 3.5-litre car, but retired because he holed the bottom of the engine. Maserati had ambitions to win the Sports Car Championship, but they could see it slipping from their grasp.

Another failure followed in the Nürburgring 1,000Km race in which both 450S entries retired. The sole finisher was a 300S that Fangio/Moss took over to finish fifth. At Le Mans Moss/Schell co-drove a 450S, with very aerodynamic coupé body designed by Frank Costin (responsible for Grand Prix Vanwall bodies). Zagato constructed it, but made a mess of the job and put the ventilation openings in the wrong places. The cockpit was hot and fume-filled, the wipers lifted off the screen at speed and it was overgeared. Its drivers were relieved when a rear universal joint seized, but, unfortunately, the same problem eliminated the standard 450S of Behra/Simon while it was leading.

The two 450S entries led the six-hour Swedish Grand Prix at Kristianstâd on 11 August and although one retired, Moss/Behra went on to win from a Ferrari and a works 300S. With one race to go, the 622-mile (1,000km) Venezuelan Grand Prix on 3 November, Maserati had a chance, albeit an outside one, of winning the Championship. Sadly, the race proved a disaster for Modena: all three 450S cars, which included a private entry, and the sole works 300S were eliminated. Ferrari won the race and the Championship.

At the end of the year Maserati withdrew from racing for financial reasons, partly, but not entirely, because of a deal to export machine tools to the Argentine that went sour after the fall of the Péron government. The V12 car developed for the 3,000cc Sports Car Championship of 1958 was unraced, but in 1959 Moss drove the new 2-litre Tipo 60 'Bird-cage' car, so called because of its chassis consisting of a multiplicity of small-section tubes, to a win at Rouen. The *Camoradi* team and other private organisations raced the 3-litre Tipo 61 version with success in 1960–61 and the last competition Maserati built by the original company was the Tipo 65 that ran at Le Mans in 1965.

Lotus Eleven

1956–58

One of the greatest Lotus triumphs was at Le Mans in 1957 when Cliff Allison and Keith Hall drove this 750cc Climax-powered car to a class victory and a win in the Index of Performance. After 1957 Lotus never performed well with sports cars at Le Mans. (LAT)

Colin Chapman's early cars created a sensation in the motor sport world. His Mark III Austin Seven-based 750 Formula car was the fastest of its type in 1951, mainly because of an ingenious modification to the induction manifolding that he claimed as his own, but in fact originated in Australia; his Mark VI of 1952–53, a short, stubby little sports-racer was vaunted for its space-frame construction, but it was not fully triangulated as a good space-frame should be; then in 1954 Chapman raced the futuristic, aerodynamic Mark VIII, the fastest British 1,500cc sports car of its day with much stiffer space-frame and bodywork evolved by Frank Costin.

In 1955 Lotus raced the Mark IX with MG and Coventry Climax engines. The works cars had a more rigid space-frame chassis designed by Gilbert McIntosh, like Frank Costin a de Havilland aircraft-

The Mark VIII and Chapman's most hectic weekend

The 1954 Lotus Mark VIII possessed an immensely stiff space-frame chassis, albeit in prototype form a rather impractical one as it was necessary to strip the engine of all ancillaries, together with the cylinder head, before it could be removed from the chassis. It had a very aerodynamic body, the work of Frank Costin, who designed it without wind tunnel facilities, but there is little doubt that the Bristol 450 influenced the design approach. The car's biggest weakness was the push-rod MG/Morris engine that developed only 85bhp or thereabouts, far lower than the output of Continental rivals, factors that the aerodynamics and low weight could not compensate for fully.

Chapman raced the car as often as possible during the year and he decided to compete over the British August Bank Holiday Weekend in the 1,500cc race at the Nürburgring in the Eifel Mountains before the German Grand Prix, practising on the Saturday and racing on the Sunday morning. He would then drive back to England to compete at both Brands Hatch and Crystal Palace on the Monday. At this time was he was still working full-time for the British Aluminium Company.

On the Friday he drove the Lotus to work in

Colin Chapman with the prototype Mark VIII in the 1,500cc sports car race at Silverstone in July 1954, the day of the British Grand Prix when he defeated Hans Herrmann (works Porsche 550). By this stage in the season the Mark VIII was looking decidedly scruffy. (T.C. March/FotoVantage)

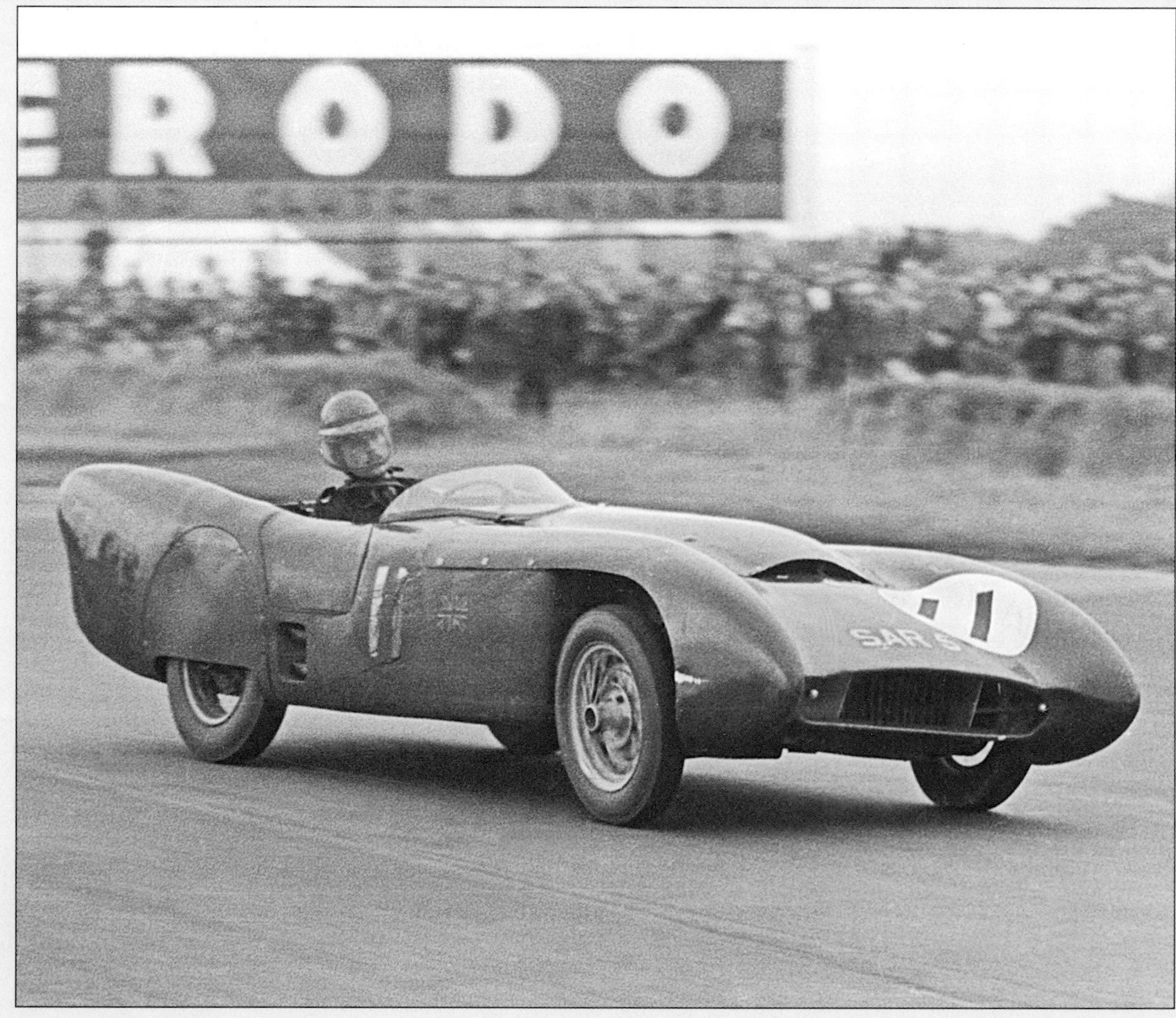

Central London, parked it in St James's Square just off Pall Mall, changed from overalls to suit in the nearby gentleman's lavatory and went to work for the day. In the evening, he changed back from suit to overalls in the same lavatory, drove off to pick up his close associate Mike Costin (later co-founder of Cosworth) and then set off to Dover to catch the cross-Channel ferry. They arrived in time for practice, but in the race on this very bumpy and difficult circuit the de Dion tube broke. After this had been welded up, the intrepid duo set off for Calais, but a broken linkage in the rear suspension caused delays.

Chapman arrived at Brands Hatch in Kent in time to run in the heat of his race, but started from the back of the grid because he had not practised. He worked his way up to second place, the Lotus's engine lost a cylinder and he sputtered on to take fourth place. The cylinder head gasket had failed and this had to be changed before Chapman could set off for the Crystal Palace.

I was at the Crystal Palace that day and knew that Chapman had been competing in Germany and intended to run at Brands Hatch. As the time for the start of his race approached, Chapman had not arrived. His small team became more and more anxious and I joined them as they wandered down to the competitors' entrance, where we found that the gate was locked. At the last moment, as the cars were going out to line up for the starting grid, Chapman screeched up to the gate.

He had no horn, so he revved the engine furiously, and after what seemed minutes – but could only have been seconds – a workman unlocked the gate and Chapman accelerated away to join the other starters. He retired on the second lap because of an engine misfire. He immediately returned to Brands Hatch for the final of his race and took over Nigel Allen's car, a newly delivered Mark VIII that had also run at the Nürburgring. Once again he retired with a sick engine.

The poor running of the Mark VIIIs in these two British races was because the engines had been set up to run on German low octane fuel at the 2,000ft (600-metre) altitude of the German circuit. It may have been an overcrowded weekend during which Chapman simply tried to do too much, but he displayed his ambition and his raw enthusiasm for motor racing and the publicity obtained by Lotus was by no means unfavourable.

man, and again bodywork designed by Costin, shorter and lighter than the 1954 cars. The team ran at Le Mans for the first time, but the Mark IX was disqualified when Chapman reversed back on to the circuit after an off-course excursion without awaiting the marshals' signal. The 13 customer Mark IXs had simpler chassis like that of the Mark VI and Lotus also built the Mark X with the Bristol 2-litre engine.

Lotus achieved International fame in 1956 with the Eleven, a direct development of the earlier cars, with multi-tubular space-frame chassis, swing-axle and coil spring/damper unit front suspension, together with a de Dion axle suspended on coil springs at the rear. Steering was by rack-and-pinion and on the serious competition cars, which were the majority, there were Girling disc brakes, mounted inboard at the rear. The Costin-designed body was still lower and shorter and the rear wings had only a slight finned outline.

Front and rear, the body hinged to good access to the mechanical components and there were drop-down doors for driver and passenger. The *Le Mans*, the serious competition model favoured by most buyers, had a streamlined head fairing, a Plexiglass wrap-round screen on the driver's side and metal tonneau cover over the left side. For the *Le Mans*, Lotus used the 1,098cc (72.4×66.7mm) single overhead camshaft Coventry Climax FWA engine, developing in more highly tuned form 83bhp at 6,800rpm. The works team, *Team Lotus*, and some private owners had cars powered by the interim 1,460cc (76.2×80mm) Climax FWB single-cam engine developing around 100bhp.

Lotus fitted a gearbox combining an Austin A30 casing with Lotus close-ration internals, but later in 1956 the MGA gearbox was substituted. The wheelbase had been reduced from 7ft 3.5in (2,220mm) for the 1955 car to 7ft 1in (2,160mm) and the track was narrower at 3ft 10.5in (1,180mm). Length had been reduced from 11ft 8in (3,555mm) to 11ft 2in (3,405mm). The Eleven was about 180 pounds (80kg) lighter. Top speed of an 85 *Le Mans* with high gearing was around 125mph (201kph) and acceleration from 0–60mph (96.5kph) took about ten seconds.

The Eleven was a highly competitive package that private owners could buy at a modest price and assemble themselves. There was purchase tax on completed cars sold in the UK and, in any event, the tiny Lotus works at Tottenham Lane, Hornsey was not able to cope with assembly of more than a few cars. The company bought in chassis, bodies and most of the other components and sold them on as a 'kit'. Once the car was assembled, the owner could go racing on more or less even terms with his contemporaries.

Essential to Lotus success was the Coventry Climax

toured mainland Europe competing almost very weekend), *Team Lotus* ran in major British events, shorter Continental races (the OSCAs were usually faster) and at Le Mans. *Team Lotus* entered three cars in the 1956 24 Hours race, new cars, strengthened for this endurance event. The 1,500cc car retired, as did one of the 1,100s after a collision at the beginning of the *Mulsanne Straight* with a large dog that was ingested through the air intake and into the engine bay as though into a mincing machine. Bicknell/Jopp finished a very satisfactory seventh overall and won the 1,100cc class.

The front row of the starting grid for the 1,500cc heat of the British Empire Trophy at Oulton Park in April 1956, when the Lotus Eleven made its racing debut. From right to left of the photograph are Chapman (works Eleven), Les Leston (Cooper), Ivor Bueb (Écurie Demi-Litre Cooper) and Mike Hawthorn (Écurie Demi-Litre Lotus). In the second row right to left are Salvadori (works Cooper), Jim Russell (works Cooper) and Reg Bicknell (Team Lotus Eleven). Moss (works-loaned Cooper), Chapman, Salvadori and Hawthorn took the first four places in the handicap final. (T.C. March/FotoVantage)

FWA engine and, later, the twin overhead camshaft four-cylinder and V8 designs from this company. Kieft was the first to use the FWA engine in its glass-fibre-bodied sports cars in 1954 and later that year Richard Steed took delivery of a Mark VIII Lotus in which he installed an FWA engine. Although the first works Mark IX in 1955 was MG-powered, thereafter Lotus used the Climax engine, as did Cooper in their rear-engined sports cars. The two marques were very closely matched in 1955 and 1956, especially when the Coopers were works cars driven by the likes of Bueb, Brabham and Salvadori.

The pendulum swung later in 1956, partly because Cooper concentrated increasingly on Formula 2 single-seaters and partly because the Eleven was a superior, better-handling car. The availability of Lotus cars, and other makes including Elva, with engines producing a reliable, consistent power output and no expensive tuning hassle led to the severe decline in support for Formula 3 500cc single-seater racing. In this category most cars were Coopers and prospects of success without a very expensively developed and maintained Norton 'Manx' engine were nil.

While most private owners ran in British events (save for the intrepid David Piper and Bob Hicks who

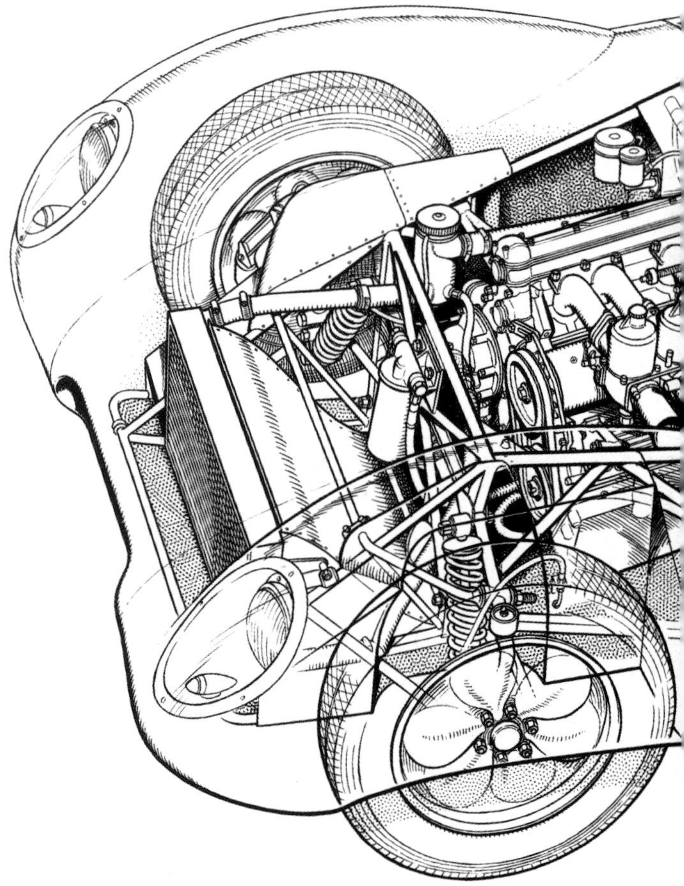

For 1957 Lotus produced the Eleven Series 2 with front suspension by double wishbones, and the upper wishbone acting as an anti-roll bar, as on Chapman's new, but largely unsuccessful Formula 2 car. The new Coventry Climax FPF 4-cylinder twin-cam 1,475cc (81.2×71.1mm) engine developing 142bhp at 6,750rpm powered a few cars and some works cars had the latest 'wobbly-web' magnesium-alloy, centre-lock disc wheels. The cars were available with the original type of body for British races or, in compliance with the new International Appendix C regulations, wider chassis, hood and full-width regulation height Plexiglas windscreen.

Two works cars and two private entries ran at Le Mans in June. The most significant was the works car with Climax FWC single-cam 744cc (76.2×45.2mm) engine. Driving it well within rev limits, Cliff Allison/Keith Hall finished 14th overall, winning both the 750cc class and the Index of Performance, categories that were previously a French stronghold. The 1,100cc cars took first, second and fourth places in their class.

The Eleven continued in unchanged form in 1958 and Lotus had now introduced the 15 intended to take engines of 1,500cc upwards and these cars formed the main thrust of the works sports car entries. Two 15s and four Elevens ran at Le Mans in 1958, but the only finisher was the works 750cc car of Stacey/Dickson, 20th and last after an off-course excursion and a lot of time wasted in the pits while the car was repaired. During its three-year production run Lotus built over 300 Elevens, the model transformed the fortunes of Lotus, changed the face of racing in Britain and put the company on the world motor racing map.

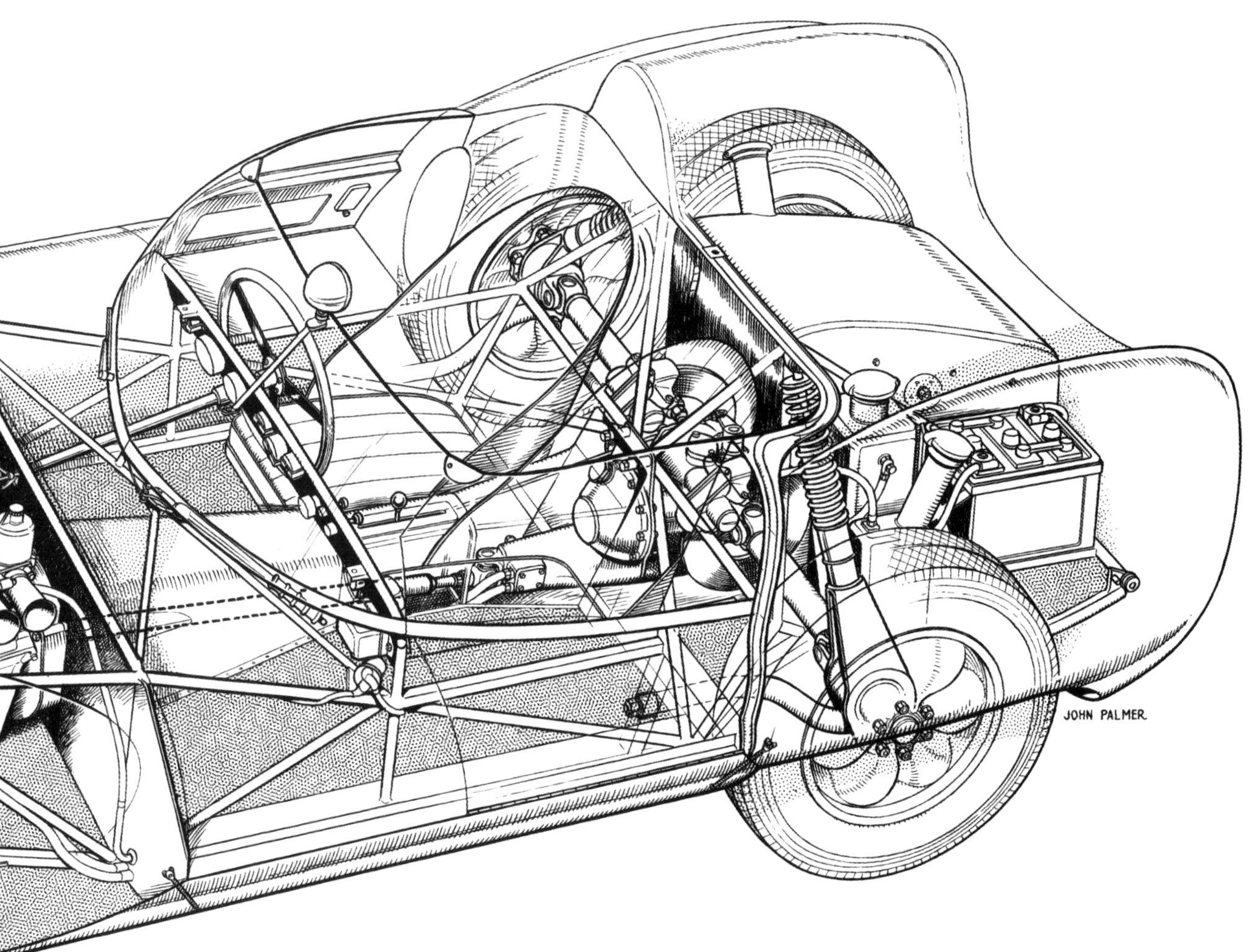

The Lotus Eleven seen in 1957 works form with twin overhead camshaft 1,500cc Climax FPF engine, wishbone front suspension and 'wobbly-web' alloy wheels. (LAT)

Aston Martin DBR1

1956–59

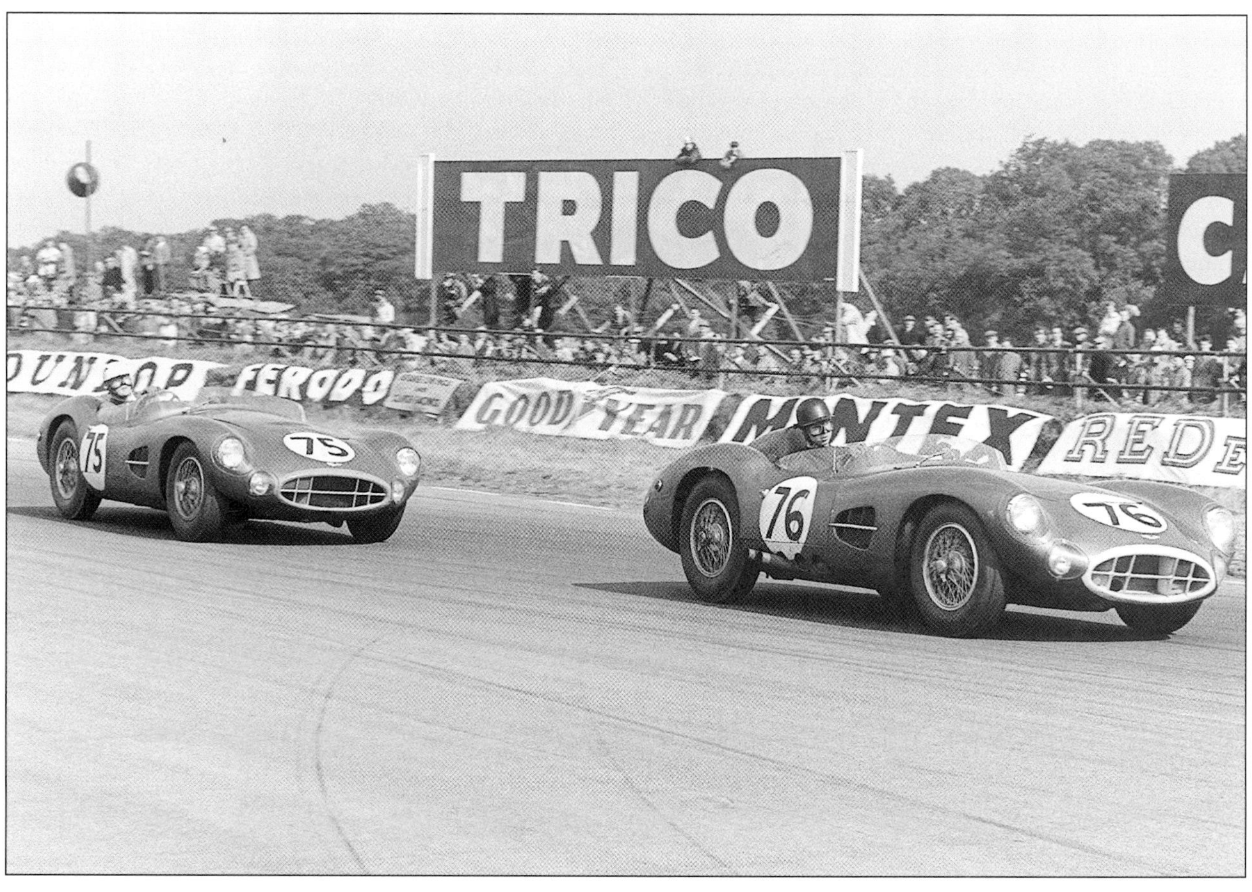

Tony Brooks (DBR1) leads Noel Cunningham-Reid (DBR2) in the sports car race at the International Trophy meeting in September 1957. An easy way of distinguishing the two models was that the DBR1 had the exhausts emerging on the right and on the DBR2 they emerged on the left. (T.C. March/FotoVantage)

John Wyer, who from 1957 was General Manager of Aston Martin-Lagonda, had been well aware of the deficiencies of the DB3S and, within the team's limited budget, work had started on a successor in 1955. There was no logical reason why the DBR1 retained a 3,000cc engine, save for David Brown's ambition to compete with a 2,500cc version in Formula 1. Engineer Ted Cutting was responsible for the complete design. In 1957 form the DBR1 had an engine with the same dimensions as the DB3S, 83×90mm (2,922cc) and a similar twin-plug cylinder head, but there was a new aluminium-alloy block. With three Weber twin-choke 45DCO carburettors, power output was 240bhp at 6,250rpm.

Transmission was by a triple-plate clutch and a five-speed non-synchromesh David Brown CG537 gearbox with straight-toothed constant-mesh gears engaged by dogs. The gearbox was mounted transversely in unit with the final drive and above it was a ZF limited slip differential. The gearbox was truly awful, with a tendency to stick in gear and difficulty in changing down because of the reluctance of the gears to engage. David Brown Gears had built the gearbox and it was appalling that Brown's own company supplied such an unreliable major component.

The chassis was a multi-tubular space-frame constructed from small-diameter chrome-molybdenum tubing; it was much more rigid than its predecessor and complete with bulkhead weighed 116 pounds (52.6kg), 50 pounds (22.7kg) less than that of the DB3S. The wheelbase had been increased to 7ft 6in (2,285mm) and the track to 4ft 3.5in (1,310mm). Front and rear suspension was similar to that of the DB3S and there was rack-and-pinion steering.

Aston Martin used Girling disc brakes, without servo assistance and very handsome Borrani 16-inch (406mm) centre-lock wire wheels with triple-eared knock-off hubs. The body, a more aerodynamic version of that of the DB3S, was panelled in 20-gauge magnesium-alloy, very thin and easily damaged. Dry weight was 15.75cwt (800kg), the same as claimed by Ferrari for the 3-litre *Testa Rossa*. Compared to its ageing predecessor, it was a vast improvement in every respect.

The first DBR1 had a 2,493cc (83×76.8mm) engine to comply with the 1956 Prototype regulations at Le Mans. Parnell/Brooks held fourth place for several hours, but the DBR1 ran its bearings just over an hour before the finish. At the start of 1957 Aston Martin had only the first car and it was not until the 132-mile (212km) Spa Grand Prix in May that the team was able to field two 3-litre cars. Tony Brooks revelled in the high speeds and fast curves of Spa-Francorchamps, he was brilliant in the wet and won with his DBR1 at 103.97mph (167.29kph). Salvadori battled with the weather and the privately entered Jaguar D-types, but finished second with his DBR1.

On 26 May Aston achieved an outstanding and totally unexpected success. Two DBR1s and a DB3S in experimental form with 2,992cc (84×90mm) engine and wishbone front suspension ran in the Nürburgring 1,000Km race. Tony Brooks, partnered by Noel Cunningham-Reid, took the lead at the start, dropped behind Moss with a 450S Maserati and when this lost a wheel on lap eight, took the lead again. The DBR1 stayed in front for the remainder of this 44-lap race, pursued by the works Ferraris, and won by a margin of over four minutes. Cunningham-Reid says, "Tony was a much faster driver than I was, but I was quick enough not to lose too much ground while I was at the wheel."

Aston Martin fielded three cars at Le Mans, two DBR1s and the new DBR2. The DBR2 was a relatively cheap and easy car to build and combined the 1955 Lagonda backbone chassis with the six-cylinder 3,670cc (92×92mm) twin overhead camshaft engine that was to power the production DB4 announced at the 1958 Earls Court Show. For Aston Martin the race was a disaster. For many hours Brooks/Cunningham-Reid (DBR1) held second place behind the *Écurie Ecosse* Jaguar D-type of Flockhart/Bueb, but Brooks crashed on the Sunday morning. The other two Aston Martins retired.

Later in 1957 Aston Martin ran in only minor races. In August three cars appeared at a three-hour race at Spa. Cunningham-Reid (DBR2) crashed in practice and non-started. Brooks drove a DBR1 that had a new cylinder head with the valves at an angle of 95 degrees and a power output of 252bhp at 6,000rpm. His oil pressure was fluctuating, but he won at 118.56mph (190.76kph) from Masten Gregory (3.8-litre Ferrari). Salvadori (DBR1) finished fourth with his gearbox jammed in fourth. In September Salvadori (DBR2) won the sports car race at the International Trophy

The line-up of works Aston Martins at the 1957 Nürburgring 1,000Km race. Number 14 is the DBR1 which Tony Brooks and Noel Cunningham-Reid drove to a surprise win, defeating the works Ferrari and Maserati teams. Roy Salvadori/Les Leston finished sixth with DBR1 number 12 and half-brothers Peter and Graham Whitehead took ninth place with DB3S number 15. (LAT)

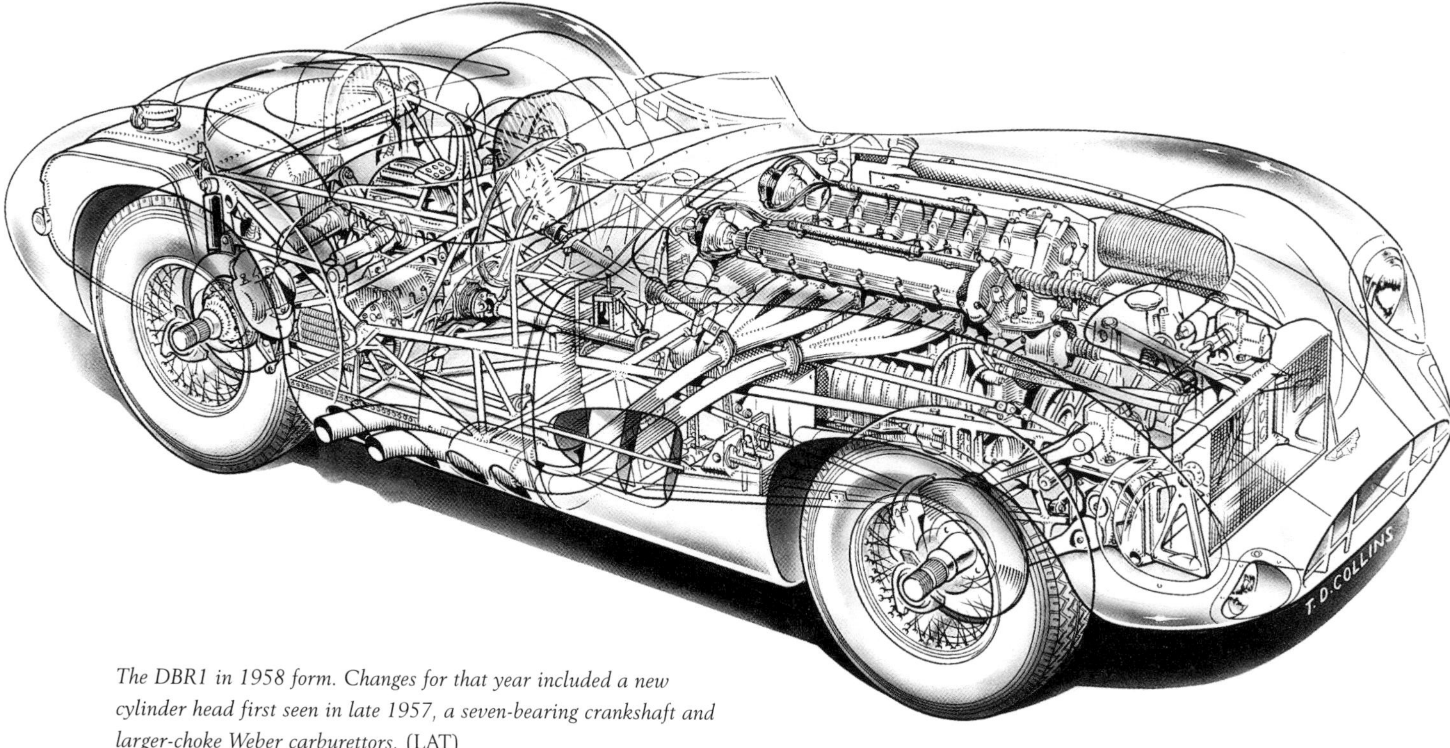

The DBR1 in 1958 form. Changes for that year included a new cylinder head first seen in late 1957, a seven-bearing crankshaft and larger-choke Weber carburettors. (LAT)

meeting at Silverstone from Archie Scott-Brown (Lister-Jaguar), but the Lister was suffering from rear suspension problems.

From 1958 there was a 3,000cc capacity limit in World Sports Car Championship events and racing became a straight fight between Aston Martin and Ferrari. Following Maserati's withdrawal from racing, Stirling Moss rejoined the Aston Martin team. In 1958 the DBR1s had the 95-degree cylinder head, larger-choke Weber 50DCO carburettors, a seven-bearing crankshaft and a power output of about 255bhp, but were detuned to 240/245bhp for endurance races. In minor races the team continued to race the DBR2s, now in 3,910cc (95×92mm) form and developing 284bhp at 5,500rpm.

The year started badly and, with the exception of one major race, continued badly. At Sebring the two DBR1s were highly competitive, but both retired. Salvadori/Shelby were eliminated because of a broken front chassis member (on their car, the first DBR1, this was bolted, while on later cars it was welded). The DBR1 of Moss/Brooks succumbed to the almost inevitable gearbox trouble.

A new development was the DBR3 with 2,991cc (92×75mm) oversquare engine based on that of the DB4. Engineer Tadek Marek had been hoping for 300bhp, but with six Weber single-choke 48DOE carburettors it developed only 258bhp at 7,000rpm. Moss drove the car in the sports car race at the International Trophy meeting at Silverstone in May, but retired because of bearing failure. Aston Martin abandoned the project.

The Targa Florio, on 11 May, was a Championship round and Moss persuaded the team to enter a DBR1 for himself and Brooks. It was a wasted effort, as there had been insufficient time for preparation and training. Moss buckled a wheel on the first lap, lost more time while a broken crankshaft damper was changed and then resumed the race, breaking the lap record twice before retiring because of the almost inevitable gearbox failure.

Aston Martin entered three DBR1s in the Nürburgring 1,000Km race on 1 June. Moss set the pace and led for the first ten laps before handing over to Jack Brabham. Brabham's only experience of the DBR1 was three laps in practice at the German circuit and it was not a car that he adjusted to easily. After three laps he handed back to Moss, but by the time the DBR1 was back in the race, it had dropped to third place. Moss fought back and by the finish he and Brabham had an advantage of four minutes over the first of the Ferrari *Testa Rossas*. The other two DBR1s retired.

The Le Mans race was another debacle and all three DBR1s were eliminated. Gendebien/Phil Hill won the race for Ferrari, but Peter and Graham Whitehead brought their private DB3S across the line in second place, almost 100 miles (161km) behind the winners.

The last round in the Championship was the Tourist Trophy, revived at Goodwood on 13 September, a four-hour race counting for only half-points. Moss/Brooks, Salvadori/Brabham and Shelby/Lewis-Evans took the first three places with their DBR1s. Two of the DBR1s had 2,992cc (84×90mm) engines that were to be standard in 1959. Aston Martin took second place in the Championship.

Aston Martin entered Formula 1 in 1959 and intended to run the DBR1s only at Le Mans. The Sebring organisers offered to pay all of Aston Martin's expenses, so the team sent a DBR1 for Salvadori/Shelby. They retired because of a broken gear-lever. Stirling Moss wanted to repeat his Nürburgring victory and he paid the costs of running the prototype DBR1 with Jack Fairman as co-driver. When Moss stopped after 17 laps, he led by 5½ minutes, but six laps later Fairman spun the DBR1 into a ditch, he was a strong man and levered the car out by using his back. Moss rejoined in fourth place and after a fast chase, he and Fairman won by a margin of 41 seconds.

For Le Mans the DBR1s had rounded and higher rear bodywork, partially enclosed front wheels, valances over the rear wheels and a long exhaust system that ran under the cockpit to the tail (roasting the driver's feet *en route*). Moss was the hare, partnered by the plodding Fairman, and after they retired because of a broken valve, Salvadori/Shelby and Trintignant/Frère took the first two places – mainly because the Ferrari drivers had revved their cars into the ground during the first few hours.

It was the win that David Brown had long coveted and victory in the Championship was now in his sights. Three DBR1s ran in the six-hour Tourist Trophy at Goodwood on 5 September. Despite another fire in the pits, when the leading DBR1 of Moss/Salvadori was set ablaze during a refuelling stop, Moss (who took over from Fairman/Shelby) won the race at 89.41mph (143.86kph) from Bonnier/von Trips (Porsche) and a Ferrari shared by four different drivers. Feltham took the Championship with 24 points to the 22 of Ferrari. It had been a long, hard road and shortly afterwards David Brown announced the withdrawal of the team from sports car racing.

In 1959 on Aston Martin's 11th post-war appearance at Le Mans, the team eventually won with this DBR1 driven by Roy Salvadori and Carroll Shelby. Changes to the cars for this race included a rerouted exhaust, which burnt the drivers' feet, and valances over the rear wheels. (LAT)

Roy Salvadori's win at Le Mans in 1959

In 1956 Aston Martin introduced the improved DBR1 and we raced this on a regular basis from the start of the 1957 season. It handled better because of the much more rigid space-frame chassis and improved weight distribution and the redesigned engine was a match for any of its rivals – especially after the imposition of a 3-litre capacity limit in World Sports Car Championship events from 1958 onwards. The one weak aspect of the DBR1 was the gearbox – made by David Brown transmissions – which had a tendency, or perhaps, more accurately, an inevitability to jam in gear.

Aston Martin entered Formula 1 racing in 1959 and although this occupied much of the team's efforts, David Brown made a powerful entry at Le Mans. Carroll Shelby partnered me, I had driven with him many times previously, and as we were about the same height there were no difficulties over seating position. The race was a straightforward battle between the Aston Martin DBR1s and the Ferrari *Testa Rossas* and the cars were very evenly matched, notwithstanding the Ferrari's higher maximum speed.

While Stirling Moss acted as the 'hare' of the team, I drove a steady race, waiting for the opposition to crack. In the Aston Martin team there was a superb relationship between the drivers and Reg Parnell (team manager) and John Wyer (technical director). It was very different at Ferrari, where there were constant arguments between the drivers and racing manager Tavoni. This certainly helped our chances, as did Stirling's superb driving that probably lured the Ferrari team into over-stressing their cars.

After six hours' racing I took the lead and Carroll and I held it for another four hours or so when our DBR1 developed a bad rear-end vibration. I made two quick pit stops and no problem could be traced and as the vibration worsened, so I lapped slower and slower. The atmosphere in our pit was now rather fraught, but when I stopped to refuel and hand over to Carroll, the vibration was traced to a damaged offside rear tyre. By the time Carroll rejoined the race, we had lost 12 to 15 minutes and were now three laps behind the Ferrari of Phil Hill/Gendebien.

In the pits John Wyer tried to calm me down and told me that he was convinced that the leading Ferrari would retire like the other two team *Testa Rossas*. When I was back at the wheel, I lapped very fast to make up lost ground, while conserving the DBR1 as much as possible. By 11am on the Sunday morning, we had closed within a lap of the Ferrari, but there seemed no likelihood that we could catch and pass it. Then the Ferrari came into the pits in a cloud of steam, completed another lap and retired.

I eased back, but I worried about imagined moans and groans from the engine and whines from the transmission. I was driving as much as permitted by the regulations because Carroll was suffering from a stomach bug. When the flag fell at 4pm, we were still in the lead and were just over six miles ahead of the second surviving DBR1 driven by Maurice Trintignant/Paul Frère.

I had burnt my right foot very badly from the heat of the exhaust of the DBR1, which for this race had been rerouted under the cockpit, and I still have the scars. All I wanted to do was sleep and I deliberately missed the presentation at the circuit. It was very much of an anti-climax. When Aston Martin won the Tourist Trophy at Goodwood, despite the car I was sharing with Stirling catching fire when I came into the pits to refuel, the team clinched its win in the World Sports Car Championship.

Roy Salvadori, Aston Martin's longest serving driver after his win with a DB3S at the British Grand Prix meeting at Aintree in 1955. (T.C. March/FotoVantage)

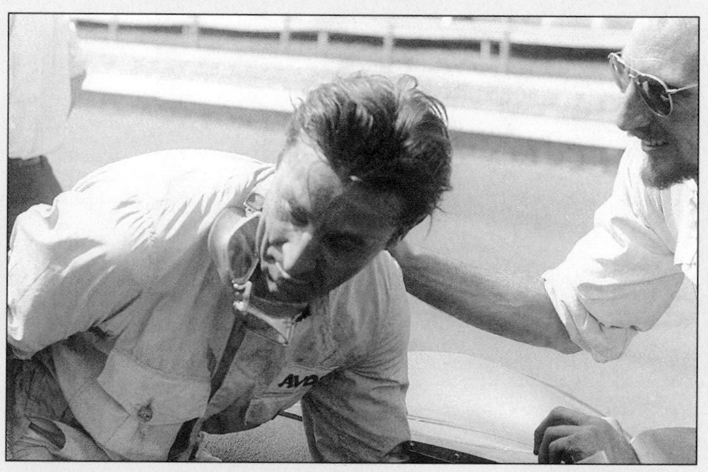

Lister-Jaguar
1957–59

The Lister-Bristol made its racing debut in the hands of Archie Scott-Brown in the unlimited capacity sports car race at the British Grand Prix meeting at Silverstone in July in 1954. Scott-Brown finished fifth overall and won the 2,000cc class. Here he leads Cliff Davis (Tojeiro-Bristol) and is about to lap the Jaguar C-type of John Manussis. (T.C. March/FotoVantage)

The Lister-Jaguar was one of the most successful sports-racing cars of the late 1950s. Like so many British competition cars of the period, it was based on a simple twin-tubular chassis, but far more sophisticated than most of its rivals. Lister, an engineering company in Cambridge, built one of the best-handling cars of its time, preparation of its Bristol and, later, Jaguar engines by Don Moore was outstanding and the driving of Archie Scott-Brown, who handled the works cars, was world-class.

Brian Lister raced Cooper-MG and Tojeiro-JAP sports cars before deciding that however enthusiastic he was and however much he enjoyed motor racing, he was not really cut out to be a racing driver and he would do far better to let his friend, Archie Scott-Brown take the wheel. Scott-Brown was physically handicapped, he had been born with a right arm that had only a vestigial forearm with partial palm and thumb, giving very poor grip of the steering wheel and although he was of normal height from the waist up, he had very short legs and measured barely five feet.

Despite his unprepossessing physique, he became one of the fastest drivers of his generation, quick and fearless, he had a great feel for the cars he drove, coupled with a wonderful sense of balance. He was also a great personality, liked and respected by his fellow drivers and outstandingly popular with the press and the public. He had no 'hang-ups' about his handicap, but his path to international racing was not easy. In 1954, Lister's first year with cars of its own manufacture, Scott-Brown's racing licence was suspended because of a medical enquiry. After less than two months, it was restored, but the authorities in Italy never let him compete there.

The Lister chassis was based on two three-inch steel-alloy tubes in kite-shaped planform, with similar cross-members, and boxed at the front by fabricated uprights to mount the double wishbone and coil spring front suspension; at the back of the chassis, drilled fabricated uprights carried the differential, inboard-mounted brakes and the de Dion axle located by twin radius-rods and a central sliding block. The first car had an MG 1,500cc engine and gearbox and it was fitted with a very simple aluminium-alloy body.

This first car performed adequately, but the Bristol-powered car that appeared in the sports car race at the British Grand Prix meeting at Silverstone on 17 July 1954 was sensational. Scott-Brown won the 2-litre class, finished fifth overall and beat many cars of larger capacity, including the three ex-works *Écurie Ecosse* C-type Jaguars. For the rest of the season and throughout 1955 Scott-Brown and the Lister, apart from the occasional mechanical failure, dominated the 2-litre sports class of British racing.

Lister supplied a number of cars with minor chassis changes to private buyers, in 1955 with very distinctive twin-tailfin bodies and in 1956 with the very low, smooth so-called 'flat-iron' bodies. A Maserati 2-litre engine powered the 1956 works car and although it was unreliable and scored only three wins, Scott-Brown was always fastest in his class. Lister built a 1,500cc Formula 2 car in late 1956, but it never ran under its own power.

For 1957 Lister decided to race a Jaguar-powered car and it proved the most successful of the Jaguar-powered hybrids – Lister included, there were four main Jaguar-powered makes, HWM, Cooper and Tojeiro. The Lister-Jaguar followed the specification of the earlier cars, but was strengthened throughout, and had a two-inch (51mm) wider rear track. Lister used Girling disc brakes, still inboard at the rear and Dunlop alloy disc wheels (in place of the original wire-spoked wheels) and these were bolt-on or fitted with quick-release hubs according to whether wheel changes might be necessary during the race. The body was similar to that of the 'flat-iron'.

The Lister handled better than any of its rivals and, this coupled with Scott-Brown's lurid driving style, consisting of more time spent time power-sliding the car than in a straight line, made it almost invincible in British events. The green car with distinctive yellow stripe and Archie at the wheel, ran in 14 short British races won 11.

Scott-Brown was beaten in one race. In the 44-mile sports car race at the International Trophy meeting at Silverstone in September 1957 Scott-Brown and Salvadori (Aston Martin DBR2) had a race-long battle and the Aston Martin driver won by a narrow margin. After the race it was discovered that the Lister's rear springs had settled enough to allow the de Dion tube to hit its bump stops, affecting the rear-end adhesion. In late 1957 Lister produced a revised and much improved Formula 2 car, but although it appeared at this Silverstone meeting, the works never raced it.

Over the winter Scott-Brown and a Lister with 3,781cc engine travelled out to compete in the Tasman series of races. Competing against mainly single-seaters, Scott-Brown ran in seven races: he won two, finished second in two, sixth in one after spinning off and retired twice. Demand for Lister-Jaguar chassis was considerable and Geo Lister & Sons Ltd laid down a production run for the 1958 season. These production cars had the wheelbase increased by 1.75 inches (28mm) to 7ft 6.75in (2,305mm), the track was wider front and rear and there were modifications aimed mainly at strengthening the chassis, together with a new body, these days known as the 'knobbly'.

The body was built in magnesium-alloy or aluminium

-alloy and it had a very low bonnet, curving smoothly over the engine and falling away to a low scuttle. International racing regulations prescribed a minimum windscreen height of ten inches (25.4mm) and the arrangement devised by Lister allowed a mounting of the screen lower than the bonnet so that the driver could look over it rather than through it. Buyers included Briggs Cunningham, one of whose cars had a Chervrolet engine, *Écurie Ecosse* and *Équipe Nationale Belge*. Bruce Halford also raced a Jaguar-powered Lister based on an earlier chassis.

World Sports Car Championship events were limited to cars of 3,000cc, although many other, mainly shorter, races were still run for cars of unlimited capacity. The Listers performed badly at Championship level, mainly because of the persistent unreliability of the 3-litre version of the Jaguar D-type. The make's successes in short-distance events with the 3,781cc engine were numerous, but a tragic accident was to set off the chain of events that brought the marque's racing career to an end.

Scott-Brown flew out to the United States to drive a 3-litre Cunningham-entered car in the Sebring 12 Hours race on 22 March. On the fourth lap the Lister slowed abruptly because of piston failure, Gendebien (works Ferrari) hit the Lister and rode up over the tail – the left front wheel of the Ferrari left a tread-mark on Scott-Brown's shoulder. Subsequently, two Cunningham Listers were fitted with 3,781cc Jaguar D-type engines and they dominated the Sports Car Club of America's Championship.

In the UK, Scott-Brown scored wins at Snetterton and Goodwood, but in his heat of the British Empire Trophy the Lister broke a steering arm – Lister made an urgent modification to prevent a recurrence. For the final he took over the car usually driven by Bruce Halford and finished third behind two Aston Martins. Scott-Brown won again at Aintree, but in the 73-mile (117km) sports car race at Silverstone in May Kansan Masten Gregory with the *Écurie Ecosse* car beat Scott-Brown into second place by 30 seconds. Afterwards

The Lister-Jaguar in its 1958, slightly modified form, popularly known as the 'knobbly'. Lister built a number of these cars for private teams and private owners and they remained remarkably successful, despite the tragic death of Archie Scott-Brown. (Brian Lister/James A. Allington)

In the sports car race at the International Trophy meeting at Silverstone in September 1957 Roy Salvadori (Aston Martin DBR2) leads Archie Scott-Brown (Lister-Jaguar). Salvadori won the race, but the main reason for the Lister's defeat was rear suspension problems causing loss of adhesion. (T.C. March/FotoVantage)

In 1959 Lister raced new Jaguar-powered cars with very bulbous bodies designed by Frank Costin. Drivers disliked the bodywork and the Jaguar engine was unreliable in 3-litre form. This is the works car of Bueb/Halford at Le Mans; they retired because of the inevitable engine failure. (LAT)

Scott-Brown said that he had driven as hard as he could, but was unable to match Gregory's speed. He was puzzled and upset by this.

In the 132-mile (212km) Spa Grand Prix held on 18 May Scott-Brown and Gregory met up again. Gregory was fastest in practice, in the race they battled furiously and there seemed to be a greater edge to the battle than mere rivalry. On a damp track Scott-Brown lost control at *Clubhouse Bend*, grazed the Dick Seaman Memorial, glanced along the Clubhouse wall, hit a road sign that broke the right-hand suspension, careered on down a slope, the car rolled and caught fire. Scott-Brown suffered severe burns to which he succumbed the following day. Gregory won from Paul Frère and Carroll Shelby (works Aston Martins).

Brian Lister lost all enthusiasm for racing and, probably, he should have withdrawn at this point, as he originally contemplated. The Listers failed at Le Mans and a special single-seater built for *Écurie Ecosse* to run against Indianapolis cars in the Two Worlds Trophy at Monza was dismally slow. Stirling Moss drove a works car to a win in the sports race at the British Grand Prix meeting at Silverstone in July, but Gregory crashed heavily, writing off the *Écurie Ecosse* car. In British events only limited success was gained during the remainder of the year.

Aerodynamacist Frank Costin designed a very bulbous body for the 1959 car and this was built with both Jaguar and Chevrolet Corvette engines. Cunningham ran two of the new cars in the United States. The works drivers were Ivor Bueb and Bruce Halford. The 1959 Lister, the last of the 'big banger' sports cars, proved no real match for the latest lightweight, smaller-capacity Cooper Monacos and Lotus 15s and both cars retired at Le Mans because of engine failure.

On 26 July Bueb and Halford crashed in a Formula 2 race at Clermont-Ferrand. Both suffered bad injuries and Ivor Bueb died six days later. Brian Lister withdrew from racing immediately. Private owners continued to race Listers, mainly the 1958 'knobblys', for several years. The Lister-Jaguar's success was short-lived, but Scott-Brown and these fantastic cars live on in the memories of many enthusiasts.

Ludovico Scarfiotti and Mike Parkes shared this Ferrari 330P3 berlinetta at Le Mans in 1966. The car is seen early in the race with the headlamp patches still in place. Scarfiotti crashed the car early on the Sunday morning when he collided with a Matra reversing back on to the track. (LAT)

In 1967 Ferrari raced the much-improved 330P4 cars. This is Chris Amon at the wheel of his P4 spyder in the BOAC 500 race at Brands Hatch. He and co-driver Jackie Stewart finished second to the Phil Hill/Mike Spence Chaparral 2F and clinched the Prototype Championship for Ferrari. (LAT)

Above: *Ford scored their second successive win at Le Mans in 1967. Dan Gurney and A.J. Foyt drove this Shelby American Mark IV to a win at an average of 135.482mph (217.991kph).* (Ford Motor Company) Opposite top: *The Porsche 908 coupé in 1968 form with long-tail (langheck) body. During the year the long-tail version failed to win a single Championship race. They were far less stable than the short-tail cars, used on slower circuits, and these won two races in 1968.* (Porsche Werkfoto) Opposite bottom: *Porsche prepared the 908.03 Spyders, not the entrants, in 1970–71. This is the car that Siffert/Redman drove to a win in the 1970 Targa Florio. The photograph is believed to have been taken at the Porsche factory, but the building in the background looks ripe for redevelopment.* (Porsche Werkfoto)

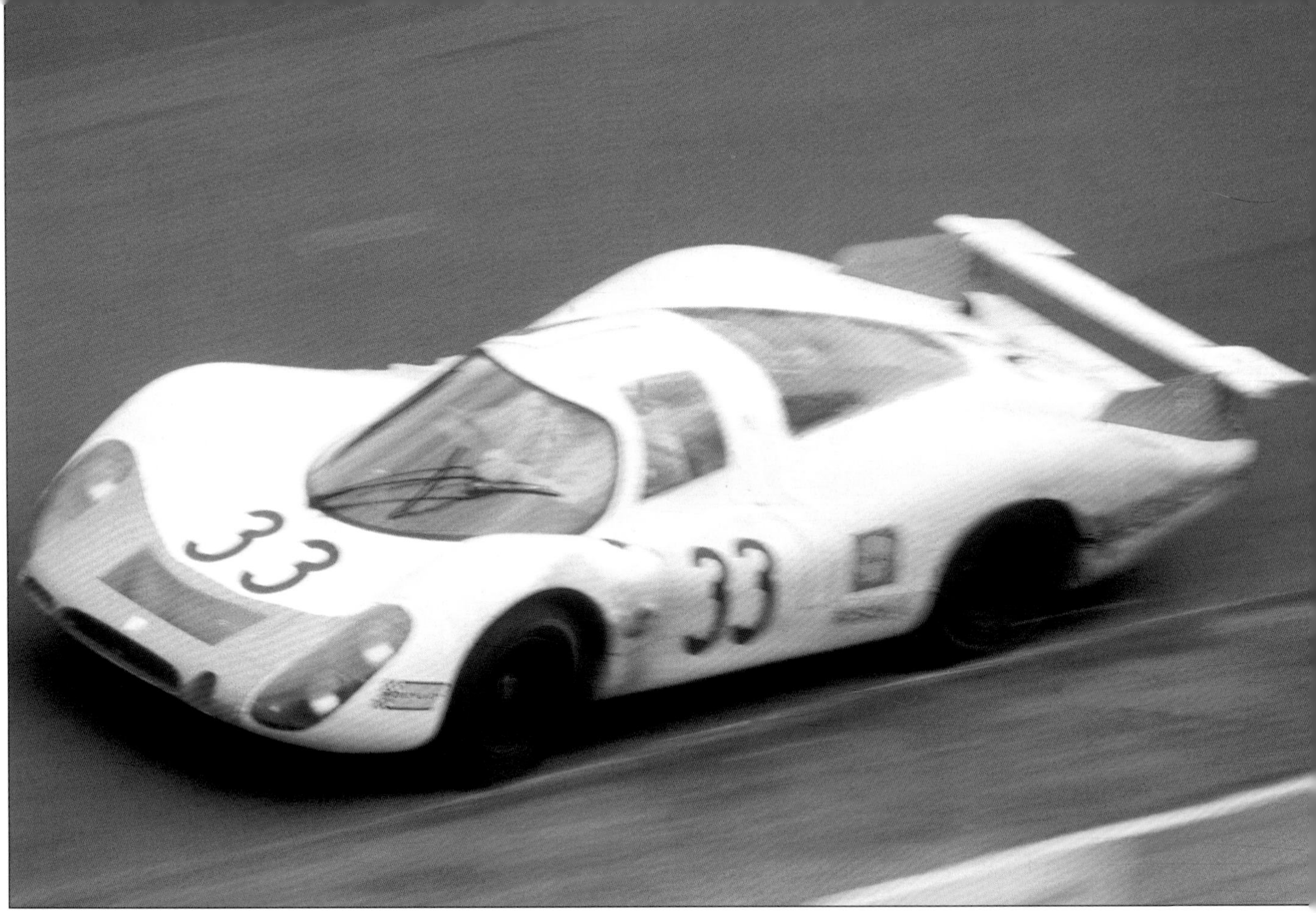
33
33

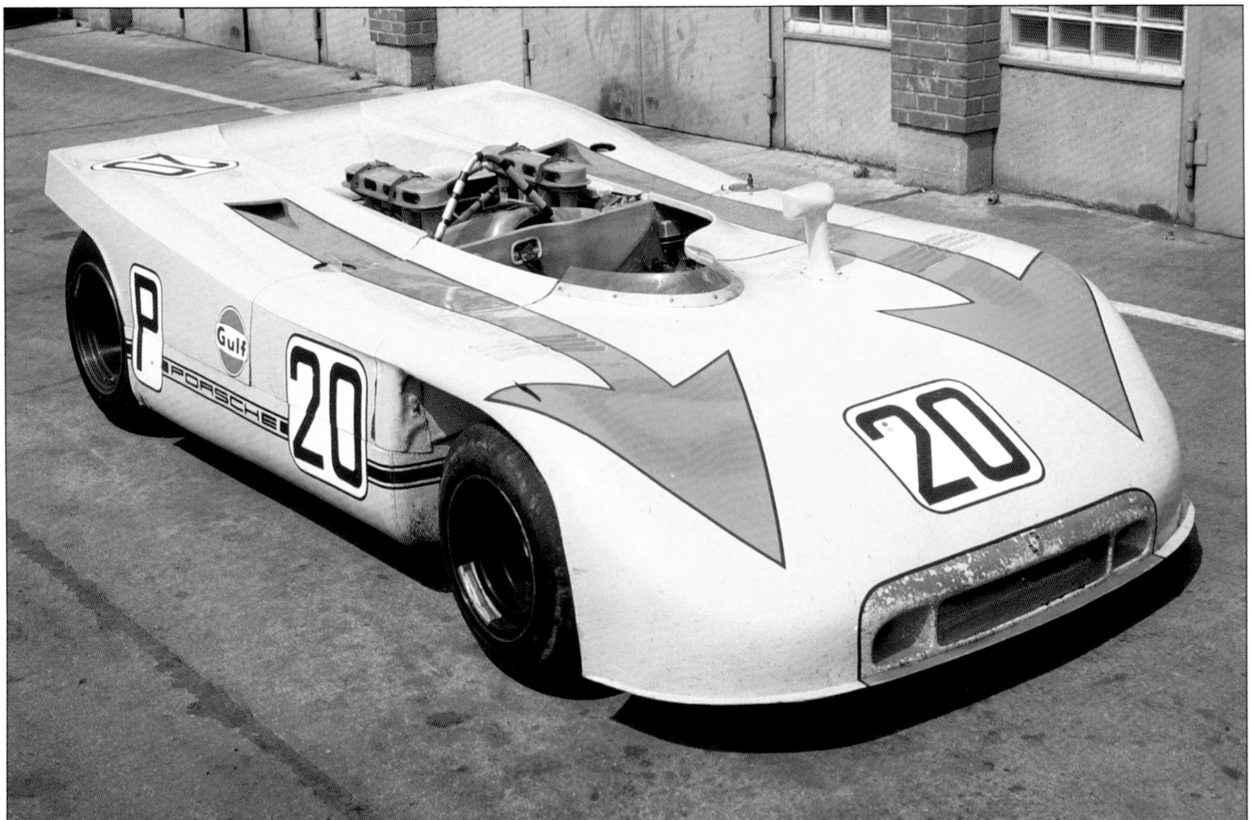
P
Gulf
PORSCHE
20
20

The 4.5-litre 917 that Richard Attwood and Hans Herrmann drove to Porsche's first win at Le Mans in 1970. It is seen during a routine pit stop on the Sunday morning of the race. It won through consistent driving and the failure of faster 917s; those of the Gulf team in particular.

Bob Wollek and John Burton drove Canon Camera-sponsored Chevron B21s in the 1972 European 2-litre Constructors' Championship. Here Wollek is at the wheel of his B21 in practice for the Barcelona round of the Championship held in October on the magnificent Montjuich Park road circuit. He set joint fastest lap, but failed to finish. Chevron finished second to Abarth in the Championship. (LAT)

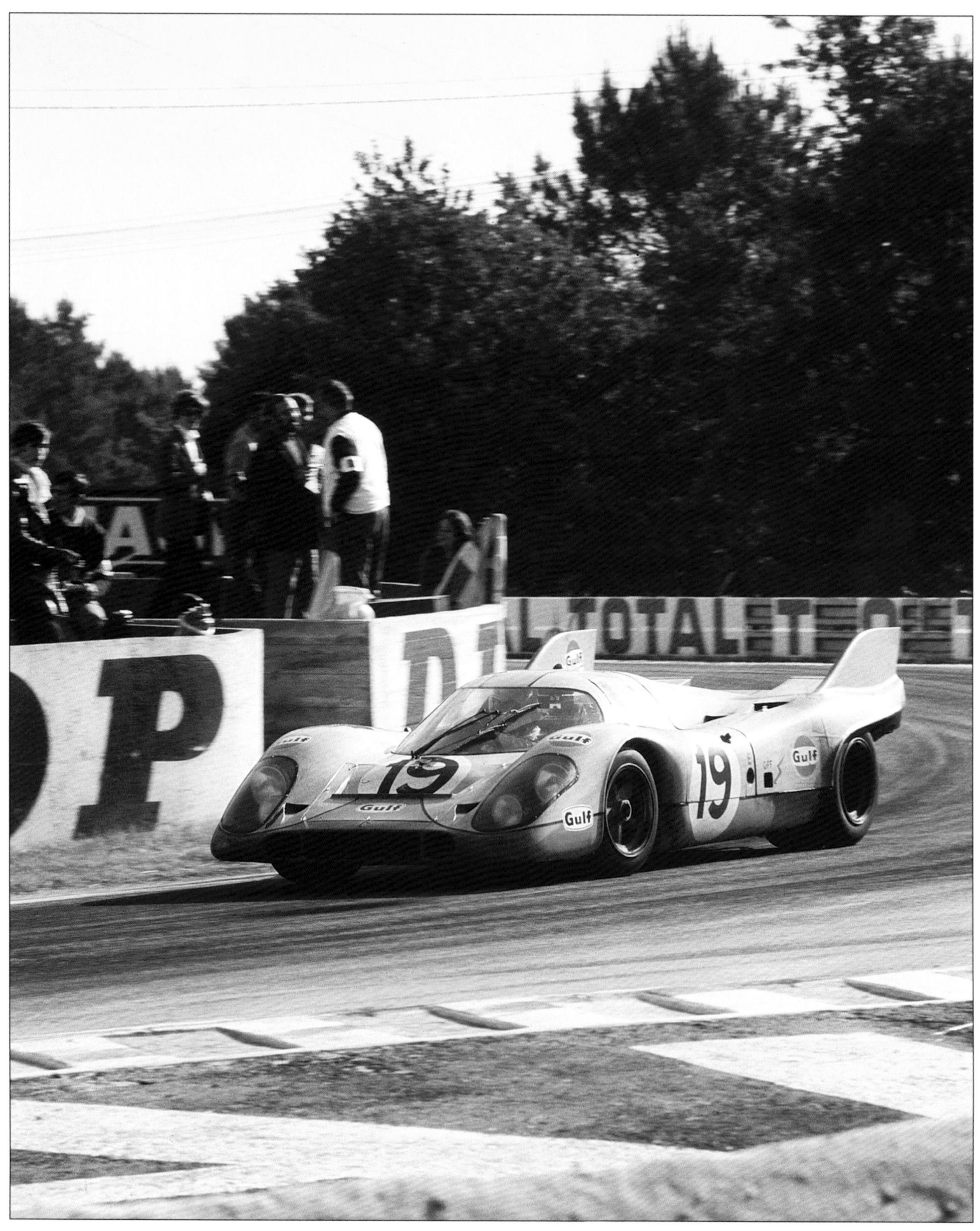

Although the Gulf-Porsche team failed to win at Le Mans in 1970-71, in the latter year Herbert Müller/Richard Attwood drove a superb race with this 917 to finish second, despite mechanical problems. They were catching the leading Martini-entered 917 when the two teams agreed not to race against each other. (LAT)

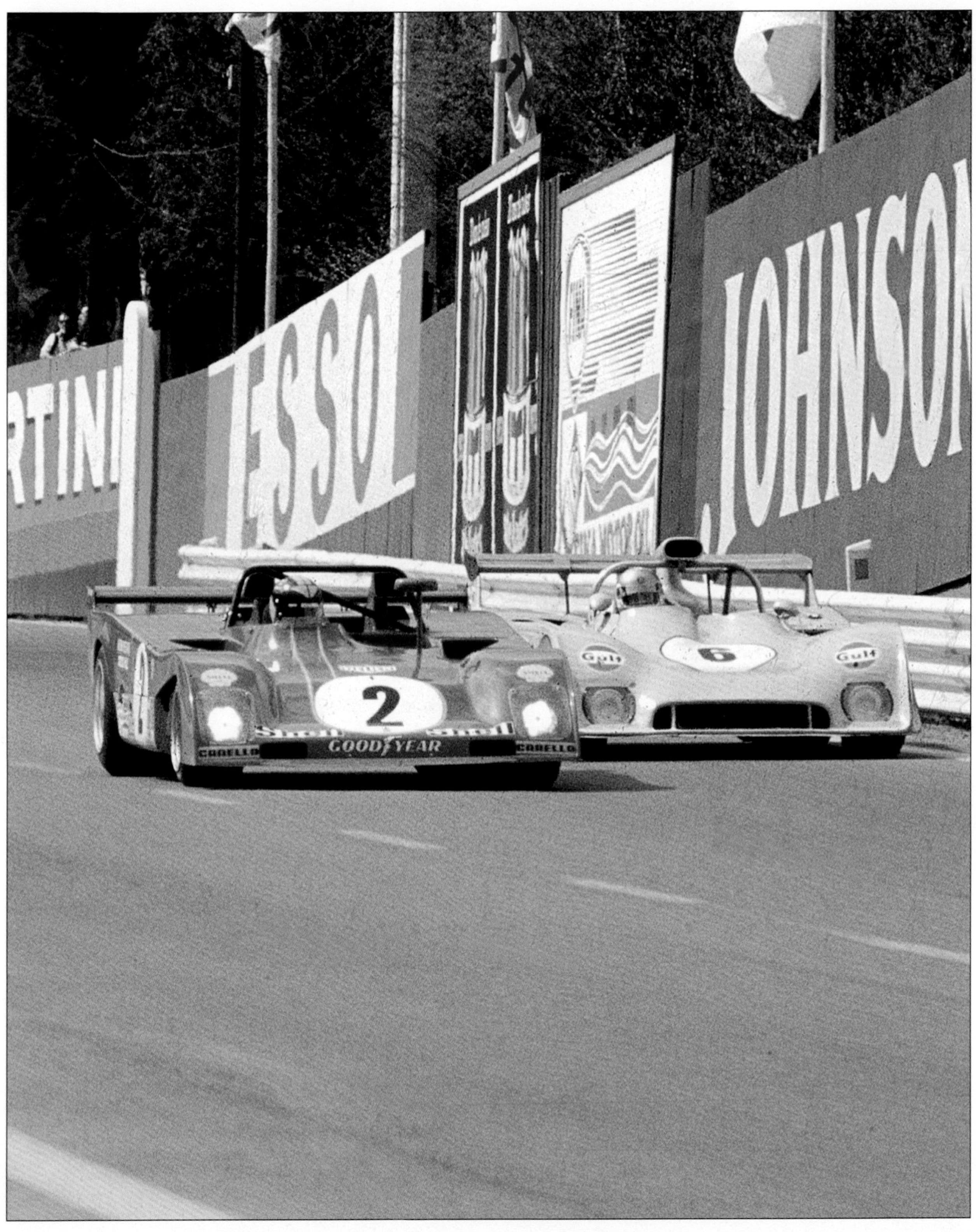

Spa 1,000Km race, 1973: on the very fast run from La Source hairpin to Eau Rouge corner, Carlos Pace with his 312PB Ferrari hurtles past the Gulf-Mirage-Ford of Schuppan/Ganley. Both Ferraris retired, the surviving Matra finished a poor third and the Gulf-Mirage-Fords took the first two places. (LAT)

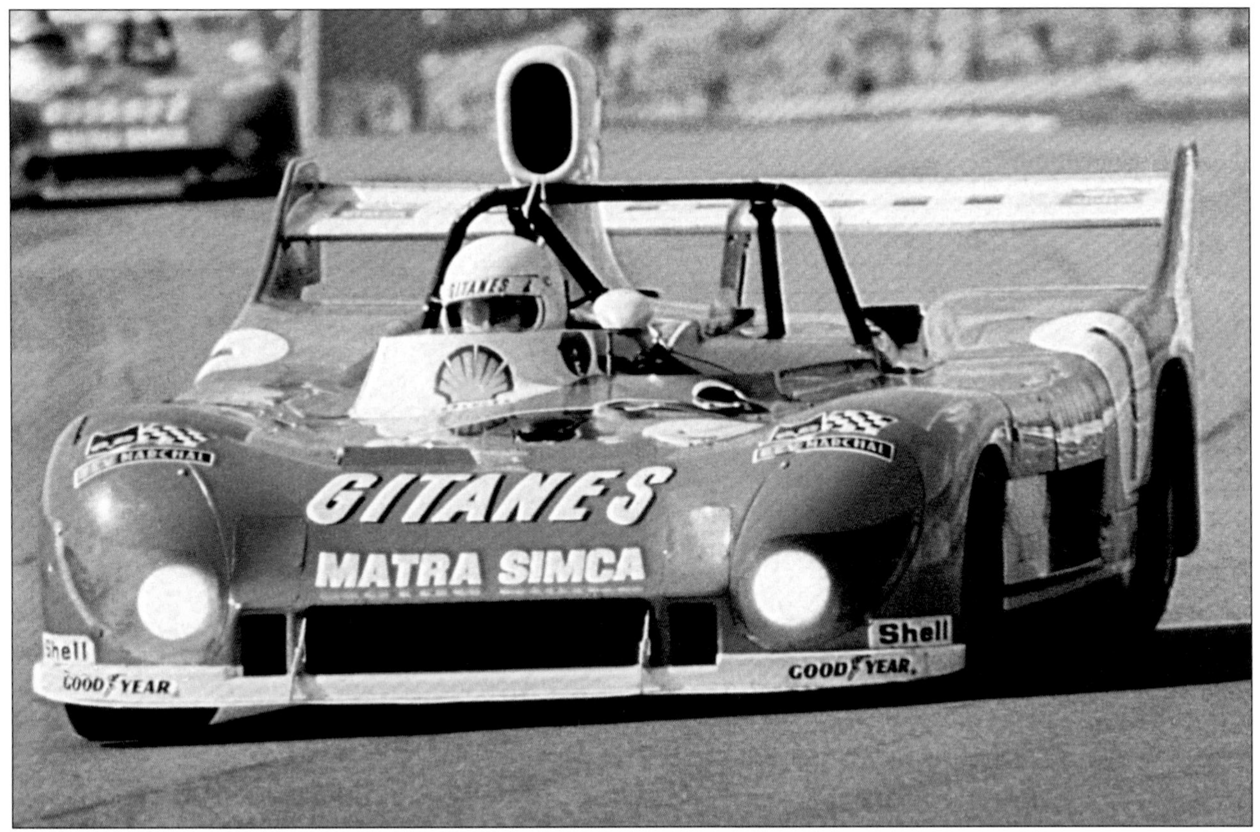

In the absence of serious opposition, Matra completely dominated sports car racing in 1974. In early laps of that year's British Airways 1,000Km race at Brands Hatch the MS670C of Jean-Pierre Jarier/Jean-Pierre Beltoise leads the similar car of Henri Pescarolo/Gérard Larrousse. They took the first two places.

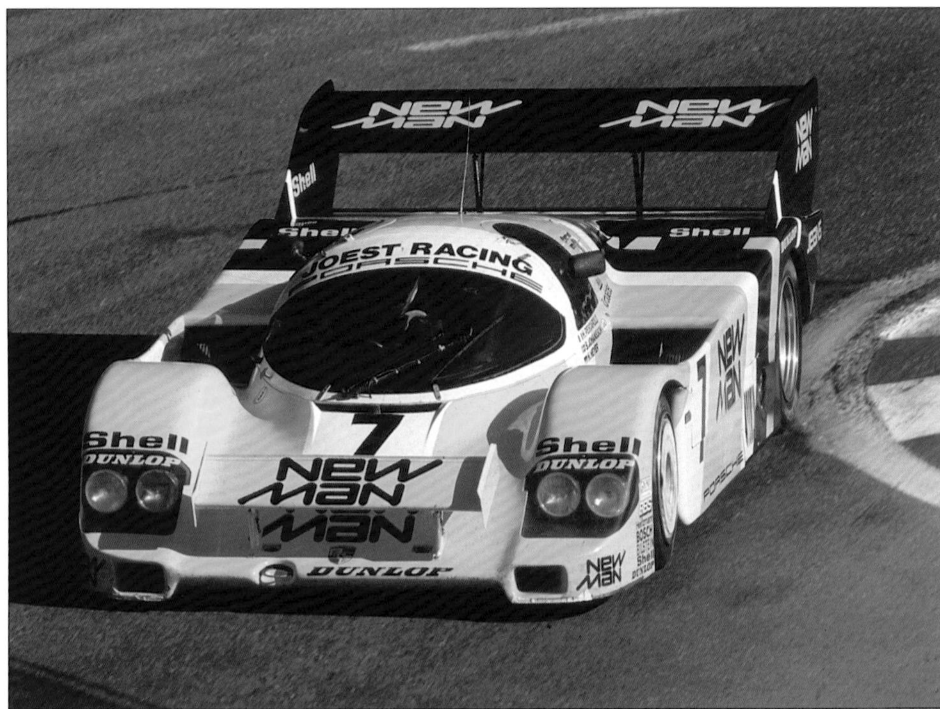

In the 1985 Spa 1,000Km race Ludwig/Barilla finished third with this 956B Porsche sponsored by New Man. The race was cut short after the fatal accident to Stefan Bellof at the wheel of another Porsche. (LAT)

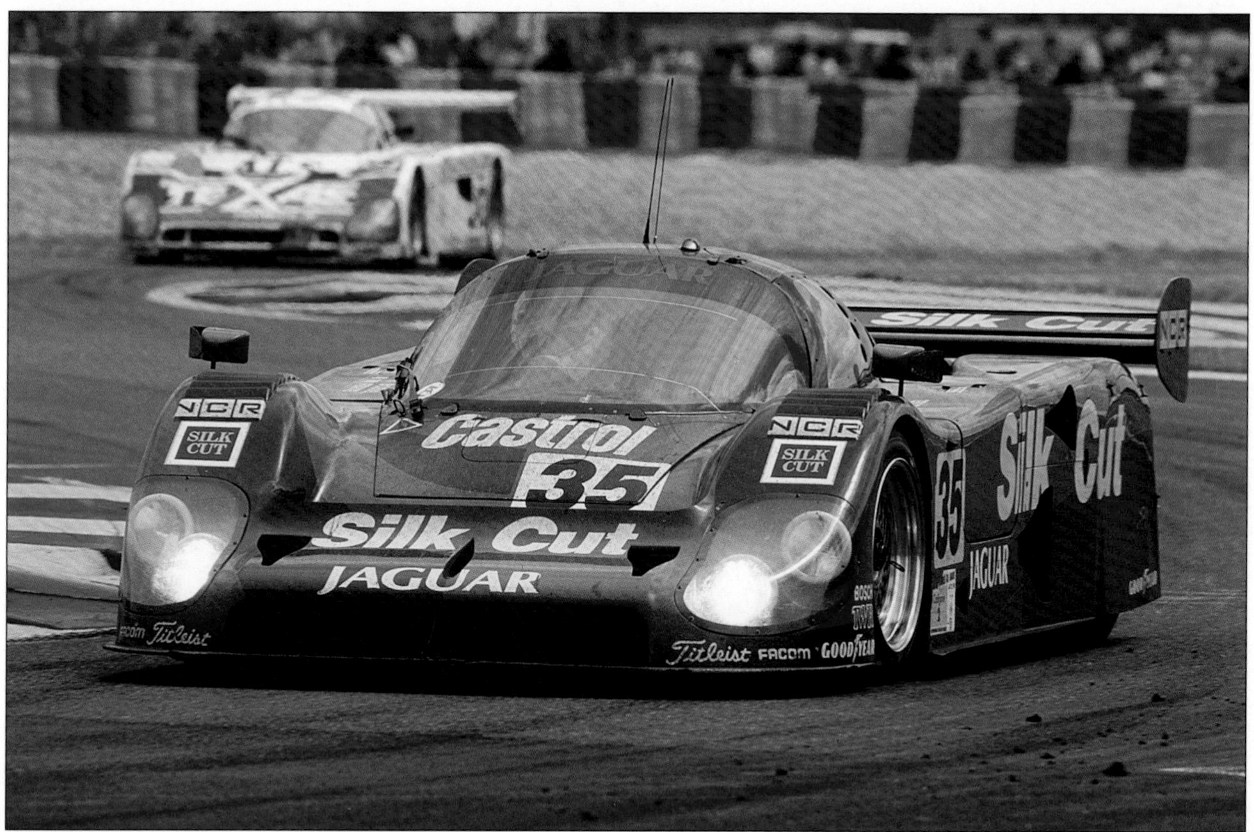

Le Mans in 1991 proved a great disappointment for Jaguar and the race was won by a lightweight turbocharged Toyota. The XJR-12s finished second, third and fourth. This is the second-placed car of Jones/Boesel/Ferté. (LAT)

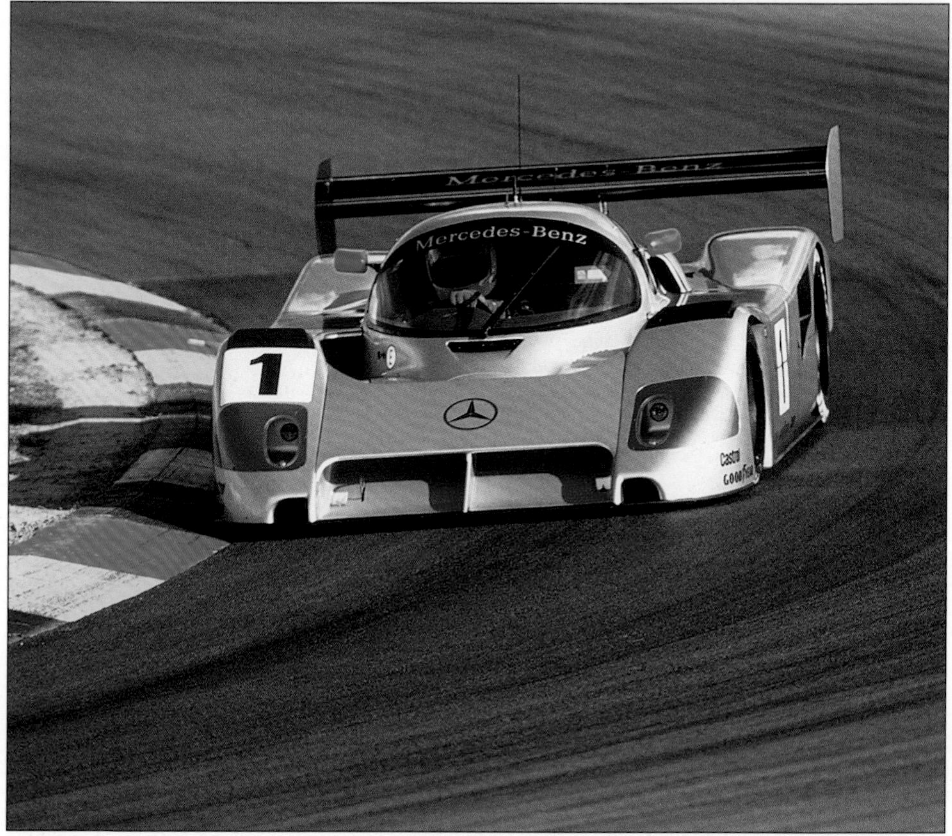

In 1991 the new 3.5-litre 291 Mercedes-Benz (née Sauber) entries proved disappointing. Jochen Mass/Michael Schumacher did, however, drive this car to a win in the Nürburgring race. (Daimler Chrysler)

Ferrari V12 *Testa Rossa*

1958–60

Mike Hawthorn, seen here at the wheel, and Wolfgang von Trips drove this works 250TR Testa Rossa into second place behind Moss/Brabham (Aston Martin DBR1) in the 1958 Nürburgring 1,000Km race. In the background is an abandoned Lotus Eleven. (FotoVantage)

During 1956–57 Ferrari had raced a new breed of V12 cars, originally the work of former Lancia engineer Andrea Fraschetti, who was killed during a testing accident at Modena in April 1957. In 1956 Ferrari raced the 290 *Mille Miglia* cars with 3,490cc single cam per bank V12 engines alongside the Tipo 860 *Monzas* and although they were beautifully balanced, good handling cars, they were not really fast enough.

For 1957 Ferrari switched to four overhead camshaft cars and progressively enlarged the engine capacity. First came a four-cam version of the 290 and then the 3,780cc (76×69.5mm) Tipo 315 *Sport* and the 4,023cc (77×72mm) Tipo 335 *Sport*. The Jaguar D-types still dominated Le Mans and Ferrari faced stiff opposition from Maserati in other races, but with wins at Buenos Aires, in the Mille Miglia and at Caracas Maranello won the Sports Car Championship for the fourth time.

Although these Ferraris still had a good racing life ahead of them, the FIA had indicated that there would be an engine capacity limit in Championship events from 1958 onwards, but failed to specify what it would be. Some thought that it would be 3,500cc to accommodate the Jaguar D-type engine, others, including Ferrari, opted for 3,000cc. The final decision, 3000cc, was not made until October 1957, by when the new Ferrari had been tested and developed.

Ferrari considered whether he should build a 3-litre version of the V6 *Dino* car or opt for a fairly simple V12. Although a 3-litre V6 car, the *Dino* 296S with

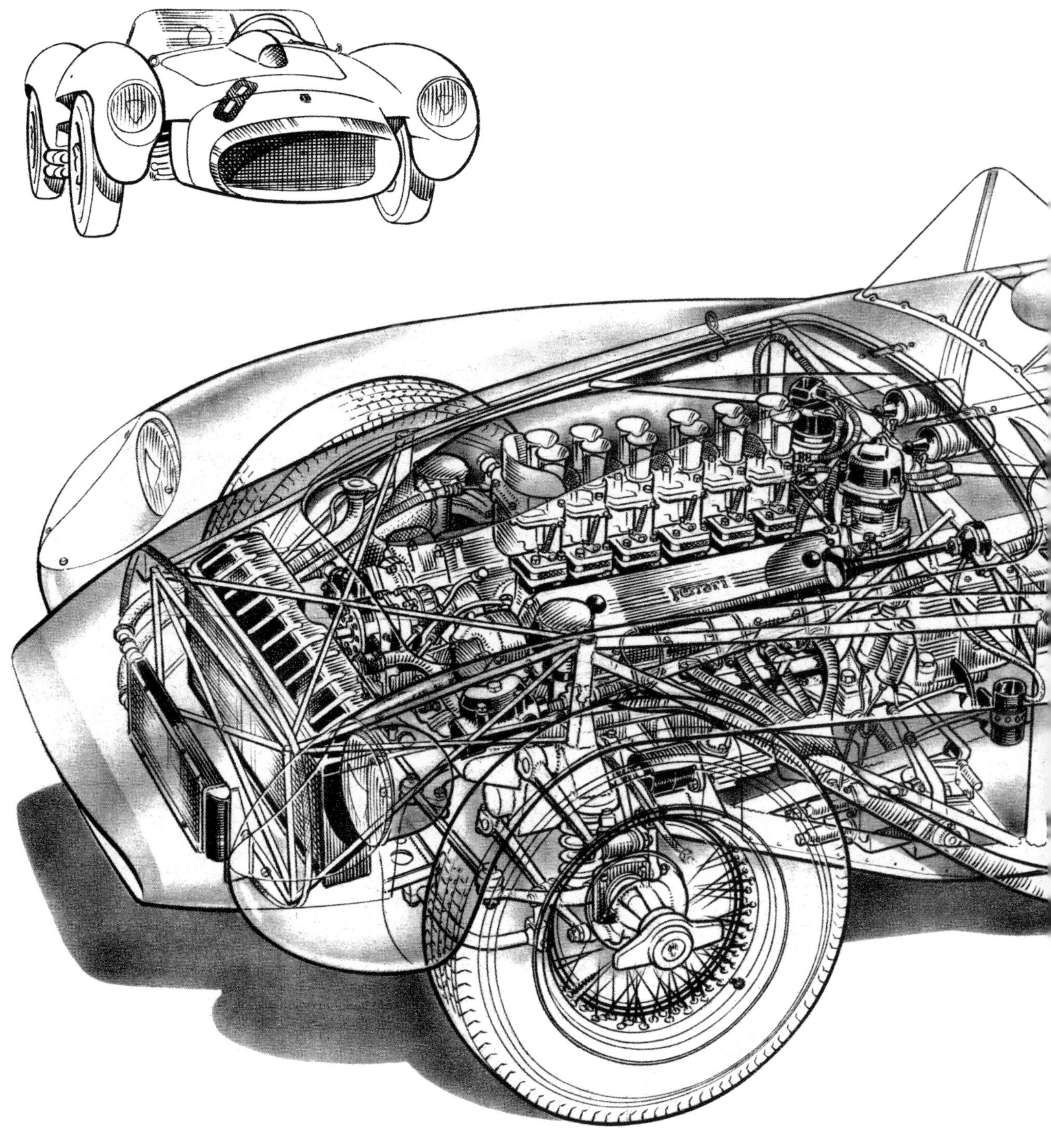

2,962.08cc (85×87mm) engine, was raced by Hawthorn at Silverstone in May 1958, this was just a 'one-off' experiment. The final decision was to race a car powered by a developed version of the Colombo-derived 250GT 3-litre engine and with that model's four-speed gearbox in unit with the engine.

The first prototype ran in the Nürburging 1,000Km race on 26 May 1957. It used the 290MM ladder-type, tubular 7ft 8.5-in (2,350mm) wheelbase chassis and had independent front suspension by double wishbones and coil springs and a de Dion rear axle suspended on a transverse leaf spring. The body was similar to that of the other 1957 works cars. Gendebien was due to drive the new car with Masten Gregory, but he switched to

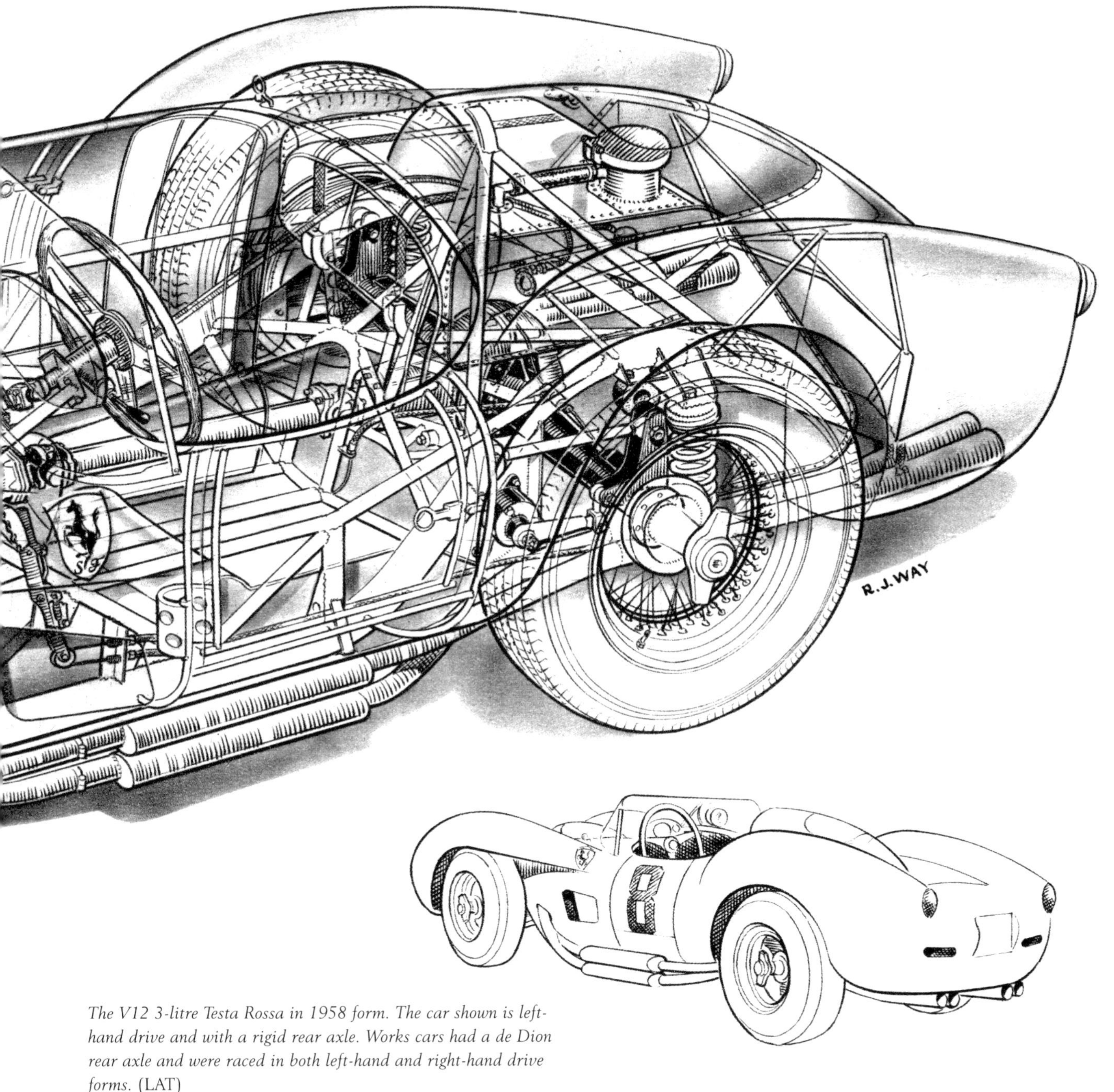

The V12 3-litre Testa Rossa in 1958 form. The car shown is left-hand drive and with a rigid rear axle. Works cars had a de Dion rear axle and were raced in both left-hand and right-hand drive forms. (LAT)

another car and so Carlo Morolli took his place. He had never sat in the car and his pre-race experience was restricted to a few blasts up and down the pit road.

Gregory drove quite a fast race, but Morolli, usually an OSCA driver, was overwhelmed by the power of the car and the responsibility. They eventually took tenth place. Ferrari developed a four overhead camshaft version of the 3-litre engine, but eventually settled on the single-cam layout, with the bottom end of the engine strengthened and the sparking plugs moved outside, near the exhaust valves, permitting the installation of six Weber twin-choke 38DCN carburettors in the vee of the engine.

A second prototype used the lighter four-cylinder

2-litre *Testa Rossa* chassis with wheelbase extended from 7ft 4.5in (2,250mm) to 7ft 8.5in (2,350mm) and a rigid rear axle suspended on coil springs. There was new and distinctive bodywork by Scaglietti with long sloping nose and cutaway front wings. This and the Nürburgring prototype were entered at Le Mans, the latter with four-cam engine. Both had a capacity of 3,117cc (75.0×58.8mm). The four-cam car non-started following piston failure while being warmed up. Gendebien and Trintignant ran well with the new car until it retired with piston failure just after midnight. Ferrari was struggling with a bad batch of pistons.

Both prototypes ran at Kristianstâd and Caracas and in Venezuela von Trips/Seidel and Trintignant/Gendebien drove them into third and fourth places. Ferrari announced the definitive 250 *Testa Rossa* at his press conference in November. The specification included the 2,953cc engine developing 300bhp at 7,200rpm, a strengthened four-speed gearbox; works cars would be raced with either rigid or de Dion rear axle and left or right-hand steering, but customer cars would have a rigid rear axle and left-hand steering.

Maserati had been forced to withdraw from racing, so Ferrari faced little opposition in 1958, except when Aston Martin deigned to race and the British beat the *Testa Rossas* only once. In the first Championship race, the Buenos Aires 1,000Km event on 26 January, Musso crashed the car he was sharing with Gendebien on the first lap, but Phil Hill/Peter Collins and Mike Hawthorn/Wolfgang von Trips took first two places ahead of Moss/Behra (Porsche). Aston Martin ran in the Sebring 12 Hours race on 22 March, but both DBR1s retired and Hill/Collins and Musso/Gendebien took the first two places.

The Targa Florio was a round in the Championship and Ferrari faced a single DBR1 that retired early in the race and Behra/Scarlatti with 1,587cc Porsche who gave the Ferrari drivers a hard time and finished in second place just under six minutes behind Musso/Gendebien with the winning *Testa Rossa*. Hawthorn/von Trips and Hill/Collins finished third and fourth, while the fourth entry driven by Munaron/Seidel retired after Seidel slid off into a rocky field, splitting the sump and losing all the engine oil.

With three successive wins Maranello was brimming with confidence when they arrived at the Nürburgring for the 1,000Km race on 1 June, even though Moss was driving for Aston and a DBR1 had won the race in 1957. Moss won again for Aston Martin, but it was a hard-fought victory, as co-driver Brabham was inexperienced with the DBR1 and was much slower than Moss. By the finish Moss had pulled out a lead of nearly four minutes and was followed across the line by the complete Ferrari team in the order Hawthorn/Collins, von Trips/Gendebien, Hill/Musso and Seidel/Munaron.

The works DBR1s retired at Le Mans and the Jaguars were unreliable in 3-litre form – except the works-prepared car of Hamilton/Bueb, which was in a secure second place on the Sunday morning when Hamilton crashed. Phil Hill/Gendebien drove a cautious race, much of it held in the wet, and won at a slow 106.056mph (170.914kph), 100 miles ahead of the private Aston Martin of Peter and Graham Whitehead. Hawthorn/Collins retired their *Testa Rossa* with a damaged gearbox caused by violent gear-changes after the clutch failed, while Seidel overshot *Arnage* with the car he was sharing with von Trips and got it bogged in mud.

Ferrari had won the World Sports Car Championship for the fifth time and did not compete in the final round the Tourist Trophy at Goodwood on 13 September, a four-hour race counting only for half-points. The final results of the Championship were Ferrari, 38 points; Aston Martin, 16 points; Porsche, 4 points. During 1958 the works Ferrari team had raced the two prototypes in updated form and two new cars. Ferrari also sold 19 production cars to private entrants.

For 1959 Ferrari introduced a modified works car, the TR59, although the true 1959 works cars differed quite substantially from that displayed at Ferrari's press conference in December 1958. There were three new TR59 team cars, plus a further two completed in April, with a new multi-tubular space-frame, right-hand-drive chassis. The engine had coil valve springs instead of the original hairpin-type and a power output of 306bhp at 7,400rpm. Lubrication was now dry-sump to prevent oil surge starving the bearings.

The engine was moved four inches (100mm) to the left in the chassis to line up with a new five-speed trans-axle with magnesium-alloy casing and designed by Colotti. Ferrari fitted Dunlop disc brakes and used Dunlop instead of Englebert tyres. The bodies were a new design by Pinin Farina, built by former Maserati bodybuilder Fantuzzi and more conventional in shape than those used in 1958. Ferrari had resolved not to build any more customer cars.

Following the deaths of Musso and Collins, and the retirement of Hawthorn, Ferrari recruited a new team of drivers, Tony Brooks, Jean Behra, Dan Gurney, together with ex-Lotus driver Cliff Allison. Hill and Gendebien remained with the team. Loss of interest in sports car racing had reduced the number of rounds in the Championship to five. Aston Martin intended to compete only at Le Mans (but there was an early change of mind) and otherwise, the only serious opposition came from the works 1,587cc Porsches.

Cliff Allison and the 1960 Targa Florio

In the 1960 Targa Florio I was partnered with Richie Ginther, which was not very sensible as he was short and I was very tall. He was also the test driver and they built the cars round him. I just could not drive the car and I told Tavoni, "Look, I'll do a practice lap in it, but racing this thing is just out of the question, I just cannot get into it." Tavoni said that they would take the covering off the seat, do this, do that, but it still didn't fit. The problem in making the cockpit any roomier was that a tube of about three-inch diameter ran across just behind the seat.

The Ferrari people told me that they would have to make a major chassis modification and I told them that if they wanted me to drive the car, they'd have to do just that. I actually went and got my case and I was walking down the road to Cefalu to get a taxi to the airport when Tavoni came running along and said, "No, no, no, we'll alter the car."

So they had to make a major modification by moving the tube back. The car that we were driving was a brand-new TRI60 and in practice there was a terrific bang as I went along the straight, I swerved the car across the road and it felt okay. It wasn't until I had slowed down a little bit that I realised that one of the front tyres had blown, it was the left tyre, and I was heading straight for the abutment of a bridge. I switched the car into a field and I ended up right across the other side in a ditch.

I walked back to the road and got a lift back to the pits in the next Ferrari that passed. It felt quite hairy after my accident. After practice I returned to the car with the mechanics and they were pleased to find that nothing had broken on the car. "It was only a blown tyre", they said, but for me, it was a very nasty experience.

We took over another, older *Testa Rossa* for the race. I did the first stint and when I came into the pits to hand over to Richie, we were in fourth place behind a trio of Porsche entries. Richie took over from me, but only a kilometre from the pits he tried to pass a slower car on the outside, went off the road and hit a tree. The car was sitting there on its tail, with its nose pointing upwards.

Cliff Allison, a former Lotus works driver, who joined Ferrari in 1959 and stayed with the team until he had a bad crash in practice for the 1960 Monaco Grand Prix. (LAT)

At Sebring on 21 March the sole Aston Martin entry retired and a TR59 shared by Gurney/Daigh/Hill/Gendebien won from another TR59 driven by Behra/Allison. At the Targa Florio on 24 May the Ferrari drivers were unhappy with the awkward gear-change on the new five-speed gearbox and were worried about Porsche lap times, for the German cars were almost as fast as the Ferraris and needed one less refuelling stop in this 626-mile (1,007km) race. The Gendebien/Hill and Gurney/Allison cars retired because of transmission problems. The Behra/Brooks car was withdrawn after both drivers had crashed it. Porsche entries took the first three places.

The Gurney/Allison TR59 in the Targa Florio had a revised engine with larger-choke Weber 42DCN carburettors, modified valve timing and was said to develop 330bhp at 7,700rpm. Two of the entries were in this form at the Nürburgring. None of the Ferrari drivers could match the speed of Stirling Moss with the sole Aston Martin and, despite the handicap of co-driver

Fairman who put the DBR1 into a ditch and then had to lever it out with his back, the British car won by a margin of 41 seconds from Hill/Gendebien and Behra/Brooks, with Gurney/Allison in fifth place.

At Le Mans on 20–21 June three TR59s faced three DBR1s. The Aston Martins took the first two places, but the Ferraris were victims of the folly of racing manager Tavoni and their drivers as much as the superiority of the Aston Martins. The TR59s were undergeared, their drivers revved them into the ground in practice and the race and all Tavoni's entreaties that they should restrict revs to 7,500 were ignored.

The drivers despised the oily Tavoni, Ferrari's sycophant, and had come to treat him with contempt. In the race the high revs caused overheating and the cylinder blocks to expand; Allison, co-driving with Portuguese driver Hermanos da Silva Ramos, damaged the gearbox synchromesh rings because of clumsy gearchanges and the other two cars retired with engine problems caused by loss of water.

In the six-hour Tourist Trophy at Goodwood on 5 September a fire in the pits eliminated the leading Aston Martin, but another DBR1 shared by Shelby/Fairman/Moss won from the Porsche of von Trips/Bonnier with a Ferrari shared by Gendebien/Allison/Hill/Brooks third. The other 'surviving' Ferrari of Brooks/Gurney was pushed across the line into fifth place after a tyre failed on the penultimate lap. Ferrari pit management was poor and the *Testa Rossas* were handling atrociously, with a pronounced understeer that changed to extreme oversteer when power was applied. Aston Martin (24 points) won the Championship from Ferrari (22 points) and Porsche (21 points).

In 1960 the only opposition to Ferrari came from Porsche and the new, privately entered 2.8-litre Maserati Tipo 61 cars. Ferrari modified two cars and these are usually described as TR59/60s. The wheelbase was shortened to 7ft 5.75in (2,280mm) and the engine was mounted an inch (25.5mm) lower and slightly further back in the chassis. Because of the difficulties with the 1959 gearbox, Ferrari used a four-speed gearbox in unit with the engine. The latest Fantuzzi bodies were shorter and lower and had the ten-inch (255mm) windscreen with wipers and luggage accommodation compulsory under the latest regulations.

The Buenos Aires 1,000Km reappeared as the first race on the calendar and despite a strong challenge from a *Camoradi* Maserati driven by Gurney/Gregory, the TR59/60s of Phil Hill/Allison and von Trips/Ginther took the first two places, with the Porsche of Graham Hill/Bonnier third. Ferrari also entered a *Dino* 246 V6 car for Scarlatti and veteran Froilan Gonzalez, but this retired because of a broken magneto wire.

Ferrari missed the Sebring race on 26 March because the organisers insisted that all competitors used Amoco. The *North American Racing Team* entered one of the works TR59/60s that had competed in the Argentine for Chuck Daigh/Richie Ginther, but it retired because of a seized engine. Nethercutt/Lovely with the former's private TR59 finished third behind two works Porsche RSKs.

At the Le Mans test day on 9 April Ferrari ran the first of two new cars known as the TRI60. These cars had a shorter 7ft 4.6in (2,250mm) wheelbase, double wishbone independent rear suspension, an improved five-speed gearbox in unit with the engine and ventilated disc brakes. The weight was 1,510 pounds (685kg), about 150 pounds (68kg) lighter than the TR59/60.

Ferrari entered five cars in the Targa Florio held on 8 May and lost the Sicilian road race to Porsche yet again. One *Testa Rossa* crashed in practice and the other in the race (see SIDEBAR). Bonnier/Herrmann won with a Porsche RS60 from von Trips/Phil Hill (rear-engined Ferrari *Dino* 246) and Gendebien/Herrmann (the latter drove two cars) with another RS60.

It was much the same story in the Nürburgring 1,000Km race on 22 May. The race was run in exceptionally bad conditions, mist and drizzle worsening into thick fog. Although the *Camoradi* Maserati 'Bird-Cage' of Moss/Gregory lost time in the pits while a broken oil pipe was replaced, the drivers brought it through to win from the Porsche RS60 of Bonnier/Gendebien, with the highest placed Ferrari, the TR59/60 shared by Allison/Mairesse/Hill, a poor third.

Ferrari entered only *Testa Rossas* at Le Mans and a strong Maserati entry fell by the wayside. There was a cock-up by Tavoni and engineer Chiti over fuel consumption. The axle ratios had been slightly lowered since the Test day, Tavoni assumed there would be no significant change in fuel consumption and by the time that Chiti realised that the cars would run out of fuel two laps short of their intended pit stops and before the drivers could be warned, Hill/von Trips (TR59) did run out of fuel.

Mairesse/Ginther (TRI60) retired because of a broken drive-shaft and Gendebien/Frère (TR59/60) won the race from Ricardo Rodriguez/Pilette (TR59 entered by *North American Racing Team*). Jim Clark/Roy Salvadori finished third with the ex-works Aston Martin DBR1 entered by *The Border Reivers* team. Ferrari won the Championship yet again with 30 points to the 26 of Porsche and 11 of Maserati.

For the last year of the Sports Car Championship, Chiti engineered an improved version of the *Testa Rossa* with a new multi-tubular space-frame and very aerodynamic, twin-nostril, high-tailed body that had

The winning works TR59 Testa Rossa is parked in front of the pits before the 1959 Sebring 12 Hours race. Chuck Daigh/Dan Gurney/Phil Hill/Olivier Gendebien shared the driving. (FotoVantage)

been developed in a primitive wind-tunnel built by him at Maranello. Power output was now said to be 315bhp at 7,500rpm, the engine was lower and further back in the chassis, and transmission was by the five-speed indirect gearbox developed for the TRI60. Apart from the development prototype based on a TR60, there were two of these cars, typed the TR61, and Ferrari also raced the 246SP with a rear-mounted *Dino* V6 engine and similar styling to that of the TR61.

At Sebring in 1961 the TR61s of Hill/Gendebien and Mairesse/Baghetti/Ginther/von Trips took the first two places. In the Targa Florio Rodriguez/Mairesse drove the only TR61, but retired after Rodriguez spun off. Von Trips/Gendebien won the race with a 246SP. Gregory/Casner with a *Camoradi* 'Bird-cage' Maserati won at the Nürburgring from Pedro and Ricardo Rodriguez with a TR61. At Le Mans the TR61s of Phil Hill/Gendebien and Mairesse/Parkes took the first two places. For the Pescara Four Hours race in August Ferrari loaned a TR61 to *Scuderia Centro-Sud*. Bandini/Scarlatti won with the TR61 after Casner crashed his *Camoradi* Maserati.

Despite the change in the rules to Prototype racing in 1962, organisers accepted almost any sports or GT car in this first year of the new formula. *Scuderia Serenissima* run by Count Volpi entered its TR61 at Sebring for Joakim Bonnier and Lucien Bianchi (Graham Hill was to have driven this car, but was suffering from back trouble). They won the race after the stewards disqualified the leading TR61 of Moss/Innes Ireland entered by *North American Racing Team* for making its first refuelling stop before the minimum number of laps had been covered.

Two TR61s ran at Le Mans, but the winner was a new works Ferrari Prototype based on the *Testa Rossa* chassis, but with a 3,967cc V12 engine and known as the 330TRI/LM. Phil Hill/Gendebien were the drivers and headed a brace of Ferrari 250GTO GT cars. During the period 1958–61 Ferrari ran *Testa Rossas* in 19 races and won ten. It was a good record in itself, but what was most remarkable was that the model was at the forefront of racing for such a long period.

Lotus 23

1962–63

The Lotus 23 introduced at the 1962 London Racing Car Show was a development of the company's Formula Junior car. It was phenomenally successful and sold in very large numbers. (James A. Allington)

In 1959 Colin Chapman had introduced the Lotus 17 intended to beat the new and all-conquering Lolas in the 1,100cc class. He showed the drawings to his new engineer, Len Terry, who told him bluntly that Chapman's idea of having strut-type suspension front and rear would not work. Terry's views were completely vindicated for the 17 suffered from incurable 'stiction': under load the strut suspension units impacted on contact with the road, lost all movement and the cars became unmanageable. Lotus did not build another small-capacity sports car until 1962 and that was the radically different 23.

From 1960 onwards Lotus had been building and selling very successful cars for the single-seater 1,000cc unsupercharged Formula Junior. These had originated as a smaller-capacity version of the Lotus 18 Formula 1 car, but as development proceeded, the Formula 1 cars became much more complex, while the Junior cars remained relatively simple. The 23 was in effect a two-seater version of the 1962 Formula Junior Lotus 22 also announced at that year's London Racing Car Show.

As on the original 18, the chassis remained a multi-tubular space-frame constructed in three bays and fully triangulated, but widened to take two seats, and was generally more rigid than the single-seater versions. The top left and bottom right longitudinal tubes served as water pipes between the engine and the radiator. The front bulkhead provided mounting points for the front suspension, steering rack, battery, pedals and cross-flow radiator (with integral oil cooler). The bulkhead forming the scuttle located the steering column, instruments and gear-change. A third bulkhead, behind the driver and forming the firewall, mounted the 9-gallon fuel tank and the rear radius arms.

At the front, the suspension was similar to that of the 1961–62 Formula Junior cars, by unequal-length double wishbones and coil spring/damper units. The rear suspension was similar to that of the 1961 Formula 1 cars: upper lateral links, reversed lower wishbones, parallel radius arms and coil spring/damper units. Steering was rack-and-pinion, Girling 9.5-inch (240mm) brakes were outboard front and rear and there were Lotus 13-inch (330mm) 'wobbly-web' cast magnesium-alloy, foor-stud disc wheels.

The 23 was a very compact and light car, with 7ft 6in (2,285mm) wheelbase, 4ft 2in (1,270mm) front track and 4ft 3.5in (1,308mm) rear track. The usual power unit was a Cosworth-modified Ford 1,098cc four-cylinder developing 103bhp at 7,500rpm. Both 997cc and 1,594cc engines became available and tranmission was by either a Renault or VW-based four-speed trans-axle. There was provision for the installation of larger-capacity fuel tanks for longer races and the glass-fibre body complied with the then current Appendix J, Group 4 rules, including the compulsory luggage space provided alongside the engine.

These cars were an immediate success. *Ian Walker Racing* was the leading entrant in the model's first year and drivers included Paul Hawkins and, when he was available, Jim Clark. Clark turned in the 23's most impressive performance in the 1962 Nürburgring 1,000Km race. With Trevor Taylor as co-driver, he was at the wheel of a car powered by a new twin overhead camshaft 1,498cc engine based on the yet to be announced Ford Classic 116E cylinder block.

Light rain was falling at the start, Bruce McLaren (Aston Martin DBR1) led the field into the South Curve, but Clark with the 23 came out ahead and built up an astonishing lead. At the end of the first lap he was 27 seconds ahead, by the end of the next lap this had increased to 47 seconds and by the end of lap 8 Clark had a lead of more than two minutes. The gap began to narrow and by the end of lap 11 Willy Mairesse (4-litre Ferrari) had closed to within 42 seconds. Then the news came through that Clark had gone

Jim Clark at the wheel of an Ian Walker Racing 23 with 1,494cc Cosworth-Ford engine at Oulton Park in September 1962. Although Clark crashed in practice and had gear-engagement problems, he came through to finish second in this 50-mile race behind Innes Ireland in a 2.5-litre Climax-powered Lotus 19. (T.C. March/FotoVantage)

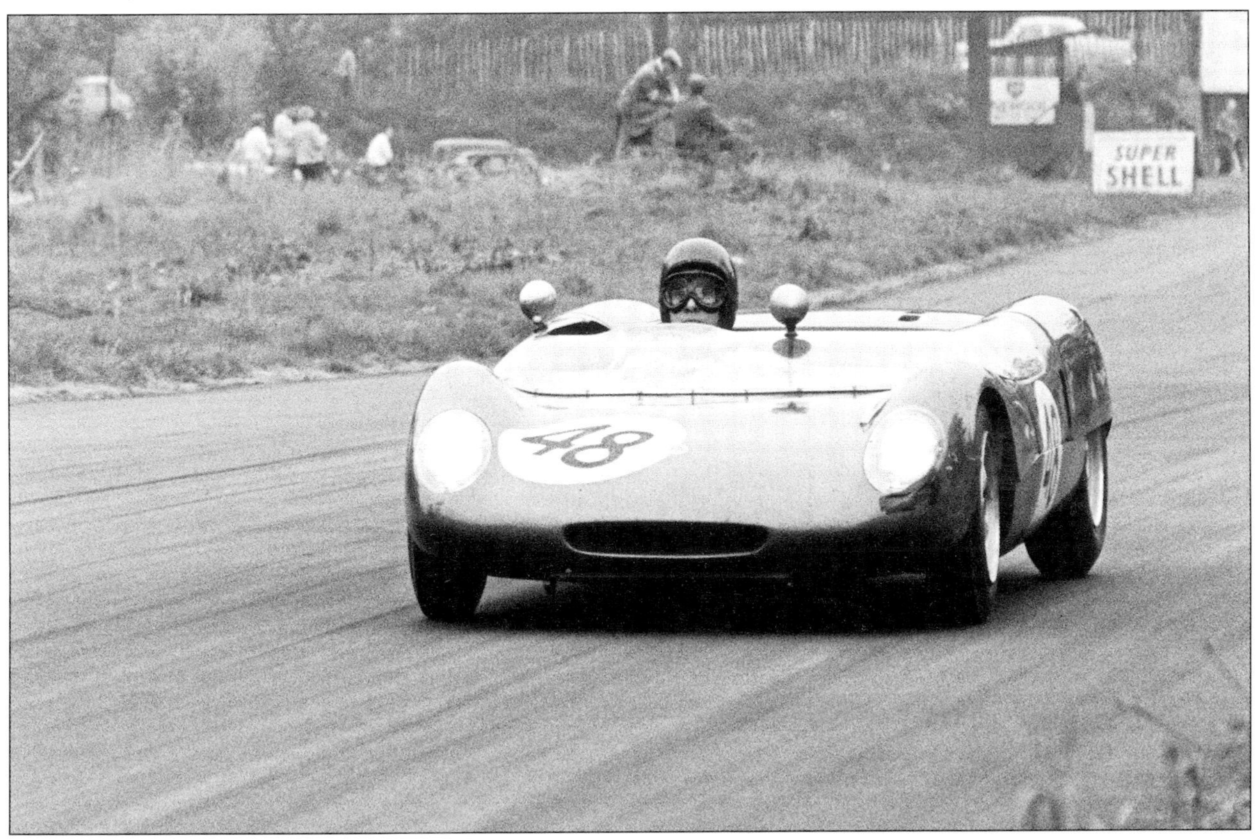

off the road at *Kesselchen*, about 7.5 miles (12km) from the pits, but was unhurt.

Later Jim Clark wrote, "[The performance of the 23] was incredible, but it could not last for ever. The exhaust manifold started to leak. I didn't notice it at first, but then I began to feel drousy. At the same time the brakes were not so good and a combination of all this led to my downfall. Coming into *Kesselchen* I changed down, but the car jumped out of gear and went into a slide. My reactions were too slow and I just couldn't correct it and went off into the bushes." No one associated with the car had expected it to finish the race, but neither did they expect Clark and the 23 to perform so well. The publicity from this 'failure' was immense and was heightened by the debacle at Le Mans.

Team Lotus and *UDT-Laystall Racing Team* each entered a Lotus 23 in the Experimental Class at Le Mans held on 23–24 June. This in fact meant the class for the new Prototypes. Both cars had high Plexiglas screens that wrapped well round the sides of the cockpit to comply with the regulations. Clark/Taylor were to drive the works car with a twin-cam 997cc engine and *UDT* had chosen Les Leston/New Zealander Tony Shelly for their 23 with Coventry Climax FWMC twin-cam 743cc unit.

The 743cc car was a clear contender for the Index of Performance, jealously guarded by Panhard and René

Seen here at Lodge Corner at Oulton Park in September 1963, Paul Hawkins finished eighth with this 1,150cc Lotus 23 and won his class in the 50-mile Sports Car race. Although Salvadori was the overall winner with a 2.7-litre Cooper Monaco-Climax, Lotus 23s took the next six places. (T.C. March/FotoVantage)

Bonnet as their own province. At scrutineering, the 23s were rejected because the fuel tanks were oversize, the turning circle was too great (it was restricted by the shallow front wheel arches), there was insufficient ground clearance and the fact that the front wheels were four-stud fixing and those at the rear six-stud. The car complied with the regulations that stated, "the method of fixation of the wheels must be the same at front and back." The method of fixation was of course the same, but the scrutineers considered that the cars should also comply with "the spirit of the regulations".

After a lengthy discussion, the scrutineers ruled that unless Lotus complied with their requirements by midday on the following day, they would not be allowed to race. Through a tremendous effort, including making the necessary parts to change the rear wheels to four-stud fixing, the chief scrutineer still rejected the 23s on the grounds that if there were six studs on the rear wheels originally, he expected to see the same number on the front. Lotus engineer Mike Costin patiently explained that the car was perfectly safe because the original layout had been designed with a view to installing the much more powerful BRM V8 engine.

Costin took the chief scrutineer by the arm and said to him, as he waved his slide rule, "If you say my car is unsafe, it means you must be qualified to say so. Perhaps we should together work out the stress calculations and I am sure that you will agree with me." Ignoring this intelligent approach, the scrutineers still rejected the cars. Colin Chapman flew out in his Piper Comanche, bringing with him Dean Delamont, the Secretary of the RAC Motor Sport Division, to support Lotus arguments, but to no avail.

It was a plot to support French motor racing interests and was widely publicised as such. After the race (in which a 702cc Panhard won the Index of Performance), the chairman of the race organisers, the *Automobile Club de l'Ouest*, made efforts to reach a financial settlement with Lotus, but Chapman considered it to be inadequate and made a vow, which he maintained, never to run works cars at Le Mans again.

For 1963 Lotus strengthened the chassis of the 23 and fitted the 1,594cc Ford-Lotus twin-cam engine as standard. In this form it was known as the 23B. *Normand Racing* ran the leading 23B team in 1963 and fielded cars for Mike Beckwith (also team manager), Tony Hegbourne and, when he was available, Jim Clark. These white cars with red and blue stripes made 49 starts and won 38 places, including 15 firsts. Other entrants scored successes worldwide, the 23/23B was one of the most successful of all Lotus sports cars and by the time that Lotus Components rolled out the last 23B in 1966, they had built 131 of both types.

Lola GT

1963

The Lola GT made its racing debut at the International Trophy meeting at Silverstone in May 1963. As Ferrari would not release John Surtees, South African Tony Maggs drove the Lola. He had not practised, so he started from the back of the grid and drove a gentle race to finish ninth. (LAT)

When Eric Broadley of Lola exhibited the Mark 6 GT Prototype at the 1963 Racing Car Show at Olympia, it was obvious that it was a major step forward in sports car design and that it had enormous potential. After building a special for the 750 Motor Club's 1172 Formula for Ford side valve-engined cars, Broadley had built outstandingly successful Climax-powered sports cars, followed up with Formula Junior cars that had achieved a modicum of success and had designed and constructed the Mark 4 Formula 1 cars; the *Bowmaker-Yeoman* team raced these cars in 1962 and with John Surtees at the wheel, they showed great promise, taking second places in the British and German Grands Prix.

The Lola GT was of monocoque construction, with a pair of large box-members linked by a steel floor pan that had small, boxed bracing members for mounting the seats and the central, remote-control gear-change. Each of the box-members, which carried the fuel, formed the door sills and had an inner face of sheet steel bent to a U-section and an outer face of duralumin sheet. Four cast magnesium-alloy formers inside each of the side-boxes had bosses to take attachments for the door frame and roof structure.

A tubular structure, mainly of square-section tubing, extending forward from the scuttle provided the mountings for the unequal-length wishbone and coil spring/damper unit front suspension and carried the cross-flow water and oil radiators and the spare wheel. The front suspension incorporated anti-dive and there

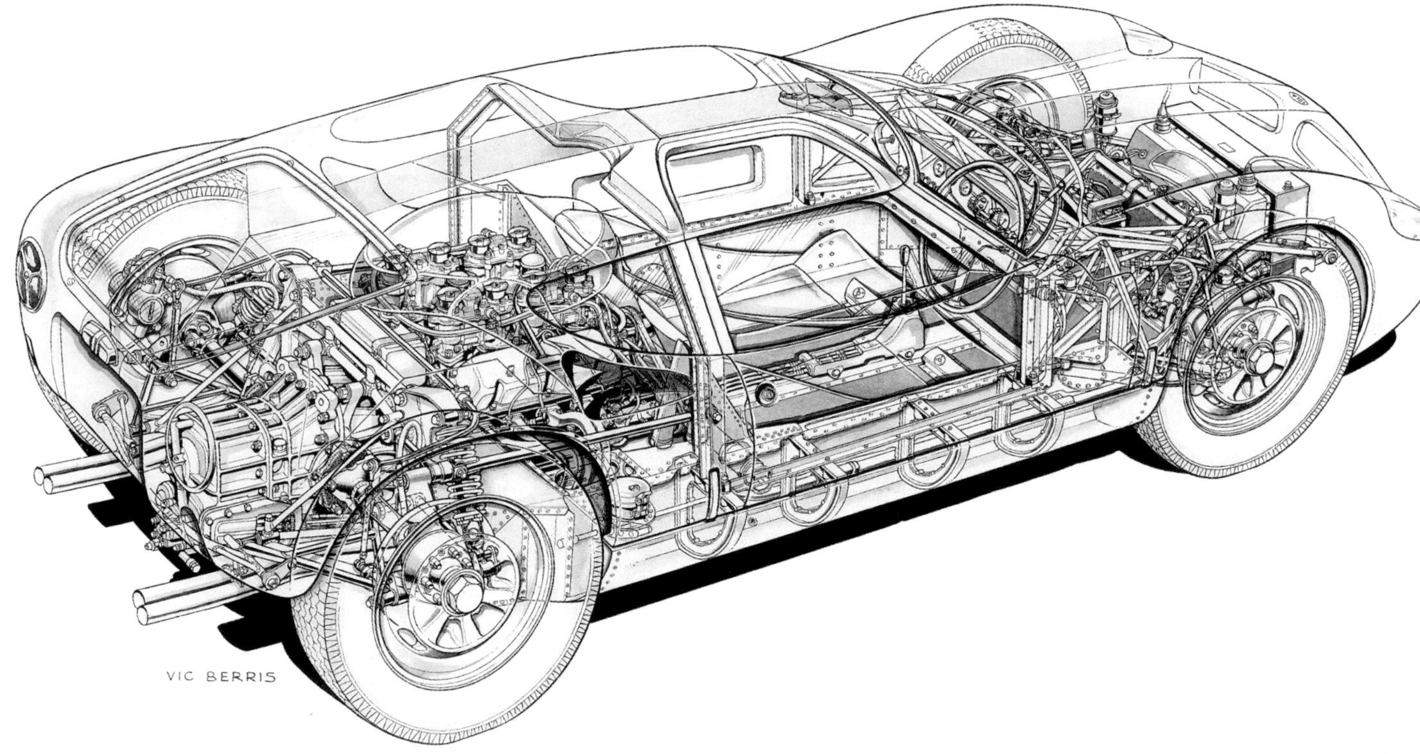

In this cutaway, maestro Vic Berris displays the details of the advanced construction of the Lola GT. It represented a major step forward in Sports Prototype design and was adopted by Ford, in less satisfactory form, as the basis of the GT40. (LAT)

was rack-and-pinion steering. From the rear of each side-box a fabricated extension terminated in a built-up pyramid box, the top of which mounted the rear coil spring/damper units.

A cantilever tubular section ran from the rear of the pyramids and there were cast-magnesium hub-carriers. These carried the A-shaped wishbones at the lower ends and the transverse links and long forward-facing radius arms at the upper ends. A Ford V8 engine was attached to the rear bulkhead of the monocoque. Behind this was Colotti four-speed trans-axle. Specialised Mouldings made the handsome glass-fibre coupé body. The GT had a 7ft 11in (2,410mm) wheelbase, together with a front and rear track of 4ft 6in (1,370mm). Dry weight was about 1,375 pounds (624kg).

Broadley tackled only a very limited season with the Lola GT and it first raced at the International Trophy meeting at Silverstone on 11 May 1963. At this event it had a 4,160cc Ford engine with Shelby modifications that included four-twin choke Weber carburettors and it developed about 260bhp at 6,500rpm. John Surtees was to drive the car, but at the last moment Ferrari refused his consent, and South African Tony Maggs took over, starting from the back of the grid without even having sat in the car before. In accordance with his instructions, he drove a gentle race to finish ninth.

Maggs/Bob Olthoff shared the car in the Nürburgring 1,000Km race on 19 May, but a loose rear wheel delayed it and engine problems caused its retirement. Lola entered two cars with Ford 4,728cc engines at Le Mans held on 15–16 June, but only one car for Attwood/Hobbs made it to the start and Hobbs crashed it on the Sunday morning. By the August Bank Holiday meeting at Brands Hatch American team *John Mecom Racing* had just taken delivery of a Lola GT, it arrived too late for practice and driver Augie Pabst completed four slow laps before retiring because of low oil pressure.

In the United States Mecom fitted the Lola with a 6-litre Chevrolet engine and Pabst drove the car in this form to a win in the Nassau Tourist Trophy. Not long after Le Mans, Eric Broadley had joined the Ford GT40 programme and although the Lola GT never had the chance to make its own mark in International racing, it formed the basis of one of the most successful of all Prototype GT cars.

Richard Attwood and the Lola GT at Le Mans

David Hobbs and I drove the Lola GT at Le Mans in 1963. It was sensational looking car and I think that it was a highly significant car in its day. Eric Broadley had entered two cars and there was a tremendous rush to get them ready and both David and I went to Lolas to help them. It was a fantastic team effort and we eventually got one car to Le Mans in time for scrutineering. Eric Broadley had not studied the regulations very closely and these required that from the interior rear view mirror there should be a clear view through the back of the car.

On the Lola in original form, the air intake was from the roof, as on all modern competition cars, into a large trunking area that fed the induction system. When you looked in the mirror, that was all you saw. Eric's reasoning probably was that the rake of the rear window was such that nothing could be seen in the rear-view mirror anyway because the view was totally distorted. The car had outside mirrors and although Eric thought that these would overcome the problem, the car failed scrutineering. When he learned this, Eric, exhausted by weeks of work on the cars, simply gave up.

Peter Jackson from Specialised Mouldings and Rob Russbrook, Eric's right-hand man were there and decided that something could be done about the situation. Eric, never seen with a cigarette in his mouth, retired to a corner and chain-smoked. Peter, Rob and the Lola mechanics hacked the whole of the rear bodywork apart, they blocked off the roof-top induction system and brought the induction through the left-hand side of the car, low down behind the door. In the rear-view mirror the driver could see only a distorted view through the Perspex, but it complied with the regulations.

The organisers saw what the team was doing and became very supportive. We passed the scrutineering deadline, but, even so, they approved the car to race. It was a time when people did not care too much about this sort of thing, it was a brand-new car and nobody gave it a chance. It was the Lola works team, but it was still an amateur effort, as the works were only a garage in Bromley. Graham Broadley drove the second car to Le Mans, but it missed scrutineering completely and it would have taken many hours to modify it.

The Lola was totally undergeared; Broadley had underestimated its performance and we were not able to achieve the top speed that we should have done. The gearbox was operated by three cables running to the gear-selector mechanism at the back, but it was a poor system and very imprecise. We knew about this and I was taking great care in changing gear. We were doing very well and we rose as high as eighth place at one stage.

In the 16th hour David Hobbs missed a gear-change going down into the *Esses*, he went off, hit the bank and the car was out of the race. I could've throttled him because of all the team effort to get the car into the race. He knew about the problem, so why go charging into a corner, knowing that you might have a selector problem?

The wreck of the Lola GT after David Hobbs missed a gear at the Esses and crashed. Although they are good friends, co-driver Richard Attwood was very angry. (LAT)

Ford GT40

1964–69

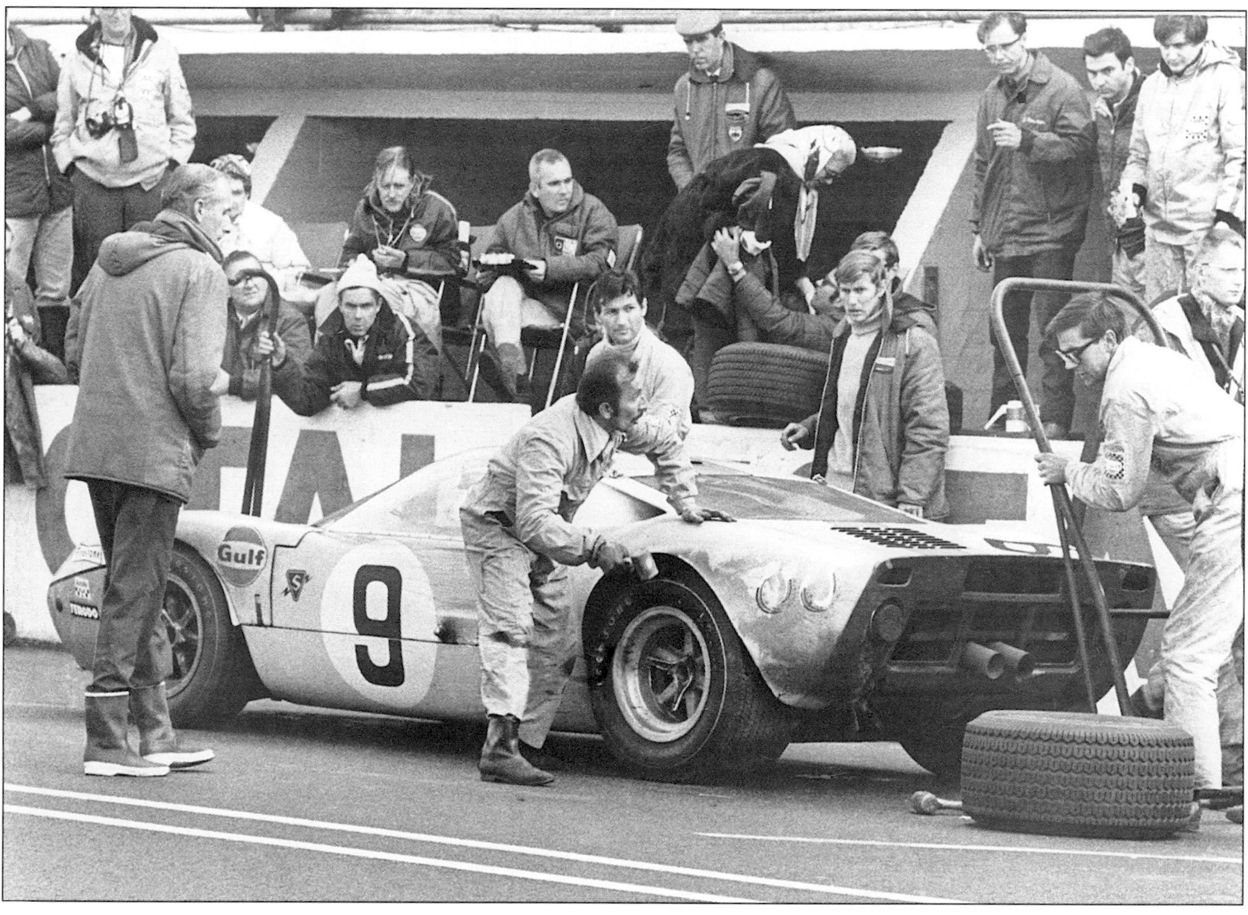

Pit stop for the winning Ford GT40 at Le Mans in 1968: in front of the car racing manager David York (in short boots) supervises operations and head mechanic Ermanno Cuoghi has just finished tightening the left rear wheel. In the back on the right are JW Automotive Technical Director John Horsman and driver Pedro Rodriguez. (Ford Motor Company)

After Ford's negotiations to buy Ferrari collapsed in May 1963, the American company set up a company to build a GT Prototype car with the intention that should be ready to race by Le Mans 1964. Already a fair amount of work had been carried out, as back in the autumn of 1962 Ford had instructed engineer Roy Lunn to start design studies for a Prototype car to be powered by the 4.2-litre V8 Indianapolis engine. Following the appearance of the very promising Lola GT in 1963, Ford arranged with Eric Broadley of Lola to take over these GT Prototypes and that he would work for them for what was, initially, to be a period of a year.

At the end of September 1963 John Wyer, formerly of Aston Martin, joined the project as Technical Director and General Manager and Ford Advanced Vehicles was set up on the Slough Trading Estate as a subsidiary of British Ford. Initially Ford appraised the Lola, made modifications to the cars and tested them extensively. These tests facilitated the design of the definitive Ford GT40 as it appeared in 1964.

The GT40 had a sheet-steel semi-monocoque chassis with square-tube stiffening and glass-fibre body panels. It was a less advanced design than its Lola predecessor. At the front suspension was by double wishbones, coil spring/damper units and an anti-roll bar. At the rear there were twin trailing arms, transverse top links, lower wishbones, coil spring/damper units and an anti-roll bar. Steering was rack-and-pinion and there were Girling disc brakes front and rear.

In accordance with the original brief, the engine was the Ford Indianapolis V8 of 4,181cc (95.5×72.9mm) with aluminium-alloy cylinder block and heads and dry sump lubrication. It was a relatively simple, unsophisticated engine developing 350bhp at 7,200rpm with four Weber twin-choke carburettors. Transmission was by a triple-plate clutch and a four-speed Colotti trans-axle. In its original form the coupé body lacked aerodynamic aids and it was painted American white and blue colours.

In early 1964 the cars were tested at the Motor Industry Research Association track near Rugby, and at Silverstone and Goodwood circuits before the team took the cars to the Le Mans Test Weekend. They proved aerodynamically unstable and both cars crashed. A rear spoiler was added, which made some improvement. To gain racing experience, a car was entered for Phil Hill/Bruce McLaren in the Nürburgring 1,000Km race. It was second fastest in practice and for a while held second place behind Surtees's Ferrari, but it was withdrawn from the race because of the failure of a rear suspension-mounting bracket, the result of incorrect welding.

Despite the obvious problems, Detroit expected a good result at Le Mans. Three cars ran, driven by Hill/McLaren, Ginther/Gregory and Attwood/Schlesser. The GT40s were second and fourth fastest in practice, although they were suffering from front-end aerodynamic lift at speed. At the end of the first hour Ginther/Gregory were leading, but dropped back and held second place place for the next three hours, before falling victim to problems with the Colotti gearbox.

Phil Hill/McLaren were delayed in the first hour because of an engine misfire, dropping back to 44th place, but climbed up to fourth after 13 hours only to retire because of gearbox trouble. Schlesser/Attwood were the slowest of the trio, but they were in sixth place when their car caught fire because of a split fuel pipe. While Wyer wanted to concentrate on development, Ford insisted that a full team should run in the Reims 12 Hours race on 5 July. Once again the GT40s battled for the lead, but all three cars were out before half-distance.

At the end of the year Ford humiliated Wyer and Ford Advanced Vehicles by transferring race-development work to the United States and race entries were entrusted to *Shelby American*. Slough built the rolling chassis for shipping to the United States and developed the existing model for production. Shelby carried out substantial modifications to the cars. His team substituted the 4,728cc (101.6×72.9mm) cast-iron block, wet-sump Ford 289 Fairlane engine and in full 'Cobra' tune this was reckoned to develop 390bhp at 7,000rpm. There was a ZF trans-axle (a modified Colotti unit was used initially) and cast alloy wheels replaced the original wire-spoked.

Shelby began the 1965 season by entering two cars in the Daytona 2,000Km race in February. There was not much in the way of opposition and Ginther/Bondurant and Miles/Ruby held the first two places until the lead car refused to fire up after a pit stop. After 27 minutes Ginther/Bondurant rejoined the race to finish third behind Miles/Ruby and Schlesser/Keck/Johnson (Cobra). Next came the Sebring 12 Hours race in late March and here McLaren/Miles were beaten into second place by the Chaparral (a much lighter sports car and not a Prototype) driven by Hall/Sharp. The second GT40 of Hill/Ginther retired because of a broken spring mounting.

Both Shelby and Wyer ran GT40s at the Le Mans Test Weekend and the Slough contribution was a new open version. It lacked the rigidity of the coupé, there was increased drag, but drivers generally preferred open cars. In 1965 Ford contested all the rounds of the Prototype Championship and despatched two cars prepared by British *Alan Mann Racing* to the Monza 1,000Km race on 25 April. It was not a successful outing, for the Fords were slower than the Ferraris that took the first two places, and McLaren/Miles were third, while the Amon/Maglioli car with 5.3-litre engine succumbed to drive-shaft problems.

Wyer entered the open GT40 for Whitmore/Bondurant in the Targa Florio on 9 May, but it was a totally unsuitable car for the Sicilian road race; it lost a wheel, resumed the race and eventually Bondurant lost control and wrecked the front suspension against a stone water trough. Four cars ran in the Nürburgring 1,000Km race on 23 May, including a 5.3-litre car entered by *Shelby* for Miles/McLaren and the open Wyer car. Only one entry survived, Amon/Maglioli who finished a poor eighth. Apart from the 7-litre Mark 2s, there were four GT40s at Le Mans, none lasted long, three retired because of blown cylinder head gaskets and one with gearbox failure.

In 1966 the GT40s for the model was homologated as a Competition GT car. Despite their poor competition record, they were the fastest cars that any private team could buy and they were widely raced. The most successful team was the American *Essex Wire Corporation*, whose cars were prepared by Wyer and managed by David Yorke, former Vanwall racing manager. Although they failed at Le Mans, where no GT40 was to finish until 1968, they achieved class wins at

Sebring, Monza and Spa. Other notable GT40 entrants included *Scuderia Filipinetti*, *Ford France* and *F. English Ltd* (Ronnie Hoare wearing another hat).

John Wyer and John Willment had bought Ford Advanced Vehicles from the parent company at the end of 1966 and the organisation became known as JW Automotive Engineering Limited. Partly because of the success of the *Essex Wire* team, Wyer was able to enter into a sponsorship deal with Gulf Oil that lasted for many years and the team's cars were painted in the distinctive pale blue and orange colours of a company that Gulf had taken over – Gulf's own dark blue was considered unsuitable. In the first races of the year the *Gulf* team ran GT40s, but at the Le Mans Test Weekend produced a new GT40-based Prototype called the Mirage M1.

Although the Mirage retained the lower, basic, steel structure of the GT40, the aluminium-alloy upper part of the body had a reduced frontal area of more streamlined shape and a more rounded cockpit area with sloping sides. Wyer installed larger-capacity engines and in its most successful form the Mirage had a 5.7-litre Ford engine developed by *Holman & Moody*.

Three GT40s ran at Le Mans in 1964, but none finished. Phil Hill/Bruce McLaren drove this car. They were delayed by ignition problems, but moved up to fourth place before retiring because of gearbox failure. (Ford Motor Company)

In most races the Mirages were overshadowed by the 7-litre Fords and works Ferraris, but in the rain-soaked Spa 1,000Km race Jacky Ickx partnered, rather inadequately, by American Dick Thompson, won easily from a 2.2-litre Porsche, the Ferrari P3/4 of Attwood/Bianchi and with the sole works P4 trailing in fifth place. It was an exceptional win that the team could not repeat during the year, but later Mirages driven by Ickx/Hawkins won the Paris 1,000Km race at Montlhéry and Ickx/Redman won the Kyalami Nine Hours race in South Africa.

When the *FIA* announced a 3-litre capacity limit for Prototypes with effect from 1968, the *Gulf* team continued to race GT40s, two newly assembled cars and a converted Mirage until their new Len Terry-designed 3-litre Mirage Prototype was ready to race in 1969. Although *Gulf* started the season with 4,728cc engines, the team carried out extensive development work during the year, adopting Gurney-Weslake cylinder heads and engines stroked to 4,942cc. The brakes were improved, as were the engine and gearbox lubrication systems and the glass-fibre body panels were reinforced by carbon-fibre. With high gearing Wyer reckoned that they were capable of 205mph (330kph).

After the GT40s failed at Daytona and Sebring, Ickx/Redman won for the team in the BOAC '500' race at Brands Hatch and Hawkins/Hobbs were the winners for *Gulf* at Monza. *Gulf* wisely missed the Targa Florio and Ickx/Hawkins were third for the team behind two works Porsche entries at the Nürburgring. Ickx/Redman (now with a 5-litre car) won the Spa 1,000Km race in the wet and Ickx, partnered by Lucien Bianchi, won again with a 5-litre car at Watkins Glen. Hobbs/Hawkins took second place for the team.

At Le Mans, postponed to 28–29 September because of strikes in France, *Gulf* entered three cars, all with 4,942cc engines and Gurney-Weslake cylinder heads. Two cars had Sullivan profile flat-tappet camshafts, while the car driven by Rodriguez/Bianchi had a special dry-deck engine with the water passages in the block welded up. Additional baffles were fitted in the sump to prevent oil surge under heavy braking. Preparation had been meticulous, with the engines running for 24 hours on the test bed with simulated gear-changes and braking. All three engines were said to develop 415bhp and in the race they were restricted to 6,000rpm (although capable of attaining 6,500rpm in top gear).

The might phalanx of four works Porsche 908s and three works-prepared, privately entered 907s proved fragile, two of the GT40s retired, but in chilly conditions, wet during the night, Rodriguez/Bianchi forged ahead to win by a margin of 45 miles (72km) from

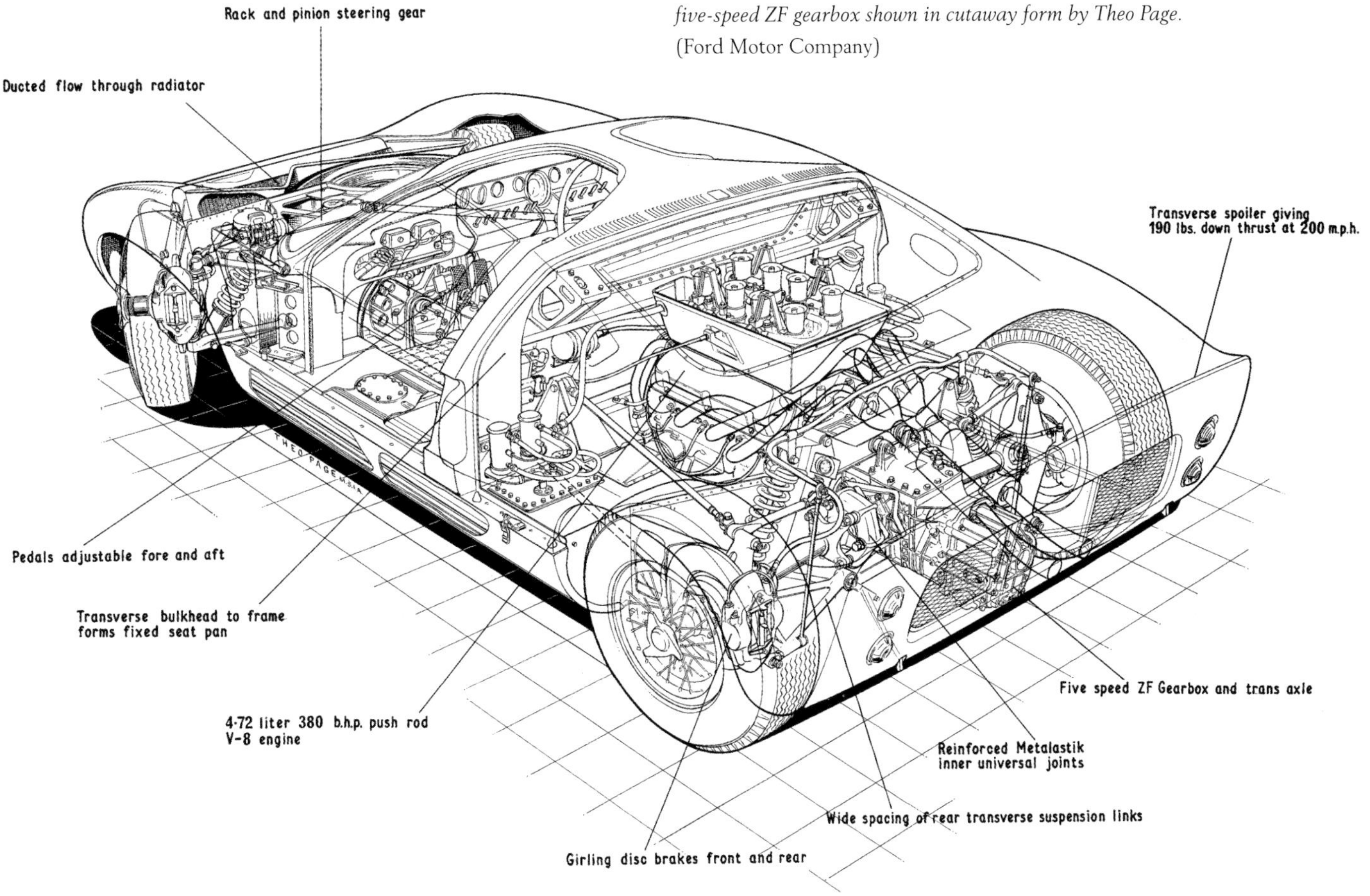

The GT40 in 1965 form with push-rod 4.7-litre engine and five-speed ZF gearbox shown in cutaway form by Theo Page. (Ford Motor Company)

Rack and pinion steering gear

Ducted flow through radiator

Transverse spoiler giving 190 lbs. down thrust at 200 m.p.h.

Pedals adjustable fore and aft

Transverse bulkhead to frame forms fixed seat pan

Five speed ZF Gearbox and trans axle

4·72 liter 380 b.h.p. push rod V-8 engine

Reinforced Metalastik inner universal joints

Wide spacing of rear transverse suspension links

Girling disc brakes front and rear

Porsche 907 and 908 entries. Only now on the fifth appearance of a GT40 at Le Mans had one of these cars finished the race and it was a very popular win.

The 3-litre Mirage first appeared in the BOAC race at Brands Hatch in April 1969, so *Gulf* entered GT40s at Daytona, where both entries were eliminated (foolishly, both Dearborn and Wyer were surprised to find that dry-deck engines worked only in cool conditions) and at Sebring the Porsche 908s were plagued by cracked chassis problems, and Ickx/Oliver with their GT40 scored an unexpected win. At Brands Hatch a single *Gulf* GT40 driven by Hobbs/Hailwood finished fifth.

Because of their reliability *Gulf* entered two GT40s at Le Mans. Porsche stumbled badly yet again and Ickx/Oliver won after a stirring battle between the young Belgian and the veteran Hans Herrmann with a rough-running Porsche 908 in the closing hours of the race. At the finish Ickx was a mere hundred yards ahead, having passed Herrmann under braking at *Mulsanne Corner* on the last lap, and was secure in the knowledge that there was nowhere that Herrmann could repass before the finishing line. It was an achievement that ranked alongside the wins by the 7-litre cars in 1966–7.

Gulf repeated their Le Mans victory in 1969 with this GT40 driven by Jacky Ickx/Jack Oliver. It was an unexpected win, for the Porsche team – on paper at least – was immensely strong. Ickx/Oliver finished only a hundred yards ahead of the Porsche 908 of Herrmann/Larrousse. (Ford Motor Company)

Lola T70

1965–69

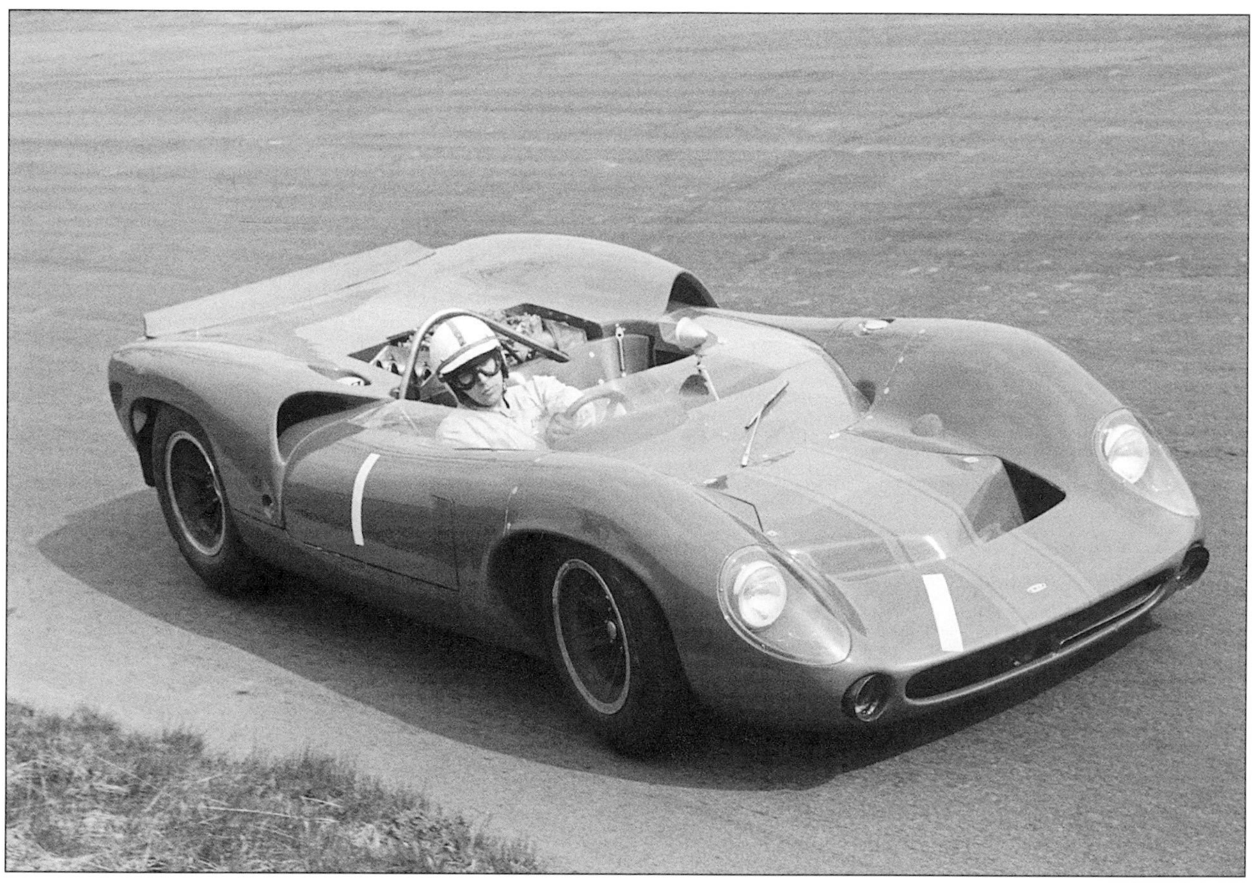

John Surtees at the wheel of his new red and green Lola T70 with Traco-developed 6.9-litre Chevrolet engine in the Tourist Trophy race at Oulton Park in April 1965. He led the first heat, but soon fell out of contention because of steering problems. (T.C. March/FotoVantage)

In the summer of 1964 Eric Broadley quit the Ford GT40 programme and formed Lola Cars Limited in premises on the Slough Trading Estate close to those of Ford Advanced Vehicles. Here Broadley built an open two-seater for the rapidly developing class that became known as Group 7. Lola exhibited the new car, the T70, at the 1965 London Racing Car Show and it proved just as a big a sensation as the Mark 6 GT two years previously.

The design was an evolution of the 1963 GT with a central sheet steel floor and 'D'-shaped sills each side, but with the fuel carried in aluminium-alloy tanks suspended from the steel sides and attached by flanges to save weight. At the rear of this structure there was a sloping rear bulkhead that formed the back to which the driver's seat was attached. The rear of the monocoque enclosed the engine, which was a semi-stressed member. At the front the monocoque tapered inwards to enclose the pedal box. The twin radiators and spare wheel were carried within the glass-fibre nose, but after the first few cars Broadley devised a box-shaped aluminium-alloy fabrication to carry the radiators.

At the front of the T70 there were magnesium-alloy suspension uprights with double wishbones and coil spring/damper units. The rear suspension consisted of lower reversed wishbones, single top links, twin radius rods each side and coil spring/damper units. There were anti-roll bars front and rear. Steering was BMC 1100 rack-and-pinion and the disc brakes were outboard front and rear. The wheelbase was 7ft 11in (2,410mm) and front and rear track 4ft 6in (1,370mm). The body was the work of Specialised Mouldings and when radiator mountings were changed, a detachable nose was fitted and this greatly improved access to front of the car. Weight was 1,375 pounds (624kg).

As first exhibited, the T70 had an Oldsmobile 4.5-litre engine and Hewland LG500 trans-axle. John Surtees took delivery of the first car for *Team Surtees* to race with the works. Initially this car was powered by a Traco-developed 5-litre Chevrolet engine, but early in the season Surtees was running the T70 with a 5.9-litre Chevrolet developing around 550bhp.

Broadley had concluded that the T70 was too heavy and after the first 15 cars they were built to Mark II specification. Instead of having a 60% steel/40% alloy monocoque, the aluminium-alloy content rose to 85% and the chassis was now riveted instead of welded. The fuel was carried in bag-tanks (because of leaks with the original alloy tanks) inserted in the sponsons and capacity had risen from 35 to 50 gallons. There were now radially ventilated brake discs and minor suspension modifications.

Race debut for the T70 was in the *Senior Service* 200 event held on a rain-inundated Silverstone at the end of March and stopped short because of the weather conditions. Surtees finished second to Clark (Lotus 30) after they both had spins – Surtees had gone off into a ditch, extricated the car and was in the pits about to retire when the race came to an end. Private teams rapidly took delivery of cars and they enjoyed a very successful year in British events, and in the United States where about 70% of the production was sold. Lola delivered about 15 T70s during the year.

The best British success was in the Guards Trophy at Brands Hatch at the end of August when Surtees and Stewart took first and third places on the aggregate of the two heats, sandwiching Bruce McLaren at the wheel of one of his own Oldsmobile-powered cars. In North America Surtees won the Player's 200 at Mosport Park in June from Jim Hall with his Chaparral. In September Surtees with his T70 won the Player's Quebec race at Mont Tremblant, but he crashed heavily in practice at Mosport Park the following weekend and suffered the severe injuries that nearly brought his racing career to an end.

Later that autumn Hansgen drove a Mecom-entered T70 to a win at Laguna Seca and second place at Las Vegas. Roy Pierpoint scored the final T70 win of the year in the Cape International Three Hours race at Killarney in South Africa. In a category which was strongly contested, the Lolas had performed well, but not as well as had been hoped.

During 1966 one of the most successful T70 entries was that of Irishman Sid Taylor whose car was driven by Denis Hulme. Successes during the year included wins at Snetterton and in the Tourist Trophy at Oulton Park, but the RAC ended Group 7 racing in mid-season and the T70s were not seen again until the first Can-Am series that started in September. Despite strong opposition from Chaparral and McLaren, Surtees won the Can-Am Cup with three victories from six races, Mont Tremblant, Riverside Raceway and Las Vegas. Dan Gurney and Mark Donohue were also Lola-mounted, and each won a round at Bridgehampton and Mosport Park respectively.

By the end of 1966 T70 production amounted to 47, but there was now no future for sales in Europe of the model in its existing form. Eric Broadley took the view that he need produce only three more cars with interchangeable bodies and the projected Mark III coupé could be homologated in the Group 4 Competition Sports Car class (minimum production of 50 cars). The *Commission Sportive Internationale* did not share Broadley's interpretation of the regulations and the Mark III coupé was regarded a Sports Prototype.

There were only minor chassis differences between the Mark III and the sports cars, but the glass-fibre body was completely new, built by Specialised Mouldings and styled by New Zealander Jim Clark who had been responsible for the original Mark 6 GT. Both front and rear sections were quickly removable, there were gull-wing doors and a full-length aluminium-alloy undertray. Lola offered what amounted to a kit to convert open T70s to Mark III coupés and production of the open T70 continued.

Seen in practice at Le Mans in 1967 is the Team Surtees Lola T70 Mark III coupé with Aston Martin 5-litre V8 engine. It was driven in the race by John Surtees and David Hobbs, but retired early because of engine failure.

With the exception of one team, all the British efforts with the Mark III were fairly amateur efforts and much the same can be said of the American entrants. The Lolas were also racing against the strongest possible opposition, the Ferrari P4s and P3/4s, the 7-litre Fords and the Chaparral. That only very limited success was gained in major events was not unexpected. The one serious British entrant was *Team Surtees*, which raced cars powered by Tadek Marek-designed works Aston Martin V8 four overhead camshaft engines of 4,510.5cc (93×83mm). Although these engines appeared to have considerable potential, they proved exceptionally fragile and were soon abandoned.

The first promising performance was in the Spa 1,000Km in May, a race run in torrentially wet conditions. Paul Hawkins, sharing the wheel of Jackie Epstein's Mark III with 5.9-litre Chevrolet engine, drove superbly. They took a fine fourth place in a race dominated by Jacky Ickx with the 5.7-litre Ford GT40-based Mirage. The Aston Martin-powered car had shown considerable speed at the Le Mans Practice Weekend, although it was overheating in cool conditions and had incipient valve problems.

Surtees/Hobbs appeared with this car at the Nürburgring 1,000Km race by when it was fitted with fuel injection and a Hewland LG600 five-speed gearbox. Although Surtees was second fastest in practice, Hobbs had a nasty moment when a wheel came off and jammed itself under the body. It did mean that he could get a spare wheel and jack from the pits and stagger back to change the wheel. The Lola-Aston Martin retired after only seven laps because of a broken rear wishbone.

Le Mans was a complete disaster for *Team Surtees*, the cars were plagued by blown cylinder head gaskets in practice and the mechanics discovered that the timimg of the fuel injection was 180 degrees out. The drivers were Surtees/Hobbs and Chris Irwin/Peter de Klerk, but neither co-driver had a chance to drive in the race. Surtees retired because of piston failure on lap three and Irwin because of a cracked crankshaft damper after about 45 minutes. The usual recriminations followed and by the Reims 12 Hours race Surtees/Hobbs were at the wheel of their Le Mans car, but now with a Chevrolet engine. Four Lolas ran in this race, they led initially, but all retired.

Broadley initially built four T70 Mark IIIB roadsters for the 1967 Can-Am series. These featured a lightened monocoque and were designed to take wider tyres (9-inch (230mm) at the front and 12-inch (305mm) at the rear). Far from properly developed, these cars were supplied, two to *Roger Penske Racing* and one each to *Team Surtees* and Dan Gurney's *All-American Racers*. There were six rounds in the 1967 Can-Am Cup and the McLaren team won every race. The Lolas were outclassed and the best performer was Mark Donohue entered by *Penske* who took two second places and a third.

The original sports-racing T70 was a very advanced design and took the technology of the 1963 GT car a stage further. With Chevrolet engines in various capacities, it was a formidable piece of machinery in European events, but enjoyed only limited success in North America where the opposition was more formidable. (LAT)

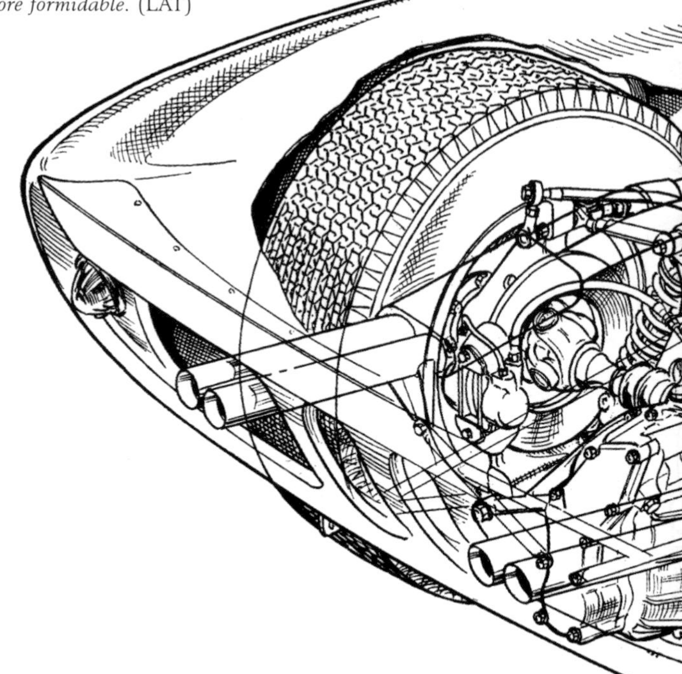

After Le Mans in 1967 the *CSI* had imposed a capacity limit of 3 litres for Group 6 Prototypes and had introduced the Group 4 category for so-called Competition Sports cars with a maximum capacity of 5 litres and a minimum production of 50. By building a few additional cars Broadley squeezed the T70 into this category. The cars usually ran with 4.9-litre Chevrolet engines, but generally were plagued by unreliability caused by the poor quality of European fuel compared with that available in the United States and most of them were running on too high a compression ratio.

Lolas ran in most of the year's Championship races, but little success was gained. In the BOAC 500 race in April Bonnier/Axelsson took sixth place. A minor, but worthwhile success was Denis Hulme's win with Sid Taylor's Mark III in the Tourist Trophy at Oulton Park in June. The 1967 race had been for saloons, so the Hulme/Taylor three victories in 1965 (with a 2-litre Brabham) and in 1966–8 amounted to a 'hat-trick'. There were successes in other minor events, but since Surtees had abandoned the T70 following its abysmal failures in 1967, there was no entrant with the facili-

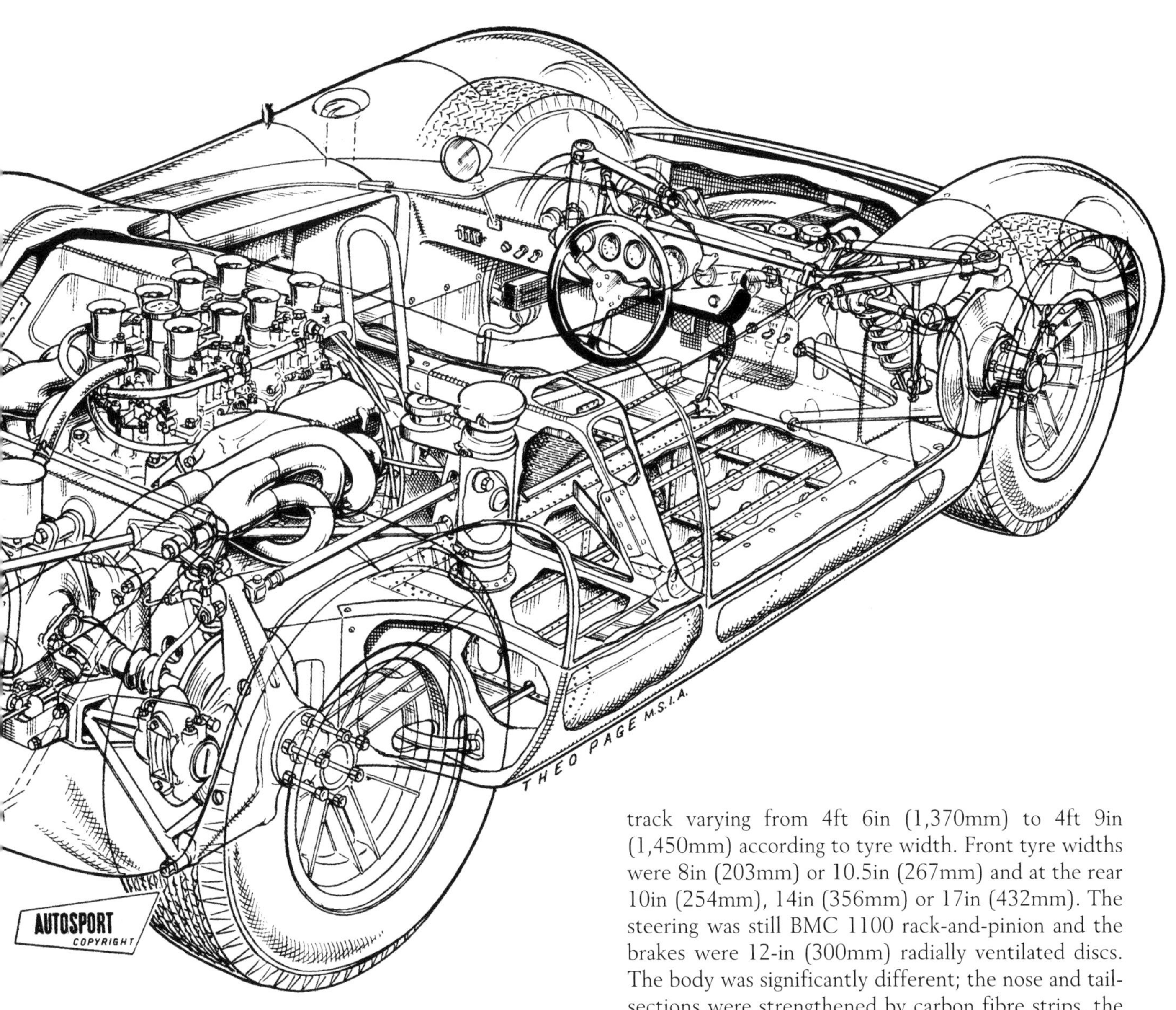

ties or the finance to fully develop the Mark IIIs and they soon became also-rans.

For 1969 Lola introduced the modified and improved Mark IIIB coupé. There was a new all-alloy bonded and riveted monocoque similar to that of the 1969 T160-series Can-Am cars. This had vastly increased torsional rigidity and, behind the cockpit, two detachable magnesium alloy castings that facilitated removal of the engine and gearbox. There was a single fuel cell in the left sill and the suspension was that of the Lola T142 Formula 5000 car. This consisted, at the front, of cast magnesium-alloy suspension uprights, double wishbones with self-aligning rubber and ball joints and coil spring/damper units. At the rear there were reversed lower wishbones, top links and lower radius arms.

The wheelbase remained 7ft 11in (2,410mm) with track varying from 4ft 6in (1,370mm) to 4ft 9in (1,450mm) according to tyre width. Front tyre widths were 8in (203mm) or 10.5in (267mm) and at the rear 10in (254mm), 14in (356mm) or 17in (432mm). The steering was still BMC 1100 rack-and-pinion and the brakes were 12-in (300mm) radially ventilated discs. The body was significantly different; the nose and tail-sections were strengthened by carbon fibre strips, the nose was nearer to the ground, there were twin head-lamps each side and conventional forward-opening doors.

In standard form the Mark IIIB had the 4.9-litre V8 Chevrolet engine in dry sump form with four twin-choke 48mm Weber carburettors and a claimed power output of 480bhp. Transmission was by a triple-plate clutch and the Hewland LG600 five-speed gearbox. Although the latest T70 was still plagued by development and engine problems, there was little other choice for the private owner who wanted to go Group 4 racing, for both the Ferrari 250LM and the Ford GT40 were obsolete. Inevitably little success was gained, but at the beginning of 1969 one remarkable Championship success was achieved.

Roger Penske Racing took delivery of two Mark IIIBs, the first not until 1 January 1969. The team expended a vast amount of time and energy in prepar-

ing this car for the Daytona 24 Hours at the beginning of February. It ran with Traco-modified, fuel injection engine developing a true 460bhp and was driven by Mark Donohue/Chuck Parsons. All the Porsche 908s ran into major mechanical problems and all five retired, as did the two *Gulf* GT40s.

When the Ickx/Oliver *Gulf* GT40 crashed and caught fire on the Sunday morning, the *Penske* Lola had spent 1 hour 19 minutes in the pits having stainless steel patches welded to its disintegrated exhaust system and had rejoined the race 40 laps in arrears. The Lola now led on the road, but it would be 90 minutes before it exceeded the distance covered by the leading GT40 before its accident. Donohue/Parsons won at the very slow average of 99.27mph (159.73kph) – the speed of the winning 2.2-litre Porsche 907 in 1968 had been 106.70mph (171.68kph).

Lothar Motschenbacher partnered by Ed Leslie took second place with a wet-sump Chevrolet-powered Mark III entered by actor James Garner's *American International Racing* team and a Pontiac Firebird took third place. It was a freak win. The best Lola results in Championship races during the remainder of the year were sixth by Motschenbacher/Leslie at Sebring, fifth by Frank Gardner/de Adamich at Monza, fifth by Bonnier/Müller at Spa – plus a very commendable second place by Bonnier/Müller in the Austrian 1,000Km race after much of the opposition had fallen by the wayside.

Australian Paul Hawkins with his Lola T70 Mark III-5-litre Chevrolet in the race for Competition Sports Cars at Oulton Park in August 1968. He finished third in this race, but won that year's RAC Sports Car Championship. Hawkins was killed when he crashed a Mark IIIB at Oulton Park in the following year's Tourist Trophy race. (T.C. March/FotoVantage)

In minor races the Mark IIIBs and the Mark IIIs performed well, for this was their true habitat. Particularly successful were Paul Hawkins and David Piper. Hawkins, who drove a works-supported car, was killed while trying to make up time lost in the pits in the Tourist Trophy at Oulton Park in May. He spun, slid across the road and hit a tree. The car caught fire and the driver perished. The writer witnessed the accident and along with the deaths of Giunti and Rodriguez in 1971 it was one of the most horrible accidents in a very dangerous period of racing. At the end of the year Piper forsook his short period of Lola ownership for a Porsche 917.

Although the Mark IIIBs and IIIs continued to appear in major and minor races over the next couple of seasons, they never again finished in the first six in a Championship race. They were good cars for private owners in short events and most disappointing of all was the total failure of the Aston Martin-powered cars with which John Surtees tried so hard in 1967. Production of the coupés amounted to 21 Mark IIIs and 23 Mark IIIBs.

David Piper and the Mark IIIB

During 1968 I had raced my Ferrari 330P3/4, but as it was a Prototype with a 4-litre engine, it was no longer eligible for World Championship events. I tried to persuade Ferrari to build me a car with a 3-litre engine, but it soon became clear that this was not practicable and I then had discussions with Peter Agg of Trojan who built the production McLaren Can-Am cars. I came close to concluding a deal, but they had production problems and they could not deliver a car until well after the start of the season. So I turned to Lola and bought a T70 Mark IIIB coupé.

I was based in Modena and had a garage opposite the Modena Autodrome, which was very useful for testing purposes and the car was delivered to me there where I traded as *Autoracing Modena*. Specialised Mouldings, at my request, supplied colour-impregnated bodywork in my usual BP light green. The colour, in fact, had nothing to do with BP, as I was sponsored by Shell, but I have always preferred lighter colours and this light green is the colour that I used when I had an agricultural machinery business.

My car had a 5-litre Traco-developed Chevrolet 5-litre engine and the usual Hewland LG600 five-speed transaxle. In my opinion, it was, technically, a very advanced car, more than a match in performance for the Ford GT40s, which were going through a second lease of life with Gurney-Weslake cylinder heads, wide wheels and ventilated discs. The Lola was a very strong car, with excellent roadholding, outboard brakes, which meant no overheating problems, and very wide wheels that used tyres of up to 10.5 inches' width at the front and 17 inches at the rear.

The IIIB had, of course, its weaknesses. The main problem was the Chevrolet engine. Lolas would often head the field at the start of a race, but drop out because of engine problems. At this time the Chevrolet V8s had cast-iron cylinder heats and they usually cracked. You needed a good supply of spare heads to get through the season. Later, of course, when Chevrolet engines were being used in Formula 5000, a lot of development work was carried out and aluminium-alloy heads became available. Towards the end of long-distance races, there could be problems with the Hewland gearbox.

There was a particular problem early in the season. Lola had lost its expert welder and in the BOAC race at Brands Hatch in April, Jo Bonnier went wide with the *Scuderia Filipinetti* IIIB at Bottom Bend, hit the safety barrier at about 100mph and cartwheeled along it, the car came to rest a total wreck. Eric Broadley came round the pits and advised me and other Mark IIIB entrants to withdraw their cars. The cause of the accident was a welding failure in a rose-joint in the rear suspension.

For many years David Piper was the leading private entrant, at first with Lotus cars, later with Ferraris and in 1969 driving a Lola T70 Mark IIIB coupé. Here he gives his impressions of racing the Lola. (Porsche Werkfoto)

Because of works drives, I ran the Lola in only a few Championship races, but I won a race at Montlhéry and took second places in the Martini Trophy, the Tourist Trophy at Oulton Park, the Prix de Salzburg and the Trophy of the Dunes at Zandvoort. Hans Herrmann drove my Lola to a win in the Solituderennen at Hockenheim. I kept the Lola until the end of 1970 (and bought it back again later). I drove it only once in 1970, in an Interserie race at Hockenheim and Richard Attwood won races with it at Montlhéry and Dijon. My Mark IIIB was also used in the making of Steve McQueen's *Le Mans* film.

Ford Mk 2 & 4

1965–67

The 7-litre Ford Mark 2 of Phil Hill/Chris Amon in early practice at Le Mans in 1965 before the spoilers on the front wings and the tail fins were added. Compare with the colour photograph on page 88. They retired in the race because of transmission problems. (Ford Motor Company)

After the GT40's unsuccessful 1964 season, Ford took two decisive steps. They acquired the Kar Kraft organisation in Detroit to develop new models and they entered into a contract with *Shelby American* to prepare the cars that would represent the works team in 1965. Extensive modifications were made to the original GT40 and the Shelby team raced these in the early part of 1965, but at Kar Kraft work was proceeding on a much faster version that appeared at Le Mans in June.

The new Mark 2 was based on standard GT40 rolling chassis built at Slough and shipped to Kar Kraft where the seating position and rear bulkhead were repositioned and the front and rear body structures were modified. This enabled Kar Kraft to install the pushrod V8 6,997cc (107.5×96.1mm) Ford Galaxie production engine that been very successful in American racing. It was a very heavy engine, weighing around 600 pounds (272kg), but modified for stock car racing with dry-sump lubrication, alloy cylinder heads and a single four-barrel Holley carburettor, power output was 475bhp at only 6,200rpm.

Notwithstanding its sheer power, it was an especially efficient engine, with a wide power band and the excellent torque of 475lb/ft at only 4,000rpm. Only a four-speed gearbox was needed and Kar Kraft decided to use the Ford T-444 all-synchromesh gearbox, with Galaxie internals in a light-alloy casing. The wheelbase was the same as for the GT40, but both front and rear track were widened and weight rose substantially to 2,505 pounds (1,136kg). In practice at Le Mans the aerodynamic stability was appalling and the Mark 2s were fitted with a spoiler under the nose, tabs on the front wings and twin tail fins.

Whereas Wyer had known that the original GT40 needed extensive development work and had constantly urged Ford to concentrate on development rather than race the cars prematurely, Detroit was still naive enough to believe that with the fastest cars on the circuit, they could win Le Mans without exhaustive testing. Of the two cars entered at Le Mans, one had been fairly rigorously tested, but the other arrived at Le Mans without having turned a wheel under its own power.

The drivers were Ken Miles/Bruce McLaren and Phil Hill/Chris Amon. The Mark 2s led away from the Le Mans start and despite the fact that Surtees (Ferrari) was in third place, it really did look that the remark so often quoted by Ford personnel, "we're going to blow them red cars right off the track" would be fulfilled. The Fords broke the lap record several times and Phil Hill finally raised it to 138.443mph (222.755kph).

At the end of the first hour the Mark 2s held first two places. After their first refuelling stop, Hill/Amon dropped back from second to 35th place because of gearbox trouble, started to climb back through the field, but retired in the seventh hour. Already Miles/McLaren, still leading at the end of the second hour, were out of the race because of transmission failure. Not a single Ford finished the race. It was a complete debacle for Detroit. Ford needed to find the reliability to match the speed of the Mark 2.

Close examination revealed that the faults in the Ford transmission were minor. On one car a grain of sand in the clutch slave cylinder had caused the piston to stick and generate heat in the throw-out bearing. This in turn had softened an oil-retaining ring in the axle and resulted in oil loss. On the other car a gear had broken because it had not been properly drilled. Ford put in hand a very intensive test and development programme. In addition to *Shelby American*, both engine developers *Holman & Moody* and British team *Alan Mann Racing* entered cars on behalf of the works in 1966.

Minor changes were made to the cars for 1966 and they became known as the Mark 2A; a shorter nose saved weight and improved aerodynamnics, more efficient radiators were fitted, there were new external brake scoops and there was improved ducting to the radiators, carburettors and brakes. Ford adopted ventilated disc brakes, but, like Ferrari, was not able to stop the discs cracking, especially prevalent during the cold night hours at Le Mans; the answer was a brake disc that could be changed almost as quickly as the pads and Ferrari, with slight modifications, copied the Ford idea.

In the Daytona 24 Hours race in February 1966 the Fords were virtually unopposed and took first, second, third and fifth places. Four 7-litre Fords faced one works Ferrari in the Sebring 12 Hours race on 26 March. Among the entries was the X-1 open 7-litre car, the cockpit of which was reckoned to be even hotter than that of the coupés; this had appeared in the 1965 Canadian Grand Prix driven by Chris Amon where it retired because of overheating and was tried in practice at Sebring with automatic transmission.

The Ferrari retired, Ken Miles/Lloyd Ruby won with the X-1 and Hansgen/Donohue took second place. Gurney/Grant had been leading by a lap, but the engine of their Mark 2 cut out on the last lap a few hundreds yards from the finish. Dan Gurney pushed the car across the line, but disqualification followed because the car had not finished under its own power. A.J. Foyt/Ronnie Bucknum drove a *Holman & Moody* Mark 2 with two-speed automatic transmission, but without the engine to assist braking, it developed an insatiable appetite for brake pads and finished 12th.

Ferrari was absent from the Le Mans Test Weekend, but Ford took it very seriously. Apart from two Mark 2s, Ford brought along the experimental 'J-car' with completely new monocoque body/chassis. This was constructed in aluminium honeycomb material sandwiched between two thin sheets of aluminium-alloy bonded with a powerful epoxy resin and riveted in high stress areas. Suspension pick-up points and other mountings and brackets were steel or aluminium alloy and bonded to the main structure.

The body was a much smoother version of the Mark 2, with low-level air intake and chopped tail reminiscent of the original Lola GT. Because of the shape of the rear decking, the rear-view mirror was mounted on the roof and the driver looked at it through a slot. Transmission was by a fully hydraulic Ford two-speed torque-converter automatic gearbox with the driver able to select drive, low or high. In most other respects the car was the same as the Mark 2, but the exhausts were grouped in fours each side instead of the crossover arrangement used on the Mark 2.

Although the car was extremely fast, it was experimental and not raced in this form. On the Saturday there was a disastrous accident when veteran American driver Walt Hansgen lost control of the car that had finished second at Sebring on the *Dunlop Bridge* bend, took to the escape road and hit the retaining wall at over 100mph. Hansgen suffered grievous injuries to which he later succumbed in the American hospital at Orléans.

Ford only made one more appearance before the Le Mans race. *Alan Mann Racing* entered a Mark 2 for John Whitmore/Frank Gardner in the Spa 1,000Km race on 22 May and they took second place to the works Ferrari of Parkes/Scarfiotti. At Le Mans Ford fielded eight Mark 2s, three entered by *Shelby American*, three by *Holman & Moody* and two by *Alan Mann Racing*. In

The experimental J-car with honeycomb construction monocoque seen in the Ford pit at the 1966 Le Mans Test Weekend. It formed the basis of the Mark 4 raced in 1967. (Ford Motor Company)

sheer numbers (and speed) Ford overwhelmed the rest of the entry and Ferrari was particularly weak, with only three cars, one entered in the name of *North American Racing Team*, and was demoralised following Surtees's abrupt departure from the team.

Although the Ferraris were lighter on tyres and more economical, the Fords streaked into the lead at the start and, apart from a very short spell on the Saturday evening following refuelling stops, they were consistently ahead. All three 330P3 Ferraris retired and although only three Fords made it to the finish, they were in the first three places in the order Amon/McLaren (*Shelby American*), Miles/Hulme (*Shelby American*) and Bucknum/Hutcherson (*Holman & Moody*). Dan Gurney set a new lap record of 142.979mph (230.053kph).

The 7-litre Prototypes did not race again in 1966, but Kar Kraft had produced an open version of the J-car with a view to running it in American events in the autumn of 1966. Sadly, veteran driver, Ken Miles was killed while testing this at Riverside Raceway in August. The 1967 Mk 4 was derived from the J-car, but the honeycomb panels incorporated much more riveting, the aerodynamics were improved, crash-resistant fuel tanks were incorporated, as was a very strong roll-over bar. Changes to the Mk 2B, as it was now known, included new glass-fibre nose and tail sections, with repositioned ducts at the front and new magnesium wheels designed to pump air across the brakes.

At the Daytona 24 Hours race in February 1967 Ford ran six Mk 2B cars, three entered by *Shelby American* and three by *Holman & Moody* (and one car in each team was called a Mercury to keep dealers for that brand placated). Although the Ford teams did not know it, they were beaten before they started. Leo Beebe, head of Ford Special Vehicles Activity, ordered that all moving parts were to be renewed for the race and the new transmission output shafts had been improperly treated. So Ford faced gearbox failure after gearbox failure and the only Mk 2B to finish was that of McLaren/Bianchi in

The winning Ford Mark 2A of McLaren/Amon takes the chequered flag at Le Mans in 1966 followed by the second-place car of Hulme/Miles. Behind them comes the Bucknum/Hutcherson car that took third place. (Ford Motor Company)

A beautifully detailed cutaway view of the 1967 Ford Mark 4 by James Allington. The Ford Mark 4 was undoubtedly one of the greatest competition sports cars of all time. (Ford Motor Company)

seventh place. Ferraris finished 1–2–3.

Only two 7-litre Fords ran at Sebring on 1 April, both *Shelby American* entries. There were no works Ferraris and although the Chaparral 2F took the lead, it fell victim to its transmission fragility. McLaren/ Andretti won with a Mk 4 on its race debut and the Mk 2B of Foyt/Ruby finished second, although it had remained stationary in the pits for half an before the chequered flag because of a broken camshaft. Just a Mark 4 and a 2B appeared at the Le Mans Test Weekend; they were the only cars to exceed 200mph (322kmh) on the *Mulsanne Straight* and McLaren with the Mk 4 was timed at 205.05mph (329.93kph).

The works Fords did not run again until Le Mans and there were seven 7-litre entries, four of them Mark 4s, three cars each entered by *Shelby American* and *Holman & Moody*, and a Mark 2B, prepared by *Holman & Moody*, but entered by *Ford France*. The Ferrari P4s were much-improved cars, reliable and fast, even if not as fast as the Fords. Accidents reduced the Ford onslaught; Ruby went off the road with the Mark 4 that he shared with Denis Hulme and during the early hours of Sunday morning a shaken Jo Schlesser, co-driver of the *Ford France* car, walked into the Ford pit to report that "there were Fords all over the road".

Andretti (*Holman & Moody* Mark 4 shared with Bianchi) locked a brake as he entered the *Esses* and crumpled the Ford into the bank; in an effort to avoid him Roger McClusky (sharing a *Holman & Moody* Mark 2B with Frank Gardner) hit the bank on the other side of the road and in avoiding both cars Schlesser also hit the bank. The Mark 2B of Hawkins/Bucknum (*Shelby American* entry) retired because of engine failure. Two Fords remained in the race and Gurney/Foyt (*Shelby American* Mark 4) won at 135.482mph (217.990kph); Ferraris were second and third and McLaren/Donohue (*Shelby American* Mark 4) finished fourth.

Although Gurney/Foyt had led for 23 hours of the race, it had been no easy victory and Scarfiotti/Parkes (Ferrari) were only three laps behind at the finish after holding second place for 13 hours. Victory was achieved by Ford's extra power, reasonable reliability and large entry. Hulme and Andretti shared a new lap record of 147.894mph (237.961kph). Immediately after the race Ford withdrew from racing and Henry Ford II financed the new Ford chicane that slightly lengthened the circuit. *Ford France* retained their Mark 2B and subsequently Schlesser/Ligier drove it to a win in the Reims 12 hours race and fourth place in the very difficult Circuit of Mugello.

It could be said of Ford that if you throw enough money at a project, it should come right – and Ford executives were aghast at the high racing budget. Even so, the Ford 7-litre cars were icons of the Prototype era and they and the P4 Ferraris provided sports car racing at its most exciting – excitement not seen again until the clash of the 917 Porsche and the 512S Ferrari in 1970.

Ferrari 330P3 & P4

1966–67

This is the P4 of Scarfiotti/Parkes that finished second in the 1967 Le Mans race. The large inlets at the front of the rear wings were absent on the 1966 P3s. (FotoVantage)

Ferrari dominated the early years of Prototype racing, in 1962 with a mixed bag of cars that included the 246SP sports-racing car, a development of the *Testa Rossa* sports-racing car fitted with a 4-litre engine and versions of the 250GTO, also with 4-litre engines. For 1963, technical director Mauro Forghieri designed and developed the 250P that combined a lengthened version of the rear-engined 246SP chassis with the V12 *Testa Rossa* engine.

In 1963 250Ps ran in four major European races and won three. At the 1963 Paris Salon, Ferrari introduced the 250LM, a fixed head coupé version of the 250P, which in production form had a 3.3-litre engine. Ferrari wanted to have the 250LM homologated as a GT car, but the FIA refused because insufficient numbers had been built. So, the 250LM became a production Prototype and proved very successful in the hands of private entrants. Its greatest achievement was a win by Jochen Rindt and Masten Gregory at Le Mans in 1965 with a car entered by *North American Racing Team*.

The Ferrari team raced 3.3-litre and 4-litre V12 Prototypes with a single cam per bank in 1964, but with four overhead camshafts in 1965. These proved very successful in the face of very fast, but fragile opposition from Ford. It was obvious that the Fords would improve in reliability and Ferrari responded to the challenge with the 330P3 Prototype. The new car retained a 3,967.4cc (77×71mm) V12 all-alloy, dry sump engine with two valves per cylinder and twin overhead camshafts per bank of cylinders chain-driven from the nose of the crankshaft. Lucas indirect fuel injection replaced the three twin-choke carburettors and power output was 420bhp at 8,000rpm.

Transmission was the usual Ferrari arrangement of a multi-plate clutch and a five-speed, all-indirect gearbox without synchromesh in unit with the final drive. The final drive ratio could be altered by changing the reduction gears. It was a gearbox that had served Ferrari well for three seasons, but by 1966 it was becoming unreliable, as it was expected to transmit about 100bhp more than when first used in 1963.

The chassis was a tubular structure, strengthened by riveted aluminium-alloy sheet and bonded glass-fibre. Although a chassis with this form of construction was not as stiff as a pure monocoque, it was much easier to construct. The front and rear suspension was still by double wishbones and coil spring/damper units front and rear. The wheelbase was unchanged at 7ft 10.5in (2,400mm), as was the track, 4ft 5.25in (1,350mm) at the front also and 4ft 4.75in (1,340mm) at the rear.

In style and function the body was vastly improved. It was slightly shorter, wider and lower than that of its predecessors, with very low nose, a very rounded and lower windscreen (permitted by a change in the Prototype regulations), the headlamps, spot lamps and indicators under a smooth Plexiglass cover each side and large air scoops behind the doors. The distinctive humped tail had rows of horizontal slats ahead and astern of the rear wheels to relieve internal high-pressure areas in the body. Ferrari claimed a dry weight of 1,558 pounds (706.5kg), only 70 pounds (32kg) more than the original 1963 250P. Maximum speed was 193mph (310kph).

John Surtees had crashed his Lola and suffered grave injuries during practice for the sports car Canadian Grand Prix in September 1965 and, initially, he was unable to take part in the development testing of the new car. Once he was fit enough, he worked closely with Forghieri, with whom he had a superb relationship, and early handling and aerodynamic problems with the P3 were soon resolved. During 1966 Ferrari was in quite serious financial trouble and was courting Fiat for financial support. Until it eventually came in 1968 with the purchase of a 49% holding, Ferrari entries often showed a lack of full commitment and sometimes the team entered only a single car.

Ferrari missed the first round of the Championship series at Daytona and Fords finished first, second, third and fifth. Ferrari sent an open P3 for Mike Parkes/Bob Bondurant to the Sebring 12 Hours race on 26 March and although they were very fast and the car was either in first or second place for most of the race, it retired in the final hour because of a broken gear-selector and Fords again took the first three places.

A single 330P3 coupé, ran in the Monza 1,000Km event on 25 April and the drivers were John Surtees, racing for the first time since his accident, and Mike Parkes. It was an unfortunate pairing, because there was no love lost between them, but they drove a superb race in appalling conditions. There were no serious Ford entries and the P3 led throughout in torrential rain. After 30 laps the P3's windscreen wiper failed, but Surtees worked out that if they increased their speed, the aerodynamics of the Ferrari would keep the screen clear. The Ferrari won easily at 103.13mph (165.94kph) from privately entered Ford GT40s, but speeds were very much lower than was usual in this race.

The Targa Florio on 8 May was another wet race and again, because of the difficulties of the circuit, there were no serious Ford entries. Ferrari sent along an open P3 for Vaccarella/Bandini and although it was not a suitable car for the race Bandini was in second place when he overturned the big Prototype on lap 7 of this ten-lap event. The works-entered 2-litre *Dino* of Guichet/Baghetti finished second behind the winning Porsche. Ferrari sent a single P3 *berlinetta* for Parkes/Scarfiotti to the Spa 1,000Km event on 22 May and, running on Firestone tyres, they won easily at 131.70mph (211.90kph) from a brace of privately entered Ford GT40s.

At the Nürburgring on 5 June Phil Hill/Joakim Bonnier scored a totally unexpected victory with the

The 330P3 of Scarfiotti/Parkes rushes through the Esses early in the 1966 Le Mans race – the headlamp patches are still in place. It was eliminated by an accident later during the night. P3s and P4s can be difficult to distinguish, but note the P3's wing mirrors and the air intake inlet let into the door, features absent on the P4. (FotoVantage)

Chevrolet-powered 2D coupé. Surtees/Parkes drove an open P3 and Surtees lapped fastest in practice at 99.60mph (160.26mph). In the race he set fastest lap, a new Prototype lap record, at 98.67mph (158.76kph), but just before the end of the first hour's racing, he shot into the pits because of a broken rear shock absorber. Parkes rejoined in 22nd place, worked the car up to eighth, handed back to Surtees, but after another rear suspension collapse, the clutch failed. Ferrari's consolation came from the second and third places by two 2-litre *Dino* coupés.

Ferrari also faced industrial disputes, rife in Italy at the time, and all the works Ferraris at Le Mans, together with the private cars looked after by the works, were less than adequately prepared. The Ferrari P3 entry consisted of *berlinettas* for Parkes/Scarfiotti and Bandini/Guichet, together with an open car driven by Rodriguez/Ginther and entered in the name of *North American Racing Team*. Facing them were eight much-improved 7-litre Fords. Surtees should have been in the team, but left Ferrari after a confrontation with team manager Dragoni orchestrated by the 'Old Man' at Maranello.

Scarfiotti was holding second place during the ninth hour when he crashed heavily. In heavy rain Schlesser (Matra-BRM) collided with a Peugeot-powered CD, went off the track and reversed back into the path of Scarfiotti who was unable to avoid him. Two hours later the P3 of Rodriguez/Ginther retired because of gear-selector problems after having overheated for some hours. The Bandini/Guichet car had also fallen back because of overheating and retired because of cylinder head gasket failure at 8.26 on the Sunday morning. Fords took the first three places and Ferrari did not race the P3s again.

The open P4 of Jackie Stewart/Chris Amon in the pits during the BOAC 500 Miles race at Brands Hatch at the end of July 1967. They finished second behind the Chaparral of Phil Hill/Mike Spence. (FotoVantage)

There is no doubt that Ferrari was badly shaken by the poor showing of the P3s in 1966 and, especially, by the defeat at Le Mans. A Ferrari had won there every year since 1960 and, interestingly, the marque was never to win there again. Work started immediately on a successor. Forghieri and the 'Old Man' contemplated developing a larger-capacity engine, but decided to stay at four litres, but with the engine in much improved form.

Engineer Franco Rocchi had developed a V12 four overhead camshaft Grand Prix engine with two inlet and one exhaust valve per cylinder and it won on its debut in the 1966 Italian Grand Prix. This was redesigned in 4-litre form for the 1967 330P4 Prototypes and features included a cylinder block of increased stiffness with cross-bolted main bearing caps and Lucas fuel injection feeding into air induction tubes located between the camshafts instead of the previous arrangement of injection between the cylinder banks. Power output was now 450bhp at 8,000rpm. Ferrari redesigned the gearbox with the gears located on two main shafts.

The chassis was wider, lighter and used the latest wide Firestone tyres. The wheelbase was the same, but the front track had been increased to 4ft 10.75in (1,490mm) and the rear track to 4ft 9.25in (1,455mm). To improve cooling, the rear brakes were now mounted outboard. The body was similar to that of the P3, but neater with small spoilers at the front and more compact tail surmounted by a flat aerofoil. Weight rose to 1,762 pounds (799kg). As before, Ferrari provided selected private teams with reworked versions of the previous year's cars. For 1967 these were the 412 (or also known as the P3/4) based on the P3s, rebodied, with carburettor engine and ZF gearbox.

In December Ferrari tested the P4 at Daytona and two months later in the 24 hours race at this circuit the Fords had serious transmission problems. Lorenzo Bandini/Chris Amon (*berlinetta*) and Ludovico Scarfiotti/Mike Parkes (*spyder*) took the first two places ahead of Rodriguez/Guichet (*North American Racing Team*-entered P3/4). Ferrari missed the Sebring race on 1 April and Ford took the first two places. Two P4s ran at the Le Mans test weekend and one was timed at 198mph (319kph).

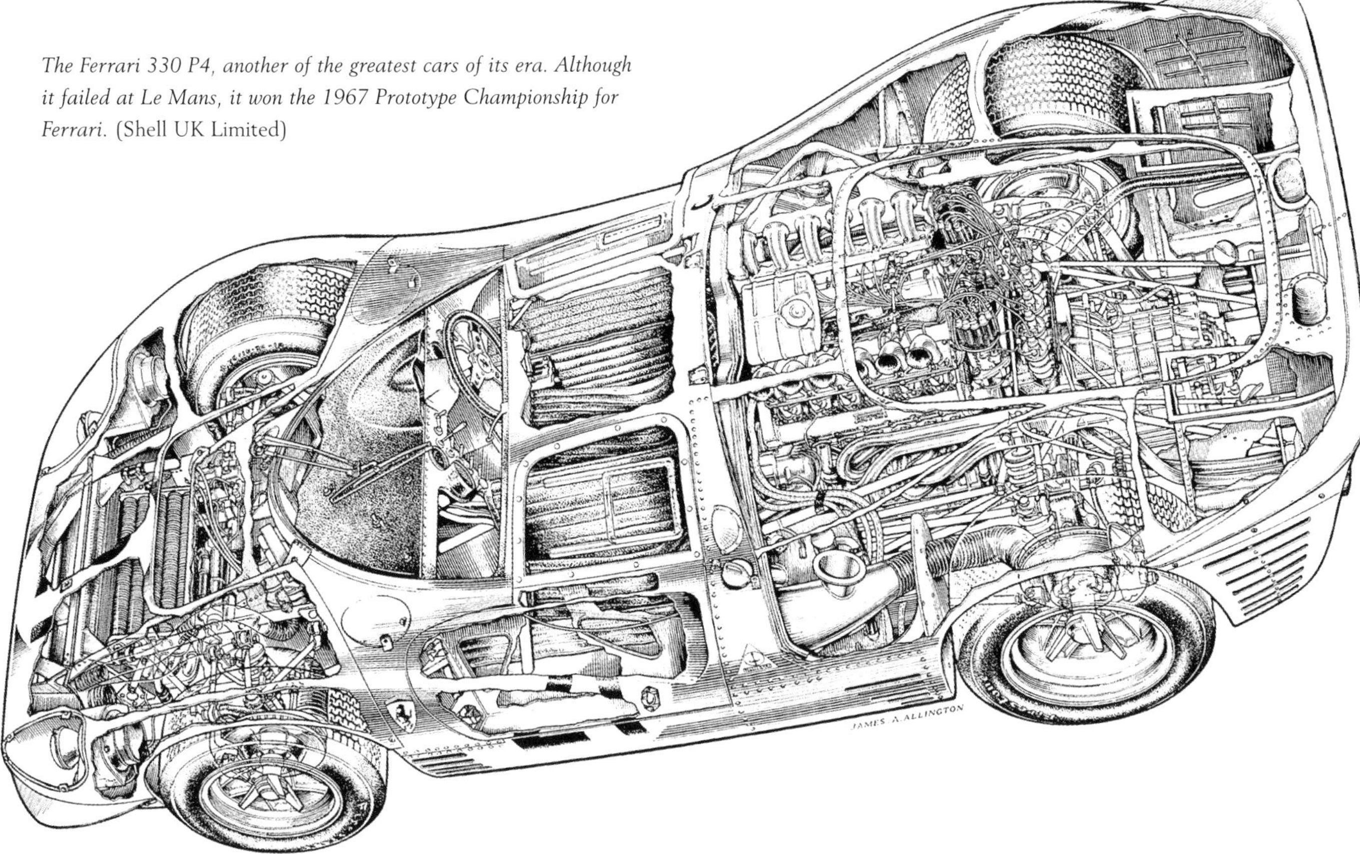

The Ferrari 330 P4, another of the greatest cars of its era. Although it failed at Le Mans, it won the 1967 Prototype Championship for Ferrari. (Shell UK Limited)

A 'soft' victory followed in the Monza 1,000Km race on 25 April. Of 41 cars entered, 17 were Ferraris of one kind or another and there were no Fords capable of challenging for victory. The P4 *berlinettas* of Amon/Bandini and Parkes/Scarfiotti finished first and second. Despite a spin into the barriers that broke a wheel and damaged the bodywork, the P3/4 entered by *Scuderia Filipinetti* for Vaccarella/Müller resumed the race after a long pit stop to finish fourth behind a Porsche. In the wet and miserable Spa 1,000Km race on 1 May the sole P4, a *berlinetta* driven by Parkes/Scarfiotti, was delayed by transmission problems and finished a poor fifth. Attwood/Bianchi with a P3/4 entered by *Maranello Concessionaires* took third place.

Ferrari sent an open P4 to the Targa Florio on 14 May for Vaccarella/Scarfiotti and although it was fastest in practice, Vaccarella crashed on the second lap. *Scuderia Filipinetti* entered their P3/4 for Müller/Guichet, but they retired because of final drive problems at the end of lap 7. Porsche took the first three places. It had been Ferrari's intention to run only a *Dino* with a 2.4-litre engine for Scarfiotti/Günther Klass in the Nürburgring 1,000Km race on 28 May, but it was withdrawn after the engine broke in practice and Porsche took the first four places.

At Le Mans held on 10–11 June there were four P4 *berlinettas* and three P3/4s (the latter now with new Ferrari five-speed trans-axles) and they faced four Mark 4 and two Mark 2B 7-litre Fords. The Fords had the edge on speed, but the Ferrari team turned in a good performance. A Ford Mark 4 driven by Gurney/Foyt won by a just over 30 miles from Scarfiotti/Parkes (works P4) and Mairesse/'Beurlys' (works P4 entered in the name of *Équipe Nationale Belge*) with the other surviving Mark 4 Ford of McLaren/Donohue fourth. The P4s of Klass/Sutcliffe and Amon/Vaccarella and the three P3/4s all retired.

Ford retired from racing after Le Mans, although there was one more round in the Championship, the BOAC '500' race in late July. The Chaparral 2F of Phil Hill/Mike Spence was firmly ensconced in the lead by the end of the fourth hour and the open P4s of Amon/Stewart, Scarfiotti/Sutcliffe and Williams/Hawkins finished second, fourth and fifth. It was enough to clinch the Prototype Championship for Ferrari with 34 points to the 32 of Porsche.

Two P4s were rebuilt for Can-Am racing, but they were underpowered compared with the opposition and failed to achieve any success. The P4 is one of the most highly regarded sports-racing cars for its appearance, the magnificent wail of the V12 engine and, one is forced to admit, the sexiness of its svelte styling.

Chaparral 2D & 2F

1966–67

The Chaparral 2D driven by Phil Hill and Joakim Bonnier scored a win in its first European race, the Nürburgring 1,000Km in 1966. Here Hill rounds the banked Karussel corner. (LAT)

Jim Hall's first Chaparral (another name for the road-runner, a member of the cuckoo family) was a front-engined sports car built by Dick Troutman and Tom Barnes in 1961. With the experience learned from this, Hall and Hap Sharp set up small workshops in Midland, Texas and built the Chaparral 2, a rear-engined sports car powered by a 'small block' 5.4-litre Chevrolet engine.

The glass-fibre-reinforced plastic monocoque chassis was the work of Andy Green, a structural engineer specialising in composite materials and employed by General Dynamics at Forth Worth. The next development was clutchless transmission devised by Hap Sharp and based on a modified Chevrolet Corvair gearbox with the help of General Motors. During 1964 the Chaparral 2 won seven of 16 races entered. General Motors over the years was to give considerable technical support to the team.

In 1965 the Sebring 12 Hours race was open to Group 7 sports cars, because the organisers thought that they would not attract sufficient Prototypes, and Jim Hall entered the Chaparral 2 for himself and Sharp. Initially Hall battled with Dan Gurney (Ford-powered Lotus 19B), but then the Chaparral stayed in front for the remainder of the race, despite a torrential rainstorm that inundated the circuit and reduced the more powerful cars to a crawl. After an hour the rain eased and soon the circuit started to dry out and Hall/Sharp went on to win at 84.72mph (136.31kph), four laps ahead of McLaren/Miles (Ford GT40). During 1965 Chaparral entered 21 races and won 16.

Chaparral entered Prototype racing in 1966 with the 2D that had the glass-fibre chassis designed for the original 2 and was powered by the Chevrolet V8 5,326cc (102×83mm) engine. This was fitted with four twin-choke carburettors of Weber-type, but made by Chevrolet. There was a separate exhaust system for each bank of cylinders and it was claimed that power output was restricted to 425bhp in the interests of reliability. The transmission was still the most interesting feature of the design.

It was not a full automatic design, but was described as a 'fluid-clutch'system. There were three forward gears, with a hydraulic coupling and a torque converter. Sliding dog clutches engaged the straight-cut gears and the driver changed gear by easing his foot on the throttle, thereby taking the loading off the dogs, and then quickly moved the gear-lever.

The body/chassis was a glass-fibre monocoque structure reinforced by metal to take localised loading and provide additional rigidity. Double wishbones and coil/spring damper units were used at the front, but at the rear the suspension was by twin trailing links, single top transfer links and reversed lower wishbones. The body of the 2D was a striking shark-profile coupé with a 'flipper' tail. The wheels had detachable rims that enabled different widths and, thus, tyre choice according to the circuit on which the car was being raced.

The 2D made its debut in the hands of Joakim Bonnier/Phil Hill in the Daytona 24 Hours race in February. The Chaparral was second fastest in practice, but it was delayed by front suspension problems, dropped to the tail of the field and retired after 14 hours' racing. By Sebring the 'flipper' tail had been deleted and there was now a prominent air intake mounted on the roof. Two cars were entered for Hall/Sharp and Bonnier/Hill, but both retired, Bonnier because of an excessive consumption of engine oil and Phil Hill (who had relieved Hap Sharp) because of transmission problems.

Chaparral next raced at the Nürburgring 1,000Km event on 5 June. This was not a Ford circuit and Ferrari sent along a single 330 P3 for Surtees/Parkes. After the Ferrari stopped at the pits with suspension problems, the Chaparral assumed a lead that it never lost, although the 2-litre Ferrari *Dinos* of Scarfiotti/Bandini and Ginther/Rodriguez harried it all the way to the finish and only 42 seconds separated the first and second-place cars. It was not a great race, but it was a great win

After the 1,000Km race, Joakim Bonnier squeezes into the cockpit alongside Phil Hill. This photograph shows clearly the 2D's gull-wing doors and the roof-top air intake. It was something of a 'fluke' win, but Chaparral added considerable interest to sports car racing at the time. (LAT)

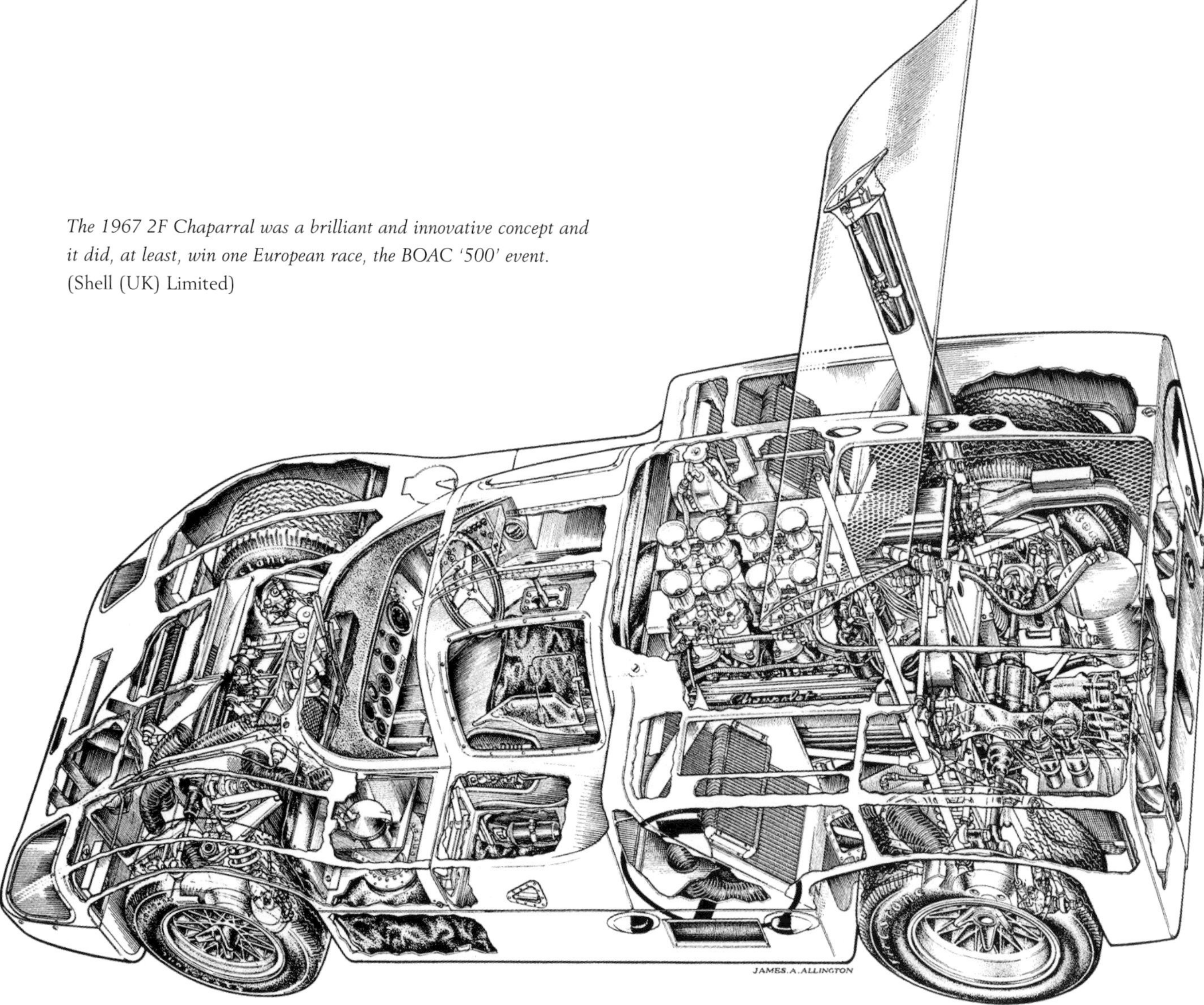

The 1967 2F Chaparral was a brilliant and innovative concept and it did, at least, win one European race, the BOAC '500' event. (Shell (UK) Limited)

for the American entrant. Hill/Bonnier drove a new 2D shipped over from the United States at Le Mans. It was never in serious contention and retired shortly before midnight because of electrical problems.

In the first official season of Can-Am racing the new Chaparral was not ready for the race at Mont Tremblant in Canada, but joined the circus at the second round at Bridgehampton. The cars were the new 2E, of similar construction to the 2D, but with a pioneering high-mounted aerofoil over the back wheels. This was hydraulically operated from a foot pedal so that when the driver depressed the pedal with his left foot, the aerofoil pivoted to an almost flat position for minimum drag on the straights; when the pressure was released, it moved into the maximum downforce position.

The Chaparrals were a match for the latest Lolas and McLarens, and turned in some excellent performances. At Bridgehampton Phil Hill was fourth, he was second at Mosport Park and then Hill and Hall were first and second in the Monterey Grand Prix at Laguna Seca. Both Chaparrals were eliminated by fuel starvation at Riverside Raceway, California. In the last round, the Stardust Grand Prix at Las Vegas, the 2Es had aerofoil problems, Hall retired and Hill finished seventh after a pit stop. Despite the speed to match the opposition, the 2Es lacked reliability and Hill was fourth in the Championship.

In 1967 Chaparral tackled a full Prototype season and both the 2D and the new 2F had a larger-capacity, aluminium-alloy block Chevrolet engine of 6,984cc (108×95.3mm) claimed to develop 575bhp at 7,000rpm. To match the extra power General Motors strengthened the gearbox, but this proved the weakest link in the Chaparral challenge and transmission problems were not resolved until late in the year. The first 2F was a 1966 2E Can-Am car, complete with side radiators and high-mounted aerofoil, modified to comply with Prototype rules. Weight with fuel was 1,800 pounds (816kg).

The team's first race was the Daytona 24 Hours and

at the Florida banked circuit Phil Hill/Mike Spence drove the 2F and Johnson/Jennings had the 2D. Hill pulled away at the start, was gradually increasing his lead and was attaining 190mph (305kph) on the banked section of the circuit. The 2F's race ended during Hill's second stint at the wheel when he lost control on loose gravel as he entered the banked section and damaged the rear suspension and chassis. The other Chaparral was never in contention and retired because of transmission failure.

In practice for Sebring the two Chaparrals were second and third fastest. Spence/Hall worked their way through to hold the lead briefly, but fell back and both Chaparrals retired because of transmission problems. It was a pattern that was to repeat itself time and time again during the European season. Mike Spence was fastest in practice for the Monza 1,000Km race on 25 April, but he and Hill retired here because of drive-shaft failure and in the Spa 1,000Km race because of the gearbox seal failure, a persistent fault.

Then the team tackled the Targa Florio on 14 May with a very unsuitable car for the tortuous Sicilian road race. Even so Phil Hill and Hap Sharp drove superbly and were in a fairly secure fourth place on lap 9 when forced to retire because of a puncture. The 2F carried only a deflated spare because of lack of space. In practice for the Nürburgring 1,000km race Mike Spence was fastest, setting an unofficial lap record, the first 100mph (161kph) lap of the circuit, five seconds faster than the existing record. At the first pit stop, Hill was leading, but after Spence took the wheel, the gearbox failed yet again.

At Le Mans Chaparral fielded two 2Fs for Hill/Spence and Johnson/Jennings. The Johnson/Jennings car succumbed to electrical problems and after holding second place early in the race Hill/Spence retired because of transmission failure that even a change of gearbox could not resolve. There remained only the BOAC '500' race at Brands Hatch on 30 July. Spence/Hill were faster than the Ferraris and took the lead after the retirement of Hulme's Lola. Despite dropping back to third place after a pit stop, they came through to win by a small margin from the Ferrari of Amon/Stewart.

Hall had solved the transmission problems, but the large-capacity Prototypes were banned at the end of 1967 and so the Chaparrals were not again raced in Europe. During 1967 and the following three seasons the team contested Can-Am racing with little success. McLaren had become increasingly dominant. The final Chaparral was the 1970 2J 'sucker' car with which Jim Hall expoloited his own and a very successful form of ground-effect by having two rear-mounted high-velocity fans driven by a two-stroke twin-cylinder engine. The fans sucked the air from under the car and kept it very close to the ground.

The 2J was in its infancy in 1970 and it was never allowed to grow up. At the end of the year the *Commision Sportive Internationale*, the rule-making body of the FIA, banned Chaparral's two-stroke engine and fans. Hall had crashed heavily at Stardust Raceway, Las Vegas in the last round of the 1968 Can-Am Championship and although he drove Chevrolet Camaros in the 1970 Trans-Am series, he reckoned that he had returned too soon. For a while Hall entered Lolas in Can-Am racing, but he realised that racing for him would never be the same after he gave up running his own cars.

Headlamps ablaze, the 7-litre Chaparral with Mike Spence at the wheel thunders down to the Esses at Le Mans in 1967. Although the car displayed tremendous speed, it retired yet again because of problems with the automatic transmission. (Ford Motor Company)

Jim Hall on ground-effect

We definitely got a jump on the competition in the aerodynamics arena in about 1964. I had built [the Chaparral 2] that had bad lift characteristics and I wanted to cure that in the winter of '63–64. I managed to do it. Then I thought, "Well, if I can eliminate lift, why can't I continue right on through zero and go negative. Why don't I push down on this thing and see if I can increase the traction?" And by golly, I was able to do that too.

Then I began to balance the car for high-speed oversteer, because a rear-drive car, if you get it balanced at low speed, if it's neutral in aero, typically goes into oversteer the faster you go. And as I dealt with this problem, the lap times dropped significantly. There was no wind tunnel involved, it was seat of the pants – and some rudimentary instrumentation: we had cables leading to graphs with pencils so that I could plot the ride height. I'd calibrate the car by putting lead in it so I knew how many pounds were needed to reduce the ride heights by the same amount.

We started measuring drag in about 1965. That's when the movable flaps came in: let's get rid of the drag on the straights but keep the downforce in the corners. When we did that, we put so much downforce on the car that we mashed it onto its own bump rubbers and into the ground. We were faster still but the ride was pretty bad. That's where the hub-mounted wing came from.

It's a pretty logical development: if we are upsetting the chassis, why not get those loads off the chassis and put them on the wheels? Gosh, that made for a nice car: the spring rates were reasonable, the ride rate was good – yet you still had the downforce. It was sad that the regs went away from that. But they did – and we did the 'sucker car' [the 2J of 1970] as a reaction to that.

Initially, I got a young boy's drawing in the mail that showed a car with a fan right in the top of it; he talked about it being a suction fan. That was always in the back of my mind, but when we began thinking about it properly we realised that if you put skirts round the car, it wasn't going to take a very big fan to do the job. We finally ended up with articulated skirts that kept a fairly narrow gap all the time. It wasn't a perfect seal – we didn't think that the scrutineers would allow that – but even so, we could reproduce the weight of the car quite easily, and that made it capable of cornering at virtually 2g. It was fantastic.

But at the end of 1970 there was a terrible outcry from the rest of the Can-Am competitors – and the *FIA* 'bandits' – about our car. They simply told us that we could not run it in 1971 – this after they had banned hub-mounted wings for '70. We had been premature going to the racetrack with the 2J, but when you think that you have something that will put you ahead of the field, you are in a big hurry to get there before any info leaks. We made a decision to go ahead and do it, learn about the car this year, and win with it the next . . .
(Reproduced with permission from *Motor Sport*.)

Jim Hall at the wheel of the Chaparral 2 in the 1965 Canadian Grand Prix, a race that he won. (LAT)

Porsche 908

1968–71

Rolf Stommelen and Jochen Neerpasch co-drove this 908 Lang *at Le Mans in 1968. This car was delayed by cooling-fan problems early in the race, but press-on determined driving brought it back up through the field to third place behind Rodriguez/Bianchi (*Gulf Ford *GT40) and Steinemann/Spoerry (Porsche 907).* (Porsche Werkfoto)

In 1961 Porsche first raced sports cars with air-cooled, horizontally opposed, 1,981cc (76×54.6mm) eight-cylinder engines similar in general design to those powering the 1962 Formula 1 cars, but with increased bore. Over the next few years the company raced Prototypes with four, six and eight cylinders and in 1966–67 fielded the very aerodynamic 910 with a six-cylinder 2-litre engine. The next stage was the 907, a car that combined the 910 multi-tubular chassis with improved aerodynamics and the eight-cylinder engine in 2,195cc (80×54.6m) form now developing 270bhp at 8,600rpm. The 907, also built in six-cylinder and eight-cylinder 2-litre forms, was raced through to mid-1968.

During 1967 Porsche had early warning of the intention of the FIA to impose a 3-litre capacity limit for Prototypes. Over the years the Porsche works entries, despite their engine capacity handicap, had been a major threat to the larger-capacity opposition on slower circuits, especially the Targa Florio, which the make had won six times. With the new capacity limit Porsche would be competing for outright victory on all circuits, especially if the company produced a car with an enlarged engine and in April 1967 work started on the 908.

Originally, the 908 had an eight-cylinder engine of 2,926cc (84×66mm), but capacity had risen to 2,996cc (85×66mm) by Le Mans in 1968. The cylinder barrels and heads were of light alloy, magnesium-alloy was used for the crankcase and there were titanium connecting rods and crankshaft, which ran in nine plain main bearings. Gears and chains from the front of the engine drove the four overhead camshafts (on the 907 they were driven by a shaft and bevel gears). Bosch fuel injection and transistorised ignition were used and there was a single distributor and twin plugs per cylinder. Initial power output was 320bhp, but by the 908's first race had risen to 335bhp.

Porsche used a small triple-plate clutch and a six-speed gearbox designed originally for a hill-climb car. It was too heavy and was replaced by a five-speed gearbox. The chassis was a steel multi-tubular space-frame structure, but by the Watkins Glen race in July 1968 Porsche had adopted a lighter aluminium-alloy chassis on one of the cars and this was used for all cars built subsequently. The front suspension was by double wishbones and Macpherson struts, with single links, reversed wishbones and radius arms at the rear. Steering was rack-and-pinion and there was right-hand drive. The 906 had a 7ft 6.55in (2,300mm) wheelbase and originally it was built in *Kurz* and *Lang* coupé forms.

Throughout 1968 Porsche's main competition came from the Group 5 Ford GT40s entered by John Wyer's *Gulf Racing* team and it was these Fords that ultimately defeated Porsche in the World Championship. Porsche 907s won the Daytona and Sebring races, but the Fords won at Brands Hatch and Monza. The 908s first appeared at the Le Mans Test Weekend and then performed disappointingly on their race debut in the Monza 1,000Km race. The *Gulf* Fords missed the Targa Florio and Elford/Maglioli won the Sicilian road race with a 907.

By the Nürburgring 1,000Km race on 19 May, the 908s were well sorted and Porsche entered two *Kurz* cars for Siffert/Elford and Mitter/Scarfiotti, as well as two 907s. Early in the race the two 908s led the two 907s with Ickx (Ford) trailing in fifth place – it was not a GT40 circuit. Two of the Porsche entries retired, the Mitter/Scarfiotti 908 and one of the 907s, but Siffert/Elford enjoyed a completely troublefree run to win by three minutes from the 907 of Herrmann/Stommelen with the Ickx/Hawkins Ford third.

The Spa 1,000Km race was a week later and in practice Porsche ran the 908 in both *Kurz* and *Lang* forms. The long-tail car was unstable through the bends and both it and the early long-tail 917s had serious aerodynamic problems that Porsche failed to acknowledge or remedy. As in 1967 the race was run in torrentially wet conditions and the *Gulf* Ford of Ickx/Redman cantered away to win by a clear lap from Mitter/Schlesser (907) and Herrmann/Stommelen (908). Neerpasch, at the wheel of the 908 he was sharing with Elford, lost control of his 908 on the *Masta Straight* and it spun wildly for 400 metres before bouncing off the banks and wrecking itself completely.

Because of strikes in France the Le Mans race was postponed until the end of September and so the next Championship race was the Watkins Glen Six Hours, an addition to the series held in July. The 908s were fitted with rear stabiliser flaps linked to the rear suspension; these were at an angle of 35 degrees on the straight, acting purely as spoilers, but on corners the flap above the outside rear wheel was raised to increase air pressure and the flap above the inside rear wheel lowered to reduce pressure. It was reckoned that the flaps worked well on fast, sweeping bends, but were of little effect on slow corners.

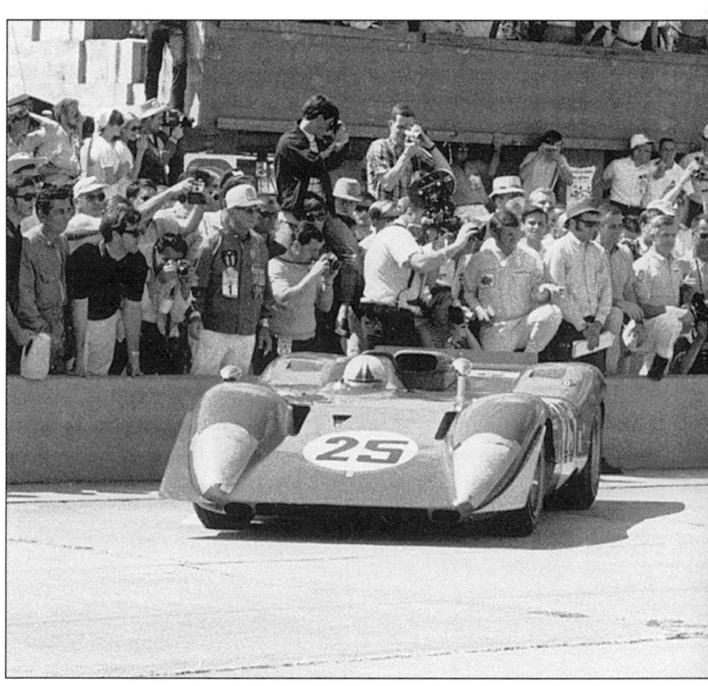

Jo Siffert (Porsche 908 Spyder) is away first at the start of the 1969 Sebring 12 Hours race; about to accelerate away are, left to right: Amon (Ferrari 312P), Donohue (Penske-entered Lola T70 Mark IIIB), Mitter (Porsche 908 Spyder) and the two Lola T70 Mark IIIs of actor James Garner's American International Racing team. (Pete Lyons)

Porsche ran four short-tail 908s at Watkins Glen, but they all had mechanical problems and Fords took the first two places. The *Gulf* Team missed the 311-mile (500km) Austrian Grand Prix at Zeltweg and the 908s were unopposed. Siffert and Herrmann/Ahrens with their *Kurz* 908s took the first two places ahead of Paul Hawkins (private Ford GT40), but both Elford and Neerpasch dropped out of contention because of mechanical problems on their 908s.

The Le Mans race was held on 28–29 September in abnormally cool conditions and it proved a straight fight between Porsche and Ford. Porsche ran four *Lang* 908s with tail fins, fixed aerofoil and spoilers, but also prepared three *Lang* 907s for private entrants as back-ups. The 908s set the pace, but fell victim to mechanical problems, two retired and the Elford/Mitter car

was disqualified because the alternator was changed contrary to race regulations. Rodriguez/Bianchi (*Gulf* Ford) won from Steinemann/Spoerry (907) with the surviving 908 shared by Stommelen and Neerpasch third. Porsche lost the World Championship to Ford by three points.

At a reception held at the Hockenheim circuit in January 1969 Porsche revealed their competition cars for 1969 and the new team manager, Rico Steinemann, formerly editor of the Swiss magazine *Powerslide* and amateur driver of 910 and 907 cars, was there to announce the details to the press. The main development was the 908 *Spyder*, a design that reflected the change in the Prototype regulations, dispensing with the requirements for minimum ground clearance, windscreen height, interior dimensions and the need to carry a spare wheel.

This short, low car, with lightweight open body, was inspired by the Porsche European Hill Climb Championship cars; it weighed only 1,390 pounds (630kg) and was claimed to have a maximum speed of 175mph (280kph). The 908 *Normal*, as it was now known, weighed 1,452 pounds (658kg) and the 200mph (320kph) 908 *Lang* had a weight of 1,496 pounds (678kg). The *Spyder* was used in most races and Porsche did not race the *Normal* at all. The *Gulf* GT40s were now uncompetitive, except at Le Mans, and the main opposition came from the new and very fast Ferrari 312P Prototypes.

Porsche entered five *Lang* 908s in the first Championship race, the Daytona 24 Hours, and suffered the first of two great humiliations. All the 908s were plagued by cracked exhaust systems and all retired because of camshaft drive failure. The result was that was that Lola T70 coupés took the first two places. It was much the same story at Sebring on 22 March. Porsche entered five 908 *Spyders* and all suffered problems, mainly cracked chassis. Ickx/Oliver scored an unexpected win with their *Gulf* Ford, the 312P Ferrari driven by Amon/Andretti took second place with more than its fair share of problems and the 908s were third, fifth and seventh.

After this second humiliation, Porsche scored a succession of wins. In the BOAC '500' race at Brands Hatch the 908 *Spyders* of Siffert/Redman, Elford/Attwood and Mitter/Schütz took the first three places ahead of the Ferrari 312P of Amon/Rodriguez. Ferrari put up a strong fight at Monza in the 1,000Km race on 25 April, but 908 *Langs* driven by Siffert/Redman and Herrmann/Ahrens finished first and second. No Ferraris ran in the 447-mile (720km) Targa Florio, Porsche entered six 908 *Spyders* and the only opposition came from Alfa Romeo with two 2-litre 33/2s and one with a 2.5-litre engine. In a steam-roller result 908s took the first four places.

In the Spa 1,000Km race on 11 May Siffert/Redman won with a 908 *Lang* from the Ferrari 312P of Rodriguez/David Piper, after a furious duel between Siffert and Rodriguez, a repeat of the battle between them at Monza. Ferrari might have won, if Piper had been able to match the lap times of his team-mate. Other 908s finished third and fourth and the race was

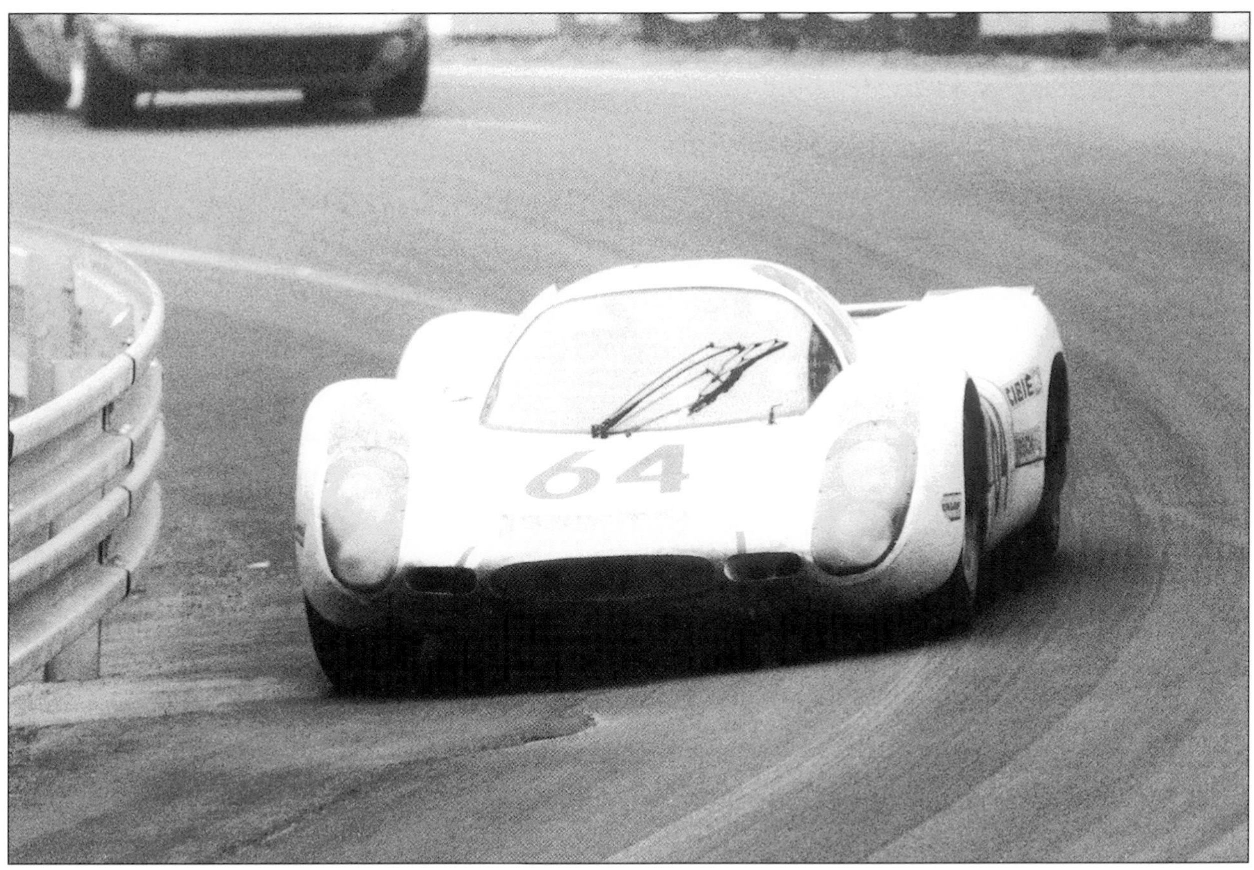

Porsche entered six cars at Le Mans in 1969 and three of these were long-tail 908s. The 908s were faster than the Gulf Ford GT40s but suffered mechanical problems. In the closing stages of the race Hans Herrmann (co-driving with Gérard Larrousse) with this very rough-running 908, battled with Jacky Ickx (Ford GT40) and was beaten into second place by a very small margin. (Porsche Werkfoto)

marked by the debut of the Porsche 917.

At the Nürburgring 1,000Km race Porsche introduced an improved version of the *Spyder* known as the 908.2, with smoother body, slightly raised glass-fibre surround to the cockpit instead of a windscreen, and a faired-in cockpit. There were small fixed spoilers at the rear because the fully movable flippers for which the car had been designed had been part of the ban on movable aerodynamic devices imposed by the *FIA* at the Monaco Grand Prix. Aerodynamic instability caused two of these cars to crash in practice and only one started the race. Siffert/Redman with an ordinary *Spyder* won from Herrmann/Stommelen (908.02) and Elford/Ahrens with another ordinary *Spyder*.

There was a very mixed works Porsche entry at Le Mans: two 917s, three 908 *Lang* coupés and a 908.02 with long tail and high fins. Siffert, co-driving with Redman, had reckoned – correctly – that with its good acceleration and braking resulting from low weight and now fully sorted handling, it would be a match for the 908 coupés. The main opposition came from the Ferrari 312Ps, raced in coupé form, and the *Gulf* Ford GT40s, which had endurance if not pace. For the last time the race began with the traditional Le Mans start and because of the French Presidential elections the start was brought forward to 2pm from 4pm.

Both Ferraris were soon out of contention, just before the four-hour mark Siffert/Redman retired because of gearbox trouble, Schütz crashed the *Lang* he was sharing with Mitter, the Lins/Kauhsen 908 was eliminated by clutch failure and both 917s retired. So, Ickx/ Oliver with their GT40 led from the 908 of Herrmann/ Larrousse that was sick and off-tune. As the race drew to a close, the two cars battled for the lead, but on the very last lap Ickx passed Herrmann under braking for *Mulsanne Corner* and there was nowhere before the finishing line that Herrmann could repass. At the chequered flag Herrmann was only 100 yards behind the Ford and Porsche suffered another humiliation.

There remained two rounds in the Championship. Porsche 908 *Spyders* took first three places in the Watkins Glen Six Hours race and in the Austrian 1,000Km race on the newly opened Österreichring

In 1970–71 Porsche raced the very light 908.03 Spyders in the Targa Florio and Nürburgring races. This is Siffert/Redman in the 1970 Targa Florio, which they won by over two minutes from another 908.03 driven by Gulf team-mates Rodriguez/Kinnunen. (Porsche Werkfoto)

917s finished first and third. Porsche won the Championship with 45 points to the 25 of Ford. In 1970–71 Porsche relied mainly on the 917s, but the racing career of the 908 was not yet over.

Well aware of the unsuitability of the 917s for the Targa Florio and the Nürburgring, Porsche developed the 908.03, with aluminium-alloy multi-tubular space-frame, suspension similar to that of the standard 908s, polyurethane body, 13-inch wheels and with the usual 908 engine and gearbox. Every effort was made to keep weight down by the use of titanium and other light material and the weight was only 1,200 pounds (545kg). The cars were entered in the name of *Gulf Racing Team* and subsidiary Austrian company, *Porsche Konstruktionen AG*, but all preparation work was carried out at Zuffenhausen.

In the 1970 Targa Florio the *Gulf*-entered 908.03s of Siffert/Redman and Rodriguez/Kinnunen took the first two places ahead of Vaccarella/Giunti with a works 5-litre Ferrari 512S. Elford/Ahrens and Herrmann/Attwood with *Porsche Konstruktionen*-entered cars took the first two places in the Nürburgring 1,000Km race from Surtees/Vaccarella with a works 512S.

For 1971 the 908.03s were largely unchanged, apart from larger 15-inch wheels, twin tail fins and an increase in weight to 1,246 pounds (565kg). The best engines now developed 375bhp. All the 908.3s were eliminated in the 1971 Targa Florio and 3-litre Alfa Romeo Tipo 33/3s, cars that had vastly improved since 1970, took the first three places. At the Nürburgring on 30 May the 908.03s redeemed themselves and Elford/Larrousse (*International Martini Racing Team*), Rodriguez/Siffert (*Gulf*) and Marko/van Lennep (*Martini*) finished 1–2–3.

At the end of 1971 Porsche sold the 908.03s to selected private customers and as late as 1975 these cars were still racing in Championship events with turbocharged 2,142cc 911 six-cylinder engines. At Le Mans in 1972 a 908 *Lang* refurbished at the works, supported by works mechanics 'on holiday' and driven by Jöst/Weber/Casoni took third place behind the winning Matras. The 908 was not always a winner, but it enjoyed a long and remarkably successful racing career.

Chevron B16, B19 & B21

1969–72

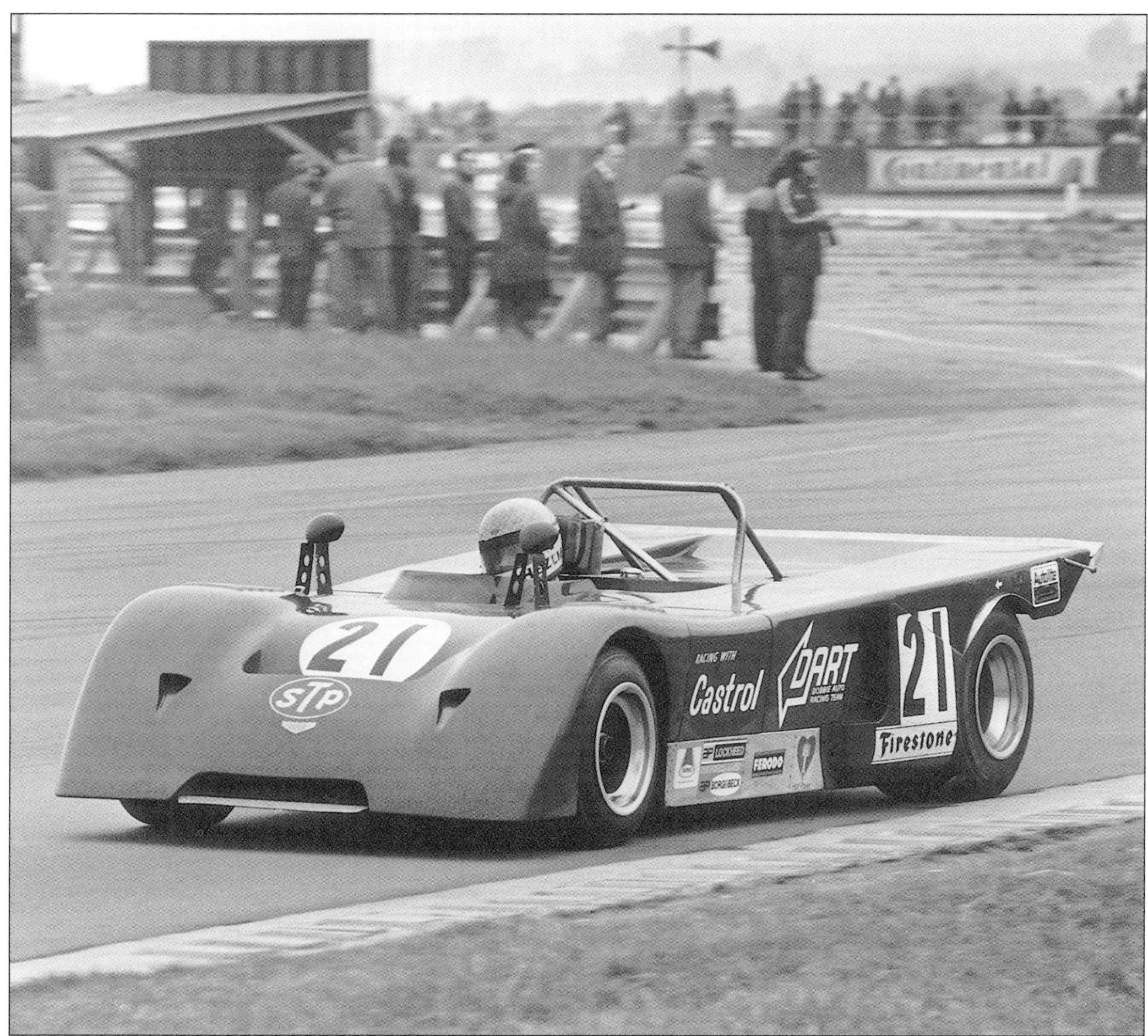

Dutch driver Toine Hezemans with this B19 entered by the DART team won the round of the 2-litre European Constructors' Championship at Silverstone in June 1971. (LAT)

Derek Bennett was an exceptionally able engineer and if he had not died prematurely, his achievements in the motor racing world would have been infinitely greater and his company would have survived very much longer. He was a man with a hyperactive mind, constantly tackling engineering problems, anxious for the next challenge. As someone so mentally preoccupied, he appeared unassuming and reserved.

When Bennett, born in Manchester on 28 November 1933, was growing up there was little opportunity for higher education. As was common, he left school at 15 and after an apprenticeship with an electrical engineering firm, worked from a series of lock-up garages, repairing cars, rebuilding wrecks and building himself a Midget racer. Circuit racing attracted him, he competed a number of times and then built the first two cars that were to bear the Chevron name. Desperate to find a suitable name for his cars, he noticed one of those roadside signs that indicate a sharp bend, a chevron, and he chose that name.

Bennett's first outing with the Clubmen's Formula Chevron B1 (the type number was retrospective) was at Kirkistown in Ireland in July 1965 and he won the race. This success, together with the interest of would-be buyers, gave Derek the impetus to take more spacious premises in a former mill in Bolton. Here, in 1966, Derek built four more cars, designated the B2, for the Clubmen's Formula and a series of GT coupés from the B3 through to the definitive B8. There were 11 of the earlier cars and 44 B8s with 2-litre BMW engines built between 1968 and 1970 and homologated as a Group 5 Competition Sports Car. In addition Chevron built the B12 with Repco 3-litre engines for John Woolfe.

In August 1969 the B16 made its racing debut. During its first shakedown tests the engine was still the 2-litre BMW, but a 1.6-litre Cosworth FVA developing about 210bhp had been fitted by the time it first raced. Transmission was by a Hewland FT200 five-speed trans-axle. The B19 had a central, box-type monocoque constructed in square-section tubing and stiffened by spot-welded alloy sheets on the upper and inner sides of the sills and with space-frames front and rear, that at the rear carrying the engine and gearbox. The front suspension was by double wishbones and coil spring/damper units.

For the rear suspension Bennett used upper and lower forward-mounted radius arms, short top locating links and coil spring/damper units, a layout based on Brabham components, which Chevron used for some years. Bennett had taken a hand in the styling of earlier Chevron bodies, but the glass-fibre body of the B16 was the work of Jim Clark of Specialised Mouldings and he evolved a very low coupé resembling the Ferrari P4. The B16 had a 7ft 9in (2,360mm) wheelbase, front and rear track of 4ft 4in (1,370mm) and a dry weight of 1267 pounds (575kg).

Brian Redman, who had previously raced the BRM-powered B5, and Chevron director David Bridges, were at the wheel of the B16s entered in the Nürburgring 500Km race for 2,000cc Prototypes and Competition Sports cars in September 1969. There were handling problems in practice and although these were not resolved, Redman took pole position and was achieving 150mph (241kph) on the fastest part of the circuit. He led throughout the race and rather demoralised Abarth drivers crossed the line in the next three places. Bridges had a more difficult race and finished seventh.

Bennett thought that the handling problems were suspension-related, but he soon realised that it was the aerodynamics and large spoilers added to the tail solved the problem. In 1970 B16s cars competed at an International level in both the Sports Car Championship and the newly inaugurated European 2-Litre Constructors' Championship. Most cars had the 1.8-litre Cosworth FVC engine developing 230bhp at 9,500rpm and in this form the B16 was homologated in late 1970 as a Competition Sports Car. Two cars had 2-litre BMW engines and these together with the Mazda rotary-engined car entered by *Levi's International Racing* remained in the Prototype category.

Redman drove a new red, works B16 in the 25-lap Embassy Trophy at Thruxton on Easter Sunday 1970. He took pole position, but Siffert with David Piper's 4.5-litre Porsche 917 powered ahead and crossed the line four seconds ahead of Redman. Three B16s ran in the BOAC 1,000Km race at Brands Hatch on 12 April, but none performed well. The first round of the 2-Litre Championship was at the Paul Ricard circuit in southern France in April. Redman could not match the speed of Jo Bonner's Lola, but won this 203-mile (326km race) after Bonnier had mechanical problems.

John Burton with his B16-FVA won the next round of the Championship at Hameenlinna in Finland, but it was a poorly supported race. The Mazda-powered car first appeared in the Spa 1,000Km race in May and Duprez/Vernaeve drove it into 15th place, second in class. Redman built up a good lead over Bonnier in the 2-litre race at the Salzburgring later in May, but ran out of fuel. A week later Duprez/Vernaeve ran in the Nürburgring 1,000Km race and despite starter motor problems took tenth place and class second.

At the 2-litre Championship round at Anderstorp in Sweden in June Redman crashed in practice because of handling problems, but finished second to Bonnier with the works Lola in both heats. Three Chevron B16s ran at Le Mans on 13–14 June, two nominally works-entered FVC-powered cars and the Mazda-engined car, but all retired. At Hockenheim, another event run in two heats and totalling 253 miles (407km), Redman was again second to Bonnier.

Redman was unavailable for the Mugello race in July and so Vic Elford took his place. The works B16 developed a leak in a bag-tank and Elford suffered petrol burns, as a result of which he lost concentration and crashed. Bonnier missed this race and Merzario (Abarth) was the winner. Next came the Coppa di Enna in August and on this very fast circuit Redman with the B16 was outpaced and third on the aggregate of the two heats behind Bonnier and Merzario.

In an effort to find greater straight-line speed Bennett devised the B19 *Spyder*, with low, lighter and lithe aluminium-alloy body. Redman drove this in the

A works Chevron B16 at Silverstone in 1970. This Chevron model had beautifully balanced lines apart from the rear spoilers that resolved handling difficulties. (FotoVantage)

Nürburgring 500Km race on 6 September and led until three-quarters race-distance when the car caught fire. Elford (works B16 coupé) came through to win from Merzario by just over a minute.

The final round of the Championship was the Trophée des Ardennes at Spa-Francorchamps on 20 September and here the *Spyder* was attaining 165mph (265kph) on the *Masta Straight*. Redman took pole position, battled with Bonnier throughout this 315-mile (507km) race; he took the lead to win at the very high average speed of 141.93mph (228.37kph) after Bonnier locked a brake and spun at *La Source* hairpin on the last lap. Chevron won the Championship with 52 points to the 51 of Lola.

For 1971 Bennett fitted the B16 *Spyder* with a glass-fibre body and it became known as the B19. Chris Craft drove the works B19, with support from several private teams. The works car was largely out of luck during the year and Chevron won only two rounds of the European Championship. The Lancashire-based *Red Rose Racing Team* won them both: Niki Lauda at Salzburgring in May and John Bridges in the Trophy of the Dunes at Zandvoort in September. Lola was the dominant marque, winning the Championship with 57 points to the 46 of Chevron in second place.

The 1972 2-litre car was the slightly modified B21 *Spyder* and only private teams raced these cars. At the start of the year the British teams were still using the FVC engine, but later *Red Rose Racing* used a 2-litre Cosworth Chevrolet Vega-based engine. Austrian Dieter Quester had a B21 with a 2-litre BMW engine reckoned to develop 275bhp. The Chevrons were competitive, but they won only two of the year's nine races. In the Tauernpokal at the Salzburgring in May Quester won from Hine (*Red Rose* entry) and John Burton with his Canon Cameras-sponsored car was the winner in Spain. Chevron again took second place in the Championship with 109 points to the 112 of Abarth.

The 2-litre Championship continued in 1973, but was waning in popularity because of European Interserie racing, and the larger-capacity sports cars appealed so much more to spectators. It was, however, still the main focus of Chevron sports car racing. The 1973 2-litre car was the B23 *Spyder*, slightly modified and with more pronouncedly wedge-shaped body. The usual engines were Alan Smith-developed versions of the FVC, but Alfa Romeo, Schnitzer BMW, Tecno and Hart BDA engines were also used. Throughout the series the Chevrons proved no match for the latest Lola T292s.

The first round of the Championship was at the Paul Ricard Circuit in April and the *Red Rose* B23s with Smith FVC engines of John Lepp and John Burton took the first two places. It was an encouraging start to the season, but Chevron failed to score another win. Lepp was second at Misano in Italy, Burton second at Imola and then Martin Raymond second at the Nürburgring and the Österreichring, good enough to give the Bolton marque second place in the Championship to Lola. Chevrons raced in many other major races and an exceptionally good performance was that of John Burton/John Bridges who finished third overall in the Nürburgring 1,000Km race in May.

In December Bennett dispatched the new B26 2-litre car with full monocoque centre-section and parallel link rear suspension to the Springbok series in South Africa. In the Kyalami Nine Hours race John Watson/Ian Scheckter set a cracking pace with the new car; they were leading by half-distance, but fell back because of overheating and finished fifth. In subsequent races there was a 2-litre capacity limit and Watson/Scheckter won the Cape Three Hours race. Because of the International fuel crisis the remainder of the series was cancelled.

Alpine-Renault dominated the 1974 2-Litre Sports Car Championship and won all seven rounds, but 2-litre Chevrons continued to do well in other events and probably their best performance that year was fourth place overall and a class win in the BOAC 1,000Km race at Brands Hatch. Although Bennett continued to build sports cars until his death, the company increasingly – and successfully – concentrated on single-seaters. Generally, however, there was a decline in sports car racing and Can-Am, Interserie and the 2-litre Championship (restricted to two rounds in 1975) were all abandoned.

Derek Bennett's brilliant career ended when he crashed his hang-glider on 12 March 1978 and suffered head injuries to which he succumbed ten days later without regaining consciousness. Inevitably, what Derek Bennett might have achieved as Chevron progressed remains an enigma. Chevron, as a serious marque, died shortly after its founder, although there have been attempts to keep the name alive.

Dieter Quester at the wheel of his B21 Chevron with BMW 2-litre engine seen in practice for the British round of the 1972 European 2-Litre Constructors' Championship, the Martini International Trophy at Silverstone in June. In the second part of the race held in the wet, Quester spun off. The tailfins were a mid-season addition. (FotoVantage)

Porsche 917

1969–71

Seen lined up in front of the pits before the 1970 Le Mans race is the Porsche 917 Lang driven by Larrousse/Kauhsen. This was painted in attractive, but startling, green with mauve whirls. It finished second. (Porsche Werkfoto)

For 1969 the *FIA* changed the rules so that only 25 cars had to be built for homologation in the Group 4 Competition Sports Car class. Two major teams exploited the change in the regulations by laying down 25 examples of large-capacity cars, of 4.5 to 5-litres, secure homologation and, to all intents and purposes, render the 3-litre Prototypes obsolete. For two years sports car racing achieved a peak of competitiveness and excitement with close battles fought not just between Porsche and Ferrari, but Porsche and Porsche.

Porsche took the 3-litre flat-eight air-cooled engine that powered the 908 Prototype and added four cylinders to give a capacity of 4,494cc (85×66mm). The 917, as the new model was known, had a magnesium-alloy crankcase split on the centre-line, with a pinion in the middle of the crankshaft to drive the twin overhead camshafts per bank of cylinders and the cooling fan by a train of gears. There were two plugs per cylinder fired by twin distributors. With Bosch fuel injection and ignition system similar to those of the 908, the 917 developed 550bhp at 8,500rpm.

Transmission was by a triple-plate dry clutch and a four or five-speed all-synchromesh gearbox in unit with the final drive that incorporated a limited slip differential. The multi-tubular space-frame chassis was similar in construction to that of the 908, but Porsche used aluminium-alloy tubing, and the driving position was very close to the front of the car. As on the 908, front suspension was by double wishbones and coil spring/damper units and at the rear there were wishbones, radius arms and coil spring/damper units. Sixty litres of fuel was carried in tanks in the side-members, but was good for only 50–55 minutes' racing.

The wheelbase was the same as that of the 908, but the front track was slightly wider and the rear track slightly narrower. Porsche used 15-inch magnesium-alloy wheels and there were large ventilated ATE-Dunlop disc brakes (but solid discs were substituted in 1970). The glass-fibre coupé body was built in *Lang* and *Kurz* forms and the rear spoilers formed an integral part of the body and were actuated by rods from the rear suspension.

The 917 was homologated on 1 May 1969. The aerodynamics were diabolical and the car was unstable, something that Porsche refused to recognise. The 917s first appeared at the Spa 1,000Km race on 26 May and they were a complete handful, twitching badly on the straights and using all the road through corners. Mitter/Schütz drove the sole starter and retired after a lap because of engine problems. The works drivers refused to handle these brutes in their existing form, so David Piper and Frank Gardner were asked to drive the 917 in the Nürburgring 1,000Km event on 1 June and after a slow, difficult race they finished eighth.

Elford/Attwood and Stommelen/Ahrens drove works *Lang* 917s at Le Mans on 14–15 June and a third car was driven by private entrant John Woolfe, with veteran works driver Herbert Linge. There was a dispute between the organisers and Porsche team manager Rico Steinemann, for the 917s were fitted with fully operative rear flaps – the form in which they were homologated, but the *FIA* had banned all movable aerodynamic devices immediately before the Monaco Grand Prix on 18 May. Eventually it was agreed that the 917s could run in homologated form, complete with flaps.

On the first lap of the race John Woolfe lost control of his 917 at *White House*, the car careered down the road on its roof, broke in two and caught fire. Woolfe suffered fatal injuries. The cause of the accident was the 917's inherent aerodynamic instability. Elford/Attwood led the race for many hours, but Elford insisted against his co-driver's wishes on driving the 917 far faster than necessary and it retired because of a split gearbox casing on the Sunday morning. The other 917 also retired on the Sunday morning because of a crankcase oil leak and exhaust problems. In October,

The two Gulf 917s of Rodriguez/Oliver and Siffert/Bell storm round Spa-Francorchamps to take the first two places in the 1971 1,000Km race. The fixed aerofoil bridging the tail on the 1971 cars can just be seen. Siffert set a new lap record at 162.09mph (260.80kph) and it remains an unbroken record for the old 8.76-mile (14.10km) circuit. (Porsche Werkfoto)

Siffert/Redman scored the 917's first win in the Austrian 1,000Km race.

John Wyer's Gulf-sponsored *JW Automotive* organisation raced the 917s in 1970–71. At a test session at the Österreichring immediately after the Austrian 1,000Km race, Wyer's deputy, John Horsman with two of the JW staff, cut away most of the rear tail with snips and rebuilt it in much shortened form with aluminium-alloy sheet and self-tapping screws. The Porsche engineering staff regarded it as sheer vandalism, but it transformed the handling and formed the basis of the 917 *Kurz* raced throughout 1970.

Dissension grew between Wyer and Porsche because the factory continued to run works cars through its Austrian subsidiary, *Porsche Konstruktionen KG* based in Salzburg. Porsche compounded their sins by first making available to Salzburg new developments, including the car with new *Lang* body seen at the Le Mans Test Weekend in April. In late 1969 a 4,907cc (86×70.4mm) engine was homologated, but this was not used until practice at Monza in April.

The usual drivers of *Gulf*'s pale blue and orange cars were Jo Siffert/Brian Redman and Pedro Rodriguez/Leo Kinnunen, while the usual Salzburg pairings were Vic Elford/Kurt Ahrens and Hans Herrmann/Richard Attwood. The only real opposition came from the Ferrari 5-litre 512S cars, but these were less reliable and had slightly inferior handling and were raced only by the works in 1970. The 512S won just one race that year, the Sebring 12 Hours, in which the 917s were plagued by wheel bearing failure.

Gulf's season started well in the Daytona 24 Hours race on 31 January–1 February and Rodriguez/Kinnunen and Siffert/Redman took the first two places. The 917s failed at Sebring on 21 March, but in the wet BOAC 1,000Km race on 12 April the 917s finished 1–2–3 in the order Rodrigeuz/Kinnunen, Elford/Hulme and Attwood/Herrmann. The Ferraris had innumerable minor problems and the highest placed was fifth. The Monza 1,000Km race on 25 April was much more closely fought and although Rodriguez/Kinnunen won, the second-place 512S was only 1min 19sec behind at the finish and other Ferraris took third and fourth places.

Porsche prepared much more nimble 908.03 3-litre cars for the Targa Florio and the Nürburgring 1,000Km race. Siffert/Redman won for *Gulf* in the Spa 1,000Km race at the high speed of 149.42mph (240.1km) and Rodriguez set a new sports car record of 160.53mph (258.29kph). The race witnessed a fantastically fierce battle for the lead between Siffert and Rodriguez, they together with Ickx (Ferrari) following immediately behind were achieving 200mph (322kph) on the *Masta Straight*, and at one time the two leading cars glanced off each other. Rodriguez/Kinnunen retired because of a seized gearbox and at the finish Ickx/Surtees were second, 2½ minutes behind Siffert/Redman.

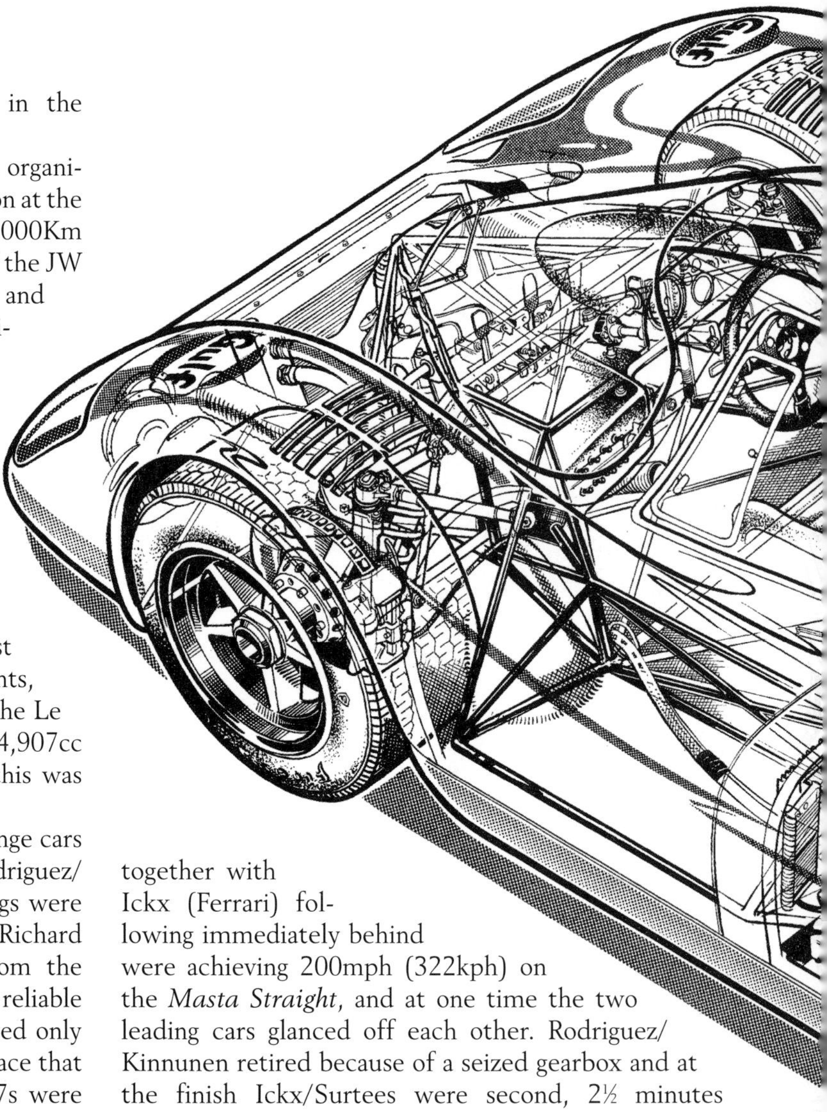

At Le Mans *Gulf* fielded three 917s, Porsche Salzburg three cars (including a *Lang*) and the *International Martini Racing Team* had a 917 *Lang* painted in pyschedelic green and mauve colours. All the *Gulf* cars retired, but Porsche scored their first win in the 24 Hours race with the Salzburg entry of Attwood/Herrmann. The last rounds of the Sports Car Manufacturers' Championship were the Watkins Glen Six Hours Race on 11 July in which Rodriguez/Kinnunen and Siffert/Redman took the first two places and the Austrian 1,000Km race on 11 October, which Siffett/Redman won from an Alfa Romeo Tipo 33/3 that was stationary in the pits because of a seized engine.

Porsche won the Championship with 63 points to the 39 of Ferrari. *Gulf* continued into 1971 with the new pairings of Siffert/Derek Bell and Rodriguez/Jack Oliver. The *International Martini Racing* team took the place of Porsche Salzburg. Porsche produced a 4,999cc 917 engine and there were new ventilated disc brakes. Body variations included a slightly longer ver-

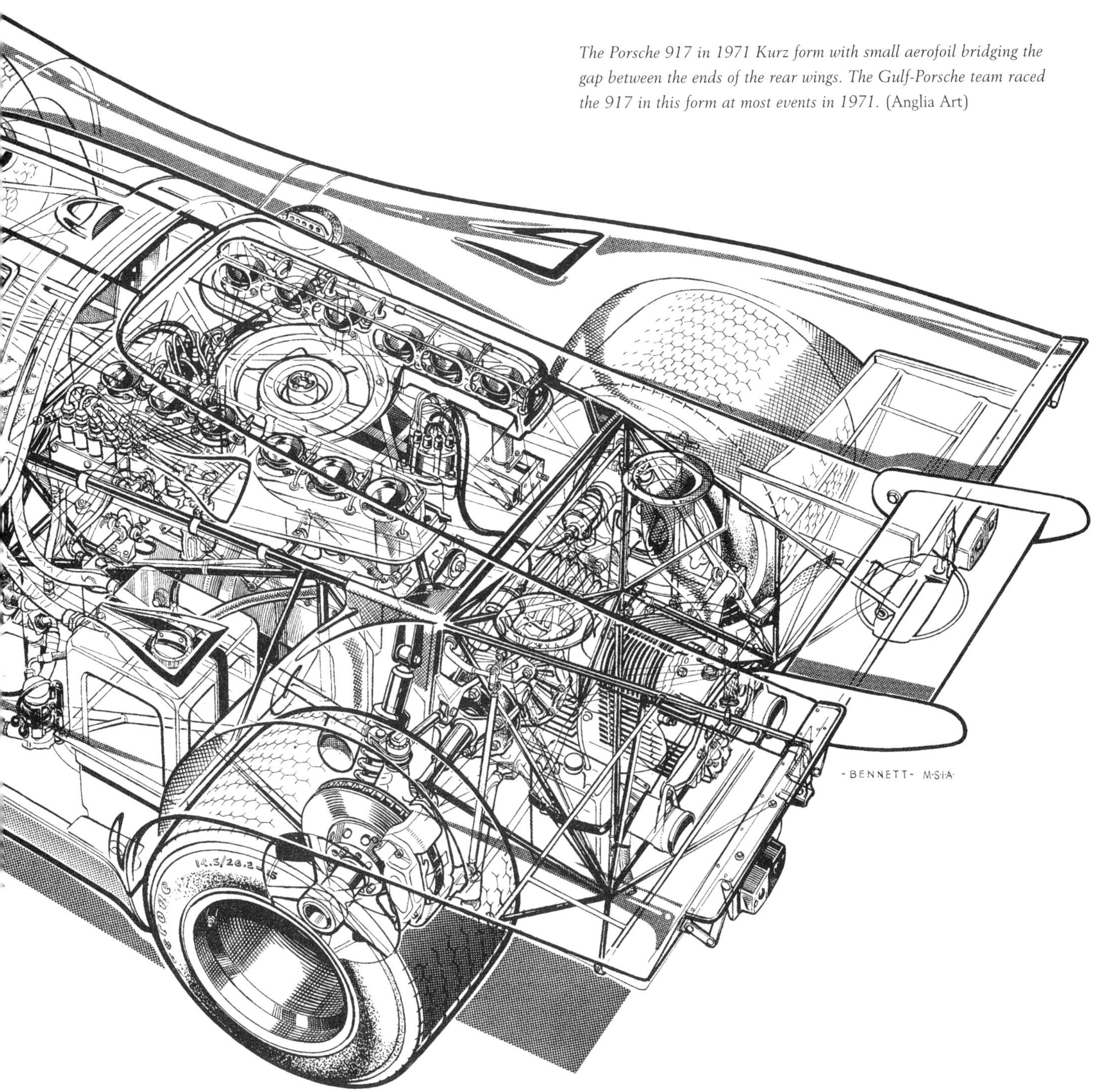

The Porsche 917 in 1971 Kurz form with small aerofoil bridging the gap between the ends of the rear wings. The Gulf-Porsche team raced the 917 in this form at most events in 1971. (Anglia Art)

sion of the *Kurz* with twin tail fins that increased speed on the straight at the expense of stability on rough surfaces and a new *Lang*, long and smooth, with the rear wheels partially enclosed and twin tail fins bridged by an aerofoil. On the usual *Kurz* model, a small aerofoil now bridged the tail.

There were 11 rounds in the 1971 Championship and *Gulf* won five. An addition to the series was the Buenos Aires 1,000Km race on 10 January and here Siffert/Bell and Rodriguez/Oliver took the first two places. Another *Gulf* victory followed at Daytona and Rodriguez/Oliver won from two private 5-litre Ferraris. At Sebring on 20 March Elford/Larrousse won for the *Martini* team after the *Gulf* cars ran into problems. All the 917s were in trouble in the BOAC 1,000Km race at Brands Hatch and a 3-litre Alfa Romeo 33/3 Prototype won from the new Ferrari 312PB Prototype driven by Ickx/Regazzoni.

Seven 917s ran at Le Mans in 1971, but there were only two finishers: this short-tail car with fins driven by Helmut Marko/Gijs van Lennep for the International Martini Racing Team won at 138.11mph (222.21kph), two laps ahead of the Gulf car of Attwood/Müller. (Porsche Werkfoto)

In the Monza 1,000Km race the *Gulf* 917s ran with tail-fin bodywork and four-speed gearboxes. There was no real opposition and Rodriguez/Oliver and Siffert/Bell took the first two places, with the third-place Alfa Romeo six laps in arrears. The *Gulf* 917s running in standard trim had another easy race in the Spa 1,000Km event on 9 May. Rodriguez/Oliver and Siffert/Bell again took the first two places; speeds had again risen and the winners averaged 154.77mph (249.02kph) including refuelling stops and Siffert set a new lap record of 162.09mph (260.80kph). As in 1970 Porsche ran 908.03s in the Targa Florio and the Nürburgring 1,000Km race.

Gulf entered three 917s in the Le Mans on 12–13 June, the latest *Lang* cars for Siffert/Bell and Rodriguez/Oliver and a 917 *Kurz* with tail fins for Attwood/Müller. There were also three cars from the *Martini* team, a *Lang* loaned by the works driven by Elford/Larrousse, a *Kurz* with tail fins entrusted to Marko/van Lennep and, again loaned by the works, an experimental high-speed bodied car developed by French aerodynamacist Charles Deutsch. It was painted in a 'Pinky and Porky' colour with dotted lines to indicate the cuts of meat formed by the carcase of a pig.

Although the *Gulf* team held the first three places after six hours' racing, they all ran into mechanical problems. By 8am on the Sunday morning Marko/van Lennep were leading from Attwood/Müller by a margin of five laps, but despite the *Martini* car's advantage, the *Gulf* drivers were steadily closing the gap and Attwood believes that they had a chance of catching and passing the leader. Porsche racing manager Rico Steinemann visited John Wyer in the *Gulf* pit and persuaded him that the teams should work together, so Attwood

Richard Attwood's win at Le Mans in 1970

In about February 1970 the Porsche factory rang me and told me that they were getting a car ready for me for Le Mans and asked me what car I would like. They offered me a choice because of the disappointment in retiring when we had such a big lead in 1969. I said, "the 5-litre engine is not proved yet, I want a 4.5 and I want a short-tail car. I want Hans Herrmann as co-driver. That will do me and we will have a good chance to win the race."

Herrmann was the oldest guy driving for the team, he and Larrousse with a 908 had finished second in 1969, narrowly beaten by Ickx and Oliver with a Wyer GT40, but I didn't realise at the time just how much he wanted to win Le Mans. I had experienced the gearbox weakness and I wanted a car with a less torquey engine and I wanted a good co-driver. Porsche wanted me to drive with Elford, he was a star driver, but I didn't want to drive with him again after what happened in 1969.

During qualifying at Le Mans I concluded that we weren't going to win, because all the 5-litre cars were so much faster and the four-speed gearbox was more suitable for this engine. We also had a four-speed gearbox with the 4.5-litre car, but we weren't allowed to use first gear and so we had to go through *Mulsanne* and *Arnage* corners in second gear and our engine just wouldn't pull out of these in second gear.

I realised that I had made a huge mistake in choosing the 4.5-litre engine. I wrote the race off – I'm a born pessimist. We were only 14th fastest, 10.7 seconds slower in qualifying than Elford/Ahrens with the 5-litre *Lang* and it meant that 13 cars in front of us had to break and I couldn't see that happening. In the race we had a lot of trouble keeping the plugs clean because of the wet weather and I kept blipping the throttle. When I came into the pits, the tell-tale was a bit close to the margin and Herrmann didn't like that because he thought that I was jeopardising his chances of winning.

All the *Gulf* 917s, the Elford/Ahrens *Lang* and all the works Ferraris dropped out and we scored what was for me an unexpected win. At the finish we were six laps ahead of the 5-litre *Lang* entered by the *Martini* team for Larrousse/Kauhsen. As soon as Hans Herrmann won Le Mans, he retired from racing.

The civic presentation held in Stuttgart after the 1970 Le Mans Race, with left to right: Willi Kauhsen and Gérard Larrousse (drivers of the second-place 917), the Bürgermeister of Stuttgart, and winners Richard Attwood and Hans Herrmann. (Porsche Werkfoto)

and Müller held back and finished two laps behind the *Martini* entry.

There remained only the Austrian 1,000Km race on 27 June won by Rodriguez/Attwood and the Watkins Glen Six Hours race on 24 July in which the *Gulf* cars were plagued by punctures and finished second and third behind the Alfa Romeo 33/3 of Peterson/de Adamich in the order Siffert/van Lennep and Attwood/Bell. Porsche won the Championship with 72 points to the 51 of Alfa Romeo. Two years of brilliant racing ended when Bell/van Lennep won the Paris 1,000Km race at Montlhéry on 17 October.

From 1972 onwards Sports Car Championships would be very different with the fastest cars limited to 3-litre Prototypes. After 1971 Porsche 917s in *Spyder* form, later turbocharged, competed with great success in Can-Am racing. Total production of 917s of all types amounted to 66 cars, of which 49 survive.

Matra MS650/660 & 670

1970–74

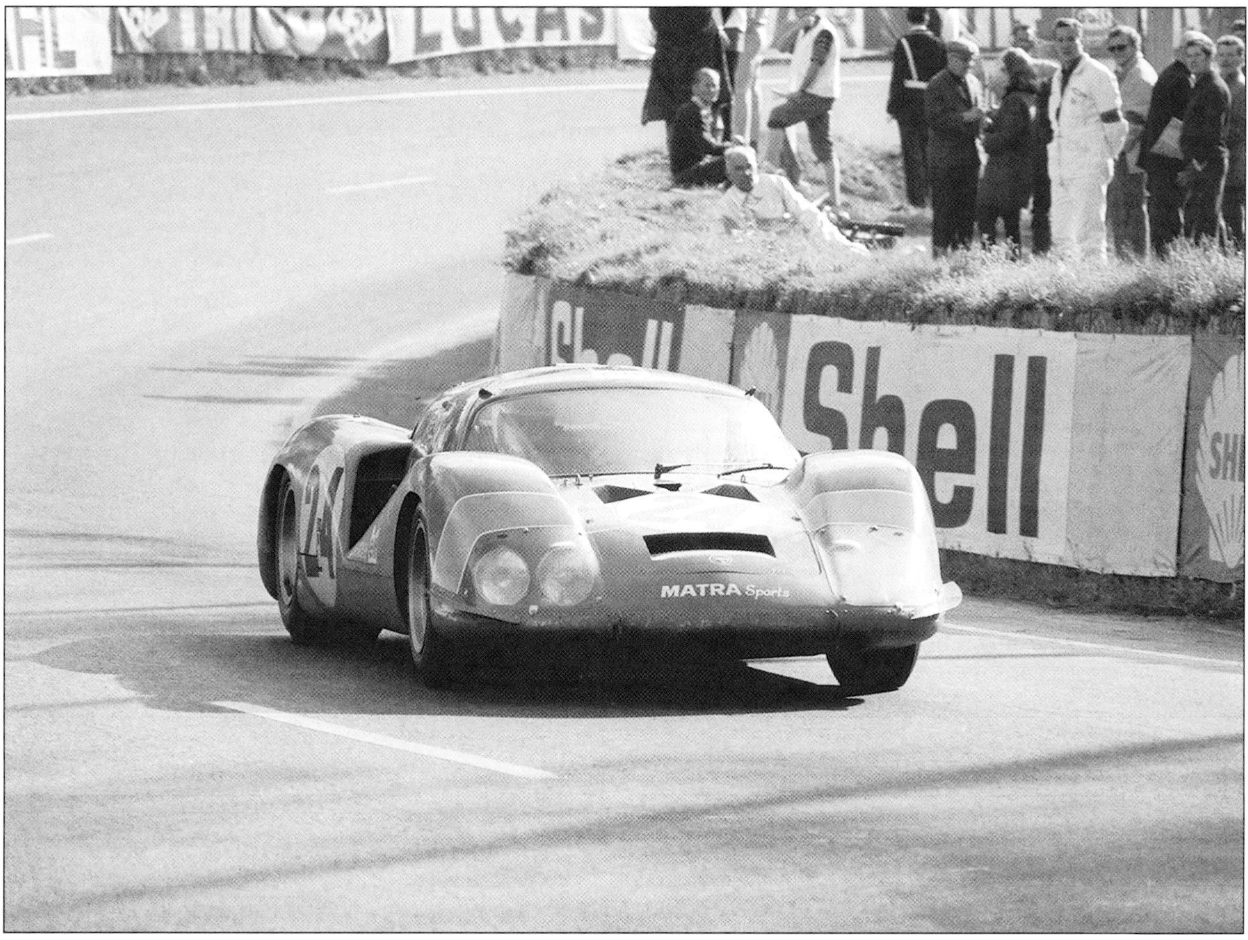

Although the Matra 630 had rather odd, angular lines, it was an exceptionally good aerodynamic design. Henri Pescarolo/'Johnny' Servoz-Gavin drove this V12-powered car at Le Mans in 1968 and for much of the race they held second or third place. They retired four hours from the finish after two punctures, the second of which wrecked the rear suspension. (LAT)

French aerospace company Engins Matra (full title Engins Mécanique Aviation-Traction) entered motor racing by chance. René Bonnet was the former partner in DB with Charles Deutsch and their Panhard-engined 750cc cars had dominated their class of sports car racing throughout the 1950s. After the partnership broke up, Bonnet built Renault-powered cars under his own name, but by 1964 his firm was in financial difficulties and Marcel Chassagny, founder of Matra, agreed a rescue take-over. Matra decided to continue manufacture of the René Bonnet Djet sports car under its own name.

Jean-Luc Lagardère, a young and enthusiastic Matra director, took charge of the project, and persuaded his co-directors that a motor racing programme was the best way to sell the production cars. Between 1964 and 1974 Matra built a vast range of competition cars, single-seaters for Formula 1, 2 and 3 (Jackie Stewart won his first Drivers' Championship in 1969 with a Cosworth-engined Matra entered by Ken Tyrrell) and Prototypes for sports car racing with BRM, Ford and, from 1968, their own V12 engine designed for both Formula 1 and Prototype racing.

All the Prototypes built between 1966 and 1968 were rather angular coupés. The 1968 M630 was powered by Matra's new V12 engine. This four overhead camshaft engine with the inlets for the induction system between the camshafts had a capacity of 2,985cc (79.7×50mm) and in its original form developed 390bhp at 10,500rpm. It powered Prototypes in three races during 1968, but retired each time. The racing staff at Matra were undecided whether the way ahead was with closed or open cars and in 1969 Matra rebuilt two M630s as open two-seaters and these were designated the MS630/650.

At Le Mans that year Matra fielded the two MS630/650s, plus the new MS650 with improved tubular chassis and longer, more steamlined tail. All three cars finished and Beltoise/Piers Courage (MS650) and Guichet/Vaccarella took fourth and fifth places. In October Jean-Pierre Beltoise/Henri Pescaralo and Rodriguez/Redman finished first and second in the poorly supported Paris 1,000Km race at Montlhéry. Chrysler France acquired the Matra car division in December 1969 and thereafter the cars raced as Matra-Simcas. In January 1970 Beltoise/Pescarolo won the non-Championship Buenos Aires 1,000Km race with the MS630/50 on its last outing.

Matra's prospects of success in 1970–71 were reduced because of the 5-litre Porsche 917 and Ferraris 512S Competition Sports Cars, and their own inefficiency did not help matters. On one notable occasion, all three Matras came into the pits at the same time, after they had rejoined the race it was realised that no one had checked the oil, so they all had to be called back in. During 1970 the cars ran at Daytona, Sebring and Brands Hatch without success and did not appear again until Le Mans. Two MS650, together with a new monocoque MS660 appeared in the 24 Hours race, but all three retired because of engine failure.

Two modified two MS650s with accommodation for a passenger, extra lighting and longer-travel suspension ran in the Tour de France in September, a race held on public roads. A passenger was carried except in the circuit tests and Matra swapped drivers halfway through because two were competing in the Canadian Grand Prix. The MS650s were fast and reliable, they faced little opposition and finished first and second in this 2000-mile (3,200km) event in the order Beltoise/Depailler/Jean Todt and Pescarolo/Jean-Pierre Jabouille/Johnny Rives. Porsche 911S entries took the next three places. In October Brabham/Cevert won the Paris 1,000Km race from a private 512S Ferrari.

In 1971 Matra ran in only two sports car races and the first of these was truly disastrous. At the Buenos Aires 1,000Km race in January the team entered a single MS660 for Beltoise/Jabouille. Beltoise ran out of fuel on the circuit and started to push the car back to the pits. He cut off the apex of corners to reduce distance and when he was close to the pits Ignazio Giunti (Ferrari 312PB) pulled out of the slipstream of the Mike Parkes's Ferrari 512M to overtake, found the Matra straddling the track and was unable to avoid a collision. Giunti was terribly burnt and injured and was dead on arrival at hospital.

Obviously, Beltoise was culpable, but so were the marshals who allowed him to push the car. At this time *Matra Sports* was still trying to do the impossible, competing in both Formula 1 and sports car racing. The next sports car appearance was at Le Mans where Amon/Beltoise drove an MS660; they were in third place by the Sunday morning, but retired because of a broken fuel-metering unit. Larrousse drove a MS660 to third place in the parochial Auvergne 186-mile (300km) race and then two MS650s ran in the Tour de France. Larrousse/Rives won for Matra, but the opposition included the Ferrari 512M of Jabouille/Juncadella who chased them hard and finished second.

Matra originally planned a full sports car season in 1972, but they had been struggling throughout 1971 with technical and parts problems in both categories in which they competed, and finally decided to run only at Le Mans. Matra entered four cars, three of which were the new MS670 with the latest MS72 V12 engine. This had the valves at a narrower angle, steel instead of titanium connecting rods and developed 450bhp at 8,400rpm, although it was detuned for Le Mans in the interests of reliability; it was more reliable and more economical than earlier versions of the V12 engine.

The wheelbase was two inches (51mm) longer at 8ft 4in (2,540mm); 13-inch (330mm) front wheels enabled the use of a lower nose-section and Girling disc brakes replaced the previous ATE components. Beltoise/Amon, Cevert/Howden Ganley and Pescarolo/ Graham Hill drove these cars and that of the last pair had a longer tail, with two boom-like structures topped by tail fins and with the aerofoil further forward than on the other cars. Jabouille/David Hobbs drove an MS660C, an improved version of the MS660 with modified suspension and reprofiled body featuring the long tail. Ferrari, who had already won the Championship, missed this race and Matra faced limited opposition.

Although Beltoise/Amon retired during the first hour, the other Matra V12s were soon in the first three places. Jabouille retired the MS660C out on the circuit because of gearbox trouble only an hour and-a-half from the finish, but Hill/Pescarolo and Cevert/Ganley took the first two places. A refurbished Porsche 908 *Lang* coupé driven by Jöst/Weber/Casoni was third, while the only surviving Alfa Romeo 33TT3 driven by Vaccarella/de Adamich finished fourth. Four mechanics

A long-awaited major success for Matra came in the 1972 Le Mans 24 Hours race when they took the first two places with MS670 cars. This is Pescarolo at the wheel of the winning car which he shared with Graham Hill. Following is the fourth-place Alfa Romeo 33TT3 of de Adamich/Vaccarella. (LAT)

and a technician had looked after each of the Matras and there was a total of 60 Matra staff at the race. The cost was astronomic, but justified by a desperately needed win to save the company's image.

Matra had entered Formula 1 in 1968 and the only win by a works car had been Chris Amon's victory in the 1971 non-Championship Argentine Grand Prix. At the end of 1972 Matra withdrew from Formula 1 to concentrate on sports car racing. In 1973 there was a season-long battle between Matra with V12 cars and Ferrari with flat-12 312PB cars and Matra now had a sufficiently strong team to maintain an edge over their Italian opposition. In the longer races Matra raced cars detuned to about 450bhp, but in the short, 1,000km (622-mile) 'sprint' races the French V12s were developing a true 475bhp. The scream of a Matra V12 at peak revs is a sound that remains unforgettable. During the year Matra used Hewland gearboxes as well as the ZFs fitted since 1966.

Only a single MS670 for Beltoise/Cevert/Pescarolo ran in the Daytona 24 Hours race on 3–4 February, but retired just after midnight because of a connecting rod through the side of the block. Ferrari had missed this race and a Porsche *Carrera* won. The second round of the Championshp was at the Vallelunga circuit near Rome in March, two cars were entered and the survivor driven by Pescarolo/Larrousse/Cevert won from the three Ferrari 312PBs. Another Matra victory followed in the Dijon 1,000Km race in April and Pescarolo/Larrousse won from a Ferrari with Cevert/Beltoise in third place.

Both Matra and Ferrari ran into problems in the Spa 1,000Km race in May, British Mirages finished first and Matra had the consolation of third place ahead of a Ferrari. Matra missed the Targa Florio, both Ferraris retired and a Porsche *Carrera* RS was the winner. The

Matras retired in the Nürburgring 1,000Km race and Ferraris took the first two places. At Le Mans four Matras faced three Ferraris. Three of the French cars were the new MS670B, with Porsche-built gearboxes to Matra specification, 13-inch wheels front and rear, lower bodywork and solid brake discs because of worries about the ventilated discs cracking.

The lead changed several times as the two teams battled, but by the 18th hour the Matra of Pescarolo/Larrousse was firmly in the lead and won from the surviving Ferrari of Merzario/Pace with the Matra of Jabouille/Jaussaud in third position. Subsequently Pescarolo/Larrousse won both the Österreichring 1,000Km race and the Watkins Glen Six Hours. There remained only the Buenos Aires race, but when this was cancelled, Matra was the winner of the World Sports Car Championship.

From 1974 onwards Ferrari concentrated on Formula 1, so Matra, now with sponsorship from Gitanes cigarettes, faced opposition only from the uncompetitive Alfa Romeo and Mirage teams and the French cars possessed both reliability and speed in most races. In the first event of the year, the Monza 1,000Km event, both cars retired shortly after the start, but thereafter the more powerful MS670C was unbeatable. The latest car had a more powerful engine, revised suspension, a Hewland TL200 trans-axle, revised suspension and lower, more aerodynamic body. Matra won the next eight races in succession. At Le Mans only the team ran the new MS680 with side-mounted radiators.

Having won the Sports Car Championship twice, Matra withdrew from racing at the end of 1974 and never raced again. Matra maintained a car division, which built co-products, including the Bagheera and Murena coupés with three seats side by side, the Matra-Simca Rancho, the Renault Espace and the Renault Avantime. Poor sales resulted in the closure of the car division in 2003, the same year that Jean-Luc Lagardère, the man behind the Matra legend, died and that a Matra Museum was opened at Vélizy.

Following Ferrari's withdrawal from sports car racing at the end of 1973, Matra completely dominated the 1974 season with their MS670C cars. Here Jacky Ickx rounds La Source hairpin in the Spa 1,000Km race with the winning car that he shared with Jean-Pierre Jarier. (LAT)

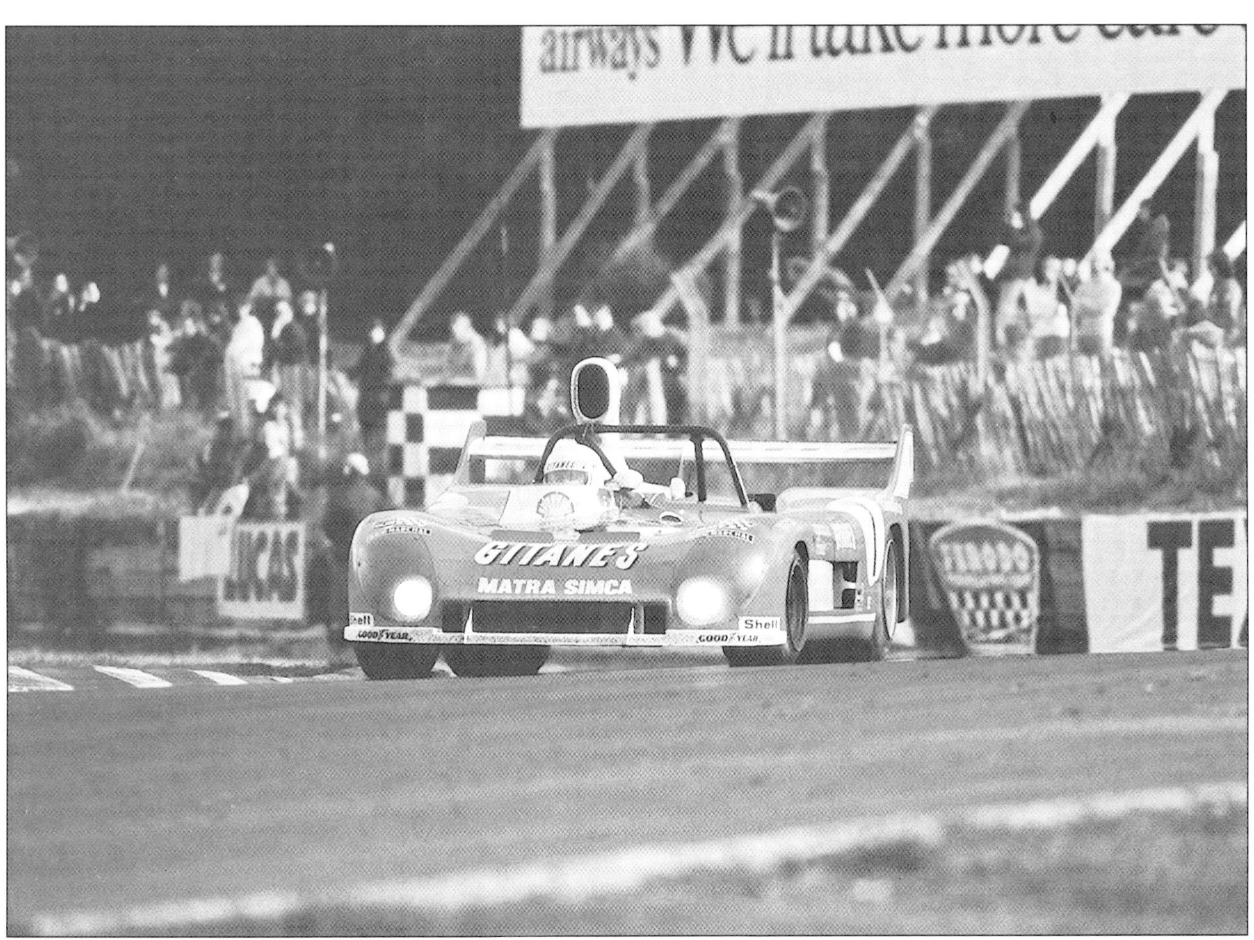

Ferrari 312PB

1971–73

As Ickx brakes hard in the 312PB which he shared with Andretti in the 1971 Sebring 12 Hours race, smoke pours from the transmission. This was the cause of the car's ultimate retirement. (Pete Lyons)

Until the current Michael Schumacher era, the 312PB was the most successful of all Ferraris and no Ferrari has had as successful a season as that enjoyed by the model in 1972 when it won every race entered. During 1970 racing was fought out between the Porsche 917 and the Ferrari 512S Competition Sports cars and for 1971 Ferrari developed the much-improved 512M that chief engineer Mauro Forghieri thought would be more than a match for the German opposition.

The 'Old Man', Enzo Ferrari, decided differently. The *FIA* had decided that Competition Sports Cars would be banned at the end of 1971 and sports car racing would primarily be for Prototypes, limited to 3 litres since the start of the 1968 season. Ferrari had raced V12 Prototypes in 1969, but then abandoned them in favour of the 512S, but other manufacturers, notably Alfa Romeo and Matra, had continued to race them. Ferrari decided to build a new Prototype derived from the 1970 3-litre 312B Grand Prix car, race and develop it in 1971 and run a full team the following year.

For the new 312PB Ferrari built the usual semi-monocoque chassis with a steel-tube space-frame stiffened by riveted aluminium-alloy panels and with a tubular structure behind the cockpot and over the engine. At the front there was the usual suspension layout of double wishbones and coil spring/damper units. The rear suspension was by lower wishbones, single upper transverse links and twin radius rods on each side. The cast-alloy front hub carriers extended backwards to form the steering arms and carry the disc brake calipers. At the rear the hub carriers incorporated the disc brake calipers.

There were wide sponsons on each side of the cockpit, that on the left containing the 120-litre (26.4-UK gallon) fuel tank, the maximum size permitted. This counterbalanced the weight of the driver (there was right-hand steering) and the sponson on the right was empty. At the front of the right sponson there was a very large filler cap from which a pipe ran down across the cockpit floor to the fuel tank. The water radiators were mounted at the rear of the sponsons. The wheelbase was 7ft 3.4in (2,220mm), front track 4ft 8.1in (1,425mm) and rear track 4ft 7.1in (1,400mm).

The horizontally opposed 12-cylinder engine had a capacity of 2,991.01cc (78.5×51.5mm) with the twin overhead camshafts per bank of cylinders gear-driven from the rear of the crankshaft. There were two valves and twin plugs per cylinder. With Lucas indirect fuel injection, the power output was 450bhp at 10,800rpm. Transmission was by a five-speed trans-axle. The very compact, wedge-shaped glass-fibre body was constructed in two parts. The nose, cockpit sides and doors hinged on pivots by the lower front wishbone mountings and the tail hinged behind the cockpit.

Ferrari sent two 312PBs to the first of the 1971 Championship races, the Buenos Aires 1,000Km, but ran only one for Giunti/Merzario. The car was second fastest in practice and Ignazio Giunti was leading when he collided with the Matra that Jean-Pierre Beltoise was pushing across the track to the pits after running out of fuel. Giunti, a very promising young Italian driver, suffered fatal burns and head injuries. It was an accident caused by sheer stupidity.

Ferrari missed the Daytona race and next entered a car for Jacky Ickx/Mario Andretti in the Sebring 12 Hours race. Again the Ferrari was second fastest in practice, it led the race, but retired because of transmission trouble. It was a race typical of the 312PB's year, very fast in practice, very fast in the race and eliminated or delayed by some misfortune or other. In the BOAC 1,000Km race at Brands Hatch the Ferrari's undoing was a slow British car, the Dulon, that spun in Ickx's path causing the young Belgian to spin and crush the Ferrari's nose against the barriers; the Ferrari rejoined the race with a new nose-section and after a furious drive Ickx/Regazzoni took second place.

At Monza the 312PB sported small tailfins to

Arturo Merzario (seen here) and rally driver Sandro Munari with this 312PB faced four works Alfa Romeo 33/TT3s in the 1972 Targa Florio. The Ferrari won by a margin of 40 seconds. (LAT)

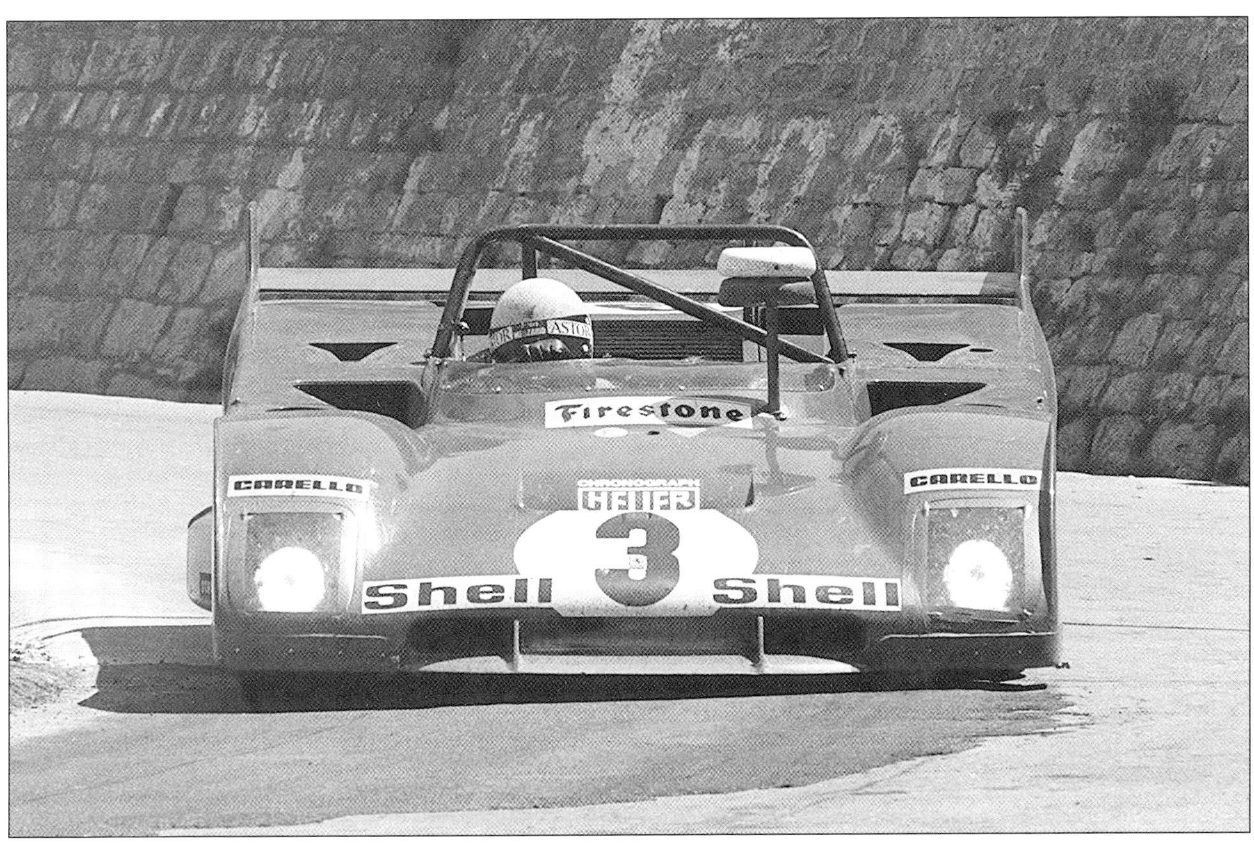

improve stability, but Ickx was forced off-line at *Lesmo* and smacked the Ferrari into the barriers and out of the race. Another accident followed at Spa-Francorchamps, where the Dulon was again the cause of the Ferrari's downfall. Driver Ridelagh pulled across the front of Regazzoni at *Stavelot*, the two cars collided and they both skidded down the course until they hit the barriers. Ferrari missed the Targa Florio and next ran at the Nürburgring where Ickx was fastest in practice and led the race – until he came into the pits with the engine boiling merrily. Inevitably the trouble was terminal and the Ferrari retired at half-distance.

Maranello missed Le Mans and the 312PB next appeared in the Austrian 1,000Km race at the Österreichring. Here Ickx/Regazzoni built up a lead of over a lap and seemed all set to win. Twenty-two laps from the finish of this 170-lap race Regazzoni lost control under braking and slammed into the barriers, probably because of suspension breakage. The final round of the Championship was the Watkins Glen Six Hours race and again the Ferrari led the race until Ickx was unable to restart after his first routine pit stop.

The 312PB had been a match for the *Gulf* 917s on all but the fastest circuits, but the bigger cars had proved less reliable than in 1970. Because of the failure of the 917s and the 312PB, the now much more reliable Alfa Romeo 33/3s had won three races. Ferrari's prospects for 1972 were excellent, but few critics expected a Maranello grand slam. On 6 November 1971 Ferrari fielded two 312PBs in the Kyalami Nine Hours race, the car raced all season and a new example with more compact body, low profile wheels and tyres and lower weight. It was a test run for the team and it had its problems, but Regazzoni/Redman and Ickx/Andretti took the first two places.

For 1972 Ferrari had built a batch of six new 312PBs so that three-car teams could be fielded without the same cars running in successive races. The 312PBs were unchanged apart from detailed modifications necessary to comply with the latest Prototype regulations. Ferrari had a strong team of drivers and the cars proved superior to the opposition, which consisted of the *Autodelta* team's latest V8 Alfa Romeo 33TT3 cars and little else. The 33TT3s were less powerful (the team's flat-12 engine was not raceworthy and would not be for a long time) and were heavier (partly because of the use of the fireproof fuel tanks designed by Carlo Chiti).

The first race, the Buenos Aires 1,000Km was on 9 January and the last of the 11 rounds was the Watkins Glen Six Hours on 22 July, an intensive season with races often inconveniently close together. Organisation had improved at Buenos Aires, but not enough. During Friday's practice 50,000 spectators crowded on to the track when the locally made Berta stopped and it took more than an hour to clear them off. The same day the police and a tractor were out on the circuit chasing a man off (there was also a dog, someone's mutt that joined in for the fun). In contrast the race was tame; Peterson/Schenken and Regazzoni/Redman took first places, ahead of two Alfa Romeos.

Reducing the Daytona Continental race to six hours from the usual 24 made this tedious, overlong event more tolerable. Ickx/Andretti and Peterson/Schenken took the first places ahead of an Alfa Romeo with the Regazzoni/Redman 312PB fourth. The results at Sebring and Brands Hatch were identical, with Ickx/Andretti and Peterson/Schenken taking the first two places ahead of an Alfa Romeo. Mario Andretti, as a good Italian boy, was one of the Old Man's favourite 'sons', but he now returned to the United States for his season's USAC racing.

So Ickx was paired with Regazzoni in the Monza 1,000Km race on 25 April and Redman with Merzario. All three cars had split final drive casings to facilitate changes of ratio and longer tails with tail fins on the trailing edge of the body bridged by an aerofoil. Heavy rain fell throughout the race and Ickx/Regazzoni won despite a long pit stop to sort out wet electrics and an alternator that caught fire. Redman spun at the *Vialone* curve, hit the barriers and was out of the race. A lap later Peterson repeated Redman's accident, but was able to drive back to the pits. After a new nose-section had been fitted and the rear suspension repaired, he and Schenken finished third.

At Spa, Redman/Merzario and Ickx/Regazzoni took the first two places, but Peterson crashed at *Les Combes*, entering the corner too quickly, unaware that it was treacherously slippery from a rain shower. *Autodelta* concentrated on preparation for the Targa Florio on 21 May where it entered four cars. Perversely, Ferrari sent only a single 312PB for Merzario and rally driver Sandro Munari. This car had the right side of the monocoque removed to accommodate a spare wheel, the softest possible suspension and an engine that gave smooth power all the way from 5,000 to 11,800rpm. The Ferrari drivers won by 24.9 seconds and humiliated Alfa Romeo.

At the Nürburgring Peterson/Schenken and Merzario/Redman took the first two places. Regazzoni crashed the car he was sharing with Ickx. Despite running at the Le Mans Test weekend, Ferrari gave the race a miss. Matras took the first two places. In the Austrian 1,000Km race the Ferraris took the first four places in the absence of the Alfa Romeos and Ickx/Andretti and Peterson/Schenken were first and second. Ferrari's domination of the Championship could not have been

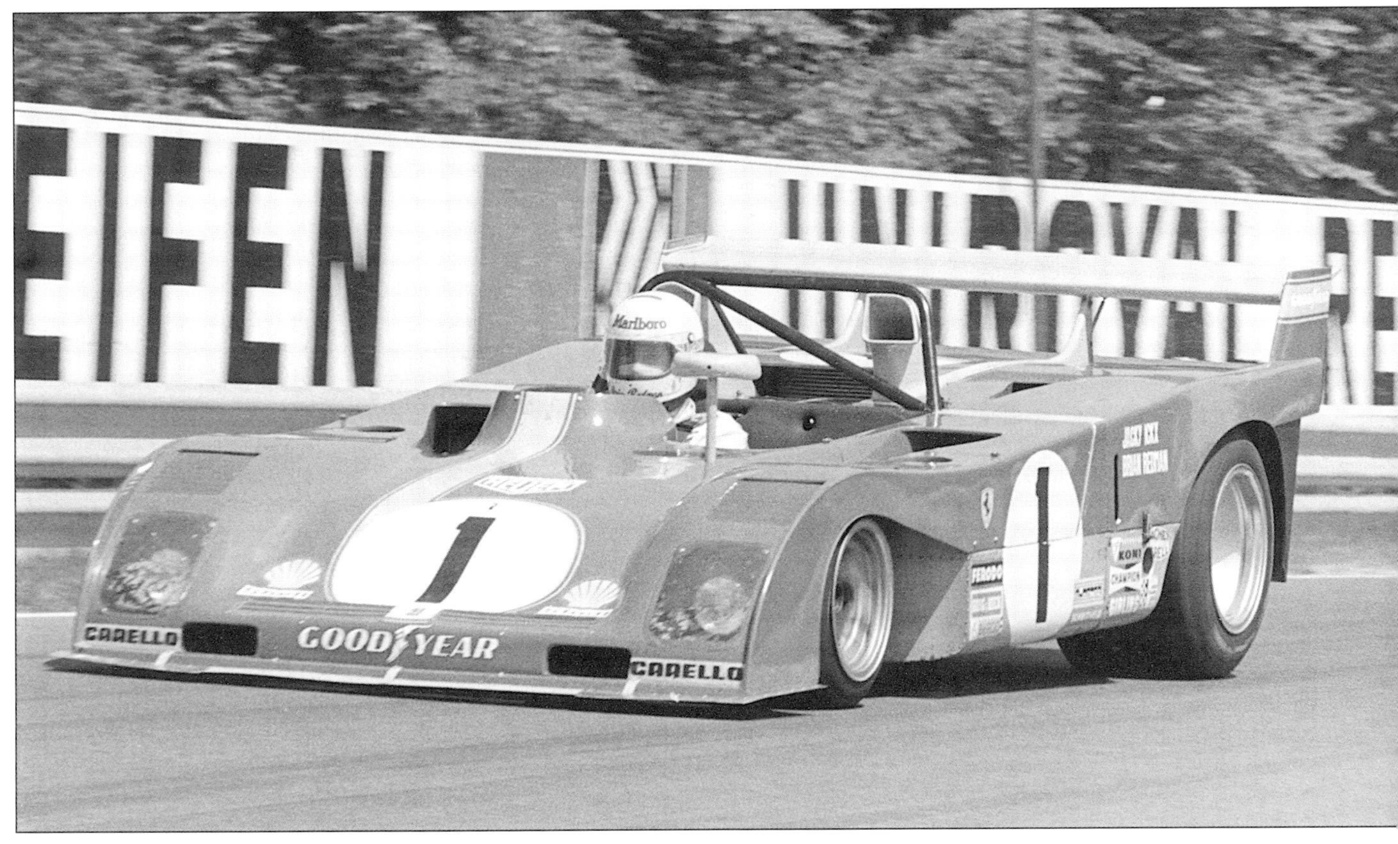

Throughout 1973 there was a fierce battle in the Sports Car Championship between Ferrari and Matra, a battle won by the French team. Here, at the Nürburgring, Jacky Ickx is at the wheel of the winning Ferrari 312PB in which he was partnered by Brian Redman. (LAT)

more complete. After the Championship series was over Ferrari ran cars in minor races, the Imola 500Km and the Kyalami Nine Hours and won both.

Ferrari raced the 312PBs again in 1973 and they now had a four-inch (100mm) longer wheelbase, higher power output and aerodynamic modifications. The handling proved unpredictable, with a tendency to switch from oversteer to understeer, and the latest Matras were slightly more powerful. Ferrari missed Daytona and the Sebring and BOAC 1,000Km races were cancelled. In their place were the Vallelunga Six Hours and the Dijon 1,000Km. Matra won them both and the Ferraris struggled to finish.

Victory in the Monza 1,000Km race meant much to Ferrari and the 312PBs took first and second places, thanks to Matra unreliability. In the Spa 1,000Km race the Ferraris and the Matras ran into problems, John Wyer-entered Ford-Mirages took the first two places, a Matra was third and the surviving Ferrari of Carlo Pace/Arturo Merzario a poor fourth. Two Ferraris, specially modified for the event, ran in the Targa Florio, but Ickx crashed the car he was sharing with Redman and Merzario (co-driving with Vaccarella) was an early victim of drive-shaft failure.

Matra missed the Sicilian road race, but reappeared in the Nürburgring 1,000Km event. The French cars ran into problems and the Ferraris of Ickx/Redman and Merzario/Pace took the first two places. At Le Mans there was a furious battle between the two marques. Ickx/Redman took the lead for Ferrari in the 11th hour, but a long pit stop dropped them to second place on the Sunday morning; they were still chasing the leading Matra when their engine failed two hours from the finish. Merzario/Pace took second place behind the leading French car.

In the Austrian 1,000Km race the Matras proved considerably faster than the Ferraris and took the first two places ahead of Ickx/Redman with their 312PB. It was a pattern that repeated itself at Watkins Glen, Matras first and second, the Ferrari of Ickx/Redman third. Ferrari still had a chance of winning the Championship, but withdrew from the final round at Buenos Aires, which was ultimately cancelled. At last Ferrari had realised the folly of trying to compete in both Formula 1 and sports car racing. After Watkins Glen no works Ferrari sports car ever raced again.

Porsche 956 & 962

1982–88

The introduction of the Group 'C' category of 1982 stimulated Porsche to introduce a new contender, the 956, that together with its successor, the 962, was to prove the most successful Porsche competition car in the make's long history. The power unit was the same flat-six that had powered Porsche's Le Mans-winning car in 1981 and was the engine that had originally been designed for Indianapolis. It was not raced there because a change of regulations made it uncompetitive.

This engine had a capacity of 2,649.6cc (92.3× 66mm), with water-cooled four-valve cylinder heads and air-cooled, Nikasil-coated cylinder barrels. There was a cast magnesium-alloy crankcase and the steel crankshaft ran in eight plain main bearings. Porsche used titanium-alloy connecting rods and forged alloy

Porsche introduced the 956 with a 2.6-litre, flat-six, twin-turbocharged engine for Group C racing in 1982. It was the same engine that the team had used to win Le Mans in 1981, and then installed in the 936. (Porsche Werkfoto)

pistons. There were gear-driven twin overhead camshafts per bank of cylinders and the vertical cooling fan was located at the front of the engine. With two KKK K26 turbochargers that had twin air-to-water intercoolers, the Bosch motronic 1.2 engine management system and a single plug per cylinder, power output was 620bhp at 8,000rpm.

Transmission was by a five-speed synchromesh gearbox with magnesium-alloy casing and aluminium-alloy bellhousing. The chassis was a tub-type monocoque with aluminium-alloy tubular roll-over cage and rear sub-frames to mount the semi-stressed engine, together with the gearbox and rear suspension. Porsche used honeycomb-aluminium sandwich construction for the pedal-box area and there were bonded Kevlar side-boxes. The body was constructed in seven panels in Kevlar reinforced by glass-fibre. For ground-effect purposes, there were venturi on each side of the central underbody. The 956 was raced with long and short tails.

Front suspension was by unequal-length wishbones and titanium rising-rate coil springs/Bilstein alloy gas shock absorbers. There were lower wishbones and parallel upper links at the rear and the coil springs were operated by fabricated rocker arms. Steering was rack-and-pinion. The 16-in (405mm) six-spoke Speedline wheels had a width of 12 inches (305mm) at the front and 15 inches (380mm) at the rear. The wheelbase was 8ft 8in (2,650mm) and the weight was 1,852 pounds (840kg). Maximum speed was 217mph (349kph).

Peter Falk was now the head of the Porsche motor sport division and for the first time Porsche raced with sponsorship, from the Rothmans tobacco company. Group C racing was characterised in its early days by a large number of potentially competitive entries, but few of which achieved anything worthwhile, largely because of inadequate funding. Porsche rapidly proved to be the dominant marque, but, initially, it was plagued by worries about the car's ability to meet the restrictive fuel consumption allowances.

The 956 made its debut in the hands of Derek Bell/Jacky Ickx in the Silverstone Six Hours race in May 1982, but they were unable to match the speed of the works Lancia LC1, a 1.4-litre turbocharged Group 6 Prototype. These cars were permitted to run in Group C only in 1982 and apart from being much lighter than the Group C cars, they had unrestricted fuel consumption. Bell/Ickx had to settle for second place. Three new cars with engines rated at 580bhp ran at Le Mans and Ickx/Bell headed a Porsche 1–2–3. Porsche had planned to withdraw after Le Mans, but carried on. Mass won a short race at the Norisring and the team also scored wins at Spa, Mount Fuji and Brands Hatch.

As the season progressed, the fuel consumption problem had been overcome by the adoption of smaller, twin KKK turbochargers, together with raised compression ratio that improved thermal efficiency. Over the winter of 1982–83 Porsche laid down a batch of 12 customer 956s and nine of these were ready by the start of the 1983 season. There were also three new works cars.

There was very little in the way of opposition to the Porsche steamroller and although the new Lancia LC2 cars were very fast, they were also very unreliable. Porsche 956s won every round of the World Endurance Championship. In two races, Monza and Brands Hatch, private entrants were the winners and defeated the works cars. A private 956 also won at Mugello in the absence of the works team.

It was very much the same story in 1984 and Porsche 956s won every round of the Championship, except the poorly supported Kyalami race in which there was only a single private 956 and Lancias took the first two places. The works Porsche team withdrew from Le Mans because of a dispute over fuel regulations, Reinhold Jöst's *New Man*-sponsored yellow and black 956 won in the hands of Wollek/Boutsen. At the end of 1984 Porsche first raced their automatic-shifting PDK (*Porsche Doppel Kupplung* – Porsche double clutch) system. Although a clutch was needed when the car moved off from rest, thereafter clutchless changes were made by a sequential lever.

Initially private owners had raced 956s in the IMSA series in the United States, but the rules changed for 1984 and it became a requirement that the pedal-box be behind the axis of the front wheels. The change was inspired by a desire to halt Porsche domination, but Zuffenhausen responded with the 962, which was, in effect a lengthened version of the 956. The front of the car was extended so that the wheels were ahead of the pedal-box and this increased the wheelbase to 9ft 0in (2,770mm). Engine capacity was increased to 2,826cc (92.3×70.4mm), there were two valves per cylinder, full air-cooling and a single massive turbocharger.

Power output in this form was 650bhp. Fuel capacity was increased to the IMSA limit of 1,200 litres. The weight was 1,852 pounds (840kg), so the cars had to be ballasted to reach the IMSA minimum weight limit of 850kg. Although the 962 failed on its first race appearance at the 1984 Daytona 24 Hours event, it then went on to win most of the races in the series. During 1985 Porsche 962s won 15 out of 16 rounds in the IMSA

By 1983 production 956s had been delivered to a number of private owners, but the Porsche works cars still remained supreme. Ickx/Mass drove this works 956 to a win in the Nürburgring 1,000Km race, the last to be held on the old circuit in the Eifel Mountains. (Porsche Werkfoto)

Championship – the exception being the Road Atlanta race in which Redman/Haywood were the winners with their *Group 44* Jaguar XJR-5.

The IMSA pedal-box regulation was adapted for Group C racing in respect of all cars manufactured after 1 January 1985. Although the factory could have continued racing the 956Bs, as they were known in their 1984 form, they decided to adapt the 962 to Group C rules and in this form it was known as the 962C. These cars were mechanically similar to the 956s, but they had larger 19-inch (480mm) wheels. Rim width was restricted to 16 inches (405mm) and Porsche had realised that larger wheels had a larger tyre 'footprint'. The works 962Cs, which used the heavy PDK gear-change system, were well over the minimum weight limit of 850kg by some 45kg (close to 100 pounds).

Initially, the 962Cs were prone to 'snap' oversteer, but this bad habit was speedily cured by suspension geometry modifications. The 1985 season was another Porsche triumph, apart from the Spa 1,000Km race, which was shortened after a collision between Ickx with a works car and Stefan Bellof with a private 956. It was bad enough to cost the life of the promising young Bellof and a Lancia won the race. Perhaps the most significant Porsche victory of the year was at Le Mans where the 956 entered by Reinhold Jöst and driven by Wollek/Barilla/'John Winter' won after an immaculately controlled race to save fuel from the *Richard Lloyd*, Canon-sponsored entry and the works 962 of Ickx/Bell.

One of the biggest problems that affected both Group C and IMSA racing during this period was that both series were largely dominated by Porsche – and if it were not for the large number of private Porsche entries, the fields would have been thin and uncompetitive. There were rising stars, Sauber and Jaguar in Group C and the Electramotive Nissans in IMSA, but initially, at least, they made little impression on Porsche superiority.

During 1986 Porsche enjoyed another very successful year in IMSA racing and won 12 of the year's races. Bob Holbert (usually partnered by Derek Bell) won six of these with *Löwenbräu* beer-sponsored cars and Price Cobb won three with Rob Dyson's car. Of the remaining five, two were won by the Lola-chassis Chevrolet GTP and one each by BMW GTP, Ford Mustang Probe and Jaguar. In European Group C racing works drivers Hans Stuck and Derek Bell used the PDK clutchless transmission in most races and Porsche entries won seven of the year's nine Championship races. The other wins were by Jaguar at Silverstone and Sauber at the Nürburgring.

Jaguar was much stronger in 1987 and the works Porsche team had lost its winning edge. Jaguar showed an advantage over Porsche in the first four races at Jerez, Jarama, Monza and Silverstone – it was only a marginal advantage, but it was enough to spell defeat. Le Mans was a very different matter, the Jaguars were still not reliable enough to last a 24 hour race and the works 962C of Bell/Stuck/Holbert won by 20 laps from a private 962C. After Le Mans the works team withdrew from racing. Zuffenhausen was well aware that a new car was needed, but there were other priorities. In IMSA racing 962s won 13 of 16 events, but a portent for the future was the Nissan victory at Miami.

In 1988 the 956/962C was in its seventh year of Championship racing. Sauber dominated most of the year's racing, but Jaguar achieved their main goal, victory at Le Mans. It was, however, a very close race. It was the only event in which Porsche entered works cars, three 962Cs, now with the Bosch Motronic 1.7 engine management system, electronically controlled turbocharger wastegates for each bank of cylinders (an idea copied from the Electramotive Nissans) and were 50bhp more powerful.

Stuck was timed in practice at Le Mans at 245mph (394kph) on the Straight and he, together with Bell and Ludwig came close to winning. Even though they lost two laps after Ludwig had run out of petrol on the course and driven the car back to the pits on the starter motor, they were only 2½ minutes behind at the finish. Nissan was now the dominant force in IMSA racing, although 962s won at Miami (Cobb/Weaver) and in the Sebring 12 Hours race (Stuck/Ludwig).

Although eclipsed by Sauber and Jaguar, the 962s and 962Cs remained the mainstay of private entries and no less than 17 were entered at Le Mans in 1989. That year Hans Stuck/Wollek finished third with a 962C behind two Mercedes-Benz entries and in 1990 Neddell/Wallace/Conrad were again third with a 962C, with another of these cars in fourth place.

This was not quite the end of Porsche presence at Le Mans. In 1994 Porsche raced a GT derivative of the 962 developed by Jochen Dauer. The company was heavily criticised for breaking the spirit, but not the letter of the rules, and modifications after the car had proved unstable in flat-bottom form, necessitated Porsche making re-application for type approval. The new cars were too heavy at just over 2,200 pounds (1,000kg) and they could not match the speed of the Toyotas. These suffered from fragile transmissions and after the Toyotas had run into trouble, Dalmas/Hailwood/Baldi won from a Toyota with the other Dalmas 962LM in third place. After this race the 962LMs were banned.

In 1996 and 1997 the Reinhold Jöst entered TWR Porsche WSC cars based on Jaguar XJR-14 chassis and with flat-six, twin-turbo, 2,994cc (95×74.4mm) engines won for Porsche at Le Mans yet again. In the meanwhile Porsche had been developing the 911 GT1-98 to compete in the new World Sportscar Championship of 1995 onwards. These flat-six, twin-turbocharged 3.2-litre coupés finished second and third at Le Mans in 1996 and two years later these cars in more highly developed form were driven to first and second places in the 24 Hours race by McNish/Aiello/Ortelli and Müller/Alzen/Wollek. It was Porsche's 13th Le Mans victory and although the company has not raced works cars since then, a return to racing by Porsche is inevitable.

During 1986 the works Rothmans-sponsored Porsche 962Cs ran in most races with PDK semi-automatic transmission. It was not, however used at Le Mans where the team used the normal five-speed synchromesh gearbox. This is the winning 962C of Hans Stuck, Derek Bell and Al Holbert (LAT)

Jaguar XJR-6/8/9 & 12

1985–91

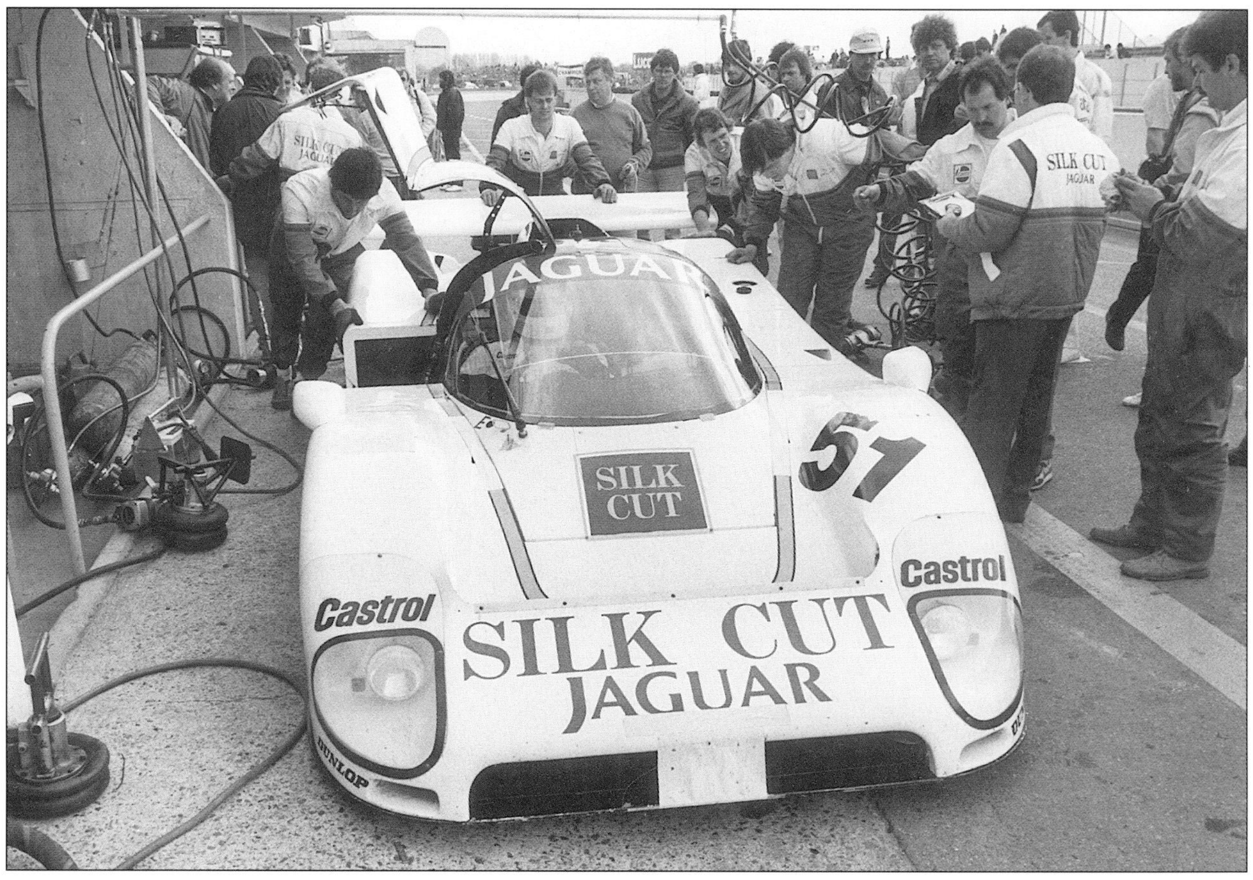

In 1986 TWR ran Jaguars at Le Mans for the first time and it was a promising first outing, although none of the cars survived to the finish. Warwick/Schlesser/Cheever drove this XJR-6 and they rose to second place before retiring after an off-course excursion by Schlesser damaged the rear suspension. (LAT)

The entry of a works Jaguar team in Group C racing was stimulated by the imminent flotation of Jaguar by the Rover Group as an independent company and by the success of Bob Tullius and his American *Group 44* team. Apart from 1968 when he ran Howmet gas-turbine cars in Prototype racing, Tullius was a staunch supporter of British marques and raced these between 1964 and 1987. Between 1982 and 1987 he entered Jaguar V12-powered cars in IMSA and Group C racing. The first *Group 44* appearance at Le Mans was in 1984, but by this time it was known that *Tom Walkinshaw Racing* would be heading the Jaguar project and he made it clear that he would be racing his own cars.

Walkinshaw had campaigned XJS coupés in the European Touring Car Championship with great success in 1982–84 and he commissioned Tony Southgate to design the new car. Typed the XJR-6, it featured a carbon-fibre chassis with Kevlar/carbon-fibre ground-effect body. (*Group 44* had used an aluminium-alloy monocoque). At the front a one-piece magnesium-alloy casting located the suspension with the inboard Koni coil spring/damper units mounted nearly horizontally. At the rear the Koni coil spring/damper units were suspended from a transverse aluminium-alloy beam that was attached to the gearbox casing, as were the lower wishbones.

Originally the XJR-6, carried fuel in three separate tanks, but by 1986 the fuel was contained in a single 99-litre bag tank installed in the space between the bulkhead and the cockpit lining. The engine was the 60-degree V12 Jaguar in 6-litre form and developing around 630bhp. The body was also Kevlar/carbon-fibre with a tall venturi either side of the engine that gave more groundforce than any of the opposition, rear wheel valances to trap escaping air and maximise venturi effect, and the tail cut off behind the rear wheels giving the cars a stubby, abbreviated appearance. Weight was the problem and at 1,985 pounds (900kg) the XJR-6 was substantially heavier than the Porsche opposition.

The new cars were not ready until well into the 1985 season and first appeared in the 1,000km (621-mile) race at Mosport in Canada; the surviving car shared by Brundle, Thackwell and Schlesser finished third. Brundle/Thackwell took fifth place at Spa, a race cut short following Stefan Bellof's fatal accident with a Porsche and both entries retired at Brands Hatch. At the flooded Fuji circuit in Japan the Jaguars, like the other European entries, were withdrawn because of the unsuitability of their tyres for these conditions. In the final round of the Championship, on the Shah Alam circuit at Selangor in Malaysia, Thackwell/Nielsen/ Lammers finished second, on the same lap as the winning Porsche.

Careful development work reduced weight and increased power for 1986 and the Jaguars, now sponsored by Gallaher's *Silk Cut* cigarette brand, were highly competitive, if far from reliable. The team failed in the Monza 'Supersprint' race, for although Schlesser/Brancatelli covered third highest distance, they were not running at the finish and were unclassified. Jaguar scored their first victory when Warwick/Cheever won the Silverstone 1,000Km race. All three cars, fitted with longer tails and lower rear wings, retired at Le Mans and after a series of mixed results that included seconds at Spa and Fuji, Jaguar finished second in the Manufacturers' Championship.

TWR developed the much-improved XJR-8 for 1987 and apart from engine capacity increased to 6,995cc and weight reduced to the minimum permitted of 850kg (1,874 pounds), there were many other changes. These included raising the rear of the engine to reduce the angle of the driveshafts and minor bodywork modifications. It proved a year of outstanding success for Jaguar, and of a total of ten races in the Championship, the team won eight. The failures came at Le Mans and the Norisring. Jaguar also won the Manufacturers' Championship.

At Le Mans the Jaguars were special XJR-8LM models that featured a new Southgate-designed short tail that was as aerodynamically efficient as the 1986 long tail. Although never able to snatch the lead, the Jaguars pushed the Porsche 962Cs hard. Win Percy crashed his Jaguar because of tyre failure and Cheever/Boesel/ Lammers were the sole Jaguar finishers in fifth place after delays caused firstly by an oil leak from the gearbox catching fire and then by losing the badly secured rear bodywork.

In 1988 Jaguar raced the improved XJR-9s in both the American IMSA series with 6-litre cars and in the Group C Championship series. In the United States Jaguar faced severe opposition from the turbocharged Nissans and in Europe the main opponents were the very competitive Mercedes-powered turbocharged 5-litre Sauber C9 cars. Sauber won at Jerez, the first race of the year (Jaguar second, on the same lap), but then Jaguar won at Jarama, Monza and Silverstone and in each of these races Sauber-Mercedes took second place.

Jaguar's main aim in 1988 was victory at Le Mans and the *TWR* team fielded five cars, two of them driven by members of the Jaguar IMSA team. Each team was managed separately, by Roger Silman for the European team and Tony Dowe for the American team. For the 24 hours race the team developed special XJR-9LM cars based on the chassis used in the short, sprint races, with rear wheel covers, the engine repositioned to reduce the centre of gravity, a new underbody and 17-inch (430mm) tyres. The main opposition came from an entry of 11 Porsche 962Cs, including three works cars. The Saubers were withdrawn after tyre failures in practice.

It proved yet another hard-fought race and the 962Cs put up a strong fight until the finish. Lammers/ Dumfries/Wallace won for Jaguar at 137.72mph

As in the 1950s, the main thrust of Jaguar's Group C programme was a win at Le Mans. It came in 1988 when Lammers/Dumfries/ Wallace drove this XJR-9LM to victory ahead of two Porsche 962Cs and with another XJR-9LM driven by Daly/Perkins/Cogan in fourth place. (LAT)

(221.59kph), but the second-place Porsche of Stuck/Bell/Ludwig finished on the same lap as the winner and another Porsche was third. Daly/Perkins/Cogan took fourth place with their XJR9-LM entered by the American team. After Le Mans Jaguar were beaten by the Saubers at Brno, the Nürburgring and Spa, but were second in each of these races and won at Brands Hatch and Fuji to clinch the Manufacturers' Championship for the second consecutive year. Jaguar team-member Martin Brundle won the Drivers' Championship.

One of the major problems with sports car-racing at this time was the poor, often non-existent cover by television – the 1988 Le Mans race was not even shown on UK TV – and lack of press exposure. Unsurprisingly Jaguar were beginning to lose interest in the *TWR* team. It should have provided a superb arena in which to publicise the marque, but failed miserably. *TWR* was developing a 3.5-litre turbocharged car (the XJR-11) to comply with forthcoming regulations, but in the meanwhile continued to race the XJR-9, which had to be modified to comply with the new regulation that no mechanical components were visible beyond the bodywork.

Jaguar's biggest problem in 1989 was the vastly improved Sauber team, which now had much greater backing from Mercedes-Benz, but there were other problems, including the high fuel consumption of the V12 engine and the shortcomings of their Dunlop tyres. Sauber set the pace, Jaguar lost out and at Le Mans there were also the Mazda, Nissan and Toyota teams to contend with. Before the start of the World Championship series, Jaguar competed in the Daytona 24 Hours and Sebring 12 Hours races and in both took second place because of mechanical problems – behind a Porsche at Daytona and behind a Nissan at Sebring.

Because of heavy fuel consumption, Jaguar could manage no higher than fifth at Suzuka and the XJR-9s retired at Dijon. Le Mans was not a round in the Championship series, but it remained the year's most prestigious race. Jaguar entered four XJR-9LMs running on 17-inch (430mm) front and 18-inch (460mm) rear wheels with Dunlop cross-ply tyres. The Jaguars displayed greater speed than in previous years and Jan Lammers was second fastest to a Sauber in qualifying. In the race they suffered major problems, including high oil consumption and transmission problems. Saubers took the first two places ahead of a Porsche and Jaguar was thrashed – their only two finishers were fourth and eighth.

The remainder of the season proved just as unsuccessful for Jaguar. After a second place at Jarama, the team ran the XJR-11 3.5-litre car at Brands Hatch, but although it was fastest in qualifying, it fell back to finish a poor fifth. The team staggered on to the last race of the year at Mexico where the XJR-9s were uncompetitive, but at least reliable, and finished fifth and sixth. In contrast Sauber had won every race entered during the year.

In 1990 Jaguar raced the 7-litre cars, slightly modified and known as XJR-12s in non-Championship events, but ran the new 3.5-litre XJR-11s, of broadly similar specification apart from the detuned Ford/Cosworth HB 3.5-litre V8 Formula 1 engine, in World Championship races. Jaguar took first two places in the Daytona race, but at Sebring the turbocharged Nissan GTP-ZXTs were first and second, with a Jaguar third. The Championship started badly at Suzuka where both XJR-11s retired and they achieved only third and fourth places at Monza. Then came Silverstone where the Jaguars took first two places on home ground and an XJR-11 finished second to a Mercedes at Spa.

After wrangles with the *FIA*, the organisers of Le Mans, the *Automobile Club de l'Ouest*, had constructed two chicanes on the *Mulsanne Straight*, to reduce speeds and so there was no direct comparison with lap times in previous years. Jaguar entered four XJR-12s, cars that were to American IMSA specification, adapted to comply with Group C rules and fitted with high-downforce wings. Mercedes had decided to give the race a miss, a decision that took away much of the interest, but there were a total of eight turbocharged Nissans and 19 Porsche 962s, including two new works-assisted cars with 3.2-litre turbocharged engines.

The Jaguar entries were superbly prepared and in the early stages of the race the XJR-11s held comfortable third, fourth, fifth and sixth places. When the leading Nissans were delayed, the Jaguars moved up and the lead cars were still second and fourth behind a Nissan at midnight. Calm reigned in the Jaguar pit, as the team was conviced that the Nissans would falter and a Jaguar would win. At 1.30am the leading Nissan retired out on the circuit because of transmission trouble, but another Nissan took the lead.

Despite the inevitable problems of the night hours, damaged bodywork, minor mechanical problems and the retirement of the car driven by Brundle/Alain Ferté/Leslie with a damaged engine after a water pump belt became detached and the engine overheated, a Jaguar now led. The leading car driven by Nielsen/Cobb, joined by Martin Brundle, had lost fourth gear and had fading brakes, but it was still comfortably ahead of the second-place Porsche. The Davy Jones/Michel Ferté/Salazar Jaguar also retired half an hour after midday on the Sunday because of terminal engine problems.

The Jaguars of Nielsen/Cobb/Brundle and Lammers/Wallace/Konrad were in first two places at the end of the 24 Hours, with Porsche 962s third and fourth and a Nissan fifth. It was not a great Le Mans victory, but was Jaguar's seventh in its history and had been the team's main goal in 1990. The rest of the year was as grim as might be expected and Mercedes-Benz won the remainder of the year's Championship races. All that Jaguar could manage were two third places.

Sports car racing continued to decline in popularity with entrants, spectators and sponsors in 1991. Jaguar raced the XJR-12s at Daytona, Sebring and Le Mans, but for Championship rounds they had the new XJR-14 cars complying with the latest regulations and powered by the Ford/Cosworth HB engine. The season devolved into a battle between Jaguar and Mercedes-Benz, both in their last season of sports car racing. Mercedes-Benz was plagued throughout the year by engine problems and both teams lost out at Le Mans.

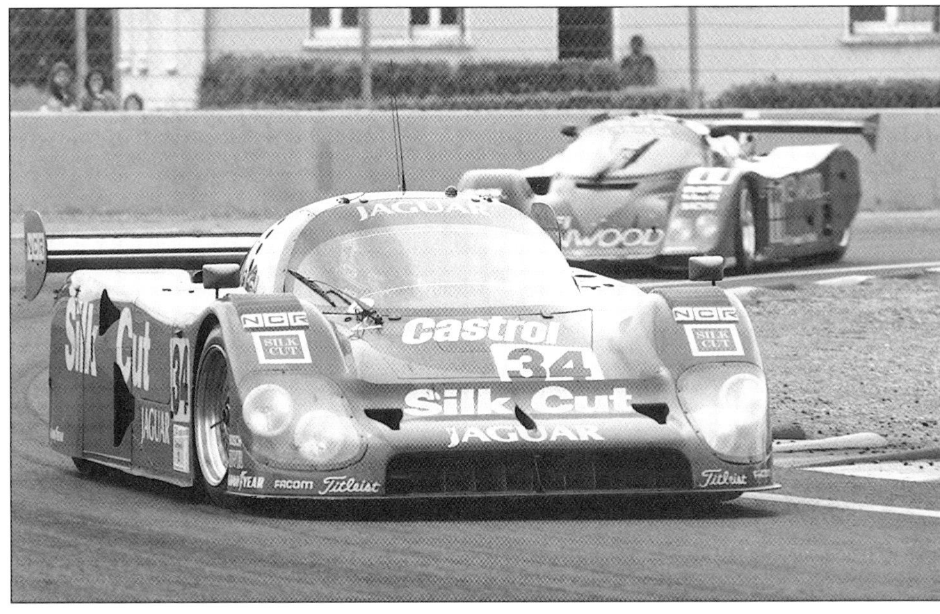

At Le Mans in 1991 Jaguar entered four XJR-12s, ballasted to comply with the new and draconian minimum weight restrictions for cars of more than 3.5 litres' capacity. The XJR-12s had 7.4-litre V12 engines. A lightweight Mazda won the race, but Jaguars took the next three places. This XJR-12 driven by Teo Fabi/Kenny Acheson/Bob Wollek finished third, despite broken exhaust problems and frontal body damage after a collision with a rabbit. (LAT)

At Daytona one XJR-11 non-started after a practice crash and the other retired, leaving victory to a Porsche. At Sebring the team fared little better, one car non-started after a collision in practice and the other finished fifth. A Peugeot 905 scored a lucky win with a Mercedes-Benz second. The first round of the Championship was, as usual at Suzuka, and although an XJR-14 was fastest in qualifying and the Jaguars led the race, both retired. By the Monza sprint, *TWR* had the XJR-14s sorted and they took the first two places. Another victory followed at Silverstone where Jaguar finished first and third.

There were concerns about the ability of the 3.5-litre cars to last the 24 hours of Le Mans; both Jaguar and Mercedes-Benz brought their latest cars to the circuit, but relied on the older cars in the race. *TWR* struggled to meet the minimum weight limit and the XJR-11s, now with 7.4-litre engines to combat the weight penalty and running on Goodyear tyres, had additional aluminium-alloy sheeting bolted to the floors, part of an effort to bring the cars up to the minimum weight. Previously the Jaguars were at least 100kg (220 pounds) lighter.

FISA gave an enormous advantage to Mazda, by being persuaded that the Japanese company's small, but exceptionally powerful rotary-engined 787B cars could run with a minimum weight of 830kg (1,830 pounds). It was a race of peculiar rules, for the ten 3.5-litre cars entered were given the first ten positions on the grid, regardless of speed and the 11th position car, Mercedes-Benz, was in fact fastest. The Jaguars were unable to match the pace of the C2 3.5-litre cars and stay within the fuel consumption limits, both Mercedes entries retired, and when the leading German car first ran into problems early on the Sunday, the Mazda of Weidler/Herbert/Gachot assumed a lead that it never lost.

The Jaguars took second, third and fourth places, with the leading car two laps behind the winner. After Le Mans, the *TWR* team ran the XJR-14s with some success, taking first two places at the Nürburgring, finishing third and fifth at Magny-Cours, sixth in Mexico and second and third at the new Autopolis circuit in Japan. *TWR* won the Team Championship and Teo Fabi and Derek Warwick took first and second places in the Drivers' Championship. The results looked good, rather better than their true merit.

Although Jaguar withdrew from racing at the end of 1991, it was not quite the end of the racing career of the cars. In modified form as the XKR-12D, the model ran in the United States, finishing second at Daytona and fourth at Sebring in 1992 and ran again at Daytona a year later when all three cars entered retired. XJR-14s formed the basis of the German *Jöst* team's *TWR*-Porsche cars that won at Le Mans in both 1996 and 1997.

Sauber-Mercedes

1985–91

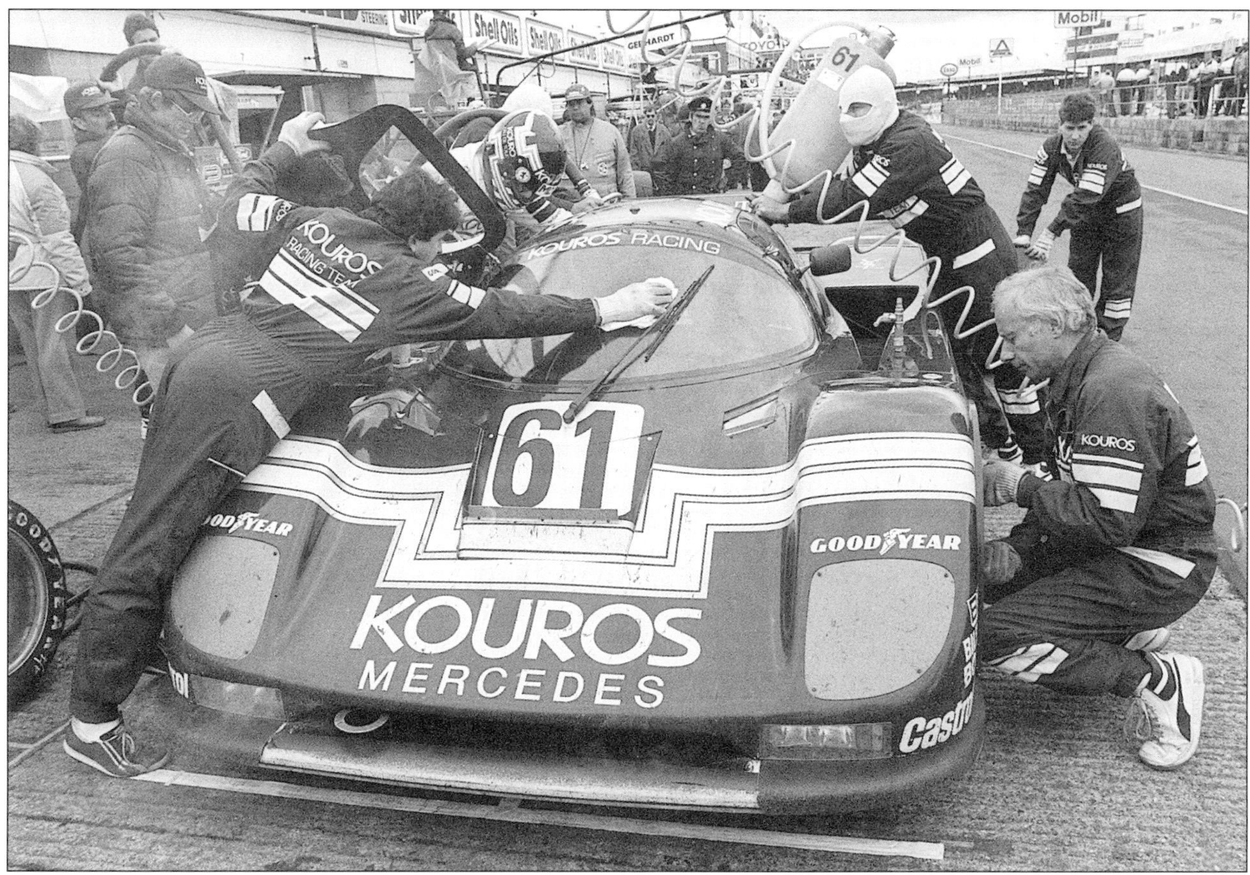

In 1986 Sauber raced with Mercedes-Benz power and Kouros sponsorship. Mike Thackwell, John Nielsen and Henri Pescarolo shared this car in the 1,000km race at Silverstone, but finished a poor eighth. The team's main problem in 1986 was inadequate ground-effect. (LAT)

Peter Sauber, based at Hinwil near Zurich, built his first sports car in 1970 and by 1981 had progressed to his own special version of the BMW M1 with tubular chassis and Swiss-built carbon-fibre body. Hans Stuck/Nelson Piquet won the 1981 Nürburgring 1,000Km race with this car. For Group C racing in 1982 Sauber built the C6 with honeycomb-aluminium chassis and the Cosworth 3.9-litre DFL engine. The Saubers, like all cars fitted with DFLs, suffered from bad engine vibration that affected ancillary components.

By 1983 Sauber had progressed to the C7 with sheet aluminium-alloy monocoque and a BMW 3.5-litre straight-six engine reckoned to be good for 475bhp. On it debut at Le Mans the new car finished ninth, behind eight Porsche entries, and after that ran in a number of other races without success. Everything then went quiet on the Sauber front until 1985 when the team reappeared at Le Mans with the C8.

The chassis of the new car was basically C7, but the power unit was the twin-turbo V8 Mercedes-Benz M117 5-litre developed under the direction of Dr Hermann Hierath, technical director of Mercedes' racing programme, and maintained by Heini Mader. At this stage Mercedes-Benz was supporting Sauber's racing programme covertly. The C7 had a completely new body with side-radiators. The overall design was the work of Leo Ress, Sauber's technical director.

The debut of the new car at Le Mans was marred by a spectacular accident. Danish driver John Nielsen was at the wheel during qualifying on the Thursday before the race when the undertray worked loose and the car became airborne over the hump at the end of the *Mulsanne Straight*. The C8 was travelling at around 220mph (a little over 350kph), it completed a loop in the air and landed back on its wheels severely damaged.

For 1986 Sauber obtained substantial sponsorship from *Kouros*, the men's toiletries brand of Yves Saint Laurent. Although it only provided sufficient finance for the team to compete in five races, it was enough for Sauber to afford a second car. The cars proved rather unreliable and lacked adequate ground-effects. There was one major success that year, however, and in typical Nürburgring weather, heavy rain and low cloud, the partnership of Mike Thackwell and Henri Pescarolo scored an unexpected win, aided by Jaguar and Porsche retirements.

Sauber developed the C9 for 1987 and this featured a much stiffer chassis reinforced by bonded aluminium-alloy panels, the ground-effect was vastly enhanced and the radiators were moved to the front to improve weight distribution. At the rear the coil spring/damper units were mounted horizontally and operated by rockers. Once again the team could only afford five races and Sauber failed to achieve a single win. There were two minor consolations during the year. Johnny Dumfries set a new lap record at Le Mans and at Spa Thackwell took pole position and led the race for a few laps.

At the end of the year *Kouros* ended their sponsorship. It was fortunate for Sauber that Mercedes-Benz now offered technical support and arranged sponsorship by its AEG Olympia business machines subsidiary. Four factory mechanics attended each race, Mercedes supplied more powerful, 700bhp engines using the very efficient Bosch Motronic 1.7 engine management system and gave assistance in developing the Hewland VGC gearbox with gears designed jointly by Mercedes and Staffs Silent Gear company.

In 1988 Sauber was able to enter two C9/88 cars, retaining a third as a spare. Drivers found the cars very demanding and they needed a great deal of sorting before they were raced. Before these were ready the team ran the older cars. During the year Sauber scored a string of victories. Schlesser/Mass/Baldi won the first race of the season, the Jerez 800km event after the failure of the Jaguars. Saubers finished second at Jarama and Monza and then second and third at Silverstone.

Le Mans was a disaster as Sauber was forced to withdraw on safety grounds after their Michelin tyres proved incapable in qualifying of coping with the combination of higher speeds and greater downforce. Schlesser/Mass won for Sauber at Brno and the Nürburgring and Baldi/Johansson took the team's fourth win of the season at Spa-Francorchamps. The team failed in the Japanese Fuji 1,000Km race, but in November Schlesser/Mass and Baldi/Johanson rounded off the year with first and second places in the Sandown Park race in Australia. Schlesser won the Drivers' Championship, but in the World Championship for Teams, Sauber was a distant second behind Jaguar.

Mercedes-Benz was sufficiently impressed with the performance of the Sauber team to sponsor them directly in 1989. The cars were painted Mercedes silver and bore a three-pointed star on the nose, although they were still called Saubers. Mercedes-Benz engine modifications included the adoption of four valves per cylinder, and power output was increased to 770bhp at 7,600rpm in race trim, enough to give them a winning edge over the Jaguar team.

The Saubers had an outstanding year, winning at Suzuka in Japan, finishing second and third at Dijon-Prenois, and then won six successive Championship races, Jarama, Brands Hatch, the Nürburgring, Donington Park, Spa-Francorchamps and Mexico City. Le Mans was not part of the Championship series, but Sauber competed and took the first two places. Sauber-Mercedes won the Teams' Championship and Jean-Louis Schlesser took the Drivers' category.

For 1990 Leo Ress developed an improved version of the C9 and this was officially known as the Mercedes-Benz C11. Engine modifications included a Bosch 1.8 electronic management system and in its latest M119 form the engine was much lighter. There was a new gearbox and the team now used Goodyear in place of Michelin tyres. The chassis was substantially stiffer and the wheelbase was longer, but it proved to be too heavy. The C11 and all future sports car chassis were made by DP Composites, run by Dave Price and based in Surrey. Changes to the body included a narrower windscreen and body.

In 1990 Sauber raced with overt works backing and the latest car was known as the Mercedes-Benz C11. This is the car shared by Jean-Louis Schlesser/Mauro Baldi in Mexico. (Daimler Chrysler AG)

The 1991 car was the C291 powered by a horizontally opposed 12-cylinder 3.5-litre engine. These cars had many problems during the year, but Jochen Mass partnered by Michael Schumacher won the Nürburgring 'sprint' race with this one. (Daimler Chrysler)

Jochen Neerpasch, then motorsport chief at Mercedes-Benz, insisted that some young blood be brought into the team, so while Jean-Louis Schlesser and Mauro Baldi drove the lead car, the second car was shared by veteran driver Jochen Mass and one of a trio of successful German Formula 3 drivers, Heinz-Harald Frentzen, Michael Schumacher and Karl Wendlinger.

It proved another exceptionally successful year for the team; Mercedes-Benz won eight races: Suzuka (C9/88), Monza (first race for the C11), Spa-Francorchamps, Dijon-Prenois, Donington Park, Montreal and Mexico City; the team's main rivals, Jaguar and Nissan, were outpaced. The Montreal race was stopped short and half-points awarded, because the manhole covers, that should have been firmly welded in place, weren't and caused havoc. Le Mans was again not part of the Championship series and Mercedes-Benz missed this race in which the Jaguars took the first two places.

At Silverstone in May the team had suffered its only defeat of the season after the mechanics went to the aid of Schumacher whose car was stranded out on the circuit during practice (disqualification followed) and Schlesser/Baldi retired because of timing chain failure. Schlesser/Baldi scored all of the team's wins except for Spa-Francorchamps where Mass/Wendlinger were the winners and Mexico City.

In the final round of the Championship Schlesser/Baldi won on the road because Mass delayed too long a stop for wet-weather tyres during a rainstorm late in the race. After the finish, however, Schlesser/Baldi were disqualified because they had taken on a tenth of a litre too much fuel at their last stop and so Mass/Schumacher became the winners. During the year Schumacher and Frentzen displayed tremendous potential, potential that, in Schumacher's case, was to be totally fulfilled in Formula 1. All three junior drivers also benefited from an immense amount of winter testing. It had been an ideal driver combination that only a confident team could risk.

Mercedes-Benz continued into 1991 with the C11 and the new C291 with 3.5-litre flat-12 engine. They had considered a wide range of configurations before choosing this layout, which best suited Leo Ress's contention that a single full-width undercar venturi was aerodynamically preferable to two ducts, one either side. It also permitted a very low centre of gravity. This engine had the very advanced TAG Electronics management system and developed 650bhp. The monocoque was a very much stronger version of its predecessors and possessed excellent aerodynamics.

In early testing it soon became obvious that the flat-12 engine was too heavy, it brought the C291 well over the 750kg minimum weight and it was underpowered compared to its rivals. At the beginning of the season it was decided that in the first few races, at least, Schlesser/Mass would share the C11, while Schumacher/Wendlinger drove the C291. In the first Championship round at Suzuka, the Peugeot team scored an unexpected and lucky win, but Schlesser/Mass took second place with a C11.

After this, the season went very badly wrong for Mercedes. Schlesser/Mass (C11) could manage no better than third in the Trofeo Caracciola at Monza. Then came Silverstone where Wendlinger/Schumacher turned in a fine performance with the C291 and finished second, the meat in the sandwich between the first and third-place 3.5-litre Jaguars. Although the C11s were the fastest cars at Le Mans, once again a Championship race, they were plagued by problems and the sole car to finish, shared by Schlesser/Mass/Ferté took a poor fifth place, despite holding a three-lap lead on the Sunday morning.

For much of the rest of the year the team was plagued by C291 engine failures caused by a faulty batch of cylinder blocks with excessivelly thin walls. Nothing further in the way of success was gained until the last race of the season at Autopolis in Japan. Here Wendlinger/Schumacher scored a surprise win with the C291, heading two Jaguars.

With interest in sports car racing waning badly, Sauber withdrew and after a year's development work, entered Formula 1 in 1993 with Mercedes-Benz-powered cars. After two seasons without substantial success, Mercedes-Benz withdrew their support from Sauber and formed an alliance with McLaren. Later Sauber used Ferrari engines and the 2004 Formula 1 car was a near-enough Ferrari clone, built with Maranello's approval.

Nissan ZX GTP & NPTI-90

1985–91

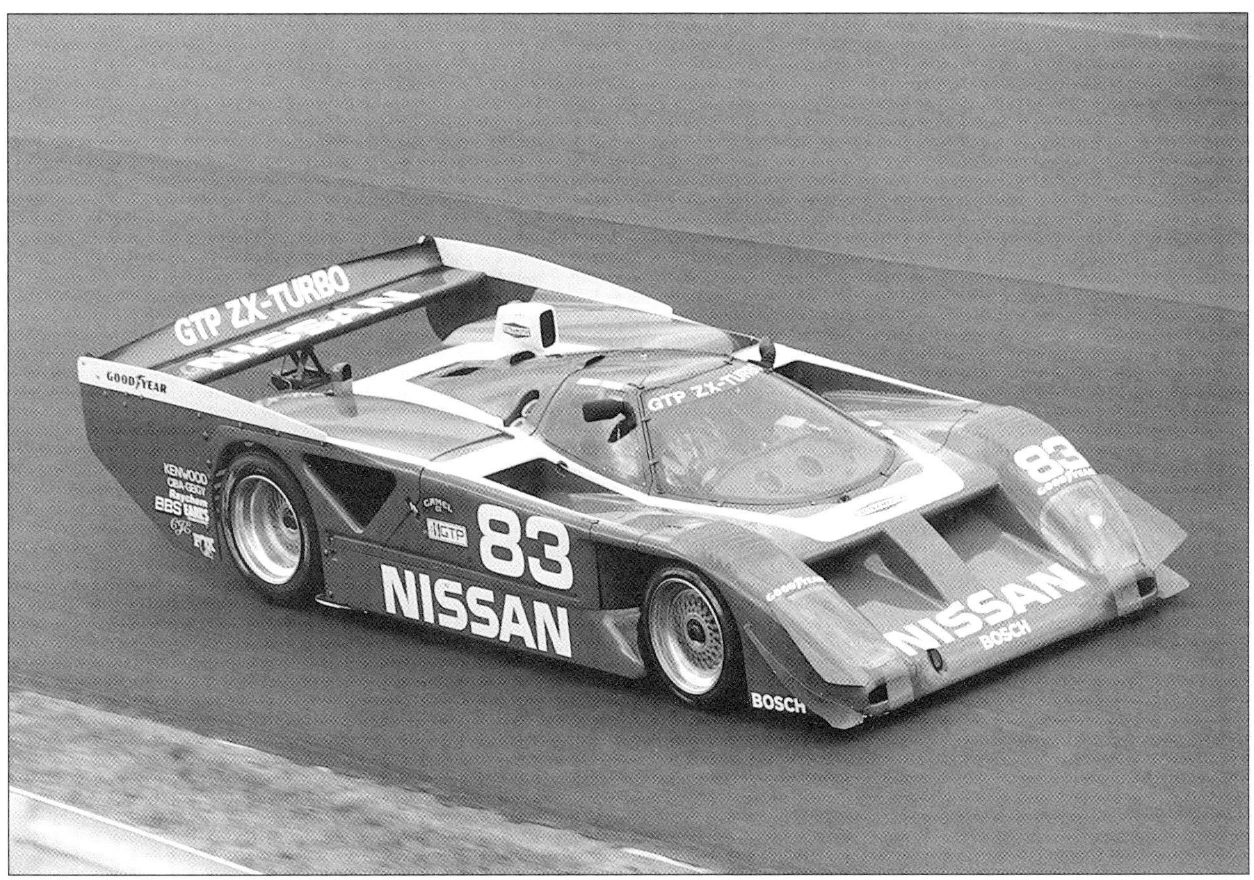

The Nissan GTP ZX-Turbo of Geoff Brabham/John Morton at Watkins Glen in July 1988. This was one of eight victories that they scored for the Electramotive team that year. (Geoffrey Hewitt)

Electramotive, founded in 1972 by Don Devendorf, became the leading Nissan dealers in California and also leading specialist in the United States in developing Nissans for competition work. When Nissan decided to enter the GTP category of American IMSA racing, they asked Electramotive to run the project on their behalf. In 1985 the American company took delivery of two T810 chassis from Lola and these were similar in most respects to the T710 cars that were supplied to the Chevrolet division of General Motors.

Lola's T810 had an exceptionally stiff honeycomb-aluminium monocoque with full-length, honeycomb side pontoons that ran from ahead of the pedal-box to the rear of the monocoque. Carbon-fibre skins strengthened the floor. A tubular steel frame mounted the engine. The front suspension was by pushrod-operation of the wisbones from inboard-mounted coil spring/damper units. At the rear there were wishbones and coil spring/damper units. The coupé bodywork was mainly carbon-fibre. The team used 13-in (330mm) ventilated disc brakes with four pistons.

The power unit was based on the production Nissan 280ZX V6, with a capacity of 2,958.9cc (87×83mm), a Garrett TO3 turbocharger and an electronic engine management system designed by Devendorf. The claimed power output was 'up to 1,000bhp at 7,600rpm'. Transmission was by a Weisman transverse five-speed gearbox. Weight was about 2,044 pounds (927kg). The wheelbase was 8ft 10.5in (2,705mm). The new car was designated the Electramotive GTP.

During 1985 Electramotive had a very difficult first

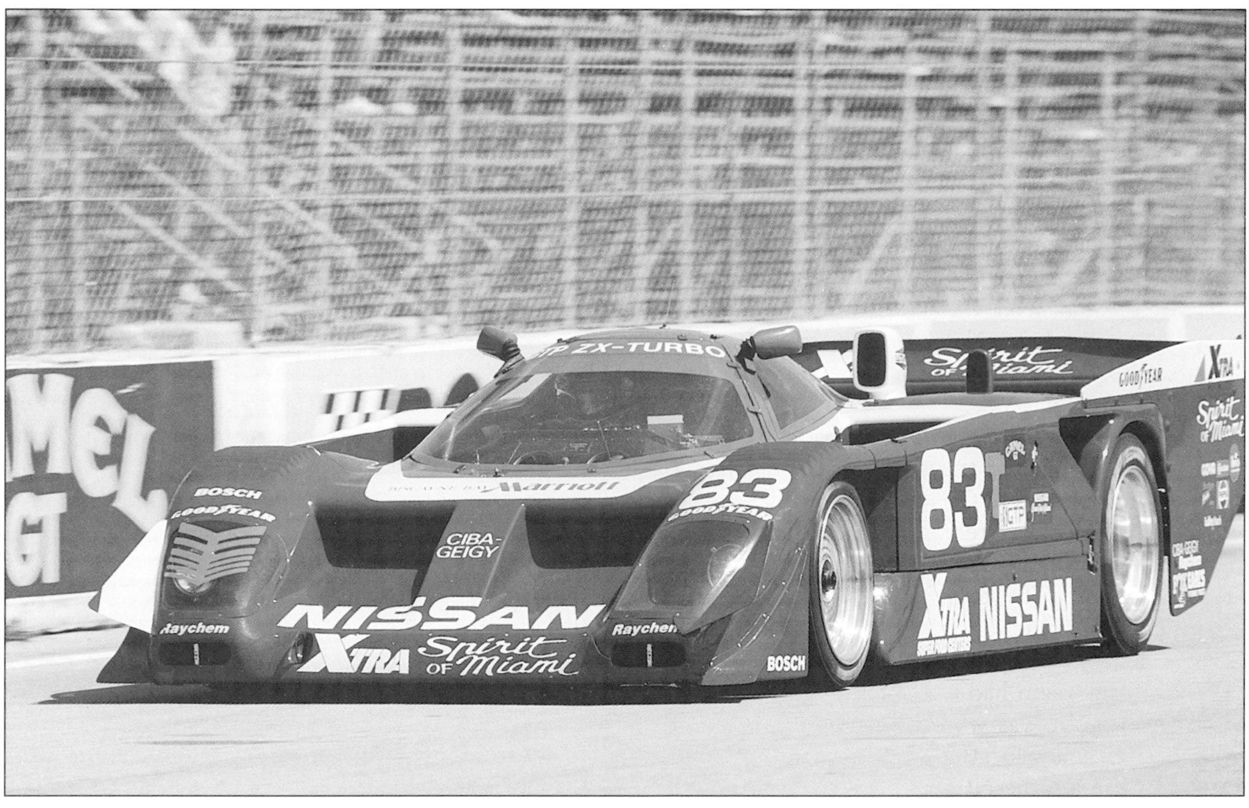

In 1989 the Nissan had another brilliant season and during the year won ten races. In the early part of the year the team continued to rely on the GTP ZX and this car is seen at the Miami race. (LAT)

season; 'Dev' Devendorf drove, partnered by Tony Adamowicz, but they had two crashes, once because of front suspension failure, and the Nissan had to be rebuilt twice. Eight races were entered, the Nissan non-started because of gearbox failure in practice on its first appearance at Riverside Raceway and the highest-placed finish was ninth at Sears Point.

An extensive development programme was carried out prior to the 1986 season and Devendorf gave up driving, bringing Geoff Brabham and E. Forbes-Robinson into the team. The team was now receiving funding direct from Nissan in Japan and the aim was a win in the IMSA Camel GT Championship, as hopefully as early 1987. The cars had originally been painted black, but now sported blue, red and white colours, with the Nissan name appearing very prominently.

The ZX showed exceptional speed in 1986, but was still unreliable. The cars were fast in practice, but something usually broke in the race. Further testing during the year resulted in redesigned front diffuser, rear bodywork and venturis. Now the Nissan was even faster and gradually reliability was improving. In the last five races of the year, the team achieved some reasonable places: third by Brabham at Portland, fourth by Forbes-Robinson in the Road America race and a shared drive to fifth place at Columbus. Brabham had been leading at Portland until a late stop for a fuel top-up.

Major changes were made for 1987; the power unit now had an aluminium-alloy block and cylinder heads, there was a smaller turbocharger with electronically controlled wastegate. New bodywork greatly increased downforce and although the top speed of the ZX was lower, it was much faster through and out of corners. The season started well for the team, with pole position and a win by Brabham/Forbes-Robinson at Miami from the Porsche 962 of Rahal/Mass. Although the team ran in 11 more races that year and took pole position four more times, the poor reliability continued, there were too many failures with Bridgestone tyres and there were several accidents.

By 1988 Electramotive was running on the much quicker Goodyear tyres, the team built its own Lola-based chassis with stronger floor and outboard front suspension that made the cars much easier to work on. The team used Hewland's latest VG-C six-speed trans-axle and although the body was similar to that of the 1987 cars, the downforce was even greater. The opposition in IMSA racing was stronger, for apart from the many Porsche 962s, the *Tom Walkinshaw Racing*-entered Jaguars were now competing in American events.

Electramotive missed the long Daytona and Sebring races, and first appeared at Miami where Geoff Brabham took pole position, but after brake problems he and co-driver John Morton were classified eighth. After that almost nothing could go wrong for the team and the ZX displayed reliability to match its speed. Brabham, usually partnered by Morton, won the next eight races in succession. There was a hiccough at Del Mar where the car was eliminated by an accident, but Brabham/Morton won the last race of the year at Tampa. Porsche beat Nissan by one point in the Manufacturers' Championship, but Brabham was Drivers' Champion.

There were few changes to the cars for 1989 and they substantially dominated the year's IMSA racing. Chip Robinson now partnered Geoff Brabham and during the year they won a total of ten races, including the Sebring 12 Hours where Arie Luyendyk shared the driving of the winning car. The team won the Manufacturers' Championship, which had been Nissan's goal, and Geoff Brabham was again Champion driver.

By 1990 the team had become *Nissan Performance Technology, Inc*; it was wholly owned by Nissan USA and moved to a new location at Vista, California. There was a new model, the NPTI-90, still with honeycomb aluminium-alloy monocoque and its designer, Trevor Harris, reckoned that it was about 80% stiffer than its predecessor because of a much wider cross-section.

The body was lower, with front-mounted radiator, an air intake in the roof and a very large aerofoil that hung from the back of the car. Drag was reduced and downforce increased. A major change was that the NPTIs were raced in 2.5-litre form to take advantage of a new IMSA rule that gave the smaller capacity class a weight advantage. Twin Garrett turbochargers were used. The wheelbase of the new car was 8ft 11.5in (2,730mm) and it weighed around 1,925 pounds (873kg).

In the early part of the season the team continued to race the 1989 cars. Both cars entered at Daytona retired because of engine problems, but thereafter the team won at Miami (first and second), Sebring (first and second), Road Atlanta and West Palm Beach. Then the new cars took over and continued their predecessors' successes at Mid-Ohio, Watkins Glen and Road America. Despite some retirements later in 1990, Brabham and Robinson took the first two places in the Drivers' Championship and Nissan won the Manufacturers' Championship for the third successive year.

For the long-distance races at the beginning of 1991 the team used Lola-based R90CK cars built to Group C rules (which were eligible for Daytona and Sebring only). A *TWR* Jaguar won at Daytona, but one of the Nissans finished second and in the Sebring 12 Hours race Brabham/Daly and Robinson/Earl took the first two places with the usual IMSA cars.

By the Road Atlanta race the NPTI had four valves per cylinder. The Jaguars were more competitive and the very light Toyotas developed and raced by Dan Gurney's *Eagle* concern were becoming a serious threat. Although the season was patchy and the team won only two more races during the year, Nissan won the Manufacturers' Championship and Brabham and Robinson were first and second in the Drivers' category. By 1992 Toyota had the upper hand and although the weight of the Nissans had been reduced by 200 pounds (91kg), they were no longer competitive and the only win was at Miami.

Nissan proposed that the American team use a new V12, but this proved hopelessly underpowered in testing and, soon afterwards, the racing programme was axed. NPTI sold off the cars, one of them finished second at Sebring and the Nissans now form the backbone of *Thundersports* racing in the United States. Nissan also raced in Europe and Japan, using March chassis for the early cars. Although no outright win was gained in Europe and the cars were largely unsuccessful, they did, from time to time, achieve some good places.

During 1990 Nissan developed the much-improved NPTI-90 and this made its racing debut in mid-season. Geoff Brabham and the NPTI-90 are seen at Mid-Ohio where the make again dominated the results. (LAT)

Bentley Speed 8

2001–03

The Bentley EXP Speed 8 was built to comply with the Le Mans LM-GTP rules, which require closed bodywork. The Audi 8RC, to which it is related, is an open car complying with Le Mans LMP rules. In 2001 two Bentleys ran at Le Mans. This car entered for Brundle/Smith/Ortelli was eliminated by failure of the gearbox compressor after 4½ hours' racing. The other Speed 8 took third place and won its class. (Bentley Motors)

Following the sale of Rolls-Royce Motors by the Vickers Group to BMW, it seemed as unlikely as ever that Bentley would return to motor racing. An agreement was, however, reached between BMW and VW that while BMW would retain Rolls-Royce, VW would acquire Bentley. Bentley came under the control of the Audi division, who are very competition-minded and, so, it did not come as too great a surprise when it was announced that Bentley would return to Le Mans in 2001.

Although the new car, known as the EXP Speed 8, was developed from the Audi R8s, which had dominated Le Mans in 2000 and 2001, it was a very different car. It was no clone of the Audi, but more 'son of the R8' and it was a case of Audi saying, "Here are the basic mechanical components, make of them what you will." The work was undertaken by *racing technology norfolk*. This company is the successor to Toyota racing specialist, *TOM'S GB*, which was acquired by Audi Sport in 1992, the Norfolk company spells its name in lower case. The result was a contender in the LM-GTP class at Le Mans that was individually engineered and developed in almost every respect.

Powering the Bentley was a 90-degree V8 engine of 3,953.5cc (85×79.2mm) with twin overhead camshafts per bank of cylinders and twin turbochargers. The camshafts were gear-driven, and there were four valves and a single plug per cylinder. There was a linerless, closed-deck, aluminium-alloy cylinder block, and a flat-plane crankshaft that ran in five plain main bearings. The Bosch fuel injection system had a coil and, originally, a single injector per cylinder. The turbochargers were the oil-cooled Garretts with a Bosch Motronic MP2.9 engine management system controlling the wastegates. No precise power output figure is available, but it was about 605bhp at 6,500rpm.

Transmission was by a carbon-fibre clutch and a transverse six-speed gearbox with a paddle-operated electro-pneumatic gear-shift. The first car had an 8ft 10.3in (2,700m)-wheelbase, but on car number two this was increased to 8ft 11.5in (2,730mm). The chassis was a monocoque formed by carbon-fibre skins over an aluminium honeycomb structure with transverse loops. The front hoop was a half-section ahead of the pedal-box and providing additional support for the front suspension; the centre hoop supported the windscreen and formed the forward roll-hoop; the rear was also a half-section, mounted on the fuel tank and formimg the rear roll-hoop.

This integral structure formed the floor, the side-panels, the scuttle, the roof, with front and rear bulkheads and bonded-in seat. The engine was bolted directly to the rear of the monocoque. The sleek closed body, constructed in carbon-fibre over aluminium or Nomex honeycomb, was designed round a windscreen of the minimum permitted size. The sidepods were bolted to the monocoque. A duct on the roof fed air to the turbochargers, and the twin water radiators were mounted slightly ahead of the engine. Front and rear suspension was by pushrods, with torsion bars at the front and coil springs at the rear.

The weight of the first car was about 2,095 pounds, rather more above the 900kg minimum weight for the LM-GTP class, but this was reduced to just above the permitted minimum by the time the cars were raced. Aerodynamics, in particular ground-effect, is one the most important aspects of a racing design. A detailed description of the Bentley's aerodynamics is contained in Ian Bamsey's excellent book (see the *Bibliography*). It suffices to say here that with a weight including driver of about 2,200 pounds, the Speed 8 produced its own weight in downforce at around 150mph (240kph).

After extensive testing, including a 24-hour test at Magny-Cours in May 2001 two Bentleys appeared at Le Mans. The team's aspirations were for both cars to finish and, if possible, one in the first six. The race was run in atrociously wet conditions, at a lower speed than expected and the fact that Bentleys' Dunlop tyres were not as effective as the Michelins fitted to the Audis, among others, was of less importance than in the dry.

Even so, Speed 8s lapped slower than their Audi rivals and they could not complete as many laps as the Audis between refuelling stops. Both Bentleys had problems with the Megaline electronic control because of rain entering the system and this affected the gear-change. It resulted in the retirement after 4½ hours of the car shared by Brundle/Guy Smith/Ortelli. After two changes of the Megaline unit, Wallace/Leitzinger/van de Poele finished third, behind two Audis and first in the LM-GTP class.

After Le Mans work started on the improved cars for the 2002 race. The capacity of the V8 engine was increased to 3,995cc (87×84mm) and with Audi FS1 direct fuel injection developed about 635bhp. Changes to the chassis were few, the nose of the car was shorter, the tail longer and the overall length was increased fractionally.

Only one car ran at Le Mans the following year. Wallace/van der Poele/Leitzinger were the drivers. Development had resulted in a quicker gear-change and improved Dunlop tyres, but the Straight 8 was slower out of corners than some of its rivals. Despite mechanical problems (including changing the front brake discs because they had become glazed) and a few minor off-course excursions, the Bentley finished fourth, 13 laps behind the winning Audi, and won the LM-GTP class.

Work again started again straight after the race on the 2003 car. It was intended to run at both Sebring and Le Mans and the cars would be using Michelin tyres. The use of the French tyres necessitated camber and steering geometry changes. Substantial changes were made to the chassis and body. The car was redesigned in 'twin-keel' form with a modified nose diffuser so that the air passing across the flat bottom of the car emitted through vertical slots in the sides of the car immediately ahead of the doors. There were pods that served to enclose the front wheels and controlled airflow at the front and minimised its interference with airflow at the rear.

In 2002 at Le Mans, Bentley entered only a single car, now with a 4-litre engine. Driven by Wallace/van de Poele/Leitzinger it took fourth place and won the LM-GTP class. Here the Bentley is accelerating away after a routine pit stop. (Bentley Motors)

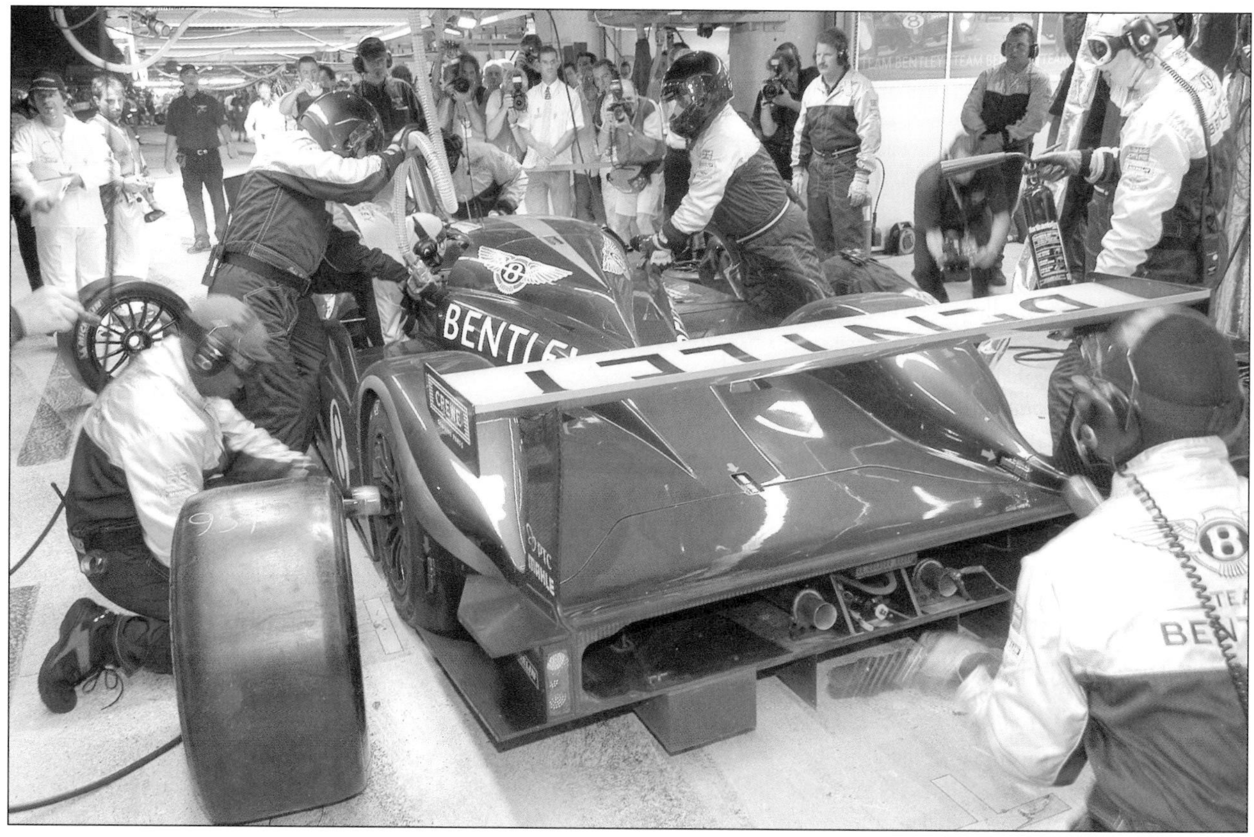

Bentley scored a fine victory at Le Mans in 2003 with a redesigned car driven by Kristensen/Capello/Smith. Here the EXP Speed 8 makes a routine pit stop. Race regulations require the car to be refuelled first and then the tyres to be changed. In practice the replacement driver must be in the seat by the completion of refuelling, as it is not practical to put the car up on its air jacks and change the wheels before this has happened. (Bentley Motors)

The driving compartment was moved rearwards so as to comply with the latest regulation requiring a wider pedal-box (the chassis tapered outwards from the front and this was the most practical way to make the change); the trans-axle and rear suspension was modified and were now more compact and the engine was closer to the rear axle. The bellhousing of the trans-axle was shortened and as a result the wheelbase was only 5mm, a fraction of an inch, longer than previously. The front overhang was very short, and the rear was lengthened. The rear suspension now incorporated torsion bars in place of coil springs.

The Bentleys were first and second fastest in qualifying for their first racing in 2003, the Sebring 12 Hours, but the scrutineers decided that the front diffusers failed to comply with the regulations, the qualifying times were disallowed and they were relegated to the back of the grid. The problem arose because at Sebring the scrutineers were using a different method of measuring the diffusers from that employed at Le Mans, and it was easily resolved. At the start the Bentleys soon moved up to third and fourth places, they could not catch the now privately entered Audis and that is where they finished in the order Herbert/Brabham/Blundell and Kristensen/Capello/Smith.

There were anxieties about running cars that were all new apart from the engine and gearbox internals in a 24 hours race, but the cars performed almost faultlessly at Le Mans. Once again the Bentleys could not run as many laps between refuelling stops as the Audis and it is suspected that the fuel pumps of the Speed 8s were unable to pick up the last litre or so of fuel. The effect of this was real tank capacity was slightly less than the 90 litres permitted under the regulations.

The Bentleys pulled away from the Audis at the rate of 2–3 seconds per lap and took first and second places. Kristensen/Capello/Smith were the winners with 377 laps to their cedit, Herbert/Brabham/Blundell took second place, two laps behind – the third-place Audi was five laps behind the winner. Bentley withdrew from racing after the win and it is unlikely that they will return in the foreseeable future. The Audis have, however, continued to race in private hands and 2004 successes included wins at Sebring, Monza and Le Mans.

Bibliography

Bamsey, Ian, *Bentley at Le Mans* (Racecar Graphic Ltd, 2004)

Berthon, Darrell, *A Racing History of the Bentley (1921-31)* (The Bodley Head, 1956)

Bianchi Anderlone, C.F., *Alfa Romeo Disco Volante* (Automobilia, 1993)

Blight, Anthony, *The French Sports Car Revolution* (Haynes, 1996)

Boschen, Lothar and Barth, Jürgen, *The Porsche Book* (Patrick Stephens, 1978)

Cherrett, Angela, *Alfa Romeo Modelo 8C 2300* (Veloce Publishing, 1992)

Clarke, R.M., *Cunningham Automobiles, 1951-55* (Brooklands Books, 1999)

Cotton, Michael, *Directory of World Sportscars: Group C and IMSA Cars from 1982* (Aston Publications)

Crombac, Gerard, *Colin Chapman, The Man and his Cars* (Patrick Stephens, 1986)

Finn, Joel E., *Ferrari Testa Rossa V12* (Osprey Publishing, 1980)

Fitzgerald, Warren W. and Merritt, Richard, F., *Ferrari, The Sports and Grand Turismo Cars* (Bond Publishing Company, 1968)

Fraichard, Georges, translated by Louis Klementaski, *The Le Mans Story* (The Bodley Head, 1954)

Fusi, Luigi, *Tutte le Vetture Alfa Romeo dal 1910* (Third Edition, Emmetigrafica, 1978)

Gunnell, John (Editor), *Standard Catalog of American Cars, 1946-1975* (Third Edition, Krause Publications, 1992)

Henry, Alan, *Mercedes in Motorsport* (Haynes Publishing, 2001)

Hull, Peter and Johnson, Norman, *The Vintage Alvis* (Third Edition, The Alvis Register, 1995)

Hull, Peter and Slater, Roy, *Alfa Romeo: A History* (Cassell & Co, 1964)

Ludvigsen, Karl, *The Mercedes-Benz Racing Cars* (Bond/Parkhurst Books, 1971)

Lurani, Giovanni, *Nuvolari*, (Cassell & Co., 1949)

Lurani, Giovanni, *Mille Miglia, 1927-57* (Automobile Year, 1981)

Morgan, Peter, *Porsche in Motorsport* (Haynes Publishing, 2000)

Moss, Stirling with Nye, Doug, *My Cars, My Life* (Patrick Stephens, 1987)

Parker, Paul, *Jaguar at Le Mans* (Haynes Publishing, 2001)

Porter, Philip, *Jaguar Sports Racing Cars* (Revised Edition, Bay View Books, 1998)

Pritchard, Anthony, *Porsche* (Pelham Books, 1969)

Pritchard, Anthony, *Sports Car Championship* (Robert Hale, 1972)

Pritchard, Anthony, *Lotus: All The Cars* (Second Edition, Aston Publications, 1992)

Pritchard, Anthony, *Aston Martin: The Post-War Competition Cars* (Aston Publications, 1991)

Pritchard, Anthony, *Scarlet Passion, Ferrari Prototypes and Competition Sports Cars, 1962-73* (Haynes Publishing, 2004)

Simons, Rainer, *BMW 328: From Roadster to Legend*, (BMW Mobile Traction, 1996)

Starkey, John, *Lola T70* (Third Edition, Veloce Publishing, 2002)

Starkey, John, *Lightning Speed, The Nissan GTP & Group C Racecars* (Gryfon Publishers, 2002)

Starkey, John, *Sauber-Mercedes, World Champions* (Gryfon Publishers, 2002)

Trow, Nigel, *Lancia Racing* (Osprey Publishing, 1987)

Venables, David, *Bugatti: A Racing History* (Haynes, 2002)

Whyte, Andrew, *Jaguar Sports Racing & Works Competition Cars from 1954* (Haynes Publishing, 1987/2003)

Index

Cars, marques, teams, body and engine manufacturers